AIR FRYER COOKB(

650 Easy and Delicious Air Fryer Recipes fo
Advanced Users

CW01590139

Alina Smith

Table of Contents

Introduction

This cookbook is comprised of a delicious collection of recipes that are suitable for all tastes. Each recipe is simple to make, full of flavor, and offers a healthier alternative to traditionally fried foods. This book is made to help ensure you get the most out of your Air Fryer

Many people have a love-hate relationship with fried foods. While they wish they could erase the calories they receive from it, they also love the taste and crunch that comes with it. That is where the air fryer comes in. The air fryer stands out from its competitors' appliances because it offers a low-fat version of normally unhealthy foods such as fried chicken, French fries and onion rings

As some healthy foods, tend to have a knock-off taste from the real deal, air fryers produce foods with a delicious taste and feel in your mouth.

The air fryer can be used in many ways to help make your hectic, daily life more manageable. Whether you want to fry, bake, grill or roast ingredients, the air fryer can do it all. It can cook without oil, prepare multiple dishes at once and its parts can be easily removed for cleaning.

Every one love the air fryer's variety of cooking options that enable them to prepare any type of meal at any time of the day

With an air fryer, you end up with healthier, low-fat dishes that make use of little to no oil. As for the flavor and texture, you have to be the judge of it. Most people say they can't taste any difference between deep-fried foods and air-fried foods. On top of all this, the device is easy to use and clean up.

Throughout the pages of this book, you will discover a variety of sweet, savory, salty, citrusy, and other delicious recipes. These flavorful dishes are hand-picked to ensure you have a hearty collection of the best recipes on hand at all times. As a result, this cookbook is the ultimate companion book to any Air Fryer. You are guaranteed to find a wonderful selection of traditional, modern and alternative recipes inside to suit any palette. There is certainly something here for everyone.

Benefits of Using an Air Fryer

Time Saving: With only 24 hours to complete everyday routine tasks, the time has become a genuinely luxury in our fast-paced lifestyle. Air Fryers are designed to save your precious cooking time by serving you crunchy snacks and fried cuisines in a matter of minutes. If you are always on a tight schedule, Air Fryer is no less than a time savior.

Protect the Food's Nutrients: Unlike deep frying, Air Fryers do not deconstruct the food's good nutrients and add on bad fats. If you think your yasai tempura (deep fried battered vegetables) are healthy, here is news for you; while they may look like they are full of nutritious elements, the deep-frying process would have destroyed the beneficial vitamins and minerals contained in the vegetables.

Superfast Heating: Unlike traditional frying method, Air Fryers takes only a few minutes to heat and prepare foods. They are always ready to make meals whenever you crave for fried foods.

Most Air Fryer models get ready in only 3 minutes to heat up properly and they can also go as high as 400 degrees F to make you crispy meals.

Keeping Cancer at Bay*:* For some oils (e.g. olive and flaxseed), their chemical structure changes in high heat causing them to transform into bad forms of fat. Additionally, since there is little oil used, there is little chances for food to produce carcinogens that activate cancer cells.

Build A Fortress for Your Heart: Eating food fried with an Air Fryer reduces the risk of heart diseases and protects your body by helping you absorb necessary nutrients. Since minimal amount of oil is used to prepare food, you can be sure that your body will not accumulate excessive fats in the long run. Instead, the optimal amount of oil used will help your body protect your heart.

Calories Are Good, But Too Much Spells Trouble*!* Fried foods are high in calories which is the leading cause of weight gain and obesity. Obesity will then lead to a plethora of killer diseases such as diabetes, cancer, stroke, sleep problems and immobility to name a few. Adopting a low-fat diet will help you maintain your weight or prevent weight loss because essentially, you are eating fewer calories. Therefore, eating Air Fryer-cooked food will support your weight loss journey.

Fat Is Not All Bad: Fat is a macronutrient – it is essential to help control inflammation, blood clotting, maintaining healthy hair and skin, prevent heart diseases, provide energy and assist in the absorption of vitamins A, D, E and K. While it is important to your bodily functions, too much of it is detrimental to health. An Air Fryer is a modern kitchen appliance that fries food using heated hot air by using at most a tablespoon of oil. This way, you are able to eat fried food without worrying about the negative effects of fatty food on your health.

Keeping Your Kidneys Clear: Consuming excess amounts of deep-fried food will impair your kidney's ability to filter our harmful fats. Therefore, eating food fried by an Air Fryer can help you lower your risks of getting kidney disease. If you are finding it difficult to quit deep-fried food cold turkey, using an Air Fryer will ease your transition to a healthier diet.

Air Fryer Maintenance

Beyond regularly cleanings, your air fryer requires some basic maintenance to make sure that it doesn't get damaged or start functioning incorrectly. This includes

- Making sure the unit is clean and free of any debris before you start cooking. If it has been a long time since you last used your air fryer, check inside. Some dust may have accumulated. If there is any food residue on the basket for pan, clean it out before you start cooking
- Inspecting the cords before each use. Never plug a damaged or frayed cord into an outlet. It can cause serious injury or even death. Make sure the cords are clean and damage-free before using your air fryer
- Make sure the air fryer is not placed close to a wall or another appliance. Air fryers need at least 4 inches of space behind them and 4 inches of space above them in order to adequately vent steam and hot air while cooking. Placing them in an enclosed space may cause the fryer to overheat
- Make sure the air fryer is placed upright, on a level surface, before you start cooking.
- Visually inspect each component, including the basket, pan and handle prior to each use. If you find any damaged components, contact the manufacturer and get them replaced

Air Fryer Cooking Charts

Every air fryer may have slightly varied cooking times and temperatures, so it is best to check your air fryer manual before operating it. Ensure to cook the meats, poultry and seafood until completely cooked at a safe internal temperature

The below chart can be used for reference assuming that the food is flipped or basket shaken halftime during cooking.

Frozen Foods

FROZEN FOODS		
Type	**Temperature (Fahrenheit)**	**Cook Time (Minutes)**
Thin French Fries (20 oz)	400	14
Thick French Fries (17 oz)	400	18
Onion Rings (12 oz)	400	8
Mozarella Sticks (11 oz)	400	8
Pot Stickers (10 oz)	400	8
Fish Sticks (10 oz)	400	10
Fish Filets (10 oz)	400	14
Chicken Nuggets (12 oz)	400	10
Breaded Shrimps	400	9

Fish & Seafood

FISH & SEAFOOD		
Type	**Temperature (Fahrenheit)**	**Cook Time (Minutes)**
Fish Filets (8 oz)	400	10
Calamari (8 oz)	400	4
Salmon filets (6 oz)	380	12
Swordfish Steak	400	10
Tuna Steak	400	7 - 10
Scallops	400	5 - 7
Shrimps	400	5

Poultry

POULTRY		
Type	**Temperature (Fahrenheit)**	**Cook Time (Minutes)**
Bone-In breasts (1.25 lbs)	370	25
Boneless breasts (4 lbs)	380	12
Drumsticks (2.5 lbs)	370	20
Bone-In thighs (2 lbs)	380	22
Boneless thighs (1.25 lbs)	380	18 - 20
Bone-In Legs (1.75 lbs)	380	30
Wings (2 lbs)	400	12
Halved Game Hen (2 lbs)	390	20
Whole Chicken (6.5 lbs)	360	75
Tenders	360	8 - 10

Beef

BEEF		
Type	**Temperature (Fahrenheit)**	**Cook Time (Minutes)**
Burger (4 oz)	370	16 - 20
Filet Mignon (8 oz)	400	18
Flank Steak (1.5 lbs)	400	12
London Broil (2 lbs)	400	20 - 28
Meatballs	380	7
Bone-In Ribeye (8 oz)	400	10 - 15
Sirloin Steaks (12 oz)	400	9 - 14
Beef-Eye Round Roast(4lbs)	390	45 - 55

Vegetables

VEGETABLES		
Type	Temperature (Fahrenheit)	Cook Time (Minutes)
Asparagus (sliced)	400	5
Beets (whole)	400	40
Broccoli Florets	400	6
Brussels Sprouts(halved)	380	15
Carrots (sliced)	380	15
Cauliflower florets	400	12
Corn on cob	390	6
Eggplant (cubed)	400	15
Fennel (quartered)	370	15
Green Beans	400	5
Kale leaves	250	12
Mushrooms (sliced)	400	5
Pearl Onions	400	10
Parsnips (cubed)	380	15
Pepper (chunks)	400	15
Small baby potatoes	400	15
Potato (chunks)	400	12
Whole potatoes (baked)	400	40
Squash (chunks)	400	12
Sweet potatoes (baked)	380	30 - 35
Cherry Tomatoes	400	4
Tomatoes (halved)	350	10
Zucchini sticks	400	12

Frequently Asked Questions

#1. How much time an air fryer takes to cook frozen foods?

Answer- One of the best things to do while cooking frozen food in an air fryer is to use the knob as per the food that you are cooking. It normally takes some more time to cook frozen foods as compared to other food items

#2. Can we cook different varieties of food in an air fryer?

Answer- Yes, you can easily cook different varieties of food in an air fryer. One of the best things about cooking food in an air fryer is that it is healthy and free from oil. Items such as meat, potatoes, poultry and French fries can be easily cooked. Apart from these items you can also bake brownies and grill different vegetables.

#3. Can we add more ingredients while the food is getting cooked in an air fryer?

Answer-Yes, you can add more ingredients while the food is getting cooked in an air fryer but make sure to add the ingredients immediately otherwise the heat loss may lead to more time consumption for cooking the food

#4. Is there any specific type of oil required for air fryer?

Answer- No, there is no special oil which is required for cooking in an air fryer. You can use any type of oil such as olive oil, peanut oil, and even butter spray.

#5. How much food can be cooked at a time in an air fryer?

Answer- It all depends on the capacity of the air fryer. Most of the air fryers come with 500g of capacity and you can also see a "max" mark on the basket of the air fryer which means that the air fryer can be filled up to this mark.

#6. Do we need to preheat the air fryer?

Answer- No, there is no need to preheat the air fryer. However, pre-heating the air fryer for about 4 minutes can help in significant reduction of the cooking time

#7. What is the input power range of an air fryer?

Answer- For the European market the input power range is 220 v and for USA market it is 110 v.

#8. How many items can be cooked at a go in an air fryer?

Answer- You can easily cook two different items at a go in an air fryer but make sure to use the divider. This will help in proper cooking and less time will be consumed

#9. Is it possible to use baking paper or aluminium foil in an air fryer?

Answer- Yes, you can use a baking paper or aluminium foil but you need to make sure that appropriate space is given so that the steam can pass easily

#10. Does air fryer help in making food crispy and tasty?

Answer- Yes, the food that you cook in an air fryer is as tasty and crispy as it is with frying. One of the main reasons why air fryer cooks tasty and crispy food is because it helps in keeping the outer layer of the food crisp and the inside gets soft.

Breakfast Recipes

1. Breakfast Potatoes.

(Prep + Cooking Time: 45 Minutes **| Serves:** 4)

Ingredients:

- 1 yellow onion, chopped.
- 1 red bell pepper, chopped.
- 2-tbsp. olive oil
- 3 potatoes, cubed.
- one-tsp. sweet paprika
- one-tsp. onion powder
- one-tsp. garlic powder
- Salt and black pepper to the taste.

Directions:

1. Grease your air fryer's basket with olive oil; add potatoes, toss and season with salt and pepper.
2. Add onion, bell pepper, garlic powder, paprika and onion powder, toss well, cover and cook at 370 °F, for 30 minutes. Divide potatoes mix on plates and serve for breakfast.

Nutrition Values (Per Serving): Calories: 214; Fat: 6g; Fiber: 8g; Carbs: 15g; Protein: 4g

2. Yummy Hash.

(Prep + Cooking Time: 25 Minutes **| Serves:** 6)

Ingredients:

- 16 oz. hash browns
- 1/4-cup olive oil
- 1 egg, whisked.
- 1-cup cheddar, shredded.
- 2-tbsp. chives, chopped.
- ½-tsp. paprika
- ½-tsp. garlic powder
- Salt and black pepper to the taste.

Directions:

1. Add oil to your air fryer; heat it up at 350 °F and add hash browns.
2. Also add paprika, garlic powder, salt, pepper and egg; toss and cook for 15 minutes. Add cheddar and chives, toss; divide among plates and serve

Nutrition Values (Per Serving): Calories: 213; Fat: 7g; Fiber: 8g; Carbs: 12g; Protein: 4g

3. Fried Sandwich.

(Prep + Cooking Time: 16 Minutes **| Serves:** 2)

Ingredients:

- 2 bacon strips
- 2 English muffins, halved.
- 2 eggs
- Salt and black pepper to the taste.

Directions:

1. Crack eggs in your air fryer, add bacon on top; cover and cook at 392 °F, for 6 minutes. Heat up your English muffin halves in your microwave for a few seconds; divide eggs on 2 halves, add bacon on top, season with salt and pepper; cover with the other 2 English muffins and serve for breakfast.

Nutrition Values (Per Serving): Calories: 261; Fat: 5g; Fiber: 8g; Carbs: 12g; Protein: 4g

4. Delightful Eggs Casserole.

(Prep + Cooking Time: 35 Minutes | **Serves:** 6)

Ingredients:

- 1 lb. turkey, ground.
- 1-cup baby spinach
- 1 sweet potato, cubed.
- 12 eggs
- 2 tomatoes, chopped for serving
- 1-tbsp. olive oil
- ½-tsp. chili powder
- Salt and black pepper to the taste.

Directions:

1. Take a bowl and mix eggs with salt, pepper, chili powder, potato, spinach, turkey and sweet potato and whisk well.
2. Heat up your air fryer at 350 degrees F; add oil and heat it up
3. Add eggs mix, spread into your air fryer; cover and cook for 25 minutes. Divide among plates and serve for breakfast.

Nutrition Values (Per Serving): Calories: 300; Fat: 5g; Fiber: 8g; Carbs: 13g; Protein: 6g

5. Eggs, Sausage and Cheese Mix.

(Prep + Cooking Time: 30 Minutes | **Serves:** 4)

Ingredients:

- 10 oz. sausages; cooked and crumbled
- 1-cup milk
- 1-cup cheddar cheese, shredded.
- 1-cup mozzarella cheese, shredded.
- 8 eggs, whisked.
- Salt and black pepper to the taste.
- Cooking spray.

Directions:

1. Take a bowl and mix sausages with cheese, mozzarella, eggs, milk, salt and pepper and whisk well.
2. Heat up your air fryer at 380 degrees F; spray cooking oil, add eggs and sausage mix and cook for 20 minutes. Divide among plates and serve.

Nutrition Values (Per Serving): Calories: 320; Fat: 6g; Fiber: 8g; Carbs: 12g; Protein: 5g

6. Cheese Fried Bake.

(Prep + Cooking Time: 30 Minutes | **Serves:** 4)

Ingredients:

- 1 lb. breakfast sausage, casings removed and chopped.
- 4 bacon slices; cooked and crumbled
- 2 ½-cups cheddar cheese, shredded.
- 2-cups milk
- 2 eggs
- 3-tbsp. parsley, chopped.
- ½-tsp. onion powder
- Salt and black pepper to the taste.
- Cooking spray.

Directions:

1. Take a bowl and mix eggs with milk, cheese, onion powder, salt, pepper and parsley and whisk well.
2. Grease your air fryer with cooking spray; heat it up at 320 °F and add bacon and sausage
3. Add eggs mix; spread and cook for 20 minutes. Divide among plates and serve

Nutrition Values (Per Serving): Calories: 214; Fat: 5g; Fiber: 8g; Carbs: 12g; Protein: 12g

7. Healthy Asparagus Frittata.

(Prep + Cooking Time: 15 Minutes | **Serves:** 2)

Ingredients:

- 10 asparagus tips; steamed
- 4 eggs, whisked.
- 4-tbsp. milk
- 2-tbsp. parmesan, grated.
- Salt and black pepper to the taste.
- Cooking spray.

Directions:

1. Take a bowl and mix eggs with parmesan, milk, salt and pepper and whisk well.
2. Heat up your air fryer at 400 °F and grease with cooking spray.
3. Add asparagus, add eggs mix; toss a bit and cook for 5 minutes. Divide frittata on plates and serve for breakfast

Nutrition Values (Per Serving): Calories: 312; Fat: 5g; Fiber: 8g; Carbs: 14g; Protein: 2g

8. Egg Muffins.

(Prep + Cooking Time: 25 Minutes | **Serves:** 4)

Ingredients:

- 1 egg
- 3.5 oz. white flour
- 2 oz. parmesan, grated.
- 2-tbsp. olive oil
- 3-tbsp. milk
- 1-tbsp. baking powder.
- A splash of Worcestershire sauce

Directions:

1. Take a bowl and mix egg with flour, oil, baking powder, milk, Worcestershire and parmesan; whisk well and divide into 4 silicon muffin cups
2. Arrange-cups in your air fryer's cooking basket; cover and cook at 392, °F, for 15 minutes. Serve warm for breakfast.

Nutrition Values (Per Serving): Calories: 251; Fat: 6g; Fiber: 8g; Carbs: 9g; Protein: 3g

9. Eggs and Tomatoes.

(Prep + Cooking Time: 15 Minutes | **Serves:** 4)

Ingredients:

- 8 cherry tomatoes, halved.
- 4 eggs
- 2 oz. milk
- 2-tbsp. parmesan, grated.
- Cooking spray.
- Salt and black pepper to the taste.

Directions:

1. Grease your air fryer with cooking spray and heat it up at 200 degrees F.
2. Take a bowl and mix eggs with cheese, milk, salt and pepper and whisk
3. Add this mix to your air fryer and cook for 6 minutes. Add tomatoes; cook your scrambled eggs for 3 minutes, divide among plates and serve.

Nutrition Values (Per Serving): Calories: 200; Fat: 4g; Fiber: 7g; Carbs: 12g; Protein: 3g

10. Potato Frittata.

(Prep + Cooking Time: 30 Minutes | **Serves:** 6)

Ingredients:

- 6 oz. jarred roasted red bell peppers, chopped.
- ½-cup parmesan, grated.
- 16 potato wedges
- 3 garlic cloves, minced.
- 12 eggs, whisked.
- 6-tbsp. ricotta cheese
- 2-tbsp. parsley, chopped.
- 2-tbsp. chives, chopped.
- Salt and black pepper to the taste.
- Cooking spray.

Directions:

1. Take a bowl and mix eggs with red peppers, garlic, parsley, salt, pepper and ricotta and whisk well.
2. Heat up your air fryer at 300 °F and grease it with cooking spray
3. Add half of the potato wedges on the bottom and sprinkle half of the parmesan all over.
4. Add half of the egg mix; add the rest of the potatoes and the rest of the parmesan.
5. Add the rest of the eggs mix; sprinkle chives and cook for 20 minutes. Divide among plates and serve for breakfast

Nutrition Values (Per Serving): Calories: 312; Fat: 6g; Fiber: 9g; Carbs: 16g; Protein: 5g

11. Bacon and Tomato Breakfast.

(Prep + Cooking Time: 40 Minutes | **Serves:** 6)

Ingredients:

- 1 lb. smoked bacon, cooked and chopped.
- ½ lb. cheddar, shredded.
- 1 lb. white bread, cubed.
- ½ lb. Monterey jack, shredded.
- 1 yellow onion, chopped.
- 28 oz. canned tomatoes, chopped.
- 1/4-cup olive oil
- 8 eggs; whisked
- 2-tbsp. chives, chopped.
- 2-tbsp. stock
- ½-tsp. red pepper; crushed
- Salt and black pepper to the taste.

Directions:

1. Add the oil to your air fryer and heat it up at 350 degrees F
2. Add bread, bacon, onion, tomatoes, red pepper and stock and stir.
3. Add eggs, cheddar and Monterey jack and cook everything for 20 minutes. Divide among plates; sprinkle chives and serve.

Nutrition Values (Per Serving): Calories: 231; Fat: 5g; Fiber: 7g; Carbs: 12g; Protein: 4g

12. Biscuits Casserole Delight.

(Prep + Cooking Time: 25 Minutes | **Serves:** 8)

Ingredients:

- 12 oz. biscuits, quartered.
- ½ lb. sausage, chopped.
- 2 ½-cups milk
- 3-tbsp. flour
- A pinch of salt and black pepper
- Cooking spray.

Directions:

1. Grease your air fryer with cooking spray and heat it over 350 degrees F
2. Add biscuits on the bottom and mix with sausage.
3. Add flour, milk, salt and pepper; toss a bit and cook for 15 minutes. Divide among plates and serve for breakfast.

Nutrition Values (Per Serving): Calories: 321; Fat: 4g; Fiber: 7g; Carbs: 12g; Protein: 5g

13. Cheesy Bread.

(Prep + Cooking Time: 18 Minutes | **Serves:** 3)

Ingredients:

- 3 garlic cloves, minced.
- 1-cup mozzarella cheese, grated.
- 6 bread slices
- 5-tbsp. butter, melted.
- 6-tsp. sun dried tomato pesto

Directions:

1. Arrange bread slices on a working surface.
2. Spread butter all over; divide tomato paste, garlic and top with grated cheese.
3. Add bread slices to your heated air fryer and cook them at 350 °F, for 8 minutes. Divide among plates and serve for breakfast

Nutrition Values (Per Serving): Calories: 187; Fat: 5g; Fiber: 6g; Carbs: 8g; Protein: 3g

14. Banana Oatmeal Casserole.

(Prep + Cooking Time: 30 Minutes | **Serves:** 8)

Ingredients:

- 1 banana, peeled and mashed.
- 2-cups rolled oats
- 1/3-cup brown sugar
- 2-cups milk
- 1 egg
- ½-cup chocolate chips
- 2/3-cup blueberries
- 2-tbsp. butter
- one-tsp. baking powder.
- one-tsp. vanilla extract
- one-tsp. cinnamon powder
- Cooking spray.

Directions:

1. Take a bowl and mix sugar with baking powder, cinnamon, chocolate chips, blueberries and banana and stir.
2. Now, take a separate bowl, mix eggs with vanilla extract and butter and stir
3. Heat up your air fryer at 320 degrees F, grease with cooking spray and add oats on the bottom.
4. Add cinnamon mix and eggs mix; toss and cook for 20 minutes. Stir one more time, divide into bowls and serve for breakfast

Nutrition Values (Per Serving): Calories: 300; Fat: 4g; Fiber: 7g; Carbs: 12g; Protein: 10g

15. Ham Pie.

(Prep + Cooking Time: 35 Minutes | **Serves:** 6)

Ingredients:

- 16 oz. crescent rolls dough
- 2 eggs, whisked.
- 2-cups ham, cooked and chopped.
- 2-cups cheddar cheese, grated.
- 1-tbsp. parmesan, grated.
- Salt and black pepper to the taste.
- Cooking spray.

Directions:

1. Grease your air fryer's pan with cooking spray and press half of the crescent rolls dough on the bottom
2. Take a bowl and mix eggs with cheddar cheese, parmesan, salt and pepper; whisk well and add over dough.
3. Spread ham, cut the rest of the crescent rolls dough in strips, arrange them over ham and cook at 300 °F, for 25 minutes. Slice pie and serve for breakfast.

Nutrition Values (Per Serving): Calories: 400; Fat: 27g; Fiber: 7g; Carbs: 22g; Protein: 16

16. Quick Turkey Burrito.

(Prep + Cooking Time: 20 Minutes | **Serves:** 2)

Ingredients:

- 4 slices turkey breast already cooked
- 1/8-cup mozzarella cheese, grated.
- 1 small avocado, peeled, pitted and sliced.
- ½ red bell pepper, sliced.
- 2 eggs
- 2-tbsp. salsa
- Salt and black pepper to the taste.
- Tortillas for serving

Directions:

1. Take a bowl and whisk eggs with salt and pepper to the taste, pour them in a pan and place it in the air fryer's basket.
2. Cook at 400 °F, for 5 minutes; take pan out of the fryer and transfer eggs to a plate
3. Arrange tortillas on a working surface, divide eggs on them; also divide turkey meat, bell pepper, cheese, salsa and avocado.
4. Roll your burritos and place them in your air fryer after you've lined it with some tin foil. Heat up the burritos at 300 °F, for 3 minutes; divide them on plates and serve.

Nutrition Values (Per Serving): Calories: 349; Fat: 23g; Fiber: 11g; Carbs: 20g; Protein: 21g

17. Cinnamon Toast.

(Prep + Cooking Time: 15 Minutes | **Serves:** 6)

Ingredients:

- 1 stick butter, soft.
- 12 bread slices
- ½-cup sugar
- 1 ½-tsp. vanilla extract
- 1 ½-tsp. cinnamon powder.

Directions:

1. Take a bowl and mix soft butter with sugar, vanilla and cinnamon and whisk well.
2. Spread this on bread slices; place them in your air fryer and cook at 400 °F, for 5 minutes; divide among plates and serve for breakfast

Nutrition Values (Per Serving): Calories: 221; Fat: 4g; Fiber: 7g; Carbs: 12g; Protein: 8g

18. Simple Breakfast.

(Prep + Cooking Time: 23 Minutes | **Serves:** 4)

Ingredients:

- 7 oz. baby spinach
- 1 garlic clove, minced.
- 4 eggs
- 8 chestnuts mushrooms, halved.
- 8 tomatoes, halved.
- 4 chipolatas
- 4 bacon slices, chopped.
- Salt and black pepper to the taste.
- Cooking spray.

Directions:

1. Grease a cooking pan with the oil and add tomatoes, garlic and mushrooms.
2. Add bacon and chipolatas, also add spinach and crack eggs at the end
3. Season with salt and pepper; place pan in the cooking basket of your air fryer and cook for 13 minutes at 350 degrees F. Divide among plates and serve for breakfast.

Nutrition Values (Per Serving): Calories: 312; Fat: 6g; Fiber: 8g; Carbs: 15g; Protein: 5g

19. Smoked Sausage Breakfast.

(Prep + Cooking Time: 40 Minutes | **Serves:** 4)

Ingredients:

- 1 ½ lbs. smoked sausage, chopped and browned.
- 16 oz. cheddar cheese, shredded.
- 1-cup milk
- 4 eggs, whisked.
- 1 ½-cups grits
- 4 ½-cups water
- 1 ½-tsp. thyme, chopped.
- 1/4-tsp. garlic powder
- Cooking spray.
- A pinch of salt and black pepper

Directions:

1. Put the water in a pot; bring to a boil over medium heat, add grits, stir and cover, cook for 5 minutes and take off heat
2. Add cheese, stir until it melts and mix with milk, thyme, salt, pepper, garlic powder and eggs and whisk really well.
3. Heat up your air fryer at 300 degrees F; grease with cooking spray and add browned sausage.
4. Add grits mix; spread and cook for 25 minutes. Divide among plates and serve for breakfast

Nutrition Values (Per Serving): Calories: 321; Fat: 6g; Fiber: 7g; Carbs: 17g; Protein: 4g

20. Polenta Bites.

(Prep + Cooking Time: 30 Minutes | **Serves:** 4)

Ingredients:

For the polenta:

- 1-cup cornmeal
- 1-tbsp. butter
- 3-cups water
- Salt and black pepper to the taste.

For the polenta bites:

- 2-tbsp. powdered sugar
- Cooking spray.

Directions:

1. In a pan; mix water with cornmeal, butter, salt and pepper, stir, bring to a boil over medium heat; cook for 10 minutes, take off heat; whisk one more time and keep in the fridge until it's cold
2. Scoop 1-tbsp. of polenta, shape a ball and place on a working surface.
3. Repeat with the rest of the polenta; arrange all the balls in the cooking basket of your air fryer, spray them with cooking spray; cover and cook at 380 °F, for 8 minutes. Arrange polenta bites on plates; sprinkle sugar all over and serve for breakfast

Nutrition Values (Per Serving): Calories: 231; Fat: 7g; Fiber: 8g; Carbs: 12g; Protein: 4g

21. Mixed Bell Peppers Frittata.

(Prep + Cooking Time: 30 Minutes | **Serves:** 4)

Ingredients:

- ½ lbs. chicken sausage, casings removed and chopped.
- 1 orange bell pepper, chopped.
- 1 green bell pepper, chopped.
- 8 eggs, whisked.
- ½-cup mozzarella cheese, shredded.
- 1 sweet onion, chopped.
- 1 red bell pepper, chopped.
- 2-tbsp. olive oil
- 2-tsp. oregano, chopped.
- Salt and black pepper to the taste.

Directions:

1. Add 1-tbsp. oil to your air fryer; add sausage, heat up at 320 °F and brown for 1 minute.
2. Add the rest of the oil, onion, red bell pepper, orange and green one; stir and cook for 2 minutes more
3. Add oregano, salt, pepper and eggs; stir and cook for 15 minutes. Add mozzarella, leave frittata aside for a few minutes; divide among plates and serve.

Nutrition Values (Per Serving): Calories: 212; Fat: 4g; Fiber: 6g; Carbs: 8g; Protein: 12g

22. Rice, Almonds Pudding.

(Prep + Cooking Time: 13 Minutes | **Serves:** 4)

Ingredients:

- 1/4-cup raisins
- 1-cup brown rice
- ½-cup maple syrup
- 1/4-cup almonds
- ½-cup coconut chips
- 1-cup milk
- 2-cups water
- A pinch of cinnamon powder.

Directions:

1. Put the rice in a pan that fits your air fryer, add the water, heat up on the stove over medium high heat; cook until rice is soft and drain.
2. Add milk, coconut chips, almonds, raisins, cinnamon and maple syrup; stir well, introduce in your air fryer and cook at 360 °F, for 8 minutes. Divide rice pudding in bowls and serve

Nutrition Values (Per Serving): Calories: 251; Fat: 6g; Fiber: 8g; Carbs: 39g; Protein: 12g

23. Potatoes with Bacon.

(Prep + Cooking Time: 30 Minutes | **Serves:** 4)

Ingredients:

- 4 potatoes, peeled and cut into medium cubes
- 2 eggs, whisked.
- 6 garlic cloves, minced.
- 4 bacon slices, chopped.
- 2 rosemary springs, chopped.
- 1-tbsp. olive oil
- Salt and black pepper to the taste.

Directions:

1. In your air fryer's pan, mix oil with potatoes, garlic, bacon, rosemary, salt, pepper and eggs and whisk. Cook potatoes at 400 °F, for 20 minutes; divide everything on plates and serve for breakfast

Nutrition Values (Per Serving): Calories: 211; Fat: 3g; Fiber: 5g; Carbs: 8g; Protein: 5g

24. French Beans and Egg Mix.

(Prep + Cooking Time: 20 Minutes | **Serves:** 3)

Ingredients:

- 3 oz. French beans; trimmed and sliced diagonally
- 4 garlic cloves, minced.
- 2 eggs, whisked.
- 1-tbsp. olive oil
- ½-tsp. soy sauce
- Salt and white pepper to the taste

Directions:

1. Take a bowl and mix eggs with soy sauce, salt and pepper and whisk well.
2. Heat up your air fryer at 320 degrees F, add oil and heat it up as well.
3. Add garlic and brown for 1 minute

4. Add French beans and egg mix; toss and cook for 10 minutes. Divide among plates and serve for breakfast.

Nutrition Values (Per Serving): Calories: 182; Fat: 3g; Fiber: 6g; Carbs: 8g; Protein: 3g

25. Protein Rich Egg White Omelet.

(Prep + Cooking Time: 25 Minutes | **Serves:** 4)

Ingredients:

- 1/4-cup tomato, chopped.
- 1/4-cup mushrooms, chopped.
- 1-cup egg whites
- 2-tbsp. skim milk
- 2-tbsp. chives, chopped.
- Salt and black pepper to the taste.

Directions:

1. Take a bowl and mix egg whites with tomato, milk, mushrooms, chives, salt and pepper; whisk well and pour into your air fryer's pan. Cook at 320 °F, for 15 minutes; cool omelet down, slice, divide among plates and serve.

Nutrition Values (Per Serving): Calories: 100; Fat: 3g; Fiber: 6g; Carbs: 7g; Carbs: 4

26. Breakfast Spanish Omelet.

(Prep + Cooking Time: 20 Minutes | **Serves:** 4)

Ingredients:

- 1 potato, peeled and cubed
- ½-cup corn
- 3 eggs
- ½ chorizo, chopped.
- 1-tbsp. parsley, chopped.
- 1-tbsp. feta cheese, crumbled.
- 1-tbsp. olive oil
- Salt and black pepper to the taste.

Directions:

1. Heat up your air fryer at 350 °F and add oil.
2. Add chorizo and potatoes; stir and brown them for a few seconds.
3. Take a bowl and mix eggs with corn, parsley, cheese, salt and pepper and whisk
4. Pour this over chorizo and potatoes; spread and cook for 5 minutes. Divide omelet on plates and serve for breakfast

Nutrition Values (Per Serving): Calories: 300; Fat: 6g; Fiber: 9g; Carbs: 12g; Protein: 6g

27. Breakfast Casserole.

(Prep + Cooking Time: 40 Minutes | **Serves:** 4)

Ingredients:

- ½-cup flour
- 4-tbsp. butter
- 2-tbsp. white sugar
- 3-tbsp. brown sugar
- ½-tsp. cinnamon powder.

For the casserole:

- ½-cup milk
- 2-cups buttermilk
- 2 ½-cups white flour
- 1 ⅔-cup blueberries
- 2 eggs
- 2 eggs
- 4-tbsp. butter
- 2-tbsp. white sugar
- one-tsp. baking soda
- one-tsp. baking powder.
- Zest from 1 lemon, grated.

Directions:

1. Take a bowl and mix 2-tbsp. white sugar with 2 ½-cups white flour, baking powder, baking soda, 2 eggs, milk, buttermilk, 4-tbsp. butter, lemon zest and blueberries; stir and pour into a pan that fits your air fryer
2. In another bowls; mix 3-tbsp. brown sugar with 2-tbsp. white sugar, 4-tbsp. butter, ½-cup flour and cinnamon, stir until you obtain a crumble and spread over blueberries mix.
3. Place in preheated air fryer and bake at 300 °F, for 30 minutes. Divide among plates and serve for breakfast.

Nutrition Values (Per Serving): Calories: 214; Fat: 5g; Fiber: 8g; Carbs: 12g; Protein: 5g

28. Breakfast Shrimp Frittata.

(Prep + Cooking Time: 25 Minutes | **Serves:** 4)

Ingredients:

- ½-cup shrimp; cooked, peeled, deveined and chopped.
- ½-cup baby spinach, chopped.
- ½-cup rice; cooked
- ½-cup Monterey jack cheese, grated.
- 4 eggs
- ½-tsp. basil; dried
- Cooking spray.
- Salt and black pepper to the taste.

Directions:

1. Take a bowl and mix eggs with salt, pepper and basil and whisk.
2. Grease your air fryer's pan with cooking spray and add rice, shrimp and spinach.
3. Add eggs mix, sprinkle cheese all over and cook in your air fryer at 350 °F, for 10 minutes. Divide among plates and serve for breakfast

Nutrition Values (Per Serving): Calories: 162; Fat: 6g; Fiber: 5g; Carbs: 8g; Protein: 4g

29. Yummy Creamy Eggs.

(Prep + Cooking Time: 22 Minutes | **Serves:** 4)

Ingredients:

- 4 eggs
- 2 ham slices
- 2-tbsp. heavy cream
- 3-tbsp. parmesan, grated.
- 2-tsp. chives, chopped.
- 2-tsp. butter, soft.
- Salt and black pepper to the taste.
- A pinch of smoked paprika

Directions:

1. Grease your air fryer's pan with the butter; line it with the ham and add it to your air fryer's basket.
2. Take a bowl and mix 1 egg with heavy cream, salt and pepper, whisk well and add over ham
3. Crack the rest of the eggs in the pan, sprinkle parmesan and cook your mix for 12 minutes at 320 degrees F. Sprinkle paprika and chives all over; divide among plates and serve for breakfast

Nutrition Values (Per Serving): Calories: 263; Fat: 5g; Fiber: 8g; Carbs: 12g; Protein: 5g

30. Yummy Tofu Scramble.

(Prep + Cooking Time: 35 Minutes | **Serves:** 4)

Ingredients:

- 4-cups broccoli florets
- 2½-cup red potatoes, cubed.
- ½-cup yellow onion, chopped.
- 1 tofu block, cubed.
- 2-tbsp. extra virgin olive oil
- 2-tbsp. soy sauce

- ½-tsp. onion powder
- one-tsp. turmeric, ground.
- ½-tsp. garlic powder
- Salt and black pepper to the taste.

Directions:

1. Mix tofu with 1-tbsp. oil, salt, pepper, soy sauce, garlic powder, onion powder, turmeric and onion in a bowl; stir and leave aside
2. Now, take a separate bowl, combine potatoes with the rest of the oil, a pinch of salt and pepper and toss to coat.
3. Put potatoes in your air fryer at 350 °F and bake for 15 minutes; shaking once.
4. Add tofu and its marinade to your air fryer and bake for 15 minutes
5. Add broccoli to the fryer and cook everything for 5 minutes more. Serve right away.

Nutrition Values (Per Serving): Calories: 140; Fat: 4g; Fiber: 3g; Carbs: 10g; Protein: 14g

31. Breakfast Soufflé.

(Prep + Cooking Time: 18 Minutes | **Serves:** 4)

Ingredients:

- 4 eggs, whisked.
- 2-tbsp. parsley, chopped.
- 2-tbsp. chives, chopped.
- 4-tbsp. heavy cream
- A pinch of red chili pepper; crushed
- Salt and black pepper to the taste.

Directions:

1. Take a bowl and mix eggs with salt, pepper, heavy cream, red chili pepper, parsley and chives; stir well and divide into 4 soufflé dishes
2. Arrange dishes in your air fryer and cook soufflés at 350 °F, for 8 minutes. Serve them hot.

Nutrition Values (Per Serving): Calories: 300; Fat: 7g; Fiber: 9g; Carbs: 15g; Protein: 6g

32. Special Long Beans Omelet.

(Prep + Cooking Time: 20 Minutes | **Serves:** 3)

Ingredients:

- 4 long beans; trimmed and sliced
- 4 garlic cloves, minced.
- 3 eggs, whisked.
- 1-tbsp. olive oil
- ½-tsp. soy sauce
- A pinch of salt and black pepper

Directions:

1. Take a bowl and mix eggs with a pinch of salt, black pepper and soy sauce and whisk well.
2. Heat up your air fryer at 320 degrees F, add oil and garlic, stir and brown for 1 minute
3. Add long beans and eggs mix; spread and cook for 10 minutes. Divide omelet on plates and serve for breakfast.

Nutrition Values (Per Serving): Calories: 200; Fat: 3g; Fiber: 7g; Carbs: 9g; Protein: 3g

33. Special Hash Browns.

(Prep + Cooking Time: 30 Minutes | **Serves:** 6)

Ingredients:

- 2 lbs. hash browns
- 8 bacon slices, chopped.
- 9 oz. cream cheese
- 6 eggs
- 1-cup cheddar cheese, shredded.
- 6 green onions, chopped.
- 1 yellow onion, chopped.
- 1-cup whole milk
- Salt and black pepper to the taste.
- Cooking spray.

Directions:

1. Heat up your air fryer at 350 °F and grease it with cooking spray.
2. Take a bowl and mix eggs with milk, cream cheese, cheddar cheese, bacon, onion, salt and pepper and whisk well
3. Add hash browns to your air fryer; add eggs mix over them and cook for 20 minutes. Divide among plates and serve.

Nutrition Values (Per Serving): Calories: 261; Fat: 6g; Fiber: 9g; Carbs: 8g; Protein: 12g

34. Morning Egg Bowls.

(Prep + Cooking Time: 30 Minutes | **Serves:** 4)

Ingredients:

- 4 dinner rolls, tops cut off and insides scooped out.
- 4 eggs
- 4-tbsp. parmesan, grated.
- 4-tbsp. heavy cream
- 4-tbsp. mixed chives and parsley
- Salt and black pepper to the taste.

Directions:

1. Arrange dinner rolls on a baking sheet and crack an egg in each.
2. Divide heavy cream, mixed herbs in each roll and season with salt and pepper.
3. Sprinkle parmesan on top of your rolls; place them in your air fryer and cook at 350 °F, for 20 minutes. Divide your bread bowls on plates and serve for breakfast

Nutrition Values (Per Serving): Calories: 238; Fat: 4g; Fiber: 7g; Carbs: 14g; Protein: 7

35. Potato Hash.

(Prep + Cooking Time: 35 Minutes | **Serves:** 4)

Ingredients:

- 1 ½ potatoes, cubed.
- 1 green bell pepper, chopped.
- 1 yellow onion, chopped.
- 2 eggs
- ½-tsp. thyme; dried
- 2-tsp. olive oil
- Salt and black pepper to the taste.

Directions:

1. Heat up your air fryer at 350 degrees F; add oil, heat it up, add onion, bell pepper, salt and pepper; stir and cook for 5 minutes.
2. Add potatoes, thyme and eggs, stir, cover and cook at 360 °F, for 20 minutes. Divide among plates and serve for breakfast

Nutrition Values (Per Serving): Calories: 241; Fat: 4g; Fiber: 7g; Carbs: 12g; Protein: 7g

36. Broccoli Quiches.

(Prep + Cooking Time: 30 Minutes | **Serves:** 2)

Ingredients:

- 1 broccoli head; florets separated and steamed
- 3 carrots, chopped and steamed
- 2 oz. cheddar cheese, grated.
- 2 oz. milk
- 1 tomato, chopped.
- 2 eggs
- one-tsp. thyme, chopped.
- one-tsp. parsley, chopped.
- Salt and black pepper to the taste.

Directions:

1. Take a bowl and mix eggs with milk, parsley, thyme, salt and pepper and whisk well.
2. Put broccoli, carrots and tomato in your air fryer
3. Add eggs mix on top, spread cheddar cheese; cover and cook at 350 °F, for 20 minutes. Divide among plates and serve for breakfast

Nutrition Values (Per Serving): Calories: 214; Fat: 4g; Fiber: 7g; Carbs: 12g; Protein: 3g

37. Spinach Parcels.

(Prep + Cooking Time: 14 Minutes | **Serves:** 2)

Ingredients:

- 1 lb. baby spinach leaves; roughly chopped
- ½ lb. ricotta cheese
- 1 egg, whisked.
- 4 sheets filo pastry
- 2-tbsp. pine nuts
- Zest from 1 lemon, grated.
- Salt and black pepper to the taste.
- Greek yogurt for serving

Directions:

1. Take a bowl and mix spinach with cheese, egg, lemon zest, salt, pepper and pine nuts and stir
2. Arrange filo sheets on a working surface, divide spinach mix; fold diagonally to shape your parcels and place them in your preheated air fryer at 400 degrees F. Bake parcels for 4 minutes; divide them on plates and serve them with Greek yogurt on the side

Nutrition Values (Per Serving): Calories: 182; Fat: 4g; Fiber: 8g; Carbs: 9g; Protein: 5g

38. Veggie Burritos Breakfast.

(Prep + Cooking Time: 20 Minutes | **Serves:** 4)

Ingredients:

- ½-cup sweet potatoes; steamed and cubed
- 4 rice papers
- 7 asparagus stalks
- ½ small broccoli head; florets separated and steamed
- 8 roasted red peppers, chopped.
- A handful kale, chopped.
- 2-tbsp. water
- 2-tbsp. liquid smoke
- 2-tbsp. cashew butter
- 2-tbsp. tamari

Directions:

1. Take a bowl and mix cashew butter with water, tamari and liquid smoke and whisk well.
2. Wet rice papers and arrange them on a working surface
3. Divide sweet potatoes, broccoli, asparagus, red peppers and kale; wrap burritos and dip each in cashew mix.
4. Arrange burritos in your air fryer and cook them at 350 °F, for 10 minutes. Divide veggie burritos on plates d serve

Nutrition Values (Per Serving): Calories: 172; Fat: 4g; Fiber: 7g; Carbs: 8g; Protein: 3g

39. Baked Eggs.

(Prep + Cooking Time: 30 Minutes | **Serves:** 4)

Ingredients:

- 1 lb. baby spinach; torn
- 4 eggs
- 7 oz. ham, chopped.
- 1-tbsp. olive oil
- 4-tbsp. milk
- Cooking spray.
- Salt and black pepper to the taste.

Directions:

1. Heat up a pan with the oil over medium heat; add baby spinach, stir cook for a couple of minutes and take off heat
2. Grease 4 ramekins with cooking spray and divide baby spinach and ham in each.
3. Crack an egg in each ramekin, also divide milk, season with salt and pepper; place ramekins in preheated air fryer at 350 °F and bake for 20 minutes. Serve baked eggs for breakfast

Nutrition Values (Per Serving): Calories: 321; Fat: 6g; Fiber: 8g; Carbs: 15g; Protein: 12

40. Leek and Potato Frittata.

(Prep + Cooking Time: 28 Minutes | **Serves:** 4)

Ingredients:

- 5 oz. fromage blanc, crumbled.
- 2 gold potatoes, boiled, peeled and chopped.
- 10 eggs, whisked.
- 2 leeks, sliced.
- 1/4-cup whole milk
- 2-tbsp. butter
- Salt and black pepper to the taste.

Directions:

1. Heat up a pan that fits your air fryer with the butter over medium heat, add leeks; stir and cook for 4 minutes.
2. Add potatoes, salt, pepper, eggs, cheese and milk, whisk well; cook for 1 minute more, introduce in your air fryer and cook at 350 °F, for 13 minutes. Slice frittata, divide among plates and serve

Nutrition Values (Per Serving): Calories: 271; Fat: 6g; Fiber: 8g; Carbs: 12g; Protein: 6g

41. Breakfast Cherries Risotto.

(Prep + Cooking Time: 22 Minutes | **Serves:** 4)

Ingredients:

- 1 ½-cups Arborio rice
- ½-cup cherries; dried
- 1/3-cup brown sugar
- 2 apples; cored and sliced
- 1-cup apple juice
- 3-cups milk
- 2-tbsp. butter
- 1 ½-tsp. cinnamon powder.
- A pinch of salt

Directions:

1. Heat up a pan that fist your air fryer with the butter over medium heat, add rice; stir and cook for 4-5 minutes.
2. Add sugar, apples, apple juice, milk, cinnamon and cherries; stir, introduce in your air fryer and cook at 350 °F, for 8 minutes. Divide into bowls and serve for breakfast

Nutrition Values (Per Serving): Calories: 162; Fat: 12g; Fiber: 6g; Carbs: 23g; Protein: 8g

42. Tasty Tuna Sandwiches.

(Prep + Cooking Time: 15 Minutes | **Serves:** 4)

Ingredients:

- 3 English muffins, halved.
- 16 oz. canned tuna; drained
- 6 provolone cheese
- 2 green onions, chopped.
- 1/4-cup mayonnaise
- 1-tbsp. lemon juice
- 2-tbsp. mustard
- 3-tbsp. butter

Directions:

1. Take a bowl and mix tuna with mayo, lemon juice, mustard and green onions and stir.
2. Grease muffin halves with the butter, place them in preheated air fryer and bake them at 350 °F, for 4 minutes. Spread tuna mix on muffin halves; top each with provolone cheese, return sandwiches to air fryer and cook them for 4 minutes; divide among plates and serve for breakfast right away

Nutrition Values (Per Serving): Calories: 182; Fat: 4g; Fiber: 7g; Carbs: 8g; Protein: 6g

43. Tasty Scrambled Eggs.

(Prep + Cooking Time: 20 Minutes | **Serves:** 2)

Ingredients:

- 1 red bell pepper, chopped.
- 2 eggs
- 2-tbsp. butter
- A pinch of sweet paprika
- Salt and black pepper to the taste.

Directions:

1. Take a bowl and mix eggs with salt, pepper, paprika and red bell pepper and whisk well.
2. Heat up your air fryer at 140 degrees F; add butter and melt it
3. Add eggs mix; stir and cook for 10 minutes. Divide scrambled eggs on plates and serve for breakfast.

Nutrition Values (Per Serving): Calories: 200; Fat: 4g; Fiber: 7g; Carbs: 10g; Protein: 3g

44. Breakfast Ham Dish.

(Prep + Cooking Time: 25 Minutes | **Serves:** 6)

Ingredients:

- 4 oz. green chilies, chopped.
- 10 oz. ham, cubed.
- 4 oz. cheddar cheese, shredded.
- 6-cups French bread, cubed.
- 2-cups milk
- 5 eggs
- 1-tbsp. mustard
- Salt and black pepper to the taste.
- Cooking spray

Directions:

1. Heat up your air fryer at 350 °F and grease it with cooking spray.
2. Take a bowl and mix eggs with milk, cheese, mustard, salt and pepper and stir.
3. Add bread cubes in your air fryer and mix with chilies and ham
4. Add eggs mix; spread and cook for 15 minutes. Divide among plates and serve.

Nutrition Values (Per Serving): Calories: 200; Fat: 5g; Fiber: 6g; Carbs: 12g; Protein: 14g

45. Breakfast Burger.

(Prep + Cooking Time: 55 Minutes | **Serves:** 4)

Ingredients:

- 1 lb. beef, ground.
- 4 bread buns; for serving
- 1 yellow onion, chopped.
- 1-tbsp. cheddar cheese, grated.
- one-tsp. garlic, minced.
- one-tsp. mustard
- one-tsp. basil; dried
- one-tsp. parsley, chopped.
- one-tsp. tomato puree
- Salt and black pepper to the taste.

Directions:

1. Take a bowl and mix beef with onion, tomato puree, garlic, mustard, basil, parsley, cheese, salt and pepper; stir well and shape 4 burgers out of this mix

2. Heat up your air fryer at 400 degrees F; add burgers and cook them for 25 minutes.
3. Reduce temperature to 350 °F and bake burgers for 20 minutes more. Arrange them on bread buns and serve for a quick breakfast

Nutrition Values (Per Serving): Calories: 234; Fat: 5g; Fiber: 8g; Carbs: 12g; Protein: 4g

46. Dates Millet Pudding.

(Prep + Cooking Time: 25 Minutes | **Serves:** 4)

Ingredients:

- 4 dates; pitted
- 14 oz. milk
- ⅔-cup millet
- 7 oz. water
- Honey for serving

Directions:

1. Put the millet in a pan that fits your air fryer; add dates, milk and water; stir, introduce in your air fryer and cook at 360 °F, for 15 minutes. Divide among plates; drizzle honey on top and serve for breakfast.

Nutrition Values (Per Serving): Calories: 231; Fat: 6g; Fiber: 6g; Carbs: 18g; Protein: 6g

47. Easy Onion Frittata.

(Prep + Cooking Time: 30 Minutes | **Serves:** 6)

Ingredients:

- 1 lb. small potatoes, chopped.
- 1 oz. cheddar cheese, grated.
- ½-cup sour cream
- 2 yellow onions, chopped.
- 10 eggs, whisked.
- 1-tbsp. olive oil
- Salt and black pepper to the taste.

Directions:

1. In a large bowl; mix eggs with potatoes, onions, salt, pepper, cheese and sour cream and whisk well.
2. Grease your air fryer's pan with the oil, add eggs mix; place in air fryer and cook for 20 minutes at 320 degrees F. Slice frittata, divide among plates and serve for breakfast.

Nutrition Values (Per Serving): Calories: 231; Fat: 5g; Fiber: 7g; Carbs: 8g; Protein: 4g

48. Special Corn Flakes Casserole.

(Prep + Cooking Time: 18 Minutes | **Serves:** 5)

Ingredients:

- 2 eggs, whisked.
- 1/4-cup blueberries
- 1 ½-cups corn flakes, crumbled.
- 5 bread slices
- 1/3-cup milk
- 4-tbsp. cream cheese; whipped
- 3-tsp. sugar
- 1/4-tsp. nutmeg, ground.

Directions:

1. Take a bowl and mix eggs with sugar, nutmeg and milk and whisk well.
2. In another bowl; mix cream cheese with blueberries and whisk well
3. Put corn flakes in a third bowl.
4. Spread blueberry mix on each bread slice; then dip in eggs mix and dredge in corn flakes at the end.
5. Place bread in your air fryer's basket; heat up at 400 °F and bake for 8 minutes. Divide among plates and serve for breakfast

Nutrition Values (Per Serving): Calories: 300; Fat: 5g; Fiber: 7g; Carbs: 16g; Protein: 4g

49. Special Shrimp Sandwiches.

(Prep + Cooking Time: 15 Minutes | **Serves:** 4)

Ingredients:

- 1 ¼-cups cheddar, shredded.
- 4 whole wheat bread slices
- 6 oz. canned tiny shrimp; drained
- 2-tbsp. green onions, chopped.
- 3-tbsp. mayonnaise
- 2-tbsp. butter, soft.

Directions:

1. Take a bowl and mix shrimp with cheese, green onion and mayo and stir well.
2. Spread this on half of the bread slices; top with the other bread slices, cut into halves diagonally and spread butter on top.
3. Place sandwiches in your air fryer and cook at 350 °F, for 5 minutes. Divide shrimp sandwiches on plates and serve them for breakfast

Nutrition Values (Per Serving): Calories: 162; Fat: 3g; Fiber: 7g; Carbs: 12g; Protein: 4g

50. Blackberry French Style Toast.

(Prep + Cooking Time: 30 Minutes | **Serves:** 6)

Ingredients:

- 1-cup blackberry jam; warm
- 12 oz. bread loaf, cubed.
- 8 oz. cream cheese, cubed.
- 4 eggs
- ½-cup brown sugar
- 2-cups half and half
- one-tsp. vanilla extract
- one-tsp. cinnamon powder.
- Cooking spray.

Directions:

1. Grease your air fryer with cooking spray and heat it up at 300 degrees F
2. Add blueberry jam on the bottom, layer half of the bread cubes, then add cream cheese and top with the rest of the bread.
3. Take a bowl and mix eggs with half and half, cinnamon, sugar and vanilla; whisk well and add over bread mix. Cook for 20 minutes; divide among plates and serve for breakfast

Nutrition Values (Per Serving): Calories: 215; Fat: 6g; Fiber: 9g; Carbs: 16g; Protein: 6g

51. Buttermilk Biscuits.

(Prep + Cooking Time: 18 Minutes | **Serves:** 4)

Ingredients:

- 3/4-cup buttermilk
- 1 ¼-cup white flour
- ½-cup self-rising flour
- 4-tbsp. butter; cold and cubed+ 1-tbsp. melted butter
- 1/4-tsp. baking soda
- ½-tsp. baking powder.
- one-tsp. sugar
- Maple syrup for serving

Directions:

1. Take a bowl and mix white flour with self-rising flour, baking soda, baking powder and sugar and stir.
2. Add cold butter and stir using your hands
3. Add buttermilk, stir until you obtain a dough and transfer to a floured working surface.
4. Roll your dough and cut 10 pieces using a round cutter.
5. Arrange biscuits in your air fryer's cake pan; brush them with melted butter and cook at 400 °F, for 8 minutes. Serve them for breakfast with some maple syrup on top

Nutrition Values (Per Serving): Calories: 192; Fat: 6g; Fiber: 9g; Carbs: 12g; Protein: 3g

52. Fried Tomato Quiche.

(Prep + Cooking Time: 40 Minutes | **Serves:** 1)

Ingredients:

- ½-cup gouda cheese, shredded.
- 1/4-cup tomatoes, chopped.
- 2 eggs
- 1/4-cup milk
- 2-tbsp. yellow onion, chopped.
- Salt and black pepper to the taste.
- Cooking spray.

Directions:

1. Grease a ramekin with cooking spray
2. Crack eggs, add onion, milk, cheese, tomatoes, salt and pepper and stir. Add this in your air fryer's pan and cook at 340 °F, for 30 minutes.

Nutrition Values (Per Serving): Calories: 241; Fat: 6g; Fiber: 8g; Carbs: 14g; Protein: 6g

53. Cream Cheese Oats.

(Prep + Cooking Time: 35 Minutes | **Serves:** 4)

Ingredients:

- 1-cup steel oats
- 2 oz. cream cheese, soft.
- 3/4-cup raisins
- 1/4-cup brown sugar
- 3-cups milk
- 2-tbsp. white sugar
- 1-tbsp. butter
- one-tsp. cinnamon powder.

Directions:

1. Heat up a pan that fits your air fryer with the butter over medium heat, add oats; stir and toast them for 3 minutes.
2. Add milk and raisins; stir, introduce in your air fryer and cook at 350 °F, for 20 minutes
3. Meanwhile, in a bowl, mix cinnamon with brown sugar and stir.
4. In a second bowl; mix white sugar with cream cheese and whisk. Divide oats into bowls and top each with cinnamon and cream cheese

Nutrition Values (Per Serving): Calories: 152; Fat: 6g; Fiber: 6g; Carbs: 25g; Protein: 7g

54. Mushroom Oatmeal Breakfast.

(Prep + Cooking Time: 30 Minutes | **Serves:** 4)

Ingredients:

- 1 small yellow onion, chopped.
- ½-cup gouda cheese, grated.
- 8 oz. mushroom, sliced.
- 2 garlic cloves, minced.
- 1-cup steel cut oats
- ½-cup water
- 14 oz. canned chicken stock
- 3 thyme springs, chopped.
- 2-tbsp. extra virgin olive oil
- 2-tbsp. butter
- Salt and black pepper to the taste.

Directions:

1. Heat up a pan that fits your air fryer with the butter over medium heat, add onions and garlic; stir and cook for 4 minutes
2. Add oats, water, salt, pepper, stock and thyme; stir, introduce in your air fryer and cook at 360 °F, for 16 minutes. Meanwhile, heat up a pan with the olive oil over medium heat, add mushrooms, cook them for 3 minutes; add to oatmeal and cheese; stir, divide into bowls and serve for breakfast.

Nutrition Values (Per Serving): Calories: 284; Fat: 8g; Fiber: 8g; Carbs: 20g; Protein: 17g

55. Tasty Artichoke Frittata.

(Prep + Cooking Time: 25 Minutes | **Serves:** 6)

Ingredients:

- 3 canned artichokes hearts; drained and chopped
- 6 eggs, whisked.
- 2-tbsp. olive oil
- ½-tsp. oregano; dried
- Salt and black pepper to the taste.

Directions:

1. Take a bowl and mix artichokes with oregano, salt, pepper and eggs and whisk well.
2. Add the oil to your air fryer's pan; add eggs mix and cook at 320 °F, for 15 minutes. Divide frittata on plates and serve for breakfast

Nutrition Values (Per Serving): Calories: 136; Fat: 6g; Fiber: 6g; Carbs: 9g; Protein: 4g

56. Mushrooms and Tofu.

(Prep + Cooking Time: 20 Minutes | **Serves:** 2)

Ingredients:

- 1 tofu block; pressed and cut into medium pieces
- 1-cup panko bread crumbs
- 1 egg
- 1-tbsp. mushrooms, minced.
- ½-tbsp. flour
- Salt and black pepper to the taste.

Directions:

1. Take a bowl and mix egg with mushrooms, flour, salt and pepper and whisk well.
2. Dip tofu pieces in egg mix; then dredge them in panko bread crumbs; place them in your air fryer and cook at 350 °F, for 10 minutes. Serve them for breakfast right away

Nutrition Values (Per Serving): Calories: 142; Fat: 4g; Fiber: 6g; Carbs: 8g; Protein: 3g

57. Smoked Fried Tofu.

(Prep + Cooking Time: 22 Minutes | **Serves:** 2)

Ingredients:

- 1 tofu block; pressed and cubed
- 1/4-cup cornstarch
- 1-tbsp. smoked paprika
- Salt and black pepper to the taste.
- Cooking spray.

Directions:

1. Grease your air fryer's basket with cooking spray and heat the fryer at 370 degrees F.
2. Take a bowl and mix tofu with salt, pepper, smoked paprika and cornstarch and toss well
3. Add tofu to you air fryer's basket and cook for 12 minutes shaking the fryer every 4 minutes. Divide into bowls and serve for breakfast

Nutrition Values (Per Serving): Calories: 172; Fat: 4g; Fiber: 7g; Carbs: 12g; Protein: 4g

58. Veggie Mix.

(Prep + Cooking Time: 35 Minutes | **Serves:** 6)

Ingredients:

- 1 yellow onion, sliced.
- 3-cups milk
- 4 oz. parmesan, grated.
- 1 red bell pepper, chopped.

- 1 gold potato, chopped.
- 8 oz. brie; trimmed and cubed
- 8 eggs
- 12 oz. sourdough bread, cubed.
- 2-tbsp. olive oil
- 2-tbsp. mustard
- Salt and black pepper to the taste.

Directions:

1. Heat up your air fryer at 350 degrees F; add oil, onion, potato and bell pepper and cook for 5 minutes.
2. Take a bowl and mix eggs with milk, salt, pepper and mustard and whisk well
3. Add bread and brie to your air fryer; add half of the eggs mix and add half of the parmesan as well.
4. Add the rest of the bread and parmesan; toss just a little bit and cook for 20 minutes.
5. Divide among plates and serve for breakfast

Nutrition Values (Per Serving): Calories: 231; Fat: 5g; Fiber: 10g; Carbs: 20g; Protein: 12g

59. Mushroom Quiches.

(Prep + Cooking Time: 20 Minutes | **Serves:** 4)

Ingredients:

- 2 button mushrooms, chopped.
- 9-inch pie dough
- 1/4-cup Swiss cheese, grated.
- 1 small yellow onion, chopped.
- 3 eggs
- 1/3-cup heavy cream
- 1-tbsp. flour
- 1-tbsp. butter, soft.
- 2-tbsp. ham, chopped.
- ½-tsp. thyme; dried
- A pinch of nutmeg, ground.
- Salt and black pepper to the taste.

Directions:

1. Dust a working surface with the flour and roll the pie dough.
2. Press in on the bottom of the pie pan your air fryer has
3. Take a bowl and mix butter with mushrooms, ham, onion, eggs, heavy cream, salt, pepper, thyme and nutmeg and whisk well.
4. Add this over pie crust, spread, sprinkle Swiss cheese all over and place pie pan in your air fryer.
5. Cook your quiche at 400 °F, for 10 minutes. Slice and serve for breakfast

Nutrition Values (Per Serving): Calories: 212; Fat: 4g; Fiber: 6g; Carbs: 7g; Protein: 7g

60. Pea Tortilla.

(Prep + Cooking Time: 17 Minutes | **Serves:** 8)

Ingredients:

- ½ lb. baby peas
- ½-cup mint, chopped.
- 1 ½-cup yogurt
- 8 eggs
- 4-tbsp. butter
- Salt and black pepper to the taste.

Directions:

1. Heat up a pan that fits your air fryer with the butter over medium heat, add peas; stir and cook for a couple of minutes.
2. Meanwhile, in a bowl, mix half of the yogurt with salt, pepper, eggs and mint and whisk well
3. Pour this over the peas, toss, introduce in your air fryer and cook at 350 °F, for 7 minutes. Spread the rest of the yogurt over your tortilla; slice and serve.

Nutrition Values (Per Serving): Calories: 192; Fat: 5g; Fiber: 4g; Carbs: 8g; Protein: 7g

61. Cheesy Sandwich.

(Prep + Cooking Time: 18 Minutes | **Serves:** 1)

Ingredients:

- 2 cheddar cheese slices
- 2 bread slices
- 2-tsp. butter
- A pinch of sweet paprika

Directions:

1. Spread butter on bread slices, add cheddar cheese on one, sprinkle paprika, top with the other bread slices, cut into 2 halves; arrange them in your air fryer and cook at 370 °F, for 8 minutes; flipping them once, arrange on a plate and serve.

Nutrition Values (Per Serving): Calories: 130; Fat: 3g; Fiber: 5g; Carbs: 9g; Protein: 3g

62. Fish Tacos Breakfast.

(Prep + Cooking Time: 23 Minutes | **Serves:** 4)

Ingredients:

- 4 white fish fillets; skinless and boneless
- 4 big tortillas
- 1 red bell pepper, chopped.
- A handful mixed romaine lettuce; spinach and radicchio
- ½-cup salsa
- 1 yellow onion, chopped.
- 1-cup corn
- 4-tbsp. parmesan, grated.

Directions:

1. Put fish fillets in your air fryer and cook at 350 °F, for 6 minutes.
2. Meanwhile, heat up a pan over medium high heat, add bell pepper, onion and corn; stir and cook for 1-2 minutes
3. Arrange tortillas on a working surface, divide fish fillets, spread salsa over them; divide mixed veggies and mixed greens and spread parmesan on each at the end.
4. Roll your tacos; place them in preheated air fryer and cook at 350 °F, for 6 minutes more. Divide fish tacos on plates and serve for breakfast

Nutrition Values (Per Serving): Calories: 200; Fat: 3g; Fiber: 7g; Carbs: 9g; Protein: 5g

63. Bread Rolls.

(Prep + Cooking Time: 22 Minutes | **Serves:** 4)

Ingredients:

- 5 potatoes; boiled, peeled and mashed.
- 8 bread slices; white parts only
- 2 green chilies, chopped.
- 2 small yellow onions, chopped.
- 2 curry leaf springs
- 1 coriander bunch, chopped.
- 2-tbsp. olive oil
- ½-tsp. turmeric powder
- ½-tsp. mustard seeds
- Salt and black pepper to the taste.

Directions:

1. Heat up a pan with one-tsp. oil; add mustard seeds, onions, curry leaves and turmeric, stir and cook for a few seconds.
2. Add mashed potatoes, salt, pepper, coriander and chilies, stir well; take off heat and cool it down.
3. Divide potatoes mix into 8 parts and shape ovals using your wet hands
4. Wet bread slices with water; press in order to drain excess water and keep one slice in your palm.
5. Add a potato oval over bread slice and wrap it around it.
6. Repeat with the rest of the potato mix and bread.

7. Heat up your air fryer at 400 degrees F; add the rest of the oil, add bread rolls; cook them for 12 minutes. Divide bread rolls on plates and serve for breakfast

Nutrition Values (Per Serving): Calories: 261; Fat: 6g; Fiber: 9g; Carbs: 12g; Protein: 7g

64. Bread Pudding.

(Prep + Cooking Time: 32 Minutes | **Serves:** 4)

Ingredients:

- ½ lb. white bread, cubed.
- 1 ⅓-cup flour
- ½-cup apple, peeled; cored and roughly chopped.
- 3/4-cup milk
- 3/4-cup water
- 3/5-cup brown sugar
- 3 oz. soft butter
- 5-tbsp. honey
- 2-tsp. cinnamon powder.
- 2-tsp. cornstarch
- one-tsp. vanilla extract

Directions:

1. Take a bowl and mix bread with apple, milk with water, honey, cinnamon, vanilla and cornstarch and whisk well
2. Now, take a separate bowl, mix flour with sugar and butter and stir until you obtain a crumbled mixture.
3. Press half of the crumble mix on the bottom of your air fryer; add bread and apple mix, add the rest of the crumble and cook everything at 350 °F, for 22 minutes. Divide bread pudding on plates and serve

Nutrition Values (Per Serving): Calories: 261; Fat: 7g; Fiber: 7g; Carbs: 8g; Protein: 5g

65. Espresso Oatmeal.

(Prep + Cooking Time: 27 Minutes | **Serves:** 4)

Ingredients:

- 1-cup steel cut oats
- 2 ½-cups water
- 1-cup milk
- 2-tbsp. sugar
- 2-tsp. vanilla extract
- one-tsp. espresso powder

Directions:

1. In a pan that fits your air fryer, mix oats with water, sugar, milk and espresso powder; stir, introduce in your air fryer and cook at 360 °F, for 17 minutes.
2. Add vanilla extract, stir; leave everything aside for 5 minutes; divide into bowls and serve for breakfast

Nutrition Values (Per Serving): Calories: 261; Fat: 7g; Fiber: 6g; Carbs: 39g; Protein: 6g

66. Walnuts Pear Oatmeal.

(Prep + Cooking Time: 17 Minutes | **Serves:** 4)

Ingredients:

- 1-cup rolled oats
- ½-cup walnuts, chopped.
- 1-cup water
- ½-cup raisins
- 2-cups pear, peeled and chopped.
- 1/4-cups brown sugar
- 1-tbsp. butter, soft.
- ½-tsp. cinnamon powder.

Directions:

1. In a heat proof dish that fits your air fryer; mix milk with sugar, butter, oats, cinnamon, raisins, pears and walnuts; stir, introduce in your fryer and cook at 360 °F, for 12 minutes. Divide into bowls and serve.

Nutrition Values (Per Serving): Calories: 230; Fat: 6g; Fiber: 11g; Carbs: 20g; Protein: 5g

67. Breakfast Raspberry Rolls.

(Prep + Cooking Time: 50 Minutes | **Serves:** 6)

Ingredients:

- 3 ¼-cups flour
- 1-cup milk
- 1/4-cup sugar
- 1 egg
- 4-tbsp. butter
- 2-tsp. yeast

For the filling:

- 12 oz. raspberries
- 8 oz. cream cheese, soft.
- 1-tbsp. cornstarch
- 5-tbsp. sugar
- one-tsp. vanilla extract
- Zest from 1 lemon, grated.

Directions:

1. Take a bowl and mix flour with sugar and yeast and stir.
2. Add milk and egg, stir until you obtain a dough, leave it aside to rise for 30 minutes; transfer dough to a working surface and roll well
3. Take a bowl and mix cream cheese with sugar, vanilla and lemon zest; stir well and spread over dough.
4. In another bowl; mix raspberries with cornstarch, stir and spread over cream cheese mix.
5. Roll your dough, cut into medium pieces, place them in your air fryer; spray them with cooking spray and cook them at 350 °F, for 30 minutes. Serve your rolls for breakfast

Nutrition Values (Per Serving): Calories: 261; Fat: 5g; Fiber: 8g; Carbs: 9g; Protein: 6g

68. Delicious Doughnuts.

(Prep + Cooking Time: 28 Minutes | **Serves:** 6)

Ingredients:

- ½-cup sugar
- 2 egg yolks
- 2 and 1/4-cups white flour
- ½-cup sour cream
- 1/3-cup caster sugar
- 4-tbsp. butter, soft.
- one-tsp. cinnamon powder.
- 1 ½-tsp. baking powder.

Directions:

1. Take a bowl and mix 2-tbsp. butter with simple sugar and egg yolks and whisk well.
2. Add half of the sour cream and stir
3. In another bowls; mix flour with baking powder, stir and also add to eggs mix.
4. Stir well until you obtain a dough, transfer it to a floured working surface; roll it out and cut big circles with smaller ones in the middle
5. Brush doughnuts with the rest of the butter; heat up your air fryer at 360 degrees F; place doughnuts inside and cook them for 8 minutes.
6. Take a bowl and mix cinnamon with caster sugar and stir. Arrange doughnuts on plates and dip them in cinnamon and sugar before serving

Nutrition Values (Per Serving): Calories: 182; Fat: 3g; Fiber: 7g; Carbs: 8g; Protein: 3g

69. Yummy Ham Rolls.

(Prep + Cooking Time: 20 Minutes | **Serves:** 4)

Ingredients:

- 4 handful gruyere cheese, grated.
- 8 ham slices, chopped.
- 1 sheet puff pastry
- 4-tsp. mustard

Directions:

1. Roll out puff pastry on a working surface, divide cheese, ham and mustard, roll tight and cut into medium rounds
2. Place all rolls in air fryer and cook for 10 minutes at 370 degrees F. Divide rolls on plates and serve for breakfast.

Nutrition Values (Per Serving): Calories: 182; Fat: 4g; Fiber: 7g; Carbs: 9g; Protein: 8g

70. Cream Breakfast Tofu.

(Prep + Cooking Time: 35 Minutes | **Serves:** 4)

Ingredients:

- 1 block firm tofu; pressed and cubed
- 1-cup Greek yogurt
- 2-tbsp. soy sauce
- 1-tbsp. potato starch
- one-tsp. rice vinegar
- 2-tsp. sesame oil

Directions:

1. Take a bowl and mix tofu cubes with vinegar, soy sauce and oil, toss, and leave aside for 15 minutes.
2. Dip tofu cubes in potato starch, toss, transfer to your air fryer; heat up at 370 °F and cook for 20 minutes shaking halfway. Divide into bowls and serve for breakfast with some Greek yogurt on the side

Nutrition Values (Per Serving): Calories: 110; Fat: 4g; Fiber: 5g; Carbs: 8g; Protein: 4g

Lunch Recipes

71. Chicken Pie Recipe

(Prep + Cooking Time: 29 Minutes | **Serves:** 4)

Ingredients:

- 2 chicken thighs; boneless, skinless and cubed
- 2 potatoes, chopped.
- 2 mushrooms, chopped.
- 1 yellow onion, chopped.
- 2 puff pastry sheets
- 1 carrot, chopped.
- 1-tbsp. flour
- 1-tbsp. milk
- 1-tbsp. butter, melted.
- one-tsp. Italian seasoning
- ½-tsp. garlic powder
- one-tsp. Worcestershire sauce
- one-tsp. soy sauce
- Salt and black pepper to the taste.

Directions:

1. Heat up a pan over medium high heat, add potatoes, carrots and onion; stir and cook for 2 minutes.
2. Add chicken and mushrooms, salt, soy sauce, pepper, Italian seasoning, garlic powder, Worcestershire sauce, flour and milk; stir really well and take off heat
3. Place 1 puff pastry sheet on the bottom of your air fryer's pan and trim edge excess.
4. Add chicken mix, top with the other puff pastry sheet; trim excess as well and brush pie with butter.
5. Place in your air fryer and cook at 360 °F, for 6 minutes. Leave pie to cool down; slice and serve for breakfast

Nutrition Values (Per Serving): Calories: 300; Fat: 5g; Fiber: 7g; Carbs: 14g; Protein: 7g

72. Summer Squash Fritters.

(Prep + Cooking Time: 17 Minutes | **Serves:** 4)

Ingredients:

- 3 oz. cream cheese
- 1/3-cup carrot, grated.
- 2/3-cup bread crumbs
- A pinch of salt and black pepper
- 1 yellow summer squash, grated.
- 1 egg, whisked.
- ½-tsp. oregano; dried
- 2-tbsp. olive oil

Directions:

1. Take a bowl and mix cream cheese with salt, pepper, oregano, egg, breadcrumbs, carrot and squash and stir well.
2. Shape medium patties out of this mix and brush them with the oil
3. Place squash patties in your air fryer and cook them at 400 °F, for 7 minutes. Serve them for lunch.

Nutrition Values (Per Serving): Calories: 200; Fat: 4g; Fiber: 7g; Carbs: 8g; Protein: 6g

73. Beef Meatballs

(Prep + Cooking Time: 25 Minutes | **Serves:** 4)

Ingredients:

- ½ lb. Italian sausage, chopped.
- ½ lb. beef, ground.
- ½-cup cheddar cheese, grated.
- ½-tsp. garlic powder

- ½-tsp. onion powder
- Mashed potatoes for serving
- Salt and black pepper to the taste.

Directions:

1. Take a bowl and mix beef with sausage, garlic powder, onion powder, salt, pepper and cheese; stir well and shape 16 meatballs out of this mix.
2. Place meatballs in your air fryer and cook them at 370 °F, for 15 minutes. Serve your meatballs with some mashed potatoes on the side

Nutrition Values (Per Serving): Calories: 333; Fat: 23g; Fiber: 1g; Carbs: 8g; Protein: 20g

74. Dill and Scallops

(Prep + Cooking Time: 15 Minutes | **Serves:** 4)

Ingredients:

- 1 lb. sea scallops; debearded
- 1-tbsp. lemon juice
- 2-tsp. olive oil
- one-tsp. dill, chopped.
- Salt and black pepper to the taste.

Directions:

1. In your air fryer, mix scallops with dill, oil, salt, pepper and lemon juice; cover and cook at 360 °F, for 5 minutes. Discard unopened ones, divide scallops and dill sauce on plates and serve for lunch.

Nutrition Values (Per Serving): Calories: 152; Fat: 4g; Fiber: 7g; Carbs: 19g; Protein: 4g

75. Zucchini and Tuna Tortillas

(Prep + Cooking Time: 20 Minutes | **Serves:** 4)

Ingredients:

- 1-cup zucchini, shredded.
- 4 corn tortillas
- 6 oz. canned tuna; drained
- 1-cup cheddar cheese, grated.
- 1/3-cup mayonnaise
- 4-tbsp. butter, soft.
- 2-tbsp. mustard

Directions:

1. Spread butter on tortillas; place them in your air fryer's basket and cook them at 400 °F, for 3 minutes.
2. Meanwhile, in a bowl, mix tuna with zucchini, mayo and mustard and stir
3. Divide this mix on each tortilla, top with cheese, roll tortillas; place them in your air fryer's basket again and cook them at 400 °F, for 4 minutes more. Serve for lunch.

Nutrition Values (Per Serving): Calories: 162; Fat: 4g; Fiber: 8g; Carbs: 9g; Protein: 4g

76. Asian Chicken

(Prep + Cooking Time: 40 Minutes | **Serves:** 4)

Ingredients:

- 2 chicken breasts; skinless, boneless and sliced
- 1 yellow onion, sliced.
- ½-cup jarred cheese sauce
- 14 oz. pizza dough
- 1 ½-cups cheddar cheese, grated.
- 1-tbsp. Worcestershire sauce
- one-tsp. olive oil
- Salt and black pepper to the taste.

Directions:

1. Preheat your air fryer at 400 degrees F; add half of the oil and onions and fry them for 8 minutes, stirring once

2. Add chicken pieces, Worcestershire sauce, salt and pepper; toss, air fry for 8 minutes more, stirring once and transfer everything to a bowl.
3. Roll pizza dough on a working surface and shape a rectangle.
4. Spread half of the cheese all over, add chicken and onion mix and top with cheese sauce.
5. Roll your dough and shape into a U.
6. Place your roll in your air fryer's basket, brush with the rest of the oil and cook at 370 degrees for 12 minutes, flipping the roll halfway. Slice your roll when it's warm and serve for lunch

Nutrition Values (Per Serving): Calories: 300; Fat: 8g; Fiber: 17g; Carbs: 20g; Protein: 6g

77. Japanese Style Chicken

(Prep + Cooking Time: 18 Minutes **| Serves:** 2)

Ingredients:

- 2 chicken thighs; skinless and boneless
- 2 ginger slices, chopped.
- 3 garlic cloves, minced.
- 1/8-cup water
- 1/4-cup soy sauce
- 1/4-cup mirin
- 1/8-cup sake
- 2-tbsp. sugar
- 1-tbsp. cornstarch mixed with 2-tbsp. water
- ½-tsp. sesame oil
- Sesame seeds for serving

Directions:

1. Take a bowl and mix chicken thighs with ginger, garlic, soy sauce, mirin, sake, oil, water, sugar and cornstarch; toss well, transfer to preheated air fryer and cook at 360 °F, for 8 minutes. Divide among plates; sprinkle sesame seeds on top and serve with a side salad for lunch

Nutrition Values (Per Serving): Calories: 300; Fat: 7g; Fiber: 9g; Carbs: 17g; Protein: 10g

78. Chicken Wings

(Prep + Cooking Time: 55 Minutes **| Serves:** 4)

Ingredients:

- 3 lbs. chicken wings
- 3/4-cup potato starch
- ½-cup butter
- 1-tbsp. old bay seasoning
- one-tsp. lemon juice
- Lemon wedges for serving

Directions:

1. Take a bowl and mix starch with old bay seasoning and chicken wings and toss well.
2. Place chicken wings in your air fryer's basket and cook them at 360 °F, for 35 minutes shaking the fryer from time to time
3. Increase temperature to 400 degrees F; cook chicken wings for 10 minutes more and divide them on plates.
4. Heat up a pan over medium heat; add butter and melt it.
5. Add lemon juice; stir well, take off heat and drizzle over chicken wings. Serve them for lunch with lemon wedges on the side

Nutrition Values (Per Serving): Calories: 271; Fat: 6g; Fiber: 8g; Carbs: 18g; Protein: 18g

79. Cheesy Ravioli and Marinara Sauce.

(Prep + Cooking Time: 18 Minutes **| Serves:** 6)

Ingredients:

- 10 oz. marinara sauce
- 20 oz. cheese ravioli
- 1-cup buttermilk
- 2-cups bread crumbs
- 1/4-cup parmesan, grated.
- 1-tbsp. olive oil

Directions:

1. Put buttermilk in a bowl and breadcrumbs in another bowl
2. Dip ravioli in buttermilk, then in breadcrumbs and place them in your air fryer on a baking sheet. Drizzle olive oil over them; cook at 400 °F, for 5 minutes; divide them on plates, sprinkle parmesan on top and serve for lunch

Nutrition Values (Per Serving): Calories: 270; Fat: 12g; Fiber: 6g; Carbs: 30g; Protein: 15g

80. Cheese and Macaroni

(Prep + Cooking Time: 40 Minutes | **Serves:** 3)

Ingredients:

- 1 ½-cups favorite macaroni
- 1/4-cup parmesan, shredded.
- 1-cup chicken stock
- 3/4-cup cheddar cheese, shredded.
- ½-cup heavy cream
- ½-cup mozzarella cheese, shredded.
- Salt and black pepper to the taste.
- Cooking spray.

Directions:

1. Spray a pan with cooking spray; add macaroni, heavy cream, stock, cheddar cheese, mozzarella and parmesan but also salt and pepper; toss well, place pan in your air fryer's basket and cook for 30 minutes. Divide among plates and serve for lunch.

Nutrition Values (Per Serving): Calories: 341; Fat: 7g; Fiber: 8g; Carbs: 18g; Protein: 4g

81. Turkish Style Koftas

(Prep + Cooking Time: 25 Minutes | **Serves:** 2)

Ingredients:

- ½ lb. lean beef, minced.
- 1 leek, chopped.
- 2-tbsp. feta cheese, crumbled.
- 1-tbsp. parsley, chopped.
- 1-tbsp. cumin, ground.
- 1-tbsp. mint, chopped.
- one-tsp. garlic, minced.
- Salt and black pepper to the taste.

Directions:

1. Take a bowl and mix beef with leek, cheese, cumin, mint, parsley, garlic, salt and pepper; stir well, shape your koftas and place them on sticks
2. Add koftas to your preheated air fryer at 360 °F and cook them for 15 minutes. Serve them with a side salad for lunch.

Nutrition Values (Per Serving): Calories: 281; Fat: 7g; Fiber: 8g; Carbs: 17g; Protein: 6g

82. Egg Rolls

(Prep + Cooking Time: 25 Minutes | **Serves:** 4)

Ingredients:

- ½-cup mushrooms, chopped.
- 8 egg roll wrappers
- 1 egg, whisked.
- 2 green onions, chopped.
- ½-cup carrots, grated.
- ½-cup zucchini, grated.
- 1-tbsp. cornstarch
- 2-tbsp. soy sauce

Directions:

1. Take a bowl and mix carrots with mushrooms, zucchini, green onions and soy sauce and stir well.
2. Arrange egg roll wrappers on a working surface; divide veggie mix on each and roll well

3. Take a bowl and mix cornstarch with egg, whisk well and brush eggs rolls with this mix.
4. Seal edges, place all rolls in your preheated air fryer and cook them at 370 °F, for 15 minutes. Arrange them on a platter and serve them for lunch

Nutrition Values (Per Serving): Calories: 172; Fat: 6g; Fiber: 6g; Carbs: 8g; Protein: 7g

83. Cheering Chicken Sandwiches.

(Prep + Cooking Time: 20 Minutes | **Serves:** 4)

Ingredients:

- 2 chicken breasts; skinless, boneless and cubed
- 1 red onion, chopped.
- 4 pita pockets
- 1-cup cherry tomatoes, halved.
- 1 red bell pepper, sliced.
- 2-cups butter lettuce; torn
- ½-cup Italian seasoning
- ½-tsp. thyme; dried
- 1-tbsp. olive oil

Directions:

1. In your air fryer, mix chicken with onion, bell pepper, Italian seasoning and oil; toss and cook at 380 °F, for 10 minutes. Transfer chicken mix to a bowl; add thyme, butter lettuce and cherry tomatoes, toss well; stuff pita pockets with this mix and serve for lunch.

Nutrition Values (Per Serving): Calories: 126; Fat: 4g; Fiber: 8g; Carbs: 14g; Protein: 4g

84. Chicken Salad

(Prep + Cooking Time: 30 Minutes | **Serves:** 4)

Ingredients:

- 1 lb. chicken tenders; boneless
- 2 ears of corn; hulled
- ½ iceberg lettuce head; cut into medium strips
- ½ romaine lettuce head; cut into medium strips
- 1-cup canned black beans; drained
- 4 green onions, chopped.
- 1-cup cheddar cheese, shredded.
- 12 cherry tomatoes, sliced.
- Olive oil as needed
- 1/4-cup ranch dressing
- 3-tbsp. cilantro, chopped.
- 1-tbsp. brown sugar
- 3-tbsp. BBQ sauce
- one-tsp. sweet paprika
- ½-tsp. garlic powder
- Salt and black pepper to the taste.

Directions:

1. Put corn in your air fryer; drizzle some oil, toss, cook at 400 °F, for 10 minutes; transfer to a plate and leave aside for now
2. Put chicken in your air fryer's basket, add salt, pepper, brown sugar, paprika and garlic powder; toss, drizzle some more oil, cook at 400 °F, for 10 minutes; flipping them halfway, transfer tenders to a cutting board and chop them.
3. Cur kernels off the cob, transfer corn to a bowl; add chicken, iceberg lettuce, romaine lettuce, black beans, cheese, cilantro, tomatoes, onions, BBQ sauce and ranch dressing; toss well and serve for lunch

Nutrition Values (Per Serving): Calories: 372; Fat: 6g; Fiber: 9g; Carbs: 17g; Protein: 6g

85. Shrimp Croquettes

(Prep + Cooking Time: 18 Minutes | **Serves:** 4)

Ingredients:

- 2/3 lb. shrimp; cooked, peeled; deveined and chopped.
- 1 egg, whisked.
- 1 ½-cups bread crumbs
- 3 green onions, chopped.
- 2-tbsp. lemon juice
- 2-tbsp. olive oil
- ½-tsp. basil; dried
- Salt and black pepper to the taste.

Directions:

1. Take a bowl and mix half of the bread crumbs with egg and lemon juice and stir well.
2. Add green onions, basil, salt, pepper and shrimp and stir really well.
3. Now, take a separate bowl, mix the rest of the bread crumbs with the oil and toss well
4. Shape round balls out of shrimp mix, dredge them in bread crumbs; place them in preheated air fryer and cook the for 8 minutes at 400 degrees F. Serve them with a dip for lunch.

Nutrition Values (Per Serving): Calories: 142; Fat: 4g; Fiber: 6g; Carbs: 9g; Protein: 4g

86. Fresh Style Chicken

(Prep + Cooking Time: 32 Minutes | **Serves:** 4)

Ingredients:

- 2 chicken breasts; skinless, boneless and cubed
- 8 button mushrooms, sliced.
- 1 red bell pepper, chopped.
- 6 bread slices
- 10 oz. alfredo sauce
- 1-tbsp. olive oil
- 2-tbsp. butter, soft.
- ½-tsp. thyme; dried

Directions:

1. In your air fryer, mix chicken with mushrooms, bell pepper and oil; toss to coat well and cook at 350 °F, for 15 minutes
2. Transfer chicken mix to a bowl; add thyme and alfredo sauce, toss, return to air fryer and cook at 350 °F, for 4 minutes more.
3. Spread butter on bread slices; add it to the fryer, butter side up and cook for 4 minutes more. Arrange toasted bread slices on a platter; top each with chicken mix and serve for lunch

Nutrition Values (Per Serving): Calories: 172; Fat: 4g; Fiber: 9g; Carbs: 12g; Protein: 4g

87. Different Pasta Salad.

(Prep + Cooking Time: 22 Minutes | **Serves:** 6)

Ingredients:

- 1 lb. penne rigate; already cooked
- 1 zucchini, sliced.in half and roughly chopped.
- 1 green bell pepper; roughly chopped.
- 4 oz. brown mushrooms, halved.
- 1-cup cherry tomatoes, halved.
- ½-cup kalamata olive; pitted and halved
- 1 red onion; roughly chopped.
- 1/4-cup olive oil
- 1 orange bell pepper; roughly chopped.
- 3-tbsp. balsamic vinegar
- 2-tbsp. basil, chopped.
- one-tsp. Italian seasoning
- Salt and black pepper to the taste.

Directions:

1. Take a bowl and mix zucchini with mushrooms, orange bell pepper, green bell pepper, red onion, salt, pepper, Italian seasoning and oil; toss well, transfer to preheated air fryer at 380 °F and cook them for 12 minutes.
2. In a large salad bowl; mix pasta with cooked veggies, cherry tomatoes, olives, vinegar and basil; toss and serve for lunch

Nutrition Values (Per Serving): Calories: 200; Fat: 5g; Fiber: 8g; Carbs: 10g; Protein: 6g

88. Delicious Fajitas

(Prep + Cooking Time: 20 Minutes | **Serves:** 4)

Ingredients:

- 1 lb. chicken breasts; cut into strips
- 4 tortillas; warmed up
- 1-cup lettuce leaves; torn for serving
- 1 green bell pepper, sliced.
- 1 yellow onion, chopped.
- 1 red bell pepper, sliced.
- 1-tbsp. lime juice
- 1/4-tsp. coriander, ground.
- one-tsp. garlic powder
- 1/4-tsp. cumin, ground.
- ½-tsp. chili powder
- Salt and black pepper to the taste.
- Cooking spray.
- Salsa for serving
- Sour cream for serving

Directions:

1. Take a bowl and mix chicken with garlic powder, cumin, chili, salt, pepper, coriander, lime juice, red bell pepper, green bell pepper and onion; toss, leave aside for 10 minutes, transfer to your air fryer and drizzle some cooking spray all over.
2. Toss and cook at 400 °F, for 10 minutes. Arrange tortillas on a working surface, divide chicken mix, also add salsa, sour cream and lettuce; wrap and serve for lunch

Nutrition Values (Per Serving): Calories: 317; Fat: 6g; Fiber: 8g; Carbs: 14g; Protein: 4g

89. Fish and Kettle Chips.

(Prep + Cooking Time: 22 Minutes | **Serves:** 2)

Ingredients:

- 2 medium cod fillets; skinless and boneless
- 1/4-cup buttermilk
- 3-cups kettle chips; cooked
- Salt and black pepper to the taste.

Directions:

1. In a bowl mix fish with salt, pepper and buttermilk; toss and leave aside for 5 minutes.
2. Put chips in your food processor, crush them and spread them on a plate.
3. Add fish and press well on all sides
4. Transfer fish to your air fryer's basket and cook at 400 °F, for 12 minutes. Serve hot for lunch.

Nutrition Values (Per Serving): Calories: 271; Fat: 7g; Fiber: 9g; Carbs: 14g; Protein: 4g

90. Beef Cubes.

(Prep + Cooking Time: 22 Minutes | **Serves:** 4)

Ingredients:

- 1 lb. sirloin, cubed.
- 1 ½-cups bread crumbs
- 16 oz. jarred pasta sauce
- 2-tbsp. olive oil
- ½-tsp. marjoram; dried
- White rice; already cooked for serving

Directions:

1. Take a bowl and mix beef cubes with pasta sauce and toss well.
2. In another bowl; mix bread crumbs with marjoram and oil and stir well
3. Dip beef cubes in this mix, place them in your air fryer and cook at 360 °F, for 12 minutes. Divide among plates and serve with white rice on the side

Nutrition Values (Per Serving): Calories: 271; Fat: 6g; Fiber: 9g; Carbs: 18g; Protein: 12g

91. Awesome Buttermilk Chicken

(Prep + Cooking Time: 28 Minutes | **Serves:** 4)

Ingredients:

- 1 ½ lbs. chicken thighs
- 2-cups white flour
- 2-cups buttermilk
- 1-tbsp. baking powder.
- 1-tbsp. garlic powder
- 1-tbsp. sweet paprika
- A pinch of cayenne pepper
- Salt and black pepper to the taste.

Directions:

1. Take a bowl and mix chicken thighs with buttermilk, salt, pepper and cayenne; toss and leave aside for 6 hours.
2. Now, take a separate bowl, mix flour with paprika, baking powder and garlic powder and stir
3. Drain chicken thighs, dredge them in flour mix; arrange them in your air fryer and cook at 360 °F, for 8 minutes. Flip chicken pieces, cook them for 10 minutes more; arrange on a platter and serve for lunch.

Nutrition Values (Per Serving): Calories: 200; Fat: 3g; Fiber: 9g; Carbs: 14g; Protein: 4g

92. Tasty Turkey Burgers

(Prep + Cooking Time: 18 Minutes | **Serves:** 4)

Ingredients:

- 1 lb. turkey meat, ground.
- 1 small jalapeno pepper, minced.
- 1 shallot, minced.
- A drizzle of olive oil
- Zest from 1 lime, grated.
- one-tsp. cumin, ground.
- 2-tsp. lime juice
- one-tsp. sweet paprika
- Salt and black pepper to the taste.
- Guacamole for serving

Directions:

1. Take a bowl and mix turkey meat with salt, pepper, cumin, paprika, shallot, jalapeno, lime juice and zest; stir well, shape burgers from this mix, drizzle the oil over them; introduce in preheated air fryer and cook them at 370 °F, for 8 minutes on each side. Divide among plates and serve with guacamole on top.

Nutrition Values (Per Serving): Calories: 200; Fat: 12g; Fiber: 0g; Carbs: 0g; Protein: 12g

93. Delicious Lentils Fritters

(Prep + Cooking Time: 20 Minutes | **Serves:** 2)

Ingredients:

- 1-cup yellow lentils; soaked in water for 1 hour and drained
- 1-inch ginger piece, grated.
- 1 hot chili pepper, chopped.
- ½-cup cilantro, chopped.
- 1 ½-cup spinach, chopped.
- 1/3-cup water
- 4 garlic cloves, minced.
- 3/4-cup red onion, chopped.
- 2-tsp. olive oil

- ½-tsp. turmeric powder
- one-tsp. garam masala
- one-tsp. baking powder.
- Salt and black pepper to the taste.
- Mint chutney for serving

Directions:

1. In your blender; mix lentils with chili pepper, ginger, turmeric, garam masala, baking powder, salt, pepper, olive oil, water, cilantro, spinach, onion and garlic, blend well and shape medium balls out of this mix.
2. Place them all in your preheated air fryer at 400 °F and cook for 10 minutes. Serve your veggie fritters with a side salad for lunch.

Nutrition Values (Per Serving): Calories: 142; Fat: 2g; Fiber: 8g; Carbs: 12g; Protein: 4g

94. Succulent Turkey Breast

(Prep + Cooking Time: 57 Minutes | **Serves:** 4)

Ingredients:

- 1 big turkey breast
- 1/4-cup maple syrup
- 2-tbsp. mustard
- 1-tbsp. butter, soft.
- ½-tsp. sage; dried
- 2-tsp. olive oil
- ½-tsp. smoked paprika
- one-tsp. thyme; dried
- Salt and black pepper to the taste.

Directions:

1. Brush turkey breast with the olive oil; season with salt, pepper, thyme, paprika and sage, rub, place in your air fryer's basket and fry at 350 °F, for 25 minutes
2. Flip turkey; cook for 10 minutes more; flip one more time and cook for another 10 minutes.
3. Meanwhile, heat up a pan with the butter over medium heat, add mustard and maple syrup; stir well, cook for a couple of minutes and take off heat. Slice turkey breast, divide among plates and serve with the maple glaze drizzled on top

Nutrition Values (Per Serving): Calories: 280; Fat: 2g; Fiber: 7g; Carbs: 16g; Protein: 14g

95. Fried Thai Salad.

(Prep + Cooking Time: 15 Minutes | **Serves:** 4)

Ingredients:

- 12 big shrimp; cooked, peeled and deveined
- 1-cup red cabbage, shredded.
- 1-cup carrots, grated.
- 1 small cucumber, chopped.
- A handful cilantro, chopped.
- Juice from 1 lime
- 2-tsp. red curry paste
- A pinch of salt and black pepper

Directions:

1. In a pan, mix cabbage with carrots, cucumber and shrimp; toss, introduce in your air fryer and cook at 360 °F, for 5 minutes. Add salt, pepper, cilantro, lime juice and red curry paste; toss again, divide among plates and serve right away.

Nutrition Values (Per Serving): Calories: 172; Fat: 5g; Fiber: 7g; Carbs: 8g; Protein: 5g

96. Chinese Style Pork

(Prep + Cooking Time: 22 Minutes | **Serves:** 4)

Ingredients:

- 2 lbs. pork; cut into medium cubes
- 2 eggs
- 1-cup cornstarch
- 3-tbsp. canola oil
- one-tsp. sesame oil
- A pinch of Chinese five spice
- Salt and black pepper to the taste.
- Sweet tomato sauce for serving

Directions:

1. Take a bowl and mix five spice with salt, pepper and cornstarch and stir.
2. In another bowl; mix eggs with sesame oil and whisk well
3. Dredge pork cubes in cornstarch mix; then dip in eggs mix and place them in your air fryer which you've greased with the canola oil.
4. Cook at 340 °F, for 12 minutes; shaking the fryer once. Serve pork for lunch with the sweet tomato sauce on the side

Nutrition Values (Per Serving): Calories: 320; Fat: 8g; Fiber: 12g; Carbs: 20g; Protein: 5g

97. Asparagus and Salmon.

(Prep + Cooking Time: 33 Minutes | **Serves:** 4)

Ingredients:

- 1 lb. asparagus; trimmed
- 1 red bell pepper; cut into halves
- 4 oz. smoked salmon
- A pinch of cayenne pepper
- A pinch of sweet paprika
- A pinch of garlic powder
- 1-tbsp. olive oil
- Salt and black pepper to the taste.

Directions:

1. Put asparagus spears and bell pepper on a lined baking sheet that fits your air fryer; add salt, pepper, garlic powder, paprika, olive oil, cayenne pepper, toss to coat, introduce in the fryer; cook at 390 °F, for 8 minutes, flip and cook for 8 minutes more. Add salmon, cook for 5 minutes more; divide everything on plates and serve.

Nutrition Values (Per Serving): Calories: 90; Fat: 1g; Fiber: 1g; Carbs: 1.2g; Protein: 4g

98. Bacon Garlic Pizzas

(Prep + Cooking Time: 20 Minutes | **Serves:** 4)

Ingredients:

- 8 bacon slices, cooked and chopped.
- 1 ¼-cups cheddar cheese, grated.
- 4 garlic cloves minced
- 4 dinner rolls; frozen
- ½-tsp. oregano dried
- ½-tsp. garlic powder
- 1-cup tomato sauce
- Cooking spray.

Directions:

1. Place dinner rolls on a working surface and press them to obtain 4 ovals.
2. Spray each oval with cooking spray; transfer them to your air fryer and cook them at 370 °F, for 2 minutes
3. Spread tomato sauce on each oval, divide garlic, sprinkle oregano and garlic powder and top with bacon and cheese.
4. Return pizzas to your heated air fryer and cook them at 370 °F, for 8 minutes more. Serve them warm for lunch

Nutrition Values (Per Serving): Calories: 217; Fat: 5g; Fiber: 8g; Carbs: 12g; Protein: 4g

99. Tasty Hot Dogs.

(Prep + Cooking Time: 17 Minutes | **Serves:** 2)

Ingredients:

- 2 hot dog buns
- 2 hot dogs
- 1-tbsp. Dijon mustard
- 2-tbsp. cheddar cheese, grated.

Directions:

1. Put hot dogs in preheated air fryer and cook them at 390 °F, for 5 minutes.
2. Divide hot dogs into hot dog buns, spread mustard and cheese; return everything to your air fryer and cook for 2 minutes more at 390 degrees F. Serve for lunch

Nutrition Values (Per Serving): Calories: 211; Fat: 3g; Fiber: 8g; Carbs: 12g; Protein: 4g

100. Mouthwatering Bacon Sandwiches.

(Prep + Cooking Time: 17 Minutes | **Serves:** 4)

Ingredients:

- 8 bacon slices; cooked and cut into thirds
- 1 red bell pepper, sliced.
- 1 yellow bell pepper, sliced.
- 3 pita pockets, halved.
- 2 tomatoes, sliced.
- 1 ¼-cup butter lettuce leaves; torn
- 1/3-cup bbq sauce
- 2-tbsp. honey

Directions:

1. In a bowl, mix BBQ sauce with honey and whisk well.
2. Brush bacon and all bell peppers with some of this mix; place them in your air fryer and cook at 350 °F, for 4 minutes
3. Shake fryer and cook them for 2 minutes more. Stuff pita pockets with bacon mix, also stuff with tomatoes and lettuce; spread the rest of the BBQ sauce and serve for lunch.

Nutrition Values (Per Serving): Calories: 186; Fat: 6g; Fiber: 9g; Carbs: 14g; Protein: 4g

101. Succulent Turkey Cakes

(Prep + Cooking Time: 20 Minutes | **Serves:** 4)

Ingredients:

- 1 ¼ lbs. turkey meat, ground.
- 6 mushrooms, chopped.
- one-tsp. onion powder
- one-tsp. garlic powder
- Cooking spray.
- Tomato sauce for serving
- Salt and black pepper to the taste.

Directions:

1. In your blender, mix mushrooms with salt and pepper, pulse well and transfer to a bowl.
2. Add turkey, onion powder, garlic powder, salt and pepper; stir and shape cakes out of this mix
3. Spray them with cooking spray; transfer them to your air fryer and cook at 320 °F, for 10 minutes. Serve them with tomato sauce on the side and a tasty side salad

Nutrition Values (Per Serving): Calories: 202; Fat: 6g; Fiber: 3g; Carbs: 17g; Protein: 10g

102. Mouthwatering Chicken Kabobs

(Prep + Cooking Time: 30 Minutes | **Serves:** 2)

Ingredients:

- 2 chicken breasts; skinless, boneless and roughly cubed
- 1/4-cup honey
- 1/3-cup soy sauce
- 6 mushrooms, halved.
- 3 orange bell peppers; cut into squares
- Cooking spray.
- Salt and black pepper to the taste.

Directions:

1. Take a bowl and mix chicken with salt, pepper, honey, say sauce and some cooking spray and toss well.
2. Thread chicken, bell peppers and mushrooms on skewers; place them in your air fryer and cook at 338 °F, for 20 minutes. Divide among plates and serve for lunch.

Nutrition Values (Per Serving): Calories: 261; Fat: 7g; Fiber: 9g; Carbs: 12g; Protein: 6g

103. Cheese Burgers

(Prep + Cooking Time: 30 Minutes | **Serves:** 2)

Ingredients:

- 12 oz. lean beef, ground.
- 4 cheddar cheese slices
- 2 burger buns, halved.
- 3-tbsp. yellow onion, chopped.
- 2-tsp. mustard
- 4-tsp. ketchup
- Salt and black pepper to the taste.

Directions:

1. Take a bowl and mix beef with onion, ketchup, mustard, salt and pepper; stir well and shape 4 patties out of this mix.
2. Divide cheese on 2 patties and top with the other 2 patties
3. Place them in preheated air fryer at 370 °F and fry them for 20 minutes. Divide cheeseburger on 2 bun halves; top with the other 2 serve for lunch

Nutrition Values (Per Serving): Calories: 261; Fat: 6g; Fiber: 10g; Carbs: 20g; Protein: 6g

104. Tasty Hash Brown Toasts

(Prep + Cooking Time: 17 Minutes | **Serves:** 4)

Ingredients:

- 4 hash brown patties; frozen
- 1/4-cup cherry tomatoes, chopped.
- 1-tbsp. basil, chopped.
- 3-tbsp. mozzarella, shredded.
- 2-tbsp. parmesan, grated.
- 1-tbsp. olive oil
- 1-tbsp. balsamic vinegar

Directions:

1. Put hash brown patties in your air fryer; drizzle the oil over them and cook them at 400 °F, for 7 minutes.
2. Take a bowl and mix tomatoes with mozzarella, parmesan, vinegar and basil and stir well. Divide hash brown patties on plates; top each with tomatoes mix and serve for lunch.

Nutrition Values (Per Serving): Calories: 199; Fat: 3g; Fiber: 8g; Carbs: 12g; Protein: 4g

105. Creamy Chicken Stew Recipe.

(Prep + Cooking Time: 35 Minutes | **Serves:** 4)

Ingredients:

- 1 ½-cups canned cream of celery soup
- ½-cup heavy cream
- 2 potatoes, chopped.
- 1 egg yolk
- 1 bay leaf
- 1 thyme spring, chopped.
- 6 chicken tenders
- 1-tbsp. milk
- Salt and black pepper to the taste.

Directions:

1. Take a bowl and mix chicken with cream of celery, potatoes, heavy cream, bay leaf, thyme, salt and pepper; toss, pour into your air fryer's pan and cook at 320 °F, for 25 minutes. Leave your stew to cool down a bit; discard bay leaf, divide among plates and serve right away.

Nutrition Values (Per Serving): Calories: 300; Fat: 11g; Fiber: 2g; Carbs: 23g; Protein: 14g

106. Special Prosciutto Sandwich.

(Prep + Cooking Time: 15 Minutes | **Serves:** 1)

Ingredients:

- 2 bread slices
- 2 mozzarella slices
- 2 prosciutto slices
- 2 basil leaves
- 2 tomato slices
- one-tsp. olive oil
- A pinch of salt and black pepper

Directions:

1. Arrange mozzarella and prosciutto on a bread slice.
2. Season with salt and pepper; place in your air fryer and cook at 400 °F, for 5 minutes. Drizzle oil over prosciutto, add tomato and basil; cover with the other bread slice, cut sandwich in half and serve.

Nutrition Values (Per Serving): Calories: 172; Fat: 3g; Fiber: 7g; Carbs: 9g; Protein: 5g

107. Stuffed Portobello Mushrooms.

(Prep + Cooking Time: 30 Minutes | **Serves:** 4)

Ingredients:

- 4 big Portobello mushroom caps
- 1/4-cup ricotta cheese
- 1-cup spinach; torn
- 1/3-cup bread crumbs
- 1-tbsp. olive oil
- 5-tbsp. parmesan, grated.
- 1/4-tsp. rosemary, chopped.

Directions:

1. Rub mushrooms caps with the oil; place them in your air fryer's basket and cook them at 350 °F, for 2 minutes
2. Meanwhile, in a bowl, mix half of the parmesan with ricotta, spinach, rosemary and bread crumbs and stir well.
3. Stuff mushrooms with this mix; sprinkle the rest of the parmesan on top; place them in your air fryer's basket again and cook at 350 °F, for 10 minutes. Divide them on plates and serve with a side salad for lunch

Nutrition Values (Per Serving): Calories: 152; Fat: 4g; Fiber: 7g; Carbs: 9g; Protein: 5g

108. Veggie Toasts.

(Prep + Cooking Time: 25 Minutes | **Serves:** 4)

Ingredients:

- 1 red bell pepper; cut into thin strips
- 1-cup cremimi mushrooms, sliced.
- 4 bread slices
- 2-tbsp. butter, soft.
- 1 yellow squash, chopped.
- 2 green onions, sliced.
- 1-tbsp. olive oil
- ½-cup goat cheese, crumbled.

Directions:

1. Take a bowl and mix red bell pepper with mushrooms, squash, green onions and oil, toss; transfer to your air fryer, cook them at 350 °F, for 10 minutes; shaking the fryer once and transfer them to a bowl
2. Spread butter on bread slices; place them in air fryer and cook them at 350 °F, for 5 minutes. Divide veggie mix on each bread slice, top with crumbled cheese and serve for lunch

Nutrition Values (Per Serving): Calories: 152; Fat: 3g; Fiber: 4g; Carbs: 7g; Protein: 2g

109. Chicken Zucchini Lunch.

(Prep + Cooking Time: 30 Minutes | **Serves:** 4)

Ingredients:

- 1 lb. chicken breasts; skinless, boneless and cubed
- 2-cups cherry tomatoes, halved.
- ½-cup almonds, chopped.
- 2 garlic cloves, minced.
- 4 zucchinis; cut with a spiralizer
- one-tsp. olive oil
- Salt and black pepper to the taste.

For the pesto:

- 2-cups kale, chopped.
- 1 garlic clove
- 2-cups basil
- 3/4-cup pine nuts
- ½-cup olive oil
- 1-tbsp. lemon juice
- A pinch of salt

Directions:

1. In your food processor, mix basil with kale, lemon juice, garlic, pine nuts, oil and a pinch of salt, pulse really well and leave aside.
2. Heat up a pan that fits your air fryer with the oil over medium heat, add garlic; stir and cook for 1 minute.
3. Add chicken, salt, pepper, stir, almonds, zucchini noodles, garlic, cherry tomatoes and the pesto you've made at the beginning, stir gently; introduce in preheated air fryer and cook at 360 °F, for 17 minutes. Divide among plates and serve for lunch

Nutrition Values (Per Serving): Calories: 344; Fat: 8g; Fiber: 7g; Carbs: 12g; Protein: 16

110. Lunch Pizzas

(Prep + Cooking Time: 17 Minutes | **Serves:** 4)

Ingredients:

- 3/4-cup pizza sauce
- 2 green onions, chopped.
- 2-cup mozzarella, grated.
- 4 oz. jarred mushrooms, sliced.
- 1-cup grape tomatoes, sliced.
- 4 pitas
- 1-tbsp. olive oil
- ½-tsp. basil; dried

Directions:

1. Spread pizza sauce on each pita bread; sprinkle green onions and basil, divide mushrooms and top with cheese.
2. Arrange pita pizzas in your air fryer and cook them at 400 °F, for 7 minutes. Top each pizza with tomato slices; divide among plates and serve

Nutrition Values (Per Serving): Calories: 200; Fat: 4g; Fiber: 6g; Carbs: 7g; Protein: 3g

111. Special Sausage

(Prep + Cooking Time: 20 Minutes | **Serves:** 4)

Ingredients:

- 1 lb. sausages, sliced.
- ½-cup chicken stock
- 1/3-cup ketchup
- 1 red bell pepper; cut into strips
- ½-cup yellow onion, chopped.
- 2-tbsp. apple cider vinegar
- 2-tbsp. mustard
- 3-tbsp. brown sugar

Directions:

1. Take a bowl and mix sugar with ketchup, mustard, stock and vinegar and whisk well.
2. In your air fryer's pan; mix sausage slices with bell pepper, onion and sweet and sour mix; toss and cook at 350 °F, for 10 minutes. Divide into bowls and serve for lunch

Nutrition Values (Per Serving): Calories: 162; Fat: 6g; Fiber: 9g; Carbs: 12g; Protein: 6g

112. Chicken, Quinoa, Corn, Beans and Casserole

(Prep + Cooking Time: 40 Minutes | **Serves:** 8)

Ingredients:

- 2 jalapeno peppers, chopped.
- ½-cup cilantro, chopped.
- 6 kale leaves, chopped.
- 3-cups mozzarella cheese, shredded.
- 14 oz. canned black beans
- 12 oz. corn
- ½-cup green onions, chopped.
- 1-cup clean tomato sauce
- 1-cup clean salsa
- 1-cup quinoa; already cooked
- 3-cups chicken breast; cooked and shredded
- 2-tsp. chili powder
- 2-tsp. cumin, ground.
- 1-tbsp. garlic powder
- Cooking spray.

Directions:

1. Spray a baking dish that fits your air fryer with cooking spray, add quinoa, chicken, black beans, corn, cilantro, kale, green onions, tomato sauce, salsa, chili powder, cumin, garlic powder, jalapenos and mozzarella; toss, introduce in your fryer and cook at 350 °F, for 17 minutes. Slice and serve warm for lunch.

Nutrition Values (Per Serving): Calories: 365; Fat: 12g; Fiber: 6g; Carbs: 22g; Protein: 26

113. Air Fryer Bacon Pudding

(Prep + Cooking Time: 40 Minutes | **Serves:** 6)

Ingredients:

- 4 bacon strips, cooked and chopped.
- 2-cups corn
- 1 yellow onion, chopped.
- 1/4-cup celery, chopped.
- ½-cup red bell pepper, chopped.
- 3 eggs, whisked.
- 3-cups bread, cubed.
- ½-cup heavy cream

- 1 ½-cups milk
- 1-tbsp. butter, soft.
- 4-tbsp. parmesan, grated.
- one-tsp. thyme, chopped.
- 2-tsp. garlic, minced.
- Salt and black pepper to the taste.
- Cooking spray.

Directions:

1. Grease your air fryer's pan with cooking spray.
2. Take a bowl and mix bacon with butter, corn, onion, bell pepper, celery, thyme, garlic, salt, pepper, milk, heavy cream, eggs and bread cubes; toss, pour into greased pan and sprinkle cheese all over
3. Add this to your preheated air fryer at 320 degrees and cook for 30 minutes. Divide among plates and serve warm for a quick lunch

Nutrition Values (Per Serving): Calories: 276; Fat: 10g; Fiber: 2g; Carbs: 20g; Protein: 10g

114. Special Pancake

(Prep + Cooking Time: 20 Minutes | **Serves:** 2)

Ingredients:

- 1-cup small shrimp, peeled and deveined
- 3 eggs, whisked.
- ½-cup flour
- ½-cup milk
- 1-cup salsa
- 1-tbsp. butter

Directions:

1. Preheat your air fryer at 400 degrees F; add fryer's pan, add 1-tbsp. butter and melt it.
2. Take a bowl and mix eggs with flour and milk, whisk well and pour into air fryer's pan, spread, cook at 350 degrees for 12 minutes and transfer to a plate. Take a bowl and mix shrimp with salsa; stir and serve your pancake with this on the side.

Nutrition Values (Per Serving): Calories: 200; Fat: 6g; Fiber: 8g; Carbs: 12g; Protein: 4g

115. Corn Casserole Recipe

(Prep + Cooking Time: 25 Minutes | **Serves:** 4)

Ingredients:

- ½-cup Swiss cheese, grated.
- 1/4-cup milk
- 2-cups corn
- ½-cup light cream
- 1 egg
- 2-tbsp. butter
- 3-tbsp. flour
- Salt and black pepper to the taste.
- Cooking spray.

Directions:

1. Take a bowl and mix corn with flour, egg, milk, light cream, cheese, salt, pepper and butter and stir well.
2. Grease your air fryer's pan with cooking spray, pour cream mix; spread and cook at 320 °F, for 15 minutes. Serve warm for lunch.

Nutrition Values (Per Serving): Calories: 281; Fat: 7g; Fiber: 8g; Carbs: 9g; Protein: 6g

116. Special Gnocchi.

(Prep + Cooking Time: 27 Minutes | **Serves:** 4)

Ingredients:

- 1/4-cup parmesan, grated.
- 3 garlic cloves, minced.
- 8 oz. spinach pesto
- 1 yellow onion, chopped.
- 16 oz. gnocchi
- 1-tbsp. olive oil

Directions:

1. Grease your air fryer's pan with olive oil, add gnocchi, onion and garlic, toss; put pan in your air fryer and cook at 400 °F, for 10 minutes.
2. Add pesto, toss and cook for 7 minutes more at 350 degrees F. Divide among plates and serve for lunch

Nutrition Values (Per Serving): Calories: 200; Fat: 4g; Fiber: 4g; Carbs: 12g; Protein: 4g

117. Zucchini Casseroles.

(Prep + Cooking Time: 26 Minutes | **Serves:** 8)

Ingredients:

- 2 sweet potatoes, peeled and cut into medium wedges
- 2 yellow onions, chopped.
- 1-cup veggie stock
- 1-cup coconut milk
- 8 zucchinis; cut into medium wedges
- 4-tbsp. dill, chopped.
- 2-tbsp. olive oil
- 1-tbsp. soy sauce
- 1/4-tsp. rosemary; dried
- ½-tsp. basil, chopped.
- 1/4-tsp. thyme; dried
- Salt and black pepper to the taste.

Directions:

1. Heat up a pan that fits your air fryer with the oil over medium heat; add onion, stir and cook for 2 minutes. Add zucchinis, thyme, rosemary, basil, potato, salt, pepper, stock, milk, soy sauce and dill; stir, introduce in your air fryer; cook at 360 °F, for 14 minutes, divide among plates and serve right away.

Nutrition Values (Per Serving): Calories: 133; Fat: 3g; Fiber: 4g; Carbs: 10g; Protein: 5g

118. Pork and Potatoes Recipe

(Prep + Cooking Time: 35 Minutes | **Serves:** 2)

Ingredients:

- 2 lbs. pork loin
- 2 red potatoes; cut into medium wedges
- one-tsp. parsley; dried
- A drizzle of balsamic vinegar
- ½-tsp. garlic powder
- ½-tsp. red pepper flakes
- Salt and black pepper to the taste.

Directions:

1. In your air fryer's pan; mix pork with potatoes, salt, pepper, garlic powder, pepper flakes, parsley and vinegar; toss and cook at 390 °F, for 25 minutes. Slice pork, divide it and potatoes on plates and serve for lunch.

Nutrition Values (Per Serving): Calories: 400; Fat: 15g; Fiber: 7g; Carbs: 27g; Protein: 20g

119. Potato Salad

(Prep + Cooking Time: 35 Minutes | **Serves:** 4)

Ingredients:

- 2 lb. red potatoes, halved.
- 2 green onions, chopped.
- 1 red bell pepper, chopped.
- 3-tbsp. mustard
- 2-tbsp. olive oil
- 1/3-cup lemon juice
- Salt and black pepper to the taste.

Directions:

1. On your air fryer's basket; mix potatoes with half of the olive oil, salt and pepper and cook at 350 °F, for 25 minutes shaking the fryer once

2. Take a bowl and mix onions with bell pepper and roasted potatoes and toss.
3. In a small bowl; mix lemon juice with the rest of the oil and mustard and whisk really well. Add this to potato salad; toss well and serve for lunch

Nutrition Values (Per Serving): Calories: 211; Fat: 6g; Fiber: 8g; Carbs: 12g; Protein: 4g

120. Amazing Beef Stew.

(Prep + Cooking Time: 30 Minutes **| Serves:** 4)

Ingredients:

- 2 lbs. beef meat; cut into medium chunks
- 4 potatoes, chopped.
- 1-quart veggie stock
- 2 carrots, chopped.
- ½-tsp. smoked paprika
- A handful thyme, chopped.
- Salt and black pepper to the taste.

Directions:

1. In a dish that fits your air fryer; mix beef with carrots, potatoes, stock, salt, pepper, paprika and thyme; stir, place in air fryer's basket and cook at 375 °F, for 20 minutes. Divide into bowls and serve right away for lunch.

Nutrition Values (Per Serving): Calories: 260; Fat: 5g; Fiber: 8g; Carbs: 20g; Protein: 22g

121. Meatballs Sandwich Delight.

(Prep + Cooking Time: 32 Minutes **| Serves:** 4)

Ingredients:

- 3 baguettes, sliced more than halfway through
- 14 oz. beef, ground.
- 7 oz. tomato sauce
- 1 small onion, chopped.
- 1 egg, whisked.
- 1-tbsp. bread crumbs
- 1-tbsp. oregano, chopped.
- 1-tbsp. olive oil
- 2-tbsp. cheddar cheese, grated.
- one-tsp. thyme; dried
- one-tsp. basil; dried
- Salt and black pepper to the taste.

Directions:

1. Take a bowl and combine meat with salt, pepper, onion, breadcrumbs, egg, cheese, oregano, thyme and basil; stir, shape medium meatballs and add them to your air fryer after you've greased it with the oil.
2. Cook them at 375 °F, for 12 minutes; flipping them halfway.
3. Add tomato sauce, cook meatballs for 10 minutes more and arrange them on sliced baguettes. Serve them right away

Nutrition Values (Per Serving): Calories: 380; Fat: 5g; Fiber: 6g; Carbs: 34g; Protein: 20g

122. Special Seafood Stew

(Prep + Cooking Time: 30 Minutes **| Serves:** 4)

Ingredients:

- 3 oz. sea bass fillet; skinless, boneless and chopped.
- 14 oz. white wine
- 3 oz. water
- 2 oz. squid pieces
- 5 oz. white rice
- 7 oz. mussels
- 6 scallops
- 3.5 oz. clams
- 4 shrimp
- 4 crayfish
- 2 oz. peas
- 1 red bell pepper, chopped.
- 1-tbsp. olive oil
- Salt and black pepper to the taste.

Directions:

1. In your air fryer's pan; mix sea bass with shrimp, mussels, scallops, crayfish, clams and squid
2. Add the oil, salt and pepper and toss to coat.
3. Take a bowl and mix peas salt, pepper, bell pepper and rice and stir.
4. Add this over seafood, also add wine and water, place pan in your air fryer and cook at 400 °F, for 20 minutes; stirring halfway. Divide into bowls and serve for lunch

Nutrition Values (Per Serving): Calories: 300; Fat: 12g; Fiber: 2g; Carbs: 23g; Protein: 25g

123. Chicken and Coconut Casserole

(Prep + Cooking Time: 35 Minutes | **Serves:** 4)

Ingredients:

- 1 lb. chicken breast; skinless, boneless and cut into thin strips
- 4 lime leaves; torn
- 1 lemongrass stalk, chopped.
- 1-inch piece, grated.
- 8 oz. mushrooms, chopped.
- 4 Thai chilies, chopped.
- 6 oz. coconut milk
- 1/4-cup lime juice
- 1/4-cup cilantro, chopped.
- 1-cup veggie stock
- 4-tbsp. fish sauce
- Salt and black pepper to the taste.

Directions:

1. Put stock into a pan that fits your air fryer; bring to a simmer over medium heat, add lemongrass, ginger and lime leaves; stir and cook for 10 minutes.
2. Strain soup, return to pan, add chicken, mushrooms, milk, chilies, fish sauce, lime juice, cilantro, salt and pepper; stir, introduce in your air fryer and cook at 360 °F, for 15 minutes. Divide into bowls and serve

Nutrition Values (Per Serving): Calories: 150; Fat: 4g; Fiber: 4g; Carbs: 6g; Protein: 7g

124. Chicken Lunch Recipe.

(Prep + Cooking Time: 30 Minutes | **Serves:** 6)

Ingredients:

- 1-cup chicken, shredded.
- 1-cup shiitake mushrooms; roughly sliced
- 1 bunch kale, chopped.
- 1/4-cup chicken stock
- 3 carrots, chopped.
- Salt and black pepper to the taste.

Directions:

1. In a blender, mix stock with kale, pulse a few times and pour into a pan that fits your air fryer. Add chicken, mushrooms, carrots, salt and pepper to the taste; toss, introduce in your air fryer and cook at 350 °F, for 18 minutes.

Nutrition Values (Per Serving): Calories: 180; Fat: 7g; Fiber: 2g; Carbs: 10g; Protein: 5g

125. Tasty Stuffed Meatballs.

(Prep + Cooking Time: 20 Minutes | **Serves:** 4)

Ingredients:

- 1/3-cup bread crumbs
- 1 lb. lean beef, ground.
- 20 cheddar cheese cubes
- 1 egg
- 1-tbsp. olive oil
- 3-tbsp. milk
- 1-tbsp. ketchup
- ½-tsp. marjoram; dried
- Salt and black pepper to the taste.

Directions:

1. Take a bowl and mix bread crumbs with ketchup, milk, marjoram, salt, pepper and egg and whisk well.
2. Add beef; stir and shape 20 meatballs out of this mix
3. Shape each meatball around a cheese cube, drizzle the oil over them and rub.
4. Place all meatballs in your preheated air fryer and cook at 390 °F, for 10 minutes. Serve them for lunch with a side salad

Nutrition Values (Per Serving): Calories: 200; Fat: 5g; Fiber: 8g; Carbs: 12g; Protein: 5g

126. Italian Style Eggplant Sandwich.

(Prep + Cooking Time: 26 Minutes | **Serves:** 4)

Ingredients:

- 1 eggplant, sliced.
- 4 bread slices
- ½-cup mayonnaise
- 3/4-cup tomato sauce
- 2-cups mozzarella cheese, grated.
- ½-cup breadcrumbs
- 2-tbsp. milk
- ½-tsp. garlic powder
- ½-tsp. onion powder
- ½-tsp. Italian seasoning
- 2-tsp. parsley; dried
- Cooking spray.
- Salt and black pepper to the taste.

Directions:

1. Season eggplant slices with salt and pepper, leave aside for 10 minutes and then pat dry them well
2. Take a bowl and mix parsley with breadcrumbs, Italian seasoning, onion and garlic powder, salt and black pepper and stir.
3. In another bowl; mix milk with mayo and whisk well.
4. Brush eggplant slices with mayo mix, dip them in breadcrumbs, place them in your air fryer's basket, spray with cooking oil and cook them at 400 °F, for 15 minutes; flipping them after 8 minutes.
5. Brush each bread slice with olive oil and arrange 2 on a working surface.
6. Add mozzarella and parmesan on each, add baked eggplant slices; spread tomato sauce and basil and top with the other bread slices, greased side down. Divide sandwiches on plates; cut them in halves and serve for lunch

Nutrition Values (Per Serving): Calories: 324; Fat: 16g; Fiber: 4g; Carbs: 39g; Protein: 12g

127. Steak and Cabbage

(Prep + Cooking Time: 20 Minutes | **Serves:** 4)

Ingredients:

- ½ lb. sirloin steak; cut into strips
- 2-cups green cabbage, chopped.
- 2 green onions, chopped.
- 2 garlic cloves, minced.
- 1 yellow bell pepper, chopped.
- 1-tbsp. peanut oil
- 2-tsp. cornstarch
- Salt and black pepper to the taste.

Directions:

1. Take a bowl and mix cabbage with salt, pepper and peanut oil; toss, transfer to air fryer's basket, cook at 370 °F, for 4 minutes and transfer to a bowl
2. Add steak strips to your air fryer; also add green onions, bell pepper, garlic, salt and pepper, toss and cook for 5 minutes. Add over cabbage; toss, divide among plates and serve for lunch.

Nutrition Values (Per Serving): Calories: 282; Fat: 6g; Fiber: 8g; Carbs: 14g; Protein: 6g

128. Sweet Potato Casserole

(Prep + Cooking Time: 60 Minutes | **Serves:** 6)

Ingredients:

- 3 big sweet potatoes; pricked with a fork
- 1/3-cup coconut cream
- 1-cup chicken stock
- 1/4-tsp. nutmeg, ground.
- A pinch of cayenne pepper
- Salt and black pepper to the taste.

Directions:

1. Place sweet potatoes in your air fryer; cook them at 350 °F, for 40 minutes; cool them down, peel, roughly chop and transfer to a pan that fits your air fryer.
2. Add stock, salt, pepper, cayenne and coconut cream; toss, introduce in your air fryer and cook at 360 °F, for 10 minutes more. Divide casserole into bowls and serve

Nutrition Values (Per Serving): Calories: 245; Fat: 4g; Fiber: 5g; Carbs: 10g; Protein: 6g

129. Chicken Corn Casserole.

(Prep + Cooking Time: 40 Minutes | **Serves:** 6)

Ingredients:

- 2 lbs. chicken breasts; skinless, boneless and cubed
- 1/3-cup cilantro, chopped.
- 1-cup clean chicken stock
- 6 oz. canned coconut milk
- 3-cups corn
- 3 handfuls spinach
- 3 green onions, chopped.
- 1 ½-cups green lentils
- 2-tsp. garlic powder
- Salt and black pepper to the taste.

Directions:

1. In a pan that fits your air fryer; mix stock with coconut milk, salt, pepper, garlic powder, chicken and lentils. Add corn, green onions, cilantro and spinach; stir well, introduce in your air fryer and cook at 350 °F, for 30 minutes.

Nutrition Values (Per Serving): Calories: 345; Fat: 12g; Fiber: 10g; Carbs: 20g; Protein: 44

130. Meatballs, Tomato Sauce

(Prep + Cooking Time: 245 Minutes | **Serves:** 4)

Ingredients:

- 1 lb. lean beef, ground.
- 16 oz. tomato sauce
- 1 egg yolk
- 1/4-cup bread crumbs
- 3 green onions, chopped.
- 2 garlic cloves, minced.
- 1-tbsp. olive oil
- 2-tbsp. mustard
- Salt and black pepper to the taste.

Directions:

1. Take a bowl and mix beef with onion, garlic, egg yolk, bread crumbs, salt and pepper; stir well and shape medium meatballs out of this mix
2. Grease meatballs with the oil, place them in your air fryer and cook them at 400 °F, for 10 minutes.
3. Take a bowl and mix tomato sauce with mustard, whisk, add over meatballs; toss them and cook at 400 °F, for 5 minutes more. Divide meatballs and sauce on plates and serve for lunch

Nutrition Values (Per Serving): Calories: 300; Fat: 8g; Fiber: 9g; Carbs: 16g; Protein: 5g

Poultry Recipes

131. Italian Chicken Recipe.

(Prep + Cooking Time: 26 Minutes | **Serves:** 4)

Ingredients:

- 5 chicken thighs
- ½-cup heavy cream
- 3/4-cup chicken stock
- 1/4-cup parmesan, grated.
- ½-cup sun dried tomatoes
- 2 garlic cloves, minced.
- 1-tbsp. thyme, chopped.
- 1-tbsp. olive oil
- 2-tbsp. basil, chopped.
- one-tsp. red pepper flakes; crushed
- Salt and black pepper to the taste.

Directions:

1. Season chicken with salt and pepper, rub with half of the oil, place in your preheated air fryer at 350 °F and cook for 4 minutes
2. Meanwhile, heat up a pan with the rest of the oil over medium high heat, add thyme garlic, pepper flakes, sun dried tomatoes, heavy cream, stock, parmesan, salt and pepper; stir, bring to a simmer, take off heat and transfer to a dish that fits your air fryer.
3. Add chicken thighs on top, introduce in your air fryer and cook at 320 °F, for 12 minutes. Divide among plates and serve with basil sprinkled on top

Nutrition Values (Per Serving): Calories: 272; Fat: 9g; Fiber: 12g; Carbs: 37g; Protein: 23g

132. Chinese Chicken Wings Recipe

(Prep + Cooking Time: 2 hours 15 Minutes | **Serves:** 6)

Ingredients:

- 16 chicken wings
- 3-tbsp. lime juice
- 2-tbsp. soy sauce
- 2-tbsp. honey
- 1/4-tsp. white pepper
- Salt and black pepper to the taste.

Directions:

1. In a bowl, mix honey with soy sauce, salt, black and white pepper and lime juice, whisk well, add chicken pieces, toss to coat and keep in the fridge for 2 hours.
2. Transfer chicken to your air fryer, cook at 370 °F, for 6 minutes on each side, increase heat to 400 °F and cook for 3 minutes more. Serve hot.

Nutrition Values (Per Serving): Calories: 372; Fat: 9g; Fiber: 10g; Carbs: 37g; Protein: 24g

133. Chicken Cacciatore Recipe

(Prep + Cooking Time: 30 Minutes | **Serves:** 4)

Ingredients:

- 8 chicken drumsticks; bone-in
- 28 oz. canned tomatoes and juice; crushed
- 1 yellow onion, chopped.
- 1 bay leaf
- ½-cup black olives, pitted and sliced.
- one-tsp. garlic powder
- one-tsp. oregano; dried
- Salt and black pepper to the taste.

Directions:

1. In a heat proof dish that fits your air fryer, mix chicken with salt, pepper, garlic powder, bay leaf, onion, tomatoes and juice, oregano and olives; toss, introduce in your preheated air fryer and cook at 365 °F, for 20 minutes. Divide among plates and serve.

Nutrition Values (Per Serving): Calories: 300; Fat: 12g; Fiber: 8g; Carbs: 20g; Protein: 24g

134. Chicken Parmesan Recipe

(Prep + Cooking Time: 25 Minutes | **Serves:** 4)

Ingredients:

- 1 ½ lbs. chicken cutlets; skinless and boneless
- 2-cups tomato sauce
- 1 egg, whisked.
- 2-cups panko bread crumbs
- 1/4-cup parmesan, grated.
- 1-cup mozzarella, grated.
- 2-cups white flour
- 3-tbsp. basil, chopped.
- ½-tsp. garlic powder
- Salt and black pepper to the taste.

Directions:

1. In a bowl, mix panko with parmesan and garlic powder and stir
2. Put flour in a second bowl and the egg in a third.
3. Season chicken with salt and pepper, dip in flour, then in egg mix and in panko.
4. Put chicken pieces in your air fryer and cook them at 360 °F, for 3 minutes on each side.
5. Transfer chicken to a baking dish that fits your air fryer, add tomato sauce and top with mozzarella, introduce in your air fryer and cook at 375 °F, for 7 minutes. Divide among plates, sprinkle basil on top and serve

Nutrition Values (Per Serving): Calories: 304; Fat: 12g; Fiber: 11g; Carbs: 22g; Protein: 15g

135. Chicken Salad Recipe

(Prep + Cooking Time: 20 Minutes | **Serves:** 4)

Ingredients:

- 1 lb. chicken breast; boneless, skinless and halved
- ½-cup feta cheese, cubed.
- 8-cups lettuce leaves; cut into strips
- 1-tbsp. water
- 4-tbsp. parmesan, grated.
- 2-tbsp. lemon juice
- 1-tbsp. olive oil
- ½-tsp. anchovies, minced.
- 3/4-tsp. garlic, minced.
- 1 ½-tsp. red wine vinegar
- 1½-tsp. mustard
- Salt and black pepper to the taste.
- Cooking spray.

Directions:

1. Spray chicken breasts with cooking oil, season with salt and pepper, introduce in your air fryer's basket and cook at 370 °F, for 10 minutes; flipping halfway
2. Transfer chicken beasts to a cutting board, shred using 2 forks, put in a salad bowl and mix with lettuce leaves.
3. In your blender, mix feta cheese with lemon juice, olive oil, mustard, vinegar, garlic, anchovies, water and half of the parmesan and blend very well. Add this over chicken mix; toss, sprinkle the rest of the parmesan and serve

Nutrition Values (Per Serving): Calories: 312; Fat: 6g; Fiber: 16g; Carbs: 22g; Protein: 26

136. Creamy Chicken, Peas and Rice

(Prep + Cooking Time: 40 Minutes | **Serves:** 4)

Ingredients:

- 1 lb. chicken breasts; skinless, boneless and cut into quarters
- 3 garlic cloves, minced.
- 1-cup chicken stock
- 1/4-cup parsley, chopped.
- 2-cups peas; frozen
- 1 ½-cups parmesan, grated.
- 1 yellow onion, chopped.
- ½-cup white wine
- 1/4-cup heavy cream
- 1-cup white rice; already cooked
- 1-tbsp. olive oil
- Salt and black pepper to the taste.

Directions:

1. Season chicken breasts with salt and pepper, drizzle half of the oil over them, rub well, put in your air fryer's basket and cook them at 360 °F, for 6 minutes
2. Heat up a pan with the rest of the oil over medium high heat, add garlic, onion, wine, stock, salt, pepper and heavy cream; stir, bring to a simmer and cook for 9 minutes.
3. Transfer chicken breasts to a heat proof dish that fits your air fryer, add peas, rice and cream mix over them, toss, sprinkle parmesan and parsley all over, place in your air fryer and cook at 420 °F, for 10 minutes. Divide among plates and serve hot

Nutrition Values (Per Serving): Calories: 313; Fat: 12g; Fiber: 14g; Carbs: 27g; Protein: 44

137. Mexican Chicken Recipe

(Prep + Cooking Time: 30 Minutes | **Serves:** 4)

Ingredients:

- 1 lb. chicken breast; boneless and skinless
- 1½-cup Monterey Jack cheese, grated.
- 1/4-cup cilantro, chopped.
- 16 oz. salsa verde
- 1-tbsp. olive oil
- one-tsp. garlic powder
- Salt and black pepper to the taste.

Directions:

1. Pour salsa verde in a baking dish that fits your air fryer, season chicken with salt, pepper, garlic powder, brush with olive oil and place it over your salsa verde
2. Introduce in your air fryer and cook at 380 °F, for 20 minutes.
3. Sprinkle cheese on top and cook for 2 minutes more. Divide among plates and serve hot

Nutrition Values (Per Serving): Calories: 340; Fat: 18g; Fiber: 14g; Carbs: 32g; Protein: 18g

138. Chicken & Parsley Sauce.

(Prep + Cooking Time: 55 Minutes | **Serves:** 6)

Ingredients:

- 12 chicken thighs
- 1/4-cup red wine
- 4 garlic cloves
- ½-cup olive oil
- 1-cup parsley, chopped.
- one-tsp. oregano; dried
- A pinch of salt
- A drizzle of maple syrup

Directions:

1. In your food processor, mix parsley with oregano, garlic, salt, oil, wine and maple syrup and pulse really well.
2. In a bowl, mix chicken with parsley sauce; toss well and keep in the fridge for 30 minutes

3. Drain chicken, transfer to your air fryer's basket and cook at 380 °F, for 25 minutes; flipping chicken once. Divide chicken on plates, drizzle parsley sauce all over and serve

Nutrition Values (Per Serving): Calories: 354; Fat: 10g; Fiber: 12g; Carbs: 22g; Protein: 17g

139. Fried Japanese Duck Breasts

(Prep + Cooking Time: 30 Minutes | **Serves:** 6)

Ingredients:

- 20 oz. chicken stock
- 6 duck breasts; boneless
- 4 ginger slices
- 4-tbsp. soy sauce
- 2-tbsp. honey
- 4-tbsp. hoisin sauce
- 1½-tsp. five spice powder
- one-tsp. sesame oil
- Salt and black pepper to the taste.

Directions:

1. In a bowl, mix five spice powder with soy sauce, salt, pepper and honey, whisk, add duck breasts, toss to coat and leave aside for now
2. Heat up a pan with the stock over medium high heat, hoisin sauce, ginger and sesame oil; stir well, cook for 2-3 minutes more, take off heat and leave aside.
3. Put duck breasts in your air fryer and cook them at 400 °F, for 15 minutes. Divide among plates, drizzle hoisin and ginger sauce all over them and serve

Nutrition Values (Per Serving): Calories: 336; Fat: 12g; Fiber: 1g; Carbs: 25g; Protein: 33

140. Chicken and Green Onions Sauce Recipe.

(Prep + Cooking Time: 26 Minutes | **Serves:** 4)

Ingredients:

- 10 green onions; roughly chopped.
- 10 chicken drumsticks
- 1-cup coconut milk
- 1-inch piece ginger root, chopped.
- 1/4-cup cilantro, chopped.
- 4 garlic cloves, minced.
- 1-tbsp. lime juice
- 2-tbsp. fish sauce
- 3-tbsp. soy sauce
- one-tsp. Chinese five spice
- one-tsp. butter, melted.
- Salt and black pepper to the taste.

Directions:

1. In your food processor, mix green onions with ginger, garlic, soy sauce, fish sauce, five spice, salt, pepper, butter and coconut milk and pulse well
2. In a bowl, mix chicken with green onions mix; toss well, transfer everything to a pan that fits your air fryer and cook at 370 °F, for 16 minutes; shaking the fryer once. Divide among plates, sprinkle cilantro on top, drizzle lime juice and serve with a side salad.

Nutrition Values (Per Serving): Calories: 321; Fat: 12g; Fiber: 12g; Carbs: 22g; Protein: 20g

141. Chicken and Asparagus Recipe

(Prep + Cooking Time: 30 Minutes | **Serves:** 4)

Ingredients:

- 8 asparagus spears
- 8 chicken wings, halved.
- 1-tbsp. rosemary, chopped.
- one-tsp. cumin, ground.
- Salt and black pepper to the taste.

Directions:

1. Pat dry chicken wings, season with salt, pepper, cumin and rosemary, put them in your air fryer's basket and cook at 360 °F, for 20 minutes
2. Meanwhile, heat up a pan over medium heat, add asparagus, add water to cover, steam for a few minutes; transfer to a bowl filled with ice water, drain and arrange on plates. Add chicken wings on the side and serve.

Nutrition Values (Per Serving): Calories: 270; Fat: 8g; Fiber: 12g; Carbs: 24g; Protein: 22g

142. Chicken Thighs and Baby Potatoes

(Prep + Cooking Time: 40 Minutes | **Serves:** 4)

Ingredients:

- 8 chicken thighs
- 1 lb. baby potatoes, halved.
- 2 garlic cloves, minced.
- 1 red onion, chopped.
- 2-tbsp. olive oil
- 2-tsp. thyme, chopped.
- ½-tsp. sweet paprika
- 2-tsp. oregano; dried
- 2-tsp. rosemary; dried
- Salt and black pepper to the taste.

Directions:

1. In a bowl, mix chicken thighs with potatoes, salt, pepper, thyme, paprika, onion, rosemary, garlic, oregano and oil.
2. Toss to coat, spread everything in a heat proof dish that fits your air fryer and cook at 400 °F, for 30 minutes; shaking halfway. Divide among plates and serve

Nutrition Values (Per Serving): Calories: 364; Fat: 14g; Fiber: 13g; Carbs: 21g; Protein: 34

143. Cheese Crusted Chicken Recipe.

(Prep + Cooking Time: 25 Minutes | **Serves:** 4)

Ingredients:

- 4 bacon slices; cooked and crumbled
- 4 chicken breasts; skinless and boneless
- ½-cup avocado oil
- 1 egg, whisked.
- 1-cup asiago cheese, shredded.
- 1-cup parmesan cheese, grated.
- 1-tbsp. water
- 1/4-tsp. garlic powder
- Salt and black pepper to the taste.

Directions:

1. In a bowl, mix parmesan with garlic, salt and pepper and stir
2. In another bowl, mix egg with water and whisk well.
3. Season chicken with salt and pepper and dip each pieces into egg and then into cheese mix.
4. Add chicken to your air fryer and cook at 320 °F, for 15 minutes. Divide chicken on plates, sprinkle bacon and asiago cheese on top and serve

Nutrition Values (Per Serving): Calories: 400; Fat: 22g; Fiber: 12g; Carbs: 32g; Protein: 47

144. Chicken Breasts and Tomatoes Sauce.

(Prep + Cooking Time: 30 Minutes | **Serves:** 4)

Ingredients:

- 4 chicken breasts; skinless and boneless
- 14 oz. canned tomatoes, chopped.
- 1/4-cup balsamic vinegar
- 1/4-cup parmesan, grated.
- 1 red onion, chopped.
- 1/4-tsp. garlic powder
- Salt and black pepper to the taste.
- Cooking spray.

Directions:

1. Spray a baking dish that fits your air fryer with cooking oil, add chicken, season with salt, pepper, balsamic vinegar, garlic powder, tomatoes and cheese; toss, introduce in your air fryer and cook at 400 °F, for 20 minutes. Divide among plates and serve hot.

Nutrition Values (Per Serving): Calories: 250; Fat: 12g; Fiber: 12g; Carbs: 19g; Protein: 28

145. Herbed Chicken Recipe.

(Prep + Cooking Time: 70 Minutes | **Serves:** 4)

Ingredients:

- 1 whole chicken
- 2-tbsp. olive oil
- 1-tbsp. lemon juice
- ½-tsp. thyme; dried
- one-tsp. rosemary; dried
- one-tsp. garlic powder
- one-tsp. onion powder
- Salt and black pepper to the taste.

Directions:

1. Season chicken with salt and pepper, rub with thyme, rosemary, garlic powder and onion powder, rub with lemon juice and olive oil and leave aside for 30 minutes.
2. Put chicken in your air fryer and cook at 360 °F, for 20 minutes on each side. Leave chicken aside to cool down, carve and serve.

Nutrition Values (Per Serving): Calories: 390; Fat: 10g; Fiber: 5g; Carbs: 22g; Protein: 20g

146. Chicken and Lentils Casserole Recipe.

(Prep + Cooking Time: 1 hour 10 Minutes | **Serves:** 8)

Ingredients:

- 2 lb. chicken breasts; skinless, boneless and chopped
- 14 oz. canned tomatoes, chopped.
- 5 garlic cloves, minced.
- 1 yellow onion, chopped.
- 2 red bell peppers, chopped.
- 2-cups corn
- 2-cups Cheddar cheese, shredded.
- 1 ½-cups green lentils
- 3-cups chicken stock
- 1-cup cilantro; chopped
- 1-tbsp. garlic powder
- 2-tbsp. jalapeno pepper; chopped.
- 3-tsp. cumin, ground.
- Cooking spray.
- Salt and cayenne pepper to the taste

Directions:

1. Put the stock in a pot, add some salt, add lentils; stir, bring to a boil over medium heat, cover and simmer for 35 minutes
2. Meanwhile, spray chicken pieces with some cooking spray, season with salt, cayenne pepper and one-tsp. cumin, put them in your air fryer's basket and cook them at 370 degrees for 6 minutes. flipping half way.
3. Transfer chicken to a heat proof dish that fits your air fryer, add bell peppers, garlic, tomatoes, onion, salt, cayenne and one-tsp. cumin.
4. Drain lentils and add them to the chicken mix as well.
5. Add jalapeno pepper, garlic powder, the rest of the cumin, corn, half of the cheese and half of the cilantro, introduce in your air fryer and cook at 320 °F, for 25 minutes.
6. Sprinkle the rest of the cheese and the remaining cilantro, divide chicken casserole on plates and serve

Nutrition Values (Per Serving): Calories: 344; Fat: 11g; Fiber: 12g; Carbs: 22g; Protein: 33

147. Honey Duck Breasts Recipe.

(Prep + Cooking Time: 32 Minutes | **Serves:** 2)

Ingredients:

- 1 smoked duck breast, halved.
- 1-tbsp. mustard
- one-tsp. tomato paste
- ½-tsp. apple vinegar
- one-tsp. honey

Directions:

1. In a bowl, mix honey with tomato paste, mustard and vinegar, whisk well, add duck breast pieces, toss to coat well, transfer to your air fryer and cook at 370 °F, for 15 minutes
2. Take duck breast out of the fryer, add to honey mix, toss again, return to air fryer and cook at 370 °F, for 6 minutes more. Divide among plates and serve with a side salad.

Nutrition Values (Per Serving): Calories: 274; Fat: 11g; Fiber: 13g; Carbs: 22g; Protein: 13g

148. Duck and Veggies Recipe.

(Prep + Cooking Time: 30 Minutes | **Serves:** 8)

Ingredients:

- 1 duck, chopped.in medium pieces
- 1 small ginger piece, grated.
- 3 cucumbers, chopped.
- 2 carrots, chopped.
- 1-cup chicken stock
- 3-tbsp. white wine
- Salt and black pepper to the taste.

Directions:

1. In a pan that fits your air fryer, mix duck pieces with cucumbers, wine, carrots, ginger, stock, salt and pepper; toss, introduce in your air fryer and cook at 370 °F, for 20 minutes. Divide everything on plates and serve.

Nutrition Values (Per Serving): Calories: 200; Fat: 10g; Fiber: 8g; Carbs: 20g; Protein: 22g

149. Duck Breasts Recipe

(Prep + Cooking Time: 50 Minutes | **Serves:** 6)

Ingredients:

- 6 duck breasts, halved.
- 1/4-cup parsley, chopped.
- 2-cups mushrooms, chopped.
- 2-cups chicken stock
- ½-cup white wine
- 3-tbsp. flour
- 6-tbsp. butter, melted.
- Salt and black pepper to the taste.

Directions:

1. Season duck breasts with salt and pepper, place them in a bowl, add melted butter; toss and transfer to another bowl.
2. Combine melted butter with flour, wine, salt, pepper and chicken stock and stir well
3. Arrange duck breasts in a baking dish that fits your air fryer, pour the sauce over them, add parsley and mushrooms, introduce in your air fryer and cook at 350 °F, for 40 minutes. Divide among plates and serve.

Nutrition Values (Per Serving): Calories: 320; Fat: 28g; Fiber: 12g; Carbs: 12g; Protein: 42

150. Chicken and Simple Coconut Sauce Recipe

(Prep + Cooking Time: 22 Minutes | **Serves:** 6)

Ingredients:

- 1/4-cup coconut milk
- 3 ½ lbs. chicken breasts
- 1-cup chicken stock
- 1 ¼-cups yellow onion, chopped.
- 2-tbsp. green onions, chopped.
- 1-tbsp. olive oil
- 1-tbsp. lime juice
- 2-tsp. sweet paprika
- one-tsp. red pepper flakes
- Salt and black pepper to the taste.

Directions:

1. Heat up a pan that fits your air fryer with the oil over medium high heat, add onions; stir and cook for 4 minutes
2. Add stock, coconut milk, pepper flakes, paprika, lime juice, salt and pepper and stir well.
3. Add chicken to the pan, add more salt and pepper; toss, introduce in your air fryer and cook at 360 °F, for 12 minutes. Divide chicken and sauce on plates and serve

Nutrition Values (Per Serving): Calories: 320; Fat: 13g; Fiber: 13g; Carbs: 32g; Protein: 23g

151. Turkey, Mushrooms and Peas Casserole.

(Prep + Cooking Time: 30 Minutes | **Serves:** 4)

Ingredients:

- 2 lbs. turkey breasts; skinless, boneless
- ½-cup peas
- 1-cup chicken stock
- 1-cup cream of mushrooms soup
- 1-cup bread cubes
- 1 yellow onion, chopped.
- 1 celery stalk, chopped.
- Salt and black pepper to the taste.

Directions:

1. In a pan that fits your air fryer, mix turkey with salt, pepper, onion, celery, peas and stock, introduce in your air fryer and cook at 360 °F, for 15 minutes
2. Add bread cubes and cream of mushroom soup; stir toss and cook at 360 °F, for 5 minutes more. Divide among plates and serve hot.

Nutrition Values (Per Serving): Calories: 271; Fat: 9g; Fiber: 9g; Carbs: 16g; Protein: 7g

152. Chicken Wings and Mint Sauce Recipe

(Prep + Cooking Time: 36 Minutes | **Serves:** 6)

Ingredients:

- 18 chicken wings, halved.
- 1-tbsp. cumin, ground.
- 1-tbsp. turmeric powder
- 1-tbsp. coriander, ground.
- 1-tbsp. sweet paprika
- 2-tbsp. olive oil
- 1-tbsp. ginger, grated.
- Salt and black pepper to the taste.

For the mint sauce:

- 3/4-cup cilantro
- Juice from ½ lime
- 1-cup mint leaves
- 1 small ginger piece, chopped.
- 1-tbsp. olive oil
- 1 Serrano pepper, chopped.
- 1-tbsp. water
- Salt and black pepper to the taste.

Directions:

1. In a bowl, mix 1-tbsp. ginger with cumin, coriander, paprika, turmeric, salt, pepper, cayenne and 2-tbsp. oil and stir well
2. Add chicken wings pieces to this mix; toss to coat well and keep in the fridge for 10 minutes.
3. Transfer chicken to your air fryer's basket and cook at 370 °F, for 16 minutes; flipping them halfway.
4. In your blender, mix mint with cilantro, 1 small ginger pieces, juice from ½ lime, 1-tbsp. olive oil, salt, pepper, water and Serrano pepper and blend very well. Divide chicken wings on plates, drizzle mint sauce all over and serve

Nutrition Values (Per Serving): Calories: 300; Fat: 15g; Fiber: 11g; Carbs: 27g; Protein: 16

153. Chicken and Creamy Veggie Mix Recipe

(Prep + Cooking Time: 40 Minutes | **Serves:** 6)

Ingredients:

- 29 oz. chicken stock
- 8 oz. mushrooms, chopped.
- 40 oz. chicken pieces; boneless and skinless
- 17 oz. asparagus; trimmed
- 2-cups whipping cream
- ½-cup yellow onion, chopped.
- 3/4-cup red peppers, chopped.
- 1 bay leaf
- 3-tbsp. butter, melted.
- 3-tsp. thyme, chopped.
- Salt and black pepper to the taste.

Directions:

1. Heat up a pan with the butter over medium heat, add onion and peppers; stir and cook for 3 minutes.
2. Add stock, bay leaf, salt and pepper, bring to a boil and simmer for 10 minutes
3. Add asparagus, mushrooms, chicken, cream, thyme, salt and pepper to the taste; stir, introduce in your air fryer and cook at 360 °F, for 15 minutes. Divide chicken and veggie mix on plates and serve

Nutrition Values (Per Serving): Calories: 360; Fat: 27g; Fiber: 13g; Carbs: 24g; Protein: 47

154. Chicken Thighs and Apple.

(Prep + Cooking Time: 12 hours 30 Minutes | **Serves:** 4)

Ingredients:

- 3 apples; cored and cut into quarters
- 8 chicken thighs; bone in and skin on
- 3/4-cup apple juice
- ½-cup maple syrup
- 1-tbsp. apple cider vinegar
- 3-tbsp. onion, chopped.
- 1-tbsp. ginger, grated.
- ½-tsp. thyme; dried
- Salt and black pepper to the taste.

Directions:

1. In a bowl, mix chicken with salt, pepper, vinegar, onion, ginger, thyme, apple juice and maple syrup; toss well, cover and keep in the fridge for 12 hours
2. Transfer this whole mix to a baking dish that fits your air fryer, add apple pieces, place in your air fryer and cook at 350 °F, for 30 minutes. Divide among plates and serve warm.

Nutrition Values (Per Serving): Calories: 314; Fat: 8g; Fiber: 11g; Carbs: 34g; Protein: 22g

155. Chinese Duck Legs Recipe

(Prep + Cooking Time: 46 Minutes | **Serves:** 2)

Ingredients:

- 2 duck legs
- 2 dried chilies, chopped.
- 1 bunch spring onions, chopped.
- 4 ginger slices
- 14 oz. water
- 2-star anise
- 1-tbsp. rice wine
- 1-tbsp. olive oil
- 1-tbsp. oyster sauce
- 1-tbsp. soy sauce
- one-tsp. sesame oil

Directions:

1. Heat up a pan with the oil over medium high heat, add chili, star anise, sesame oil, rice wine, ginger, oyster sauce, soy sauce and water; stir and cook for 6 minutes
2. Add spring onions and duck legs, toss to coat, transfer to a pan that fits your air fryer, put in your air fryer and cook at 370 °F, for 30 minutes. Divide among plates and serve.

Nutrition Values (Per Serving): Calories: 300; Fat: 12g; Fiber: 12g; Carbs: 26g; Protein: 18g

156. Duck and Plum Sauce Recipe.

(Prep + Cooking Time: 42 Minutes | **Serves:** 2)

Ingredients:

- 9 oz. red plumps; stoned; cut into small wedges
- 1-cup beef stock
- 2 duck breasts
- 1 shallot, chopped.
- 1-star anise
- 2-tbsp. sugar
- 2-tbsp. red wine
- 1-tbsp. butter, melted.
- 1-tbsp. olive oil

Directions:

1. Heat up a pan with the olive oil over medium heat, add shallot; stir and cook for 5 minutes;
2. Add sugar and plums; stir and cook until sugar dissolves
3. Add stock and wine; stir, cook for 15 minutes; take off heat and keep warm for now.
4. Score duck breasts, season with salt and pepper, rub with melted butter, transfer to a heat proof dish that fits your air fryer, add star anise and plum sauce, introduce in your air fryer and cook at 360 °F, for 12 minutes. Divide everything on plates and serve

Nutrition Values (Per Serving): Calories: 400; Fat: 25g; Fiber: 12g; Carbs: 29g; Protein: 44

157. Cider Glazed Chicken Recipe

(Prep + Cooking Time: 24 Minutes | **Serves:** 4)

Ingredients:

- 6 chicken thighs; bone in and skin on
- 2 apples; cored and sliced
- 2/3-cup apple cider
- 1 sweet potato, cubed.
- 2-tbsp. honey
- 1-tbsp. butter
- 1-tbsp. olive oil
- 1-tbsp. rosemary, chopped.
- 1-tbsp. mustard
- Salt and black pepper to the taste.

Directions:

1. Heat up a pan that fits your air fryer with half of the oil over medium high heat, add cider, honey, butter and mustard, whisk well, bring to a simmer, take off heat, add chicken and toss really well
2. In a bowl, mix potato cubes with rosemary, apples, salt, pepper and the rest of the oil; toss well and add to chicken mix.
3. Place pan in your air fryer and cook at 390 °F, for 14 minutes. Divide everything on plates and serve

Nutrition Values (Per Serving): Calories: 241; Fat: 7g; Fiber: 12g; Carbs: 28g; Protein: 22g

158. Fall Fried Chicken

(Prep + Cooking Time: 30 Minutes | **Serves:** 8)

Ingredients:

- 3 lbs. chicken breasts; skinless and boneless
- 10 white mushrooms, halved.
- 1 red bell pepper, chopped.
- 1 green bell pepper
- 1 yellow onion, chopped.
- 1 garlic clove, minced.
- 1-tbsp. olive oil
- 2-tbsp. mozzarella cheese, shredded.
- Salt and black pepper to the taste.
- Cooking spray.

Directions:

1. Season chicken with salt and pepper, rub with garlic, spray with cooking spray, place in your preheated air fryer and cook at 390 °F, for 12 minutes
2. Meanwhile, heat up a pan with the oil over medium heat, add onion; stir and sauté for 2 minutes.
3. Add mushrooms, garlic and bell peppers; stir and cook for 8 minutes.
4. Divide chicken on plates, add mushroom mix on the side, sprinkle cheese while chicken is still hot and serve right away

Nutrition Values (Per Serving): Calories: 305; Fat: 12g; Fiber: 11g; Carbs: 26g; Protein: 32

159. Marinated Duck Breasts Recipe

(Prep + Cooking Time: 1 day 15 Minutes | **Serves:** 2)

Ingredients:

- 1/4-cup sherry wine
- 1-cup white wine
- 1/4-cup soy sauce
- 2 duck breasts
- 6 tarragon springs
- 2 garlic cloves, minced.
- 1-tbsp. butter
- Salt and black pepper to the taste.

Directions:

1. In a bowl, mix duck breasts with white wine, soy sauce, garlic, tarragon, salt and pepper; toss well and keep in the fridge for 1 day
2. Transfer duck breasts to your preheated air fryer at 350 °F and cook for 10 minutes; flipping halfway.
3. Meanwhile, pour the marinade in a pan, heat up over medium heat, add butter and sherry; stir, bring to a simmer, cook for 5 minutes and take off heat. Divide duck breasts on plates, drizzle sauce all over and serve

Nutrition Values (Per Serving): Calories: 475; Fat: 12g; Fiber: 3g; Carbs: 10g; Protein: 48

Chicken Breasts with Passion Fruit Sauce

(Prep + Cooking Time: 20 Minutes | **Serves:** 4)

Ingredients:

- 4 passion fruits; halved, deseeded and pulp reserved
- 4 chicken breasts
- 2-star anise
- 2 oz. maple syrup
- 1 bunch chives, chopped.
- 1-tbsp. whiskey
- Salt and black pepper to the taste.

Directions:

1. Heat up a pan with the passion fruit pulp over medium heat, add whiskey, star anise, maple syrup and chives; stir well, simmer for 5-6 minutes and take off heat.
2. Season chicken with salt and pepper, put in preheated air fryer and cook at 360 °F, for 10 minutes; flipping halfway. Divide chicken on plates, heat up the sauce a bit, drizzle it over chicken and serve

Nutrition Values (Per Serving): Calories: 374; Fat: 8g; Fiber: 22g; Carbs: 34g; Protein: 37

160. Turkey Quarters and Veggies Recipe

(Prep + Cooking Time: 44 Minutes | **Serves:** 4)

Ingredients:

- 2 lbs. turkey quarters
- 1 celery stalk, chopped.
- 1-cup chicken stock
- 1 yellow onion, chopped.
- 1 carrot, chopped.
- 3 garlic cloves, minced.
- 2 bay leaves
- 2-tbsp. olive oil
- ½-tsp. rosemary; dried
- ½-tsp. sage; dried
- ½-tsp. thyme; dried
- Salt and black pepper to the taste.

Directions:

1. Rub turkey quarters with salt, pepper, half of the oil, thyme, sage, rosemary and thyme, put in your air fryer and cook at 360 °F, for 20 minutes
2. In a pan that fits your air fryer, mix onion with carrot, garlic, celery, the rest of the oil, stock, bay leaves, salt and pepper and toss.
3. Add turkey, introduce everything in your air fryer and cook at 360 °F, for 14 minutes more. Divide everything on plates and serve

Nutrition Values (Per Serving): Calories: 362; Fat: 12g; Fiber: 16g; Carbs: 22g; Protein: 17g

161. Chicken and Cauliflower Rice Mix Recipe

(Prep + Cooking Time: 30 Minutes | **Serves:** 6)

Ingredients:

- 3 lbs. chicken thighs; boneless and skinless
- 24 oz. cauliflower rice
- 1-cup beef stock
- 3 carrots, chopped.
- 2 bay leaves
- 1/4-cup red wine vinegar
- 4 garlic cloves, minced.
- 3 bacon slices, chopped.
- 4-tbsp. olive oil
- 1-tbsp. garlic powder
- 1-tbsp. Italian seasoning
- one-tsp. turmeric powder
- Salt and black pepper to the taste.

Directions:

1. Heat up a pan that fits your air fryer over medium high heat, add bacon, carrots, onion and garlic; stir and cook for 8 minutes
2. Add chicken, oil, vinegar, turmeric, garlic powder, Italian seasoning and bay leaves; stir, introduce in your air fryer and cook at 360 °F, for 12 minutes. Add cauliflower rice and stock; stir, cook for 6 minutes more, divide among plates and serve.

Nutrition Values (Per Serving): Calories: 340; Fat: 12g; Fiber: 12g; Carbs: 16g; Protein: 8g

162. Chicken and Creamy Mushrooms Recipe

(Prep + Cooking Time: 40 Minutes | **Serves:** 8)

Ingredients:

- 8 chicken thighs
- 8 oz. cremini mushrooms, halved.
- 1/4-cup parmesan, grated.
- 3 garlic cloves, minced.
- 1-cup chicken stock
- 1/4-cup heavy cream
- 1-tbsp. mustard
- 3-tbsp. butter, melted.
- ½-tsp. thyme; dried
- ½-tsp. oregano; dried
- ½-tsp. basil; dried
- Salt and black pepper to the taste.

Directions:

1. Rub chicken pieces with 2-tbsp. butter, season with salt and pepper, put in your air fryer's basket, cook at 370 °F, for 5 minutes and leave aside in a bowl for now
2. Meanwhile, heat up a pan with the rest of the butter over medium high heat, add mushrooms and garlic; stir and cook for 5 minutes.
3. Add salt, pepper, stock, oregano, thyme and basil; stir well and transfer to a heat proof dish that fits your air fryer.
4. Add chicken, toss everything, put in your air fryer and cook at 370 °F, for 20 minutes. Add mustard, parmesan and heavy cream, toss everything again, cook for 5 minutes more, divide among plates and serve

Nutrition Values (Per Serving): Calories: 340; Fat: 10g; Fiber: 13g; Carbs: 22g; Protein: 12g

163. Coconut Creamy Chicken

(Prep + Cooking Time: 2 hours 25 Minutes **| Serves:** 4)

Ingredients:

- 4 big chicken legs
- 4-tbsp. coconut cream
- 2-tbsp. ginger, grated.
- 5-tsp. turmeric powder
- Salt and black pepper to the taste.

Directions:

1. In a bowl, mix cream with turmeric, ginger, salt and pepper, whisk, add chicken pieces, toss them well and leave aside for 2 hours.
2. Transfer chicken to your preheated air fryer, cook at 370 °F, for 25 minutes; divide among plates and serve with a side salad

Nutrition Values (Per Serving): Calories: 300; Fat: 4g; Fiber: 12g; Carbs: 22g; Protein: 20g

164. Duck and Cherries Recipe

(Prep + Cooking Time: 30 Minutes **| Serves:** 4)

Ingredients:

- 4 duck breasts; boneless, skin on and scored
- 1 jalapeno, chopped.
- 4 sage leaves, chopped.
- 1/3-cup balsamic vinegar
- ½-cup yellow onion, chopped.
- 2-cups rhubarb, sliced.
- 2-cups cherries; pitted
- ½-cup sugar
- 1/4-cup honey
- 1-tbsp. ginger, grated.
- ½-tsp. clove, ground.
- one-tsp. garlic, minced.
- ½-tsp. cinnamon powder.
- one-tsp. cumin, ground.
- Salt and black pepper to the taste.

Directions:

1. Season duck breast with salt and pepper, put in your air fryer and cook at 350 °F, for 5 minutes on each side.
2. Meanwhile, heat up a pan over medium heat, add sugar, honey, vinegar, garlic, ginger, cumin, clove, cinnamon, sage, jalapeno, rhubarb, onion and cherries; stir, bring to a simmer and cook for 10 minutes
3. Add duck breasts; toss well, divide everything on plates and serve.

Nutrition Values (Per Serving): Calories: 456; Fat: 13g; Fiber: 4g; Carbs: 64g; Protein: 31

165. Duck and Tea Sauce Recipe

(Prep + Cooking Time: 30 Minutes | **Serves:** 4)

Ingredients:

- 2 duck breast halves; boneless
- 2 ¼-cup chicken stock
- 1 ½-cup orange juice
- 3/4-cup shallot, chopped.
- 3-tbsp. butter, melted.
- 1-tbsp. honey
- 3-tsp. earl gray tea leaves
- Salt and black pepper to the taste.

Directions:

1. Season duck breast halves with salt and pepper, put in preheated air fryer and cook at 360 °F, for 10 minutes.
2. Meanwhile, heat up a pan with the butter over medium heat, add shallot; stir and cook for 2-3 minutes
3. Add stock; stir and cook for another minute.
4. Add orange juice, tea leaves and honey; stir, cook for 2-3 minutes more and strain into a bowl.
5. Divide duck on plates, drizzle tea sauce all over and serve

Nutrition Values (Per Serving): Calories: 228; Fat: 11g; Fiber: 2g; Carbs: 20g; Protein: 12g

166. Chicken and Radish Mix Recipe

(Prep + Cooking Time: 40 Minutes | **Serves:** 4)

Ingredients:

- 4 chicken things; bone-in
- 3 carrots; cut into thin sticks
- 6 radishes, halved.
- 1-cup chicken stock
- 2-tbsp. chives, chopped.
- 1-tbsp. olive oil
- one-tsp. sugar
- Salt and black pepper to the taste.

Directions:

1. Heat up a pan that fits your air fryer over medium heat, add stock, carrots, sugar and radishes; stir gently, reduce heat to medium, cover pot partly and simmer for 20 minutes
2. Rub chicken with olive oil, season with salt and pepper, put in your air fryer and cook at 350 °F, for 4 minutes. Add chicken to radish mix; toss, introduce everything in your air fryer, cook for 4 minutes more, divide among plates and serve

Nutrition Values (Per Serving): Calories: 237; Fat: 10g; Fiber: 4g; Carbs: 19g; Protein: 29

167. Duck Breasts with Endives Recipe

(Prep + Cooking Time: 35 Minutes | **Serves:** 4)

Ingredients:

- 2 duck breasts
- 6 endives; julienned
- 8 oz. white wine
- 1-tbsp. garlic, minced.
- 2-tbsp. heavy cream
- 1-tbsp. sugar
- 1-tbsp. olive oil
- 2-tbsp. cranberries
- Salt and black pepper to the taste.

Directions:

1. Score duck breasts and season them with salt and pepper, put in preheated air fryer and cook at 350 °F, for 20 minutes; flipping them halfway
2. Meanwhile, heat up a pan with the oil over medium heat, add sugar and endives; stir and cook for 2 minutes.
3. Add salt, pepper, wine, garlic, cream and cranberries; stir and cook for 3 minutes. Divide duck breasts on plates, drizzle the endives sauce all over and serve

Nutrition Values (Per Serving): Calories: 400; Fat: 12g; Fiber: 32g; Carbs: 29g; Protein: 28

168. Chicken and Peaches Recipe

(Prep + Cooking Time: 40 Minutes | **Serves:** 6)

Ingredients:

- 1 whole chicken; cut into medium pieces
- 4 peaches, halved.
- 1/3-cup honey
- 1/4-cup olive oil
- 3/4-cup water
- Salt and black pepper to the taste.

Directions:

1. Put the water in a pot, bring to a simmer over medium heat, add honey, whisk really well and leave aside
2. Rub chicken pieces with the oil, season with salt and pepper, place in your air fryer's basket and cook at 350 °F, for 10 minutes.
3. Brush chicken with some of the honey mix, cook for 6 minutes more, flip again, brush one more time with the honey mix and cook for 7 minutes more.
4. Divide chicken pieces on plates and keep warm.
5. Brush peaches with what's left of the honey marinade, place them in your air fryer and cook them for 3 minutes. Divide among plates next to chicken pieces and serve

Nutrition Values (Per Serving): Calories: 430; Fat: 14g; Fiber: 3g; Carbs: 15g; Protein: 20g

169. Pepperoni Chicken Recipe

(Prep + Cooking Time: 32 Minutes | **Serves:** 6)

Ingredients:

- 4 medium chicken breasts; skinless and boneless
- 6 oz. mozzarella, sliced.
- 2 oz. pepperoni, sliced.
- 14 oz. tomato paste
- 1-tbsp. olive oil
- one-tsp. garlic powder
- one-tsp. oregano; dried
- Salt and black pepper to the taste.

Directions:

1. In a bowl, mix chicken with salt, pepper, garlic powder and oregano and toss
2. Put chicken in your air fryer, cook at 350 °F, for 6 minutes and transfer to a pan that fits your air fryer.
3. Add mozzarella slices on top, spread tomato paste, top with pepperoni slices, introduce in your air fryer and cook at 350 °F, for 15 minutes more. Divide among plates and serve

Nutrition Values (Per Serving): Calories: 320; Fat: 10g; Fiber: 16g; Carbs: 23g; Protein: 27

170. Quick Creamy Chicken Casserole Recipe.

(Prep + Cooking Time: 22 Minutes | **Serves:** 4)

Ingredients:

- 10 oz. spinach, chopped.
- 2-cup chicken breasts; skinless, boneless and cubed
- 1 ½-cups milk
- ½-cup parmesan, grated.
- ½-cup heavy cream
- 1-cup bread crumbs
- 3-tbsp. flour
- 4-tbsp. butter
- Salt and black pepper to the taste.

Directions:

1. Heat up a pan with the butter over medium heat, add flour and stir well.
2. Add milk, heavy cream and parmesan; stir well, cook for 1-2 minutes more and take off heat
3. In a pan that fits your air fryer, spread chicken and spinach.
4. Add salt and pepper and toss.

5. Add cream mix and spread, sprinkle bread crumbs on top, introduce in your air fryer and cook at 350 for 12 minutes. Divide chicken and spinach mix on plates and serve

Nutrition Values (Per Serving): Calories: 321; Fat: 9g; Fiber: 12g; Carbs: 22g; Protein: 17g

171. Chicken and Chestnuts Mix Recipe.

(Prep + Cooking Time: 22 Minutes | **Serves:** 2)

Ingredients:

- ½ lb. chicken pieces
- 2 tortillas for serving
- 1 small yellow onion, chopped.
- 2-tbsp. chicken stock
- 2-tbsp. balsamic vinegar
- 2-tbsp. soy sauce
- 4-tbsp. water chestnuts
- 2-tsp. garlic, minced.
- A pinch of allspice, ground.
- A pinch of ginger, grated.

Directions:

1. In a pan that fits your air fryer, mix chicken meat with onion, garlic, ginger, allspice, chestnuts, soy sauce, stock and vinegar; stir, transfer to your air fryer and cook at 360 °F, for 12 minutes. Divide everything on plates and serve.

Nutrition Values (Per Serving): Calories: 301; Fat: 12g; Fiber: 7g; Carbs: 24g; Protein: 12g

172. Chinese Stuffed Chicken Recipe.

(Prep + Cooking Time: 45 Minutes | **Serves:** 8)

Ingredients:

- 1 whole chicken
- 2 red chilies, chopped.
- 4 ginger slices
- 1 yam, cubed.
- 10 wolfberries
- one-tsp. soy sauce
- 3-tsp. sesame oil
- Salt and white pepper to the taste

Directions:

1. Season chicken with salt, pepper, rub with soy sauce and sesame oil and stuff with wolfberries, yam cubes, chilies and ginger
2. Place in your air fryer, cook at 400 °F, for 20 minutes and then at 360 °F, for 15 minutes. Carve chicken, divide among plates and serve.

Nutrition Values (Per Serving): Calories: 320; Fat: 12g; Fiber: 17g; Carbs: 22g; Protein: 12g

173. Easy Duck Breasts Recipe.

(Prep + Cooking Time: 25 Minutes | **Serves:** 4)

Ingredients:

- 4 garlic heads, peeled, tops cut off and quartered
- 4 duck breasts; skinless and boneless
- 1 ½-tbsp. olive oil
- 2-tbsp. lemon juice
- ½-tsp. lemon pepper
- Salt and black pepper to the taste.

Directions:

1. In a bowl, mix duck breasts with garlic, lemon juice, salt, pepper, lemon pepper and olive oil and toss everything.
2. Transfer duck and garlic to your air fryer and cook at 350 °F, for 15 minutes. Divide duck breasts and garlic on plates and serve

Nutrition Values (Per Serving): Calories: 200; Fat: 7g; Fiber: 1g; Carbs: 11g; Protein: 17g

174. Chicken Tenders and Flavored Sauce Recipe

(Prep + Cooking Time: 20 Minutes | **Serves:** 6)

Ingredients:

- 2 lbs. chicken tenders
- ½-cup chicken stock
- 2-cups heavy cream
- 2-tbsp. parsley, chopped.
- 2-tbsp. cornstarch
- 2-tbsp. butter
- 2-tbsp. olive oil
- 2-tbsp. water
- one-tsp. onion powder
- one-tsp. sweet paprika
- one-tsp. chili powder
- 2-tsp. garlic powder
- Salt and black pepper to the taste.

Directions:

1. In a bowl, mix garlic powder with onion powder, chili, salt, pepper and paprika; stir, add chicken and toss.
2. Rub chicken tenders with oil, place in your air fryer and cook at 360 °F, for 10 minutes
3. Meanwhile, heat up a pan with the butter over medium high heat, add cornstarch, stock, cream, water and parsley; stir, cover and cook for 10 minutes. Divide chicken on plates, drizzle sauce all over and serve.

Nutrition Values (Per Serving): Calories: 351; Fat: 12g; Fiber: 9g; Carbs: 20g; Protein: 17g

175. Duck Breast with Fig Sauce Recipe

(Prep + Cooking Time: 30 Minutes | **Serves:** 4)

Ingredients:

- 2 duck breasts; skin on, halved
- 1 shallot, chopped.
- 1-cup beef stock
- ½-cup port wine
- 1-tbsp. white flour
- 1-tbsp. olive oil
- ½-tsp. thyme, chopped.
- ½-tsp. garlic powder
- 1/4-tsp. sweet paprika
- 3-tbsp. butter, melted.
- 4-tbsp. fig preserves
- Salt and black pepper to the taste.

Directions:

1. Season duck breasts with salt and pepper, drizzle half of the melted butter, rub well, put in your air fryer's basket and cook at 350 °F, for 5 minutes on each side
2. Meanwhile, heat up a pan with the olive oil and the rest of the butter over medium high heat, add shallot; stir and cook for 2 minutes.
3. Add thyme, garlic powder, paprika, stock, salt, pepper, wine and figs; stir and cook for 7-8 minutes.
4. Add flour; stir well, cook until sauce thickens a bit and take off heat.
5. Divide duck breasts on plates, drizzle figs sauce all over and serve

Nutrition Values (Per Serving): Calories: 246; Fat: 12g; Fiber: 4g; Carbs: 22g; Protein: 3g

176. Greek Chicken Recipe

(Prep + Cooking Time: 25 Minutes | **Serves:** 4)

Ingredients:

- 1 lb. chicken thighs
- ½ lb. asparagus; trimmed
- 1 zucchini; roughly chopped.
- 1 lemon sliced
- 3 garlic cloves, minced.
- Juice from 1 lemon
- 2-tbsp. olive oil
- one-tsp. oregano; dried
- Salt and black pepper to the taste.

Directions:

1. In a heat proof dish that fits your air fryer, mix chicken pieces with oil, lemon juice, oregano, garlic, salt, pepper, asparagus, zucchini and lemon slices; toss, introduce in preheated air fryer and cook at 380 °F, for 15 minutes. Divide everything on plates and serve.

Nutrition Values (Per Serving): Calories: 300; Fat: 8g; Fiber: 12g; Carbs: 20g; Protein: 18g

177. Duck Breasts and Raspberry Sauce Recipe

(Prep + Cooking Time: 25 Minutes | **Serves:** 4)

Ingredients:

- 2 duck breasts; skin on and scored
- ½-cup raspberries
- ½-cup water
- 1-tbsp. sugar
- ½-tsp. cinnamon powder.
- one-tsp. red wine vinegar
- Salt and black pepper to the taste.
- Cooking spray.

Directions:

1. Season duck breasts with salt and pepper, spray them with cooking spray, put in preheated air fryer skin side down and cook at 350 °F, for 10 minutes
2. Heat up a pan with the water over medium heat, add raspberries, cinnamon, sugar and wine; stir, bring to a simmer, transfer to your blender, puree and return to pan. Add air fryer duck breasts to pan as well; toss to coat, divide among plates and serve right away.

Nutrition Values (Per Serving): Calories: 456; Fat: 22g; Fiber: 4g; Carbs: 14g; Protein: 45

178. Duck Breasts and Mango Mix Recipe.

(Prep + Cooking Time: 1 hour 10 Minutes | **Serves:** 4)

Ingredients:

- 4 duck breasts
- 3 garlic cloves, minced.
- 1½-tbsp. lemongrass, chopped.
- 3-tbsp. lemon juice
- 2-tbsp. olive oil
- Salt and black pepper to the taste.

For the mango mix:

- 1 red onion, chopped.
- 1 mango, peeled and chopped
- 1 ½-tbsp. lemon juice
- 1-tbsp. coriander, chopped.
- 1-tbsp. sweet chili sauce
- one-tsp. ginger, grated.
- 3/4-tsp. sugar

Directions:

1. In a bowl, mix duck breasts with salt, pepper, lemongrass, 3-tbsp. lemon juice, olive oil and garlic; toss well, keep in the fridge for 1 hour, transfer to your air fryer and cook at 360 °F, for 10 minutes; flipping once.
2. Meanwhile, in a bowl, mix mango with coriander, onion, chili sauce, lemon juice, ginger and sugar and toss well
3. Divide duck on plates, add mango mix on the side and serve.

Nutrition Values (Per Serving): Calories: 465; Fat: 11g; Fiber: 4g; Carbs: 29g; Protein: 38

179. Chicken and Garlic Sauce Recipe

(Prep + Cooking Time: 30 Minutes | **Serves:** 4)

Ingredients:

- 4 chicken breasts; skin on and bone-in
- 40 garlic cloves, peeled and chopped.
- 2 thyme springs
- 1/4-cup chicken stock
- 1/4-cup dry white wine
- 2-tbsp. parsley, chopped.
- 1-tbsp. butter, melted.
- 1-tbsp. olive oil
- Salt and black pepper to the taste.

Directions:

1. Season chicken breasts with salt and pepper, rub with the oil, place in your air fryer, cook at 360 °F, for 4 minutes on each side and transfer to a heat proof dish that fits your air fryer.
2. Add melted butter, garlic, thyme, stock, wine and parsley; toss, introduce in your air fryer and cook at 350 °F, for 15 minutes more. Divide everything on plates and serve.

Nutrition Values (Per Serving): Calories: 227; Fat: 9g; Fiber: 13g; Carbs: 22g; Protein: 12g

180. Chicken and Spinach Salad Recipe

(Prep + Cooking Time: 22 Minutes | **Serves:** 2)

Ingredients:

- 2 chicken breasts; skinless and boneless
- 1 avocado; pitted, peeled and chopped
- 5-cups baby spinach
- 8 strawberries, sliced.
- 1 small red onion, sliced.
- ½-cup lemon juice
- 1/4-cup olive oil
- 1-tbsp. tarragon, chopped.
- 2-tbsp. balsamic vinegar
- 2-tsp. sweet paprika
- 2-tsp. parsley; dried
- ½-tsp. onion powder
- Salt and black pepper to the taste.

Directions:

1. Put chicken in a bowl, add lemon juice, parsley, onion powder and paprika and toss.
2. Transfer chicken to your air fryer and cook at 360 °F, for 12 minutes
3. In a bowl, mix spinach, onion, strawberries and avocado and toss.
4. In another bowl, mix oil with vinegar, salt, pepper and tarragon, whisk well, add to the salad and toss. Divide chicken on plates, add spinach salad on the side and serve

Nutrition Values (Per Serving): Calories: 240; Fat: 5g; Fiber: 13g; Carbs: 25g; Protein: 22g

181. Chicken and Apricot Sauce Recipe

(Prep + Cooking Time: 30 Minutes | **Serves:** 4)

Ingredients:

- 1 whole chicken; cut into medium pieces
- 1/4-cup white wine
- 1/4-cup apricot preserves
- 1/4-cup chicken stock
- 1-tbsp. olive oil
- 2-tbsp. white vinegar
- 2-tbsp. honey
- 1 ½-tsp. ginger, grated.
- ½-tsp. marjoram; dried
- ½-tsp. smoked paprika
- Salt and black pepper to the taste.

Directions:

1. Season chicken with salt, pepper, marjoram and paprika; toss to coat, add oil, rub well, place in your air fryer and cook at 360 °F, for 10 minutes

2. Transfer chicken to a pan that fits your air fryer, add stock, wine, vinegar, ginger, apricot preserves and honey; toss, put in your air fryer and cook at 360 °F, for 10 minutes more. Divide chicken and apricot sauce on plates and serve.

Nutrition Values (Per Serving): Calories: 200; Fat: 7g; Fiber: 19g; Carbs: 20g; Protein: 14g

182. Duck Breasts with Red Wine and Orange Sauce Recipe.

(Prep + Cooking Time: 45 Minutes | **Serves:** 4)

Ingredients:

- 2 duck breasts; skin on and halved
- ½-cup honey
- 2-cups orange juice
- 4-cups red wine
- 2-cups chicken stock
- 2-tbsp. sherry vinegar
- 2-tbsp. olive oil
- 2-tbsp. butter
- 2-tsp. pumpkin pie spice
- Salt and black pepper to the taste.

Directions:

1. Heat up a pan with the orange juice over medium heat, add honey; stir well and cook for 10 minutes.
2. Add wine, vinegar, stock, pie spice and butter; stir well, cook for 10 minutes more and take off heat
3. Season duck breasts with salt and pepper, rub with olive oil, place in preheated air fryer at 370 °F and cook for 7 minutes on each side.
4. Divide duck breasts on plates, drizzle wine and orange juice all over and serve right away

Nutrition Values (Per Serving): Calories: 300; Fat: 8g; Fiber: 12g; Carbs: 24g; Protein: 11g

183. Tea Glazed Chicken Recipe

(Prep + Cooking Time: 40 Minutes | **Serves:** 6)

Ingredients:

- 6 chicken legs
- ½-cup pineapple preserves
- ½-cup apricot preserves
- 6 black tea bags
- 1 onion, chopped.
- 1-cup hot water
- 1-tbsp. olive oil
- 1-tbsp. soy sauce
- 1/4-tsp. red pepper flakes
- Salt and black pepper to the taste.

Directions:

1. Put the hot water in a bowl, add tea bags, leave aside covered for 10 minutes; discard bags at the end and transfer tea to another bowl
2. Add soy sauce, pepper flakes, apricot and pineapple preserves, whisk really well and take off heat.
3. Season chicken with salt and pepper, rub with oil, put in your air fryer and cook at 350 °F, for 5 minutes.
4. Spread onion on the bottom of a baking dish that fits your air fryer, add chicken pieces, drizzle the tea glaze on top, introduce in your air fryer and cook at 320 °F, for 25 minutes. Divide everything on plates and serve

Nutrition Values (Per Serving): Calories: 298; Fat: 14g; Fiber: 1g; Carbs: 14g; Protein: 30

184. Chicken Thighs Recipe

(Prep + Cooking Time: 30 Minutes | **Serves:** 6)

Ingredients:

- 2 ½ lbs. chicken thighs
- 5 green onions, chopped.
- 1-tbsp. sherry wine
- 1-tbsp. soy sauce
- 2-tbsp. sesame oil
- 1/4-tsp. sugar
- ½-tsp. white vinegar
- Salt and black pepper to the taste.

Directions:

1. Season chicken with salt and pepper, rub with half of the sesame oil, add to your air fryer and cook at 360 °F, for 20 minutes
2. Meanwhile, heat up a pan with the rest of the oil over medium high heat, add green onions, sherry wine, vinegar, soy sauce and sugar; toss, cover and cook for 10 minutes. Shred chicken using 2 forks divide among plates, drizzle sauce all over and serve.

Nutrition Values (Per Serving): Calories: 321; Fat: 8g; Fiber: 12g; Carbs: 36g; Protein: 24g

185. Chicken and Capers Recipe.

(Prep + Cooking Time: 30 Minutes | **Serves:** 2)

Ingredients:

- 4 chicken thighs
- ½-cup chicken stock
- 4 garlic cloves, minced.
- 1 lemon, sliced.
- 4 green onions, chopped.
- 3-tbsp. butter, melted.
- 3-tbsp. capers
- Salt and black pepper to the taste.

Directions:

1. Brush chicken with butter, sprinkle salt and pepper to the taste, place them in a baking dish that fits your air fryer.
2. Also add capers, garlic, chicken stock and lemon slices, toss to coat, introduce in your air fryer and cook at 370 °F, for 20 minutes; shaking halfway. Sprinkle green onions, divide among plates and serve

Nutrition Values (Per Serving): Calories: 200; Fat: 9g; Fiber: 10g; Carbs: 17g; Protein: 7g

186. Chicken Breasts and BBQ Chili Sauce Recipe.

(Prep + Cooking Time: 30 Minutes | **Serves:** 6)

Ingredients:

- 6 chicken breasts; skinless and boneless
- 1-cup pear jelly
- 1/4-cup honey
- 2-cups chili sauce
- 2-cups ketchup
- one-tsp. chili powder
- one-tsp. mustard powder
- one-tsp. garlic powder
- ½-tsp. liquid smoke
- one-tsp. sweet paprika
- Salt and black pepper to the taste.

Directions:

1. Season chicken breasts with salt and pepper, put in preheated air fryer and cook at 350 °F, for 10 minutes.
2. Meanwhile, heat up a pan with the chili sauce over medium heat, add ketchup, pear jelly, honey, liquid smoke, chili powder, mustard powder, sweet paprika, salt, pepper and the garlic powder; stir, bring to a simmer and cook for 10 minutes. Add air fried chicken breasts; toss well, divide among plates and serve.

Nutrition Values (Per Serving): Calories: 473; Fat: 13g; Fiber: 7g; Carbs: 39g; Protein: 33

187. Lemony Chicken

(Prep + Cooking Time: 40 Minutes | **Serves:** 6)

Ingredients:

- 1 whole chicken; cut into medium pieces
- Zest from 2 lemons, grated.
- Juice from 2 lemons
- 1-tbsp. olive oil
- Salt and black pepper to the taste.

Directions:

1. Season chicken with salt, pepper, rub with oil and lemon zest, drizzle lemon juice, put in your air fryer and cook at 350 °F, for 30 minutes; flipping chicken pieces halfway. Divide among plates and serve with a side salad.

Nutrition Values (Per Serving): Calories: 334; Fat: 24g; Fiber: 12g; Carbs: 26g; Protein: 20g

188. Chicken and Black Olives Sauce Recipe

(Prep + Cooking Time: 18 Minutes | **Serves:** 2)

Ingredients:

- 1 chicken breast cut into 4 pieces
- 3 garlic cloves, minced.
- 2-tbsp. olive oil

For the sauce:

- 1/4-cup parsley, chopped.
- 1-cup black olives; pitted
- 1-tbsp. lemon juice
- 2-tbsp. olive oil
- Salt and black pepper to the taste.

Directions:

1. In your food processor, mix olives with salt, pepper, 2-tbsp. olive oil, lemon juice and parsley, blend very well and transfer to a bowl.
2. Season chicken with salt and pepper, rub with the oil and garlic, place in your preheated air fryer and cook at 370 °F, for 8 minutes. Divide chicken on plates, top with olives sauce and serve

Nutrition Values (Per Serving): Calories: 270; Fat: 12g; Fiber: 12g; Carbs: 23g; Protein: 22g

189. Veggie Stuffed Chicken Breasts Recipe.

(Prep + Cooking Time: 25 Minutes | **Serves:** 4)

Ingredients:

- 4 chicken breasts; skinless and boneless
- 3 tomatoes, chopped.
- 1 red onion, chopped.
- 1 zucchini, chopped.
- 2 yellow bell peppers, chopped.
- 1-cup mozzarella, shredded.
- 2-tbsp. olive oil
- one-tsp. Italian seasoning
- Salt and black pepper to the taste.

Directions:

1. Mix a slit on each chicken breast creating a pocket, season with salt and pepper and rub them with olive oil.
2. In a bowl, mix zucchini with Italian seasoning, bell peppers, tomatoes and onion and stir
3. Stuff chicken breasts with this mix, sprinkle mozzarella over them, place them in your air fryer's basket and cook at 350 °F, for 15 minutes. Divide among plates and serve

Nutrition Values (Per Serving): Calories: 300; Fat: 12g; Fiber: 7g; Carbs: 22g; Protein: 18g

Fish and Seafood Recipes

190. Salmon with Mash and Capers.

(Prep + Cooking Time: 30 Minutes | **Serves:** 4)

Ingredients:

- 4 salmon fillets; skinless and boneless
- 1-tbsp. capers; drained
- 2-tsp. olive oil
- Juice from 1 lemon
- Salt and black pepper to the taste.

For the potato mash:

- 1 lb. potatoes, chopped.
- ½-cup milk
- 1-tbsp. dill; dried
- 2-tbsp. olive oil

Directions:

1. Put potatoes in a pot, add water to cover, add some salt, bring to a boil over medium high heat, cook for 15 minutes; drain, transfer to a bowl; mash with a potato masher, add 2-tbsp. oil, dill, salt, pepper and milk, whisk well and leave aside for now.
2. Season salmon with salt and pepper, drizzle 2-tsp. oil over them, rub, transfer to your air fryer's basket, add capers on top, cook at 360 °F and cook for 8 minutes. Divide salmon and capers on plates; add mashed potatoes on the side, drizzle lemon juice all over and serve

Nutrition Values (Per Serving): Calories: 300; Fat: 17g; Fiber: 8g; Carbs: 12g; Protein: 18g

191. Trout Fillet & Orange Sauce

(Prep + Cooking Time: 20 Minutes | **Serves:** 4)

Ingredients:

- 4 spring onions, chopped.
- 4 trout fillets; skinless and boneless
- 1-tbsp. ginger, minced.
- 1-tbsp. olive oil
- Salt and black pepper to the taste.
- Juice and zest from 1 orange

Directions:

1. Season trout fillets with salt, pepper, rub them with the olive oil, place in a pan that fits your air fryer, add ginger, green onions, orange zest and juice; toss well, place in your air fryer and cook at 360 °F, for 10 minutes. Divide fish and sauce on plates and serve right away.

Nutrition Values (Per Serving): Calories: 239; Fat: 10g; Fiber: 7g; Carbs: 18g; Protein: 23g

192. Tasty Catfish

(Prep + Cooking Time: 30 Minutes | **Serves:** 4)

Ingredients:

- 4 cat fish fillets
- 1-tbsp. olive oil
- 1-tbsp. lemon juice
- 1-tbsp. parsley, chopped.
- A pinch of sweet paprika
- Salt and black pepper to the taste.

Directions:

1. Season catfish fillets with salt, pepper, paprika, drizzle oil, rub well, place in your air fryer's basket and cook at 400 °F, for 20 minutes; flipping the fish after 10 minutes. Divide fish on plates, drizzle lemon juice all over, sprinkle parsley and serve.

Nutrition Values (Per Serving): Calories: 253; Fat: 6g; Fiber: 12g; Carbs: 26g; Protein: 22g

193. Asian Style Halibut.

(Prep + Cooking Time: 40 Minutes | **Serves:** 3)

Ingredients:

- 1 lb. halibut steaks
- 1 garlic clove, minced.
- 2/3-cup soy sauce
- 1/4-cup sugar
- 1/4-cup orange juice
- ½-cup mirin
- 2-tbsp. lime juice
- 1/4-tsp. ginger, grated.
- 1/4-tsp. red pepper flakes; crushed

Directions:

1. Put soy sauce in a pan; heat up over medium heat, add mirin, sugar, lime and orange juice, pepper flakes, ginger and garlic; stir well, bring to a boil and take off heat
2. Transfer half of the marinade to a bowl, add halibut, toss to coat and leave aside in the fridge for 30 minutes.
3. Transfer halibut to your air fryer and cook at 390 °F, for 10 minutes; flipping once. Divide halibut steaks on plates; drizzle the rest of the marinade all over and serve hot

Nutrition Values (Per Serving): Calories: 286; Fat: 5g; Fiber: 12g; Carbs: 14g; Protein: 23g

194. Shrimp and Crab Recipe.

(Prep + Cooking Time: 35 Minutes | **Serves:** 4)

Ingredients:

- 1 lb. shrimp, peeled and deveined
- 1-cup crabmeat; flaked
- 1-cup green bell pepper, chopped.
- 1-cup celery, chopped.
- 1-cup mayonnaise
- ½-cup yellow onion, chopped.
- 2-tbsp. breadcrumbs
- 1-tbsp. butter, melted.
- one-tsp. sweet paprika
- one-tsp. Worcestershire sauce
- Salt and black pepper to the taste.

Directions:

1. Take a bowl and mix shrimp with crab meat, bell pepper, onion, mayo, celery, salt, pepper and Worcestershire sauce; toss well and transfer to a pan that fits your air fryer
2. Sprinkle bread crumbs and paprika, add melted butter, place in your air fryer and cook at 320 °F, for 25 minutes; shaking halfway. Divide among plates and serve right away

Nutrition Values (Per Serving): Calories: 200; Fat: 13g; Fiber: 9g; Carbs: 17g; Protein: 19g

195. Mouthwatering Cod Steaks with Plum Sauce.

(Prep + Cooking Time: 30 Minutes | **Serves:** 2)

Ingredients:

- 2 big cod steaks
- 1-tbsp. plum sauce
- ½-tsp. ginger powder
- 1/4-tsp. turmeric powder
- ½-tsp. garlic powder
- Salt and black pepper to the taste.
- Cooking spray.

Directions:

1. Season cod steaks with salt and pepper, spray them with cooking oil, add garlic powder, ginger powder and turmeric powder and rub well
2. Place cod steaks in your air fryer and cook at 360 °F, for 15 minutes; flipping them after 7 minutes.
3. Heat up a pan over medium heat, add plum sauce; stir and cook for 2 minutes. Divide cod steaks on plates, drizzle plum sauce all over and serve

Nutrition Values (Per Serving): Calories: 250; Fat: 7g; Fiber: 1g; Carbs: 14g; Protein: 12g

196. Air Fried Cod

(Prep + Cooking Time: 22 Minutes | **Serves:** 4)

Ingredients:

- 2 cod fish; 7 oz. each
- 3 spring onions, chopped.
- 1-cup water
- A drizzle of sesame oil
- 4 ginger slices
- 1-tbsp. sugar
- 3-tbsp. olive oil
- 2-tbsp. coriander, chopped.
- 4-tbsp. light soy sauce
- one-tsp. dark soy sauce
- Salt and black pepper to the taste.

Directions:

1. Season fish with salt, pepper, drizzle sesame oil, rub well and leave aside for 10 minutes
2. Add fish to your air fryer and cook at 356 °F, for 12 minutes.
3. Meanwhile, heat up a pot with the water over medium heat, add dark and light soy sauce and sugar; stir, bring to a simmer and take off heat.
4. Heat up a pan with the olive oil over medium heat, add ginger and green onions; stir, cook for a few minutes and take off heat. Divide fish on plates, top with ginger and green onions, drizzle soy sauce mix, sprinkle coriander and serve right away

Nutrition Values (Per Serving): Calories: 300; Fat: 17g; Fiber: 8g; Carbs: 20g; Protein: 22g

197. Special Tuna and Chimichurri Sauce

(Prep + Cooking Time: 18 Minutes | **Serves:** 4)

Ingredients:

- 1 lb. sushi tuna steak
- 2 avocados; pitted, peeled and sliced
- 1 jalapeno pepper, chopped.
- 6 oz. baby arugula
- 3 garlic cloves, minced.
- ½-cup cilantro, chopped.
- 1/3-cup olive oil+ 2-tbsp.
- 1 small red onion, chopped.
- 3-tbsp. balsamic vinegar
- 2-tbsp. parsley, chopped.
- 2-tbsp. basil, chopped.
- one-tsp. red pepper flakes
- one-tsp. thyme, chopped.
- Salt and black pepper to the taste.

Directions:

1. Take a bowl and mix ⅓-cup oil with jalapeno, vinegar, onion, cilantro, basil, garlic, parsley, pepper flakes, thyme, salt and pepper; whisk well and leave aside for now.
2. Season tuna with salt and pepper, rub with the rest of the oil; place in your air fryer and cook at 360 °F, for 3 minutes on each side
3. Mix arugula with half of the chimichuri mix you've made and toss to coat. Divide arugula on plates, slice tuna and also divide among plates; top with the rest of the chimichuri and serve.

Nutrition Values (Per Serving): Calories: 276; Fat: 3g; Fiber: 1g; Carbs: 14g; Protein: 20g

198. Shrimp and Cauliflower Recipe.

(Prep + Cooking Time: 22 Minutes | **Serves:** 2)

Ingredients:

- 1 lb. shrimp, peeled and deveined
- 4 bacon slices; cooked and crumbled
- 1/4-cup heavy cream
- 8 oz. mushrooms; roughly chopped
- ½-cup beef stock
- 1 cauliflower head; riced
- 2 garlic cloves, minced.
- 1-tbsp. butter
- 1-tbsp. parsley; finely chopped.
- 1-tbsp. chives, chopped.
- A pinch of red pepper flakes
- Salt and black pepper to the taste.
- Cooking spray.

Directions:

1. Season shrimp with salt and pepper, spray with cooking oil, place in your air fryer and cook at 360 °F, for 7 minutes.
2. Meanwhile, heat up a pan with the butter over medium heat, add mushrooms; stir and cook for 3-4 minutes.
3. Add garlic, cauliflower rice, pepper flakes, stock, cream, chives, parsley, salt and pepper; stir, cook for a few minutes and take off heat. Divide shrimp on plates, add cauliflower mix on the side, sprinkle bacon on top and serve

Nutrition Values (Per Serving): Calories: 245; Fat: 7g; Fiber: 4g; Carbs: 6g; Protein: 20g

199. Mouthwatering Salmon and Avocado Salsa.

(Prep + Cooking Time: 40 Minutes | **Serves:** 4)

Ingredients:

- 4 salmon fillets
- 1-tbsp. olive oil
- ½-tsp. chili powder
- one-tsp. garlic powder
- one-tsp. cumin, ground.
- one-tsp. sweet paprika
- Salt and black pepper to the taste.

For the salsa:

- 1 avocado; pitted, peeled and chopped.
- 1 small red onion, chopped.
- 2-tbsp. cilantro, chopped.
- Juice from 2 limes
- Salt and black pepper to the taste.

Directions:

1. Take a bowl and mix salt, pepper, chili powder, onion powder, paprika and cumin; stir, rub salmon with this mix, drizzle the oil, rub again, transfer to your air fryer and cook at 350 °F, for 5 minutes on each side.
2. Meanwhile, in a bowl, mix avocado with red onion, salt, pepper, cilantro and lime juice and stir. Divide fillets on plates, top with avocado salsa and serve

Nutrition Values (Per Serving): Calories: 300; Fat: 14g; Fiber: 4g; Carbs: 18g; Protein: 16

200. Cod Fillets with Grapes and Fennel Salad

(Prep + Cooking Time: 25 Minutes | **Serves:** 2)

Ingredients:

- 2 black cod fillets; boneless
- 1-cup grapes, halved.
- ½-cup pecans
- 1 fennel bulb; thinly sliced
- 1-tbsp. olive oil
- Salt and black pepper to the taste.

Directions:

1. Drizzle half of the oil over fish fillets; season with salt and pepper, rub well, place fillets in your air fryer's basket; cook for 10 minutes at 400 °F and transfer to a plate.
2. Take a bowl and mix pecans with grapes, fennel, the rest of the oil, salt and pepper; toss to coat, add to a pan that fits your air fryer and cook at 400 °F, for 5 minutes. Divide cod on plates; add fennel and grapes mix on the side and serve.

Nutrition Values (Per Serving): Calories: 300; Fat: 4g; Fiber: 2g; Carbs: 32g; Protein: 22g

201. Tabasco Shrimp Recipe

(Prep + Cooking Time: 20 Minutes | **Serves:** 4)

Ingredients:

- 1 lb. shrimp, peeled and deveined
- 2-tbsp. olive oil
- 2-tbsp. water
- one-tsp. oregano; dried
- ½-tsp. smoked paprika
- ½-tsp. parsley; dried
- one-tsp. red pepper flakes
- one-tsp. Tabasco sauce
- Salt and black pepper to the taste.

Directions:

1. Take a bowl and mix oil with water, Tabasco sauce, pepper flakes, oregano, parsley, salt, pepper, paprika and shrimp and toss well to coat
2. Transfer shrimp to your preheated air fryer at 370 °F and cook for 10 minutes shaking the fryer once. Divide shrimp on plates and serve with a side salad

Nutrition Values (Per Serving): Calories: 200; Fat: 5g; Fiber: 6g; Carbs: 13g; Protein: 8g

202. Asian Style Salmon

(Prep + Cooking Time: 1 hour 15 Minutes | **Serves:** 2)

Ingredients:

- 2 medium salmon fillets
- 6-tbsp. honey
- 6-tbsp. light soy sauce
- 3-tsp. mirin
- one-tsp. water

Directions:

1. Take a bowl and mix soy sauce with honey, water and mirin, whisk well, add salmon, rub well and leave aside in the fridge for 1 hour.
2. Transfer salmon to your air fryer and cook at 360 °F, for 15 minutes; flipping them after 7 minutes
3. Meanwhile, put the soy marinade in a pan, heat up over medium heat; whisk well, cook for 2 minutes and take off heat. Divide salmon on plates, drizzle marinade all over and serve

Nutrition Values (Per Serving): Calories: 300; Fat: 12g; Fiber: 8g; Carbs: 13g; Protein: 24g

203. East Trout and Butter Sauce

(Prep + Cooking Time: 20 Minutes | **Serves:** 4)

Ingredients:

- 4 trout fillets; boneless
- 3-tbsp. chives, chopped.
- 6-tbsp. butter
- 2-tbsp. olive oil
- 2-tsp. lemon juice
- 3-tsp. lemon zest, grated.
- Salt and black pepper to the taste.

Directions:

1. Season trout with salt and pepper, drizzle the olive oil, rub, transfer to your air fryer and cook at 360 °F, for 10 minutes; flipping once.
2. Meanwhile, heat up a pan with the butter over medium heat, add salt, pepper, chives, lemon juice and zest, whisk well; cook for 1-2 minutes and take off heat. Divide fish fillets on plates, drizzle butter sauce all over and serve

Nutrition Values (Per Serving): Calories: 300; Fat: 12g; Fiber: 9g; Carbs: 27g; Protein: 24g

204. Oriental Fish Recipe

(Prep + Cooking Time: 22 Minutes | **Serves:** 4)

Ingredients:

- 2 lbs. red snapper fillets; boneless
- 1 yellow onion, chopped.
- 3 garlic cloves, minced.
- 1-tbsp. lemon juice
- 1-tbsp. tamarind paste
- 2-tbsp. water
- 1-tbsp. oriental sesame oil
- 1-tbsp. ginger, grated.
- 3-tbsp. mint, chopped.
- ½-tsp. cumin, ground.
- Salt and black pepper to the taste.

Directions:

1. In your food processor, mix garlic with onion, salt, pepper, tamarind paste, sesame oil, ginger, water and cumin, pulse well and rub fish with this mix.
2. Place fish in your preheated air fryer at 320 °F and cook for 12 minutes; flipping fish halfway. Divide fish on plates, drizzle lemon juice all over, sprinkle mint and serve right away

Nutrition Values (Per Serving): Calories: 241; Fat: 8g; Fiber: 16g; Carbs: 17g; Protein: 12g

205. Vinaigrette and Cod

(Prep + Cooking Time: 25 Minutes | **Serves:** 4)

Ingredients:

- 4 cod fillets; skinless and boneless
- 12 cherry tomatoes, halved.
- 8 black olives; pitted and roughly chopped
- 1 bunch basil, chopped.
- 2-tbsp. lemon juice
- 2-tbsp. olive oil
- Salt and black pepper to the taste.
- Cooking spray.

Directions:

1. Season cod with salt and pepper to the taste; place in your air fryer's basket and cook at 360 °F, for 10 minutes; flipping after 5 minutes
2. Meanwhile, heat up a pan with the oil over medium heat, add tomatoes, olives and lemon juice; stir, bring to a simmer, add basil, salt and pepper; stir well and take off heat. Divide fish on plates and serve with the vinaigrette drizzled on top

Nutrition Values (Per Serving): Calories: 300; Fat: 5g; Fiber: 8g; Carbs: 12g; Protein: 8g

206. Tangy Saba Fish

(Prep + Cooking Time: 18 Minutes | **Serves:** 1)

Ingredients:

- 4 Saba fish fillet; boneless
- 3 red chili pepper, chopped.
- 2-tbsp. olive oil
- 2-tbsp. garlic, minced.
- 2-tbsp. lemon juice
- Salt and black pepper to the taste.

Directions:

1. Season fish fillets with salt and pepper and put in a bowl.
2. Add lemon juice, oil, chili and garlic toss to coat, transfer fish to your air fryer and cook at 360 °F, for 8 minutes; flipping halfway. Divide among plates and serve with some fries.

Nutrition Values (Per Serving): Calories: 300; Fat: 4g; Fiber: 8g; Carbs: 15g; Protein: 15g

207. Salmon Thyme and Parsley

(Prep + Cooking Time: 25 Minutes | **Serves:** 4)

Ingredients:

- 4 salmon fillets; boneless
- 1 yellow onion, chopped.
- 4 parsley springs
- 3 tomatoes, sliced.
- 4 thyme springs
- 3-tbsp. extra virgin olive oil
- Juice from 1 lemon
- Salt and black pepper to the taste.

Directions:

1. Drizzle 1-tbsp. oil in a pan that fits your air fryer; add a layer of tomatoes, salt and pepper, drizzle 1 more-tbsp. oil, add fish, season them with salt and pepper, drizzle the rest of the oil, add thyme and parsley springs, onions, lemon juice, salt and pepper, place in your air fryer's basket and cook at 360 °F, for 12 minutes shaking once. Divide everything on plates and serve right away.

Nutrition Values (Per Serving): Calories: 242; Fat: 9g; Fiber: 12g; Carbs: 20g; Protein: 31

208. Flavored Fried Salmon

(Prep + Cooking Time: 1 hour 8 Minutes | **Serves:** 2)

Ingredients:

- 2 salmon fillets
- 1/3-cup water
- 3 scallions, chopped.
- 1/3-cup brown sugar
- 1/3-cup soy sauce
- 2-tbsp. lemon juice
- 2-tbsp. olive oil
- ½-tsp. garlic powder
- Salt and black pepper to the taste.

Directions:

1. Take a bowl and mix sugar with water, soy sauce, garlic powder, salt, pepper, oil and lemon juice, whisk well, add salmon fillets; toss to coat and leave aside in the fridge for 1 hour
2. Transfer salmon fillets to the fryer's basket and cook at 360 °F, for 8 minutes flipping them halfway. Divide salmon on plates; sprinkle scallions on top and serve right away.

Nutrition Values (Per Serving): Calories: 300; Fat: 12g; Fiber: 10g; Carbs: 23g; Protein: 20g

209. Creamy-Shrimp and Veggies

(Prep + Cooking Time: 40 Minutes | **Serves:** 4)

Ingredients:

- 1 lb. shrimp, peeled and deveined
- 1 yellow onion, chopped.
- 2 garlic cloves, minced.
- 1-cup heavy cream
- 1 spaghetti squash; cut into halves
- 8 oz. mushrooms, chopped.
- 1/4-cup butter, melted.
- 1-cup parmesan cheese, grated.
- 1 asparagus bunch; cut into medium pieces
- 2-tbsp. olive oil
- one-tsp. red pepper flakes; crushed
- 2-tsp. Italian seasoning
- Salt and black pepper to the taste.

Directions:

1. Place squash halves in you air fryer's basket; cook at 390 °F, for 17 minutes; transfer to a cutting board, scoop insides and transfer to a bowl
2. Put water in a pot, add some salt, bring to a boil over medium heat, add asparagus, steam for a couple of minutes; transfer to a bowl filled with ice water, drain and leave aside as well.
3. Heat up a pan that fits your air fryer with the oil over medium heat, add onions and mushrooms; stir and cook for 7 minutes
4. Add pepper flakes, Italian seasoning, salt, pepper, squash, asparagus, shrimp, melted butter, cream, parmesan and garlic; toss and cook in your air fryer at 360 °F, for 6 minutes. Divide everything on plates and serve.

Nutrition Values (Per Serving): Calories: 325; Fat: 6g; Fiber: 5g; Carbs: 14g; Protein: 13g

210. Halibut and Sun-Dried Tomatoes

(Prep + Cooking Time: 20 Minutes | **Serves:** 2)

Ingredients:

- 2 medium halibut fillets
- 6 sun dried tomatoes, chopped.
- 2 small red onions, sliced.
- 1 fennel bulb, sliced.
- 9 black olives, pitted and sliced.
- 4 rosemary springs, chopped.
- 2 garlic cloves, minced.
- ½-tsp. red pepper flakes; crushed
- 2-tsp. olive oil
- Salt and black pepper to the taste.

Directions:

1. Season fish with salt, pepper, rub with garlic and oil and put in a heat proof dish that fits your air fryer.
2. Add onion slices, sun dried tomatoes, fennel, olives, rosemary and sprinkle pepper flakes, transfer to your air fryer and cook at 380 °F, for 10 minutes. Divide fish and veggies on plates and serve.

Nutrition Values (Per Serving): Calories: 300; Fat: 12g; Fiber: 9g; Carbs: 18g; Protein: 30

211. Salmon & Chives Vinaigrette

(Prep + Cooking Time: 22 Minutes | **Serves:** 4)

Ingredients:

- 4 salmon fillets; boneless
- 1/3-cup maple syrup
- 3-tbsp. balsamic vinegar
- 2-tbsp. chives, chopped.
- 2-tbsp. dill, chopped.
- 1-tbsp. olive oil
- Salt and black pepper to the taste.

Directions:

1. Season fish with salt and pepper, rub with the oil, place in your air fryer and cook at 350 °F, for 8 minutes; flipping once
2. Heat up a small pot with the vinegar over medium heat, add maple syrup, chives and dill; stir and cook for 3 minutes. Divide fish on plates and serve with chives vinaigrette on top.

Nutrition Values (Per Serving): Calories: 270; Fat: 3g; Fiber: 13g; Carbs: 25g; Protein: 10g

212. Peas and Cod Fillets.

(Prep + Cooking Time: 20 Minutes | **Serves:** 4)

Ingredients:

- 4 cod fillets; boneless
- 2 garlic cloves, minced.
- 2-cups peas
- 2-tbsp. parsley, chopped.
- 4-tbsp. wine
- ½-tsp. sweet paprika
- ½-tsp. oregano; dried
- Salt and pepper to the taste

Directions:

1. In your food processor mix garlic with parsley, salt, pepper, oregano, paprika and wine and blend well.
2. Rub fish with half of this mix, place in your air fryer and cook at 360 °F, for 10 minutes
3. Meanwhile, put peas in a pot, add water to cover, add salt, bring to a boil over medium high heat, cook for 10 minutes; drain and divide among plates. Also divide fish on plates, spread the rest of the herb dressing all over and serve

Nutrition Values (Per Serving): Calories: 261; Fat: 8g; Fiber: 12g; Carbs: 20g; Protein: 22g

213. Italian Barramundi Fillets

(Prep + Cooking Time: 18 Minutes | **Serves:** 4)

Ingredients:

- 2 barramundi fillets; boneless
- 1/4-cup black olives, chopped.
- 1/4-cup green olives; pitted and chopped
- 1/4-cup cherry tomatoes, chopped.
- 1-tbsp. lemon zest
- 2-tbsp. lemon zest
- 1-tbsp. olive oil+ 2-tsp.
- 2-tbsp. parsley, chopped.
- 2-tsp. Italian seasoning
- Salt and black pepper to the taste.

Directions:

1. Rub fish with salt, pepper, Italian seasoning and 2-tsp. olive oil, transfer to your air fryer and cook at 360 °F, for 8 minutes; flipping them halfway.
2. Take a bowl and mix tomatoes with black olives, green olives, salt, pepper, lemon zest and lemon juice, parsley and 1-tbsp. olive oil and toss well. Divide fish on plates; add tomato salsa on top and serve

Nutrition Values (Per Serving): Calories: 270; Fat: 4g; Fiber: 2g; Carbs: 18g; Protein: 27

214. Salmon & Blackberry Glaze.

(Prep + Cooking Time: 43 Minutes | **Serves:** 4)

Ingredients:

- 4 medium salmon fillets; skinless
- 1-inch ginger piece, grated.
- 12 oz. blackberries
- 1/4-cup sugar
- 1-cup water
- Juice from ½ lemon
- 1-tbsp. olive oil
- Salt and black pepper to the taste.

Directions:

1. Heat up a pot with the water over medium high heat, add ginger, lemon juice and blackberries; stir, bring to a boil, cook for 4-5 minutes; take off heat, strain into a bowl, return to pan and combine with sugar.
2. Stir this mix, bring to a simmer over medium low heat and cook for 20 minutes
3. Leave blackberry sauce to cool down, brush salmon with it, season with salt and pepper, drizzle olive oil all over and rub fish well.

4. Place fish in your preheated air fryer at 350 °F and cook for 10 minutes; flipping fish fillets once. Divide among plates, drizzle some of the remaining blackberry sauce all over and serve

Nutrition Values (Per Serving): Calories: 312; Fat: 4g; Fiber: 9g; Carbs: 19g; Protein: 14g

215. Special Salmon Recipe

(Prep + Cooking Time: 35 Minutes | **Serves:** 4)

Ingredients:

- 1 ½ lbs. salmon fillets; skinless and boneless
- 1 lb. medium beets, sliced.
- 1/4-cup lemon juice
- 4-cups mixed baby greens
- 6-tbsp. olive oil
- 1-tbsp. chives, chopped.
- 1-tbsp. parsley, chopped.
- 1-tbsp. fresh tarragon, chopped.
- 3-tbsp. shallots, chopped.
- 1-tbsp. grated lemon zest
- Salt and pepper to the taste

Directions:

1. Take a bowl and mix beets with ½-tbsp. oil and toss to coat
2. Season them with salt and pepper, arrange them on a baking sheet; introduce in the oven at 450 °F and bake for 20 minutes.
3. Take beets out of the oven, add salmon on top, brush it with the rest if the oil and season with salt and pepper.
4. Take a bowl and mix chives with parsley and tarragon and sprinkle 1-tbsp. of this mix over salmon.
5. Introduce in the oven again and bake for 15 minutes.
6. Meanwhile, in a boil with shallots with lemon peel, salt, pepper and lemon juice and the rest of the herbs mixture and stir gently
7. Combine 2-tbsp. of shallots dressing with mixed greens and toss gently. Take salmon out of the oven, arrange on plates, add beets and greens on the side, drizzle the rest of the shallot dressing on top and serve right away

Nutrition Values (Per Serving): Calories: 312; Fat: 2g; Fiber: 2g; Carbs: 2g; Protein: 4g

216. Creamy Salmon Recipe

(Prep + Cooking Time: 20 Minutes | **Serves:** 4)

Ingredients:

- 4 salmon fillets; boneless
- ½-cup coconut cream
- 1/3-cup cheddar cheese, grated.
- 1-tbsp. olive oil
- 1 ½-tsp. mustard
- Salt and black pepper to the taste.

Directions:

1. Season salmon with salt and pepper, drizzle the oil and rub well.
2. Take a bowl and mix coconut cream with cheddar, mustard, salt and pepper and stir well.
3. Transfer salmon to a pan that fits your air fryer; add coconut cream mix, introduce in your air fryer and cook at 320 °F, for 10 minutes. Divide among plates and serve

Nutrition Values (Per Serving): Calories: 200; Fat: 6g; Fiber: 14g; Carbs: 17g; Protein: 20g

217. Lemon Sole & Swiss Chard

(Prep + Cooking Time: 24 Minutes | **Serves:** 4)

Ingredients:

- 2 bunches Swiss chard, chopped.
- 4 sole fillets; boneless
- 4 white bread slices, quartered.
- 1/4-cup walnuts, chopped.

- 2 garlic cloves, minced.
- 1/4-cup parmesan, grated.
- 1/4-cup lemon juice
- 3-tbsp. capers
- 4-tbsp. olive oil
- 4-tbsp. butter
- one-tsp. lemon zest, grated.
- Salt and black pepper to the taste.

Directions:

1. In your food processor, mix bread with walnuts, cheese and lemon zest and pulse well.
2. Add half of the olive oil, pulse really well again and leave aside for now
3. Heat up a pan with the butter over medium heat, add lemon juice, salt, pepper and capers; stir well, add fish and toss it.
4. Transfer fish to your preheated air fryer's basket, top with bread mix you've made at the beginning and cook at 350 °F, for 14 minutes.
5. Meanwhile, heat up another pan with the rest of the oil, add garlic, Swiss chard, salt and pepper; stir gently, cook for 2 minutes and take off heat. Divide fish on plates and serve with sautéed chard on the side

Nutrition Values (Per Serving): Calories: 321; Fat: 7g; Fiber: 18g; Carbs: 27g; Protein: 12g

218. Mustard Salmon Recipe

(Prep + Cooking Time: 20 Minutes **| Serves:** 1)

Ingredients:

- 1 big salmon fillet; boneless
- 1-tbsp. maple extract
- 1-tbsp. coconut oil
- 2-tbsp. mustard
- Salt and black pepper to the taste.

Directions:

1. Take a bowl and mix maple extract with mustard, whisk well, season salmon with salt and pepper and brush salmon with this mix.
2. Spray some cooking spray over fish; place in your air fryer and cook at 370 °F, for 10 minutes; flipping halfway. Serve with a tasty side salad

Nutrition Values (Per Serving): Calories: 300; Fat: 7g; Fiber: 14g; Carbs: 16g; Protein: 20g

219. Simple Squid and Guacamole

(Prep + Cooking Time: 16 Minutes **| Serves:** 2)

Ingredients:

- 2 medium squids; tentacles separated and tubes scored lengthwise
- 1-tbsp. olive oil
- Juice from 1 lime
- Salt and black pepper to the taste.

For the guacamole:

- 1 red onion, chopped.
- 2 avocados; pitted, peeled and chopped.
- 2 red chilies, chopped.
- 1 tomato, chopped.
- 1-tbsp. coriander, chopped.
- Juice from 2 limes

Directions:

1. Season squid and squid tentacles with salt, pepper, drizzle the olive oil all over, put in your air fryer's basket and cook at 360 °F, for 3 minutes on each side
2. Transfer squid to a bowl; drizzle lime juice all over and toss.
3. Meanwhile, put avocado in a bowl, mash with a fork, add coriander, chilies, tomato, onion and juice from 2 limes and toss. Divide squid on plates, top with guacamole and serve

Nutrition Values (Per Serving): Calories: 500; Fat: 43g; Fiber: 6g; Carbs: 7g; Protein: 20g

220. Salmon and Orange Marmalade Recipe

(Prep + Cooking Time: 25 Minutes | **Serves:** 4)

Ingredients:

- 1 lb. wild salmon; skinless, boneless and cubed
- 2 lemons, sliced.
- 1/3-cup orange marmalade
- 1/4-cup balsamic vinegar
- 1/4-cup orange juice
- A pinch of salt and black pepper

Directions:

1. Heat up a pot with the vinegar over medium heat; add marmalade and orange juice; stir, bring to a simmer, cook for 1 minute and take off heat.
2. Thread salmon cubes and lemon slices on skewers, season with salt and black pepper, brush them with half of the orange marmalade mix, arrange in your air fryer's basket and cook at 360 °F, for 3 minutes on each side. Brush skewers with the rest of the vinegar mix; divide among plates and serve right away with a side salad

Nutrition Values (Per Serving): Calories: 240; Fat: 9g; Fiber: 12g; Carbs: 14g; Protein: 10g

221. Salmon and Lemon Relish Recipe.

(Prep + Cooking Time: 40 Minutes | **Serves:** 2)

Ingredients:

- 2 salmon fillets; boneless
- 1-tbsp. olive oil
- Salt and black pepper to the taste.

For the relish:

- 1 Meyer lemon; cut in wedges and then sliced
- 1/4-cup olive oil
- 1 shallot, chopped.
- 2-tbsp. parsley, chopped.
- 1-tbsp. lemon juice

Directions:

1. Season salmon with salt and pepper, rub with 1-tbsp. oil, place in your air fryer's basket and cook at 320 °F, for 20 minutes; flipping the fish halfway
2. Meanwhile, in a bowl, mix shallot with the lemon juice, a pinch of salt and black pepper; stir and leave aside for 10 minutes.
3. Now, take a separate bowl, mix marinated shallot with lemon slices, salt, pepper, parsley and 1/4-cup oil and whisk well. Divide salmon on plates, top with lemon relish and serve

Nutrition Values (Per Serving): Calories: 200; Fat: 3g; Fiber: 3g; Carbs: 23g; Protein: 19g

222. Tilapia & Chives Sauce

(Prep + Cooking Time: 18 Minutes | **Serves:** 4)

Ingredients:

- 4 medium tilapia fillets
- 1/4-cup Greek yogurt
- 2-tbsp. chives, chopped.
- 2-tsp. honey
- Juice from 1 lemon
- Salt and black pepper to the taste.
- Cooking spray.

Directions:

1. Season fish with salt and pepper, spray with cooking spray, place in preheated air fryer 350 °F and cook for 8 minutes; flipping halfway.

2. Meanwhile, in a bowl, mix yogurt with honey, salt, pepper, chives and lemon juice and whisk really well. Divide air fryer fish on plates, drizzle yogurt sauce all over and serve right away.

Nutrition Values (Per Serving): Calories: 261; Fat: 8g; Fiber: 18g; Carbs: 24g; Protein: 21g

223. Roasted Cod & Prosciutto.

(Prep + Cooking Time: 20 Minutes | **Serves:** 4)

Ingredients:

- 4 medium cod filets
- 1/4-cup butter, melted.
- 2 garlic cloves, minced.
- 1 shallot, chopped.
- 3-tbsp. prosciutto, chopped.
- 1-tbsp. parsley, chopped.
- 2-tbsp. lemon juice
- one-tsp. Dijon mustard
- Salt and black pepper to the taste.

Directions:

1. Take a bowl and mix mustard with butter, garlic, parsley, shallot, lemon juice, prosciutto, salt and pepper and whisk well.
2. Season fish with salt and pepper; spread prosciutto mix all over, put in your air fryer and cook at 390 °F, for 10 minutes. Divide among plates and serve

Nutrition Values (Per Serving): Calories: 200; Fat: 4g; Fiber: 7g; Carbs: 12g; Protein: 6g

224. Special Swordfish and Mango Salsa

(Prep + Cooking Time: 16 Minutes | **Serves:** 2)

Ingredients:

- 2 medium swordfish steaks
- 1 avocado; pitted, peeled and chopped
- 1 orange, peeled and sliced
- 1 mango, chopped.
- A pinch of cumin
- A pinch of onion powder
- A pinch of garlic powder
- 1-tbsp. cilantro, chopped.
- ½-tbsp. balsamic vinegar
- 2-tsp. avocado oil
- Salt and black pepper to the taste.

Directions:

1. Season fish steaks with salt, pepper, garlic powder, onion powder and cumin and rub with half of the oil; place in your air fryer and cook at 360 °F, for 6 minutes; flipping halfway.
2. Meanwhile, in a bowl, mix avocado with mango, cilantro, balsamic vinegar, salt, pepper and the rest of the oil and stir well. Divide fish on plates; top with mango salsa and serve with orange slices on the side.

Nutrition Values (Per Serving): Calories: 200; Fat: 7g; Fiber: 2g; Carbs: 14g; Protein: 14g

225. Chinese Style Cod

(Prep + Cooking Time: 20 Minutes | **Serves:** 2)

Ingredients:

- 2 medium cod fillets; boneless
- 1-tbsp. light soy sauce.
- one-tsp. peanuts; crushed
- 2-tsp. garlic powder
- ½-tsp. ginger, grated.

Directions:

1. Put fish fillets in a heat proof dish that fits your air fryer, add garlic powder, soy sauce and ginger; toss well, put in your air fryer and cook at 350 °F, for 10 minutes. Divide fish on plates, sprinkle peanuts on top and serve.

Nutrition Values (Per Serving): Calories: 254; Fat: 10g; Fiber: 11g; Carbs: 14g; Protein: 23g

226. Stuffed Salmon Delight

(Prep + Cooking Time: 30 Minutes | **Serves:** 2)

Ingredients:

- 5 oz. tiger shrimp, peeled, deveined and chopped
- 2 salmon fillets; skinless and boneless
- 3 green onions, chopped.
- 2-cups spinach; torn
- 6 mushrooms, chopped.
- 1/4-cup macadamia nuts; toasted and chopped
- 1-tbsp. olive oil
- Salt and black pepper to the taste.

Directions:

1. Heat up a pan with half of the oil over medium high heat, add mushrooms, onions, salt and pepper; stir and cook for 4 minutes.
2. Add macadamia nuts, spinach and shrimp; stir, cook for 3 minutes and take off heat
3. Make an incision lengthwise in each salmon fillet, season with salt and pepper, divide spinach and shrimp mix into incisions and rub with the rest of the olive oil.
4. Place in your air fryer's basket and cook at 360 °F and cook for 10 minutes; flipping halfway. Divide stuffed salmon on plates and serve

Nutrition Values (Per Serving): Calories: 290; Fat: 15g; Fiber: 3g; Carbs: 12g; Protein: 31

227. Salmon and Greek Yogurt Sauce Recipe

(Prep + Cooking Time: 30 Minutes | **Serves:** 2)

Ingredients:

- 2 medium salmon fillets
- 6 lemon slices
- 1 garlic clove, minced.
- 1-cup Greek yogurt
- 1-tbsp. basil, chopped.
- ½-tsp. mint, chopped.
- ½-tsp. cilantro, chopped.
- 2-tsp. curry powder
- A pinch of cayenne pepper
- Sea salt and black pepper to the taste

Directions:

1. Place each salmon fillet on a parchment paper piece, make 3 splits in each and stuff them with basil
2. Season with salt and pepper, top each fillet with 3 lemon slices, fold parchment, seal edges, introduce in the oven at 400 °F and bake for 20 minutes.
3. Meanwhile, in a bowl, mix yogurt with cayenne pepper, salt to the taste, garlic, curry, mint and cilantro and whisk well. Transfer fish to plates, drizzle the yogurt sauce you've just prepared on top and serve right away!

Nutrition Values (Per Serving): Calories: 242; Fat: 1g; Fiber: 2g; Carbs: 3g; Protein: 3g

228. Cod with Pearl Onions Recipe

(Prep + Cooking Time: 25 Minutes | **Serves:** 2)

Ingredients:

- 14 oz. pearl onions
- 2 medium cod fillets
- 8 oz. mushrooms, sliced.
- 1-tbsp. parsley; dried
- one-tsp. thyme; dried
- Black pepper to the taste

Directions:

1. Put fish in a heat proof dish that fits your air fryer; add onions, parsley, mushrooms, thyme and black pepper; toss well, put in your air fryer and cook at 350 °F and cook for 15 minutes. Divide everything on plates and serve.

Nutrition Values (Per Serving): Calories: 270; Fat: 14g; Fiber: 8g; Carbs: 14g; Protein: 22g

229. Salmon and Avocado Sauce Recipe.

(Prep + Cooking Time: 20 Minutes | **Serves:** 4)

Ingredients:

- 4 salmon fillets; boneless
- 1 avocado; pitted, peeled and chopped
- 1/3-cup coconut milk
- 1/4-cup cilantro, chopped.
- 1-tbsp. lime zest, grated.
- 1-tbsp. lime juice
- one-tsp. garlic powder
- one-tsp. onion powder
- Salt and black pepper to the taste.

Directions:

1. Season salmon fillets with salt, black pepper and lime zest, rub well, put in your air fryer, cook at 350 °F, for 9 minutes; flipping once and divide among plates.
2. In your food processor, mix avocado with cilantro, garlic powder, onion powder, lime juice, salt, pepper and coconut milk; blend well, drizzle over salmon and serve right away

Nutrition Values (Per Serving): Calories: 260; Fat: 7g; Fiber: 20g; Carbs: 28g; Protein: 18g

230. Flavored Jamaican Salmon Recipe

(Prep + Cooking Time: 20 Minutes | **Serves:** 4)

Ingredients:

- 4-cups baby arugula
- 2-cups radish; julienned
- 4 medium salmon fillets; boneless
- 3 scallions, chopped.
- 1/4-cup pepitas; toasted
- 2-cups cabbage, shredded.
- 2-tsp. olive oil
- 4-tsp. apple cider vinegar
- 3-tsp. avocado oil
- 2-tsp. sriracha sauce
- 4-tsp. sugar
- 1 ½-tsp. Jamaican jerk seasoning
- Salt and black pepper to the taste.

Directions:

1. Take a bowl and mix sriracha with sugar, whisk and transfer 2-tsp. to another bowl
2. Combine 2-tsp. sriracha mix with the avocado oil, olive oil, vinegar, salt and pepper and whisk well.
3. Sprinkle jerk seasoning over salmon, rub with sriracha and sugar mix and season with salt and pepper.
4. Transfer to your air fryer and cook at 360 °F, for 10 minutes; flipping once.
5. Take a bowl and mix radishes with cabbage, arugula, salt, pepper, sriracha and vinegar mix and toss well. Divide salmon and radish mix on plates, sprinkle pepitas and scallions on top and serve

Nutrition Values (Per Serving): Calories: 290; Fat: 6g; Fiber: 12g; Carbs: 17g; Protein: 10g

231. Spanish Salmon Recipe.

(Prep + Cooking Time: 25 Minutes | **Serves:** 6)

Ingredients:

- 2-cups bread croutons
- 3/4-cup green olives; pitted
- 3 red bell peppers; cut into medium wedges
- 3 red onions; cut into medium wedges
- 5-tbsp. olive oil
- 6 medium salmon fillets; skinless and boneless
- 2-tbsp. parsley, chopped.
- ½-tsp. smoked paprika
- Salt and black pepper to the taste.

Directions:

1. In a heat proof dish that fits your air fryer, mix bread croutons with onion wedges, bell pepper ones, olives, salt, pepper, paprika and 3-tbsp. olive oil; toss well, place in your air fryer and cook at 356 °F, for 7 minutes
2. Rub salmon with the rest of the oil; add over veggies and cook at 360 °F, for 8 minutes. Divide fish and veggie mix on plates, sprinkle parsley all over and serve.

Nutrition Values (Per Serving): Calories: 321; Fat: 8g; Fiber: 14g; Carbs: 27g; Protein: 22g

232. Marinated Salmon Recipe.

(Prep + Cooking Time: 1 hour 20 Minutes | **Serves:** 6)

Ingredients:

- 1 whole salmon
- 1-tbsp. tarragon, chopped.
- 1-tbsp. garlic, minced.
- 1-tbsp. dill, chopped.
- 1 lemon, sliced.
- Juice from 2 lemons
- A pinch of salt and black pepper

Directions:

1. In a large fish, mix fish with salt, pepper and lemon juice; toss well and keep in the fridge for 1 hour.
2. Stuff salmon with garlic and lemon slices, place in your air fryer's basket and cook at 320 °F, for 25 minutes. Divide among plates and serve with a tasty coleslaw on the side.

Nutrition Values (Per Serving): Calories: 300; Fat: 8g; Fiber: 9g; Carbs: 19g; Protein: 27

233. Buttery Shrimp Skewers

(Prep + Cooking Time: 16 Minutes | **Serves:** 2)

Ingredients:

- 8 shrimps, peeled and deveined
- 4 garlic cloves, minced.
- 8 green bell pepper slices
- 1-tbsp. rosemary, chopped.
- 1-tbsp. butter, melted.
- Salt and black pepper to the taste.

Directions:

1. Take a bowl and mix shrimp with garlic, butter, salt, pepper, rosemary and bell pepper slices; toss to coat and leave aside for 10 minutes
2. Arrange 2 shrimp and 2 bell pepper slices on a skewer and repeat with the rest of the shrimp and bell pepper pieces.
3. Place them all in your air fryer's basket and cook at 360 °F, for 6 minutes. Divide among plates and serve right away

Nutrition Values (Per Serving): Calories: 140; Fat: 1g; Fiber: 12g; Carbs: 15g; Protein: 7g

234. Stuffed Calamari Recipe

(Prep + Cooking Time: 35 Minutes | **Serves:** 4)

Ingredients:

- 4 big calamari; tentacles separated and chopped and tubes reserved
- 5 oz. kale, chopped.
- 2 oz. canned tomato puree
- 1 yellow onion, chopped.
- 2 garlic cloves, minced.
- 1 red bell pepper, chopped.
- 1-tbsp. olive oil
- 2-tbsp. parsley, chopped.
- Salt and black pepper to the taste.

Directions:

1. Heat up a pan with the oil over medium heat; add onion and garlic; stir and cook for 2 minutes.
2. Add bell pepper, tomato puree, calamari tentacles, kale, salt and pepper; stir, cook for 10 minutes and take off heat. stir and cook for 3 minutes
3. Stuff calamari tubes with this mix, secure with toothpicks, put in your air fryer and cook at 360 °F, for 20 minutes. Divide calamari on plates; sprinkle parsley all over and serve.

Nutrition Values (Per Serving): Calories: 322; Fat: 10g; Fiber: 14g; Carbs: 14g; Protein: 22g

235. Coconut Tilapia Recipe

(Prep + Cooking Time: 20 Minutes | **Serves:** 4)

Ingredients:

- 4 medium tilapia fillets
- ½-cup cilantro, chopped.
- ½-cup coconut milk
- 2 garlic cloves, chopped.
- ½ jalapeno; chopped.
- ½-tsp. garam masala
- one-tsp. ginger, grated.
- Salt and black pepper to the taste.
- Cooking spray.

Directions:

1. In your food processor, mix coconut milk with salt, pepper, cilantro, ginger, garlic, jalapeno and garam masala and pulse really well.
2. Spray fish with cooking spray, spread coconut mix all over, rub well, transfer to your air fryer's basket and cook at 400 °F, for 10 minutes. Divide among plates and serve hot

Nutrition Values (Per Serving): Calories: 200; Fat: 5g; Fiber: 6g; Carbs: 25g; Protein: 26

236. Crusted Salmon Recipe.

(Prep + Cooking Time: 20 Minutes | **Serves:** 4)

Ingredients:

- 4 salmon fillets
- 1-cup pistachios, chopped.
- 1/4-cup lemon juice
- 1-tbsp. mustard
- 2-tbsp. honey
- one-tsp. dill, chopped.
- Salt and black pepper to the taste.

Directions:

1. Take a bowl and mix pistachios with mustard, honey, lemon juice, salt, black pepper and dill; whisk and spread over salmon.
2. Put in your air fryer and cook at 350 °F, for 10 minutes. Divide among plates and serve with a side salad

Nutrition Values (Per Serving): Calories: 300; Fat: 17g; Fiber: 12g; Carbs: 20g; Protein: 22g

237. Hawaiian Salmon Recipe

(Prep + Cooking Time: 20 Minutes | **Serves:** 2)

Ingredients:

- 20 oz. canned pineapple pieces and juice
- 2 medium salmon fillets; boneless
- 1-tbsp. balsamic vinegar
- one-tsp. onion powder
- ½-tsp. ginger, grated.
- 2-tsp. garlic powder
- Salt and black pepper to the taste.

Directions:

1. Season salmon with garlic powder, onion powder, salt and black pepper, rub well, transfer to a heat proof dish that fits your air fryer, add ginger and pineapple chunks and toss them really gently.

2. Drizzle the vinegar all over, put in your air fryer and cook at 350 °F, for 10 minutes. Divide everything on plates and serve.

Nutrition Values (Per Serving): Calories: 200; Fat: 8g; Fiber: 12g; Carbs: 17g; Protein: 20g

238. Fried Branzino

(Prep + Cooking Time: 20 Minutes | **Serves:** 4)

Ingredients:

- 4 medium branzino fillets; boneless
- Zest from 1 orange, grated.
- Zest from 1 lemon, grated.
- ½-cup parsley, chopped.
- Juice from ½ orange
- Juice from ½ lemon
- 2-tbsp. olive oil
- A pinch of red pepper flakes; crushed
- Salt and black pepper to the taste.

Directions:

1. In a large bowl; mix fish fillets with lemon zest, orange zest, lemon juice, orange juice, salt, pepper, oil and pepper flakes; toss really well, transfer fillets to your preheated air fryer at 350 °F and bake for 10 minutes; flipping fillets once. Divide fish on plates, sprinkle with parsley and serve right away.

Nutrition Values (Per Serving): Calories: 261; Fat: 8g; Fiber: 12g; Carbs: 21g; Protein: 12g

239. Red Snapper Recipe

(Prep + Cooking Time: 45 Minutes | **Serves:** 4)

Ingredients:

- 1/4 lb. okra, chopped.
- 3 garlic cloves, minced.
- 1 jalapeno, chopped.
- 1 big red snapper; cleaned and scored
- 1 red bell pepper, chopped.
- 2-tbsp. white wine
- 2-tbsp. parsley, chopped.
- 1-tbsp. butter
- 2-tbsp. olive oil
- Salt and black pepper to the taste.

Directions:

1. Take a bowl and mix jalapeno, wine with garlic; stir well and rub snapper with this mix.
2. Season fish with salt and pepper and leave it aside for 30 minutes
3. Meanwhile, heat up a pan with 1-tbsp. butter over medium heat, add bell pepper and okra; stir and cook for 5 minutes.
4. Stuff red snapper's belly with this mix; also add parsley and rub with the olive oil.
5. Place in preheated air fryer and cook at 400 °F, for 15 minutes; flipping the fish halfway. Divide among plates and serve

Nutrition Values (Per Serving): Calories: 261; Fat: 7g; Fiber: 18g; Carbs: 28g; Protein: 18g

240. Chili Salmon Recipe.

(Prep + Cooking Time: 25 Minutes | **Serves:** 12)

Ingredients:

- 1 lb. salmon, cubed.
- 1/4-cup water
- 1¼-cups coconut, shredded.
- 3 garlic cloves, minced.
- 1 egg
- 4 red chilies, chopped.
- 1/4-cup balsamic vinegar
- ½-cup honey
- 1/3-cup flour
- 2-tbsp. olive oil
- A pinch of salt and black pepper

Directions:

1. Take a bowl and mix flour with a pinch of salt and stir
2. In another bowl; mix egg with black pepper and whisk.
3. Put coconut in a third bowl.
4. Dip salmon cubes in flour, egg and coconut, put them in your air fryer's basket, cook at 370 °F, for 8 minutes; shaking halfway and divide among plates
5. Heat up a pan with the water over medium high heat, add chilies, cloves, vinegar and honey; stir very well, bring to a boil, simmer for a couple of minutes; drizzle over salmon and serve

Nutrition Values (Per Serving): Calories: 220; Fat: 12g; Fiber: 2g; Carbs: 14g; Protein: 13g

241. Fish and Couscous Recipe

(Prep + Cooking Time: 25 Minutes | **Serves:** 4)

Ingredients:

- 2½ lbs. sea bass; gutted
- 2 small fennel bulbs; cored and sliced
- 3/4-cup whole wheat couscous; cooked
- 2 red onions, chopped.
- 1/4-cup almonds; toasted and sliced
- 5-tsp. fennel seeds
- Cooking spray.
- Salt and black pepper to the taste.

Directions:

1. Season fish with salt and pepper, spray with cooking spray; place in your air fryer and cook at 350 °F, for 10 minutes.
2. Meanwhile, spray a pan with some cooking oil and heat it up over medium heat
3. Add fennel seeds to this pan; stir and toast them for 1 minute.
4. Add onion, salt, pepper, fennel bulbs, almonds and couscous; stir, cook for 2-3 minutes and divide among plates. Add fish next to couscous mix and serve right away

Nutrition Values (Per Serving): Calories: 354; Fat: 7g; Fiber: 10g; Carbs: 20g; Protein: 30

242. Honey Sea Bass Recipe.

(Prep + Cooking Time: 20 Minutes | **Serves:** 2)

Ingredients:

- ½ lb. canned lentils; drained
- 2 oz. watercress
- 2 sea bass fillets
- Juice from ½ orange
- Zest from ½ orange, grated.
- 2-tbsp. olive oil
- 2-tbsp. mustard
- 2-tsp. honey
- A small bunch of parsley, chopped.
- A small bunch of dill, chopped.
- A pinch of salt and black pepper

Directions:

1. Season fish fillets with salt and pepper, add orange zest and juice, rub with 1-tbsp. oil, with honey and mustard, rub, transfer to your air fryer and cook at 350 °F, for 10 minutes; flipping halfway.
2. Meanwhile, put lentils in a small pot, warm it up over medium heat, add the rest of the oil, watercress, dill and parsley; stir well and divide among plates. Add fish fillets and serve right away.

Nutrition Values (Per Serving): Calories: 212; Fat: 8g; Fiber: 12g; Carbs: 9g; Protein: 17g

243. Tasty Pollock Recipe

(Prep + Cooking Time: 25 Minutes | **Serves:** 6)

Ingredients:

- 4 Pollock fillets; boneless
- 1/4-cup parmesan, grated.
- ½-cup sour cream
- 2-tbsp. butter, melted.
- Salt and black pepper to the taste.
- Cooking spray.

Directions:

1. In a bowl, mix sour cream with butter, parmesan, salt and pepper and whisk well
2. Spray fish with cooking spray and season with salt and pepper.
3. Spread sour cream mix on one side of each Pollock fillet, arrange them in your preheated air fryer at 320 °F and cook them for 15 minutes. Divide Pollock fillets on plates and serve with a tasty side salad

Nutrition Values (Per Serving): Calories: 300; Fat: 13g; Fiber: 3g; Carbs: 14g; Protein: 44

244. Salmon and Avocado Salad Recipe

(Prep + Cooking Time: 30 Minutes | **Serves:** 4)

Ingredients:

- 2 medium salmon fillets
- 1 jalapeno pepper, chopped.
- 5 cilantro springs, chopped.
- 1 oz. feta cheese, crumbled.
- 4 oz. mushrooms, sliced.
- 12 cherry tomatoes, halved.
- 8 oz. lettuce leaves; torn
- 1 avocado; pitted, peeled and cubed
- 1/4-cup melted butter
- 2-tbsp. olive oil
- 2-tbsp. white wine vinegar
- Sea salt and black pepper to the taste

Directions:

1. Place salmon on a lined baking sheet, brush with 2-tbsp. melted butter, season with salt and pepper; broil for 15 minutes over medium heat and then keep warm
2. Meanwhile, heat up a pan with the rest of the butter over medium heat, add mushrooms; stir and cook for a few minutes.
3. Put tomatoes in a bowl, add salt, pepper and 1-tbsp. olive oil and toss to coat.
4. In a salad bowl; mix salmon with mushrooms, lettuce, avocado, tomatoes, jalapeno and cilantro. Add the rest of the oil, vinegar, salt and pepper, sprinkle cheese on top and serve

Nutrition Values (Per Serving): Calories: 235; Fat: 6g; Fiber: 8g; Carbs: 19g; Protein: 5g

245. Catfish Fillets Recipe

(Prep + Cooking Time: 22 Minutes | **Serves:** 4)

Ingredients:

- 2 catfish fillets
- 4 oz. Worcestershire sauce
- 2 oz. butter
- 3/4-cup catsup
- 1-tbsp. balsamic vinegar
- 1-tbsp. parsley, chopped.
- ½-tsp. garlic, minced.
- ½-tsp. jerk seasoning
- one-tsp. mustard
- Salt and black pepper to the taste.

Directions:

1. Heat up a pan with the butter over medium heat, add Worcestershire sauce, garlic, jerk seasoning, mustard, catsup, vinegar, salt and pepper; stir well, take off heat and add fish fillets.

2. Toss well, leave aside for 10 minutes; drain fillets, transfer them to your preheated air fryer's basket at 350 °F and cook for 8 minutes; flipping fillets halfway. Divide among plates, sprinkle parsley on top and serve right away

Nutrition Values (Per Serving): Calories: 351; Fat: 8g; Fiber: 16g; Carbs: 27g; Protein: 17g

246. Snapper Fillets and Veggies Recipe

(Prep + Cooking Time: 24 Minutes | **Serves:** 2)

Ingredients:

- 2 red snapper fillets; boneless
- ½-cup green bell pepper, chopped.
- ½-cup leeks, chopped.
- ½-cup red bell pepper, chopped.
- 1-tbsp. olive oil
- one-tsp. tarragon; dried
- A splash of white wine
- Salt and black pepper to the taste.

Directions:

1. In a heat proof dish that fits your air fryer; mix fish fillets with salt, pepper, oil, green bell pepper, red bell pepper, leeks, tarragon and wine; toss well everything, introduce in preheated air fryer at 350 °F and cook for 14 minutes; flipping fish fillets halfway. Divide fish and veggies on plates and serve warm.

Nutrition Values (Per Serving): Calories: 300; Fat: 12g; Fiber: 8g; Carbs: 29g; Protein: 12g

247. Black Cod & Plum Sauce

(Prep + Cooking Time: 25 Minutes | **Serves:** 2)

Ingredients:

- 2 medium black cod fillets; skinless and boneless
- 1 egg white
- ½-cup red quinoa; already cooked
- 1/4-cup water
- 1 red plum; pitted and chopped
- 2-tsp. raw honey
- 1/4-tsp. black peppercorns; crushed
- 2-tsp. whole wheat flour
- 4-tsp. lemon juice
- one-tsp. olive oil
- 2-tsp. parsley
- ½-tsp. smoked paprika

Directions:

1. Take a bowl and mix one-tsp. lemon juice with egg white, flour and 1/4-tsp. paprika and whisk well.
2. Put quinoa in a bowl and mix it with ⅓ of egg white mix
3. Put the fish into the bowl with the remaining egg white mix and toss to coat.
4. Dip fish in quinoa mix; coat well and leave aside for 10 minutes.
5. Heat up a pan with one-tsp. oil over medium heat; add peppercorns, honey and plum; stir, bring to a simmer and cook for 1 minute
6. Add the rest of the lemon juice, the rest of the paprika and the water; stir well and simmer for 5 minutes.
7. Add parsley; stir, take sauce off heat and leave aside for now.
8. Put fish in your air fryer and cook at 380 °F, for 10 minutes. Arrange fish on plates, drizzle plum sauce on top and serve.

Nutrition Values (Per Serving): Calories: 324; Fat: 14g; Fiber: 22g; Carbs: 27g; Protein: 22g

248. Delightful French Cod

(Prep + Cooking Time: 32 Minutes **| Serves:** 4)

Ingredients:

- 2 lbs. cod; boneless
- 14 oz. canned tomatoes; stewed
- 1 yellow onion, chopped.
- ½-cup white wine
- 2 garlic cloves, minced.
- 2-tbsp. butter
- 3-tbsp. parsley, chopped.
- 2-tbsp. olive oil
- Salt and black pepper to the taste.

Directions:

1. Heat up a pan with the oil over medium heat, add garlic and onion; stir and cook for 5 minutes.
2. Add wine; stir and cook for 1 minute more
3. Add tomatoes; stir, bring to a boil, cook for 2 minutes; add parsley; stir again and take off heat.
4. Pour this mix into a heat proof dish that fits your air fryer, add fish, season it with salt and pepper and cook in your fryer at 350 °F, for 14 minutes. Divide fish and tomatoes mix on plates and serve

Nutrition Values (Per Serving): Calories: 231; Fat: 8g; Fiber: 12g; Carbs: 26g; Protein: 14g

Meat Recipes

249. Provencal Pork Recipe

(Prep + Cooking Time: 25 Minutes **| Serves:** 2)

Ingredients:

- 7 oz. pork tenderloin
- 1 red onion, sliced.
- 1 yellow bell pepper; cut into strips
- 1 green bell pepper; cut into strips
- 1-tbsp. olive oil
- ½-tbsp. mustard
- 2-tsp. Provencal herbs
- Salt and black pepper to the taste.

Directions:

1. In a baking dish that fits your air fryer, mix yellow bell pepper with green bell pepper, onion, salt, pepper, Provencal herbs and half of the oil and toss well
2. Season pork with salt, pepper, mustard and the rest of the oil, toss well and add to veggies. Introduce everything in your air fryer,
3. Cook at 370 °F, for 15 minutes; divide among plates and serve

Nutrition Values (Per Serving): Calories: 300; Fat: 8g; Fiber: 7g; Carbs: 21g; Protein: 23g

250. Lamb Roast and Potatoes Recipe.

(Prep + Cooking Time: 55 Minutes **| Serves:** 6)

Ingredients:

- 4 lbs. lamb roast
- 1 spring rosemary
- 6 potatoes, halved.
- ½-cup lamb stock
- 4 bay leaves
- 3 garlic cloves, minced.
- Salt and black pepper to the taste.

Directions:

1. Put potatoes in a dish that fits your air fryer, add lamb, garlic, rosemary spring, salt, pepper, bay leaves and stock, toss, introduce in your air fryer and cook at 360 °F, for 45 minutes. Slice lamb, divide among plates and serve with potatoes and cooking juices.

Nutrition Values (Per Serving): Calories: 273; Fat: 4g; Fiber: 12g; Carbs: 25g; Protein: 29

251. Beef Fillets with Garlic Mayo Recipe

(Prep + Cooking Time: 50 Minutes **| Serves:** 8)

Ingredients:

- 3 lbs. beef fillet
- 1/4-cup tarragon, chopped.
- 2 garlic cloves, minced.
- 1/3-cup sour cream
- 1-cup mayonnaise
- 2-tbsp. mustard
- 2-tbsp. mustard
- 2-tbsp. chives, chopped.
- Salt and black pepper to the taste.

Directions:

1. Season beef with salt and pepper to the taste, place in your air fryer, cook at 370 °F, for 20 minutes; transfer to a plate and leave aside for a few minutes.
2. Take a bowl and mix garlic with sour cream, chives, mayo, some salt and pepper, whisk and leave aside.

3. In another bowl, mix mustard with Dijon mustard and tarragon, whisk, add beef, toss, return to your air fryer and cook at 350 °F, for 20 minutes more. Divide beef on plates, spread garlic mayo on top and serve

Nutrition Values (Per Serving): Calories: 400; Fat: 12g; Fiber: 2g; Carbs: 27g; Protein: 19g

252. Pork with Couscous Recipe.

(Prep + Cooking Time: 45 Minutes | **Serves:** 6)

Ingredients:

- 2 ½ lbs. pork loin; boneless and trimmed
- 2-cups couscous; cooked
- 3/4-cup chicken stock
- 2-tbsp. olive oil
- ½-tbsp. garlic powder
- ½-tbsp. sweet paprika
- 1/4-tsp. rosemary; dried
- one-tsp. basil; dried
- one-tsp. oregano; dried
- 1/4-tsp. marjoram; dried
- 2 ¼-tsp. sage; dried
- Salt and black pepper to the taste.

Directions:

1. Take a bowl and mix oil with stock, paprika, garlic powder, sage, rosemary, thyme, marjoram, oregano, salt and pepper to the taste, whisk well, add pork loin, toss well and leave aside for 1 hour.
2. Transfer everything to a pan that fits your air fryer and cook at 370 °F, for 35 minutes. Divide among plates and serve with couscous on the side

Nutrition Values (Per Serving): Calories: 310; Fat: 4g; Fiber: 6g; Carbs: 37g; Protein: 34

253. Lamb and Lemon Sauce Recipe.

(Prep + Cooking Time: 40 Minutes | **Serves:** 4)

Ingredients:

- 2 lamb shanks
- 2 garlic cloves, minced.
- 4-tbsp. olive oil
- Zest from ½ lemon
- Juice from ½ lemon
- ½-tsp. oregano; dried
- Salt and black pepper to the taste.

Directions:

1. Season lamb with salt, pepper, rub with garlic, put in your air fryer and cook at 350 °F, for 30 minutes.
2. Meanwhile, in a bowl, mix lemon juice with lemon zest, some salt and pepper, the olive oil and oregano and whisk very well. Shred lamb, discard bone, divide among plates, drizzle the lemon dressing all over and serve.

Nutrition Values (Per Serving): Calories: 260; Fat: 7g; Fiber: 3g; Carbs: 15g; Protein: 12g

254. Fennel Flavored Pork Roast Recipe

(Prep + Cooking Time: 1 hour 10 Minutes | **Serves:** 10)

Ingredients:

- 5 ½ lbs. pork loin roast; trimmed
- 1/4-cup olive oil
- 3 garlic cloves, minced.
- 2-tbsp. rosemary, chopped.
- 1-tbsp. fennel seeds
- one-tsp. fennel, ground.
- 2-tsp. red pepper; crushed
- Salt and black pepper to the taste.

Directions:

1. In your food processor mix garlic with fennel seeds, fennel, rosemary, red pepper, some black pepper and the olive oil and blend until you obtain a paste

2. Spread 2-tbsp. garlic paste on pork loin, rub well, season with salt and pepper, introduce in your preheated air fryer and cook at 350 °F, for 30 minutes.
3. Reduce heat to 300 °F and cook for 15 minutes more. Slice pork, divide among plates and serve.

Nutrition Values (Per Serving): Calories: 300; Fat: 14g; Fiber: 9g; Carbs: 26g; Protein: 22g

255. Lemony Lamb Leg Recipe

(Prep + Cooking Time: 1 hour 10 Minutes | **Serves:** 6)

Ingredients:

- 4 lbs. lamb leg
- 2 lbs. baby potatoes
- 2 springs rosemary, chopped.
- 3 garlic cloves, minced.
- 1-cup beef stock
- 2-tbsp. oregano, chopped.
- 1-tbsp. lemon rind, grated.
- 2-tbsp. olive oil
- 2-tbsp. lemon juice
- 2-tbsp. parsley, chopped.
- Salt and black pepper to the taste.

Directions:

1. Make small cuts all over lamb, insert rosemary springs and season with salt and pepper.
2. Take a bowl and mix 1-tbsp. oil with oregano, parsley, garlic, lemon juice and rind; stir and rub lamb with this mix
3. Heat up a pan that fits your air fryer with the rest of the oil over medium high heat, add potatoes; stir and cook for 3 minutes.
4. Add lamb and stock; stir, introduce in your air fryer and cook at 360 °F, for 1 hour. Divide everything on plates and serve

Nutrition Values (Per Serving): Calories: 264; Fat: 4g; Fiber: 12g; Carbs: 27g; Protein: 32

256. Lamb Shanks and Carrots Recipe.

(Prep + Cooking Time: 55 Minutes | **Serves:** 4)

Ingredients:

- 4 lamb shanks
- 1 yellow onion; finely chopped.
- 1 tomato; roughly chopped.
- 4 oz. red wine
- 6 carrots; roughly chopped.
- 2 garlic cloves, minced.
- 2-tbsp. water
- 2-tbsp. tomato paste
- 2-tbsp. olive oil
- one-tsp. oregano; dried
- Salt and black pepper to the taste.

Directions:

1. Season lamb with salt and pepper, rub with oil, put in your air fryer and cook at 360 °F, for 10 minutes
2. In a pan that fits your air fryer, mix onion with carrots, garlic, tomato paste, tomato, oregano, wine and water and toss.
3. Add lamb, toss, introduce in your air fryer and cook at 370 °F, for 35 minutes. Divide everything on plates and serve.

Nutrition Values (Per Serving): Calories: 432; Fat: 17g; Fiber: 8g; Carbs: 17g; Protein: 43

257. Beef Brisket and Onion Sauce Recipe

(Prep + Cooking Time: 2 hours 10 Minutes | **Serves:** 6)

Ingredients:

- ½ lb. celery, chopped.
- 4 lbs. beef brisket
- 1 lb. carrot, chopped.
- 1 lb. yellow onion, chopped.

- 8 earl grey tea bags
- 4-cups water
- Salt and black pepper to the taste.

For the sauce:

- ½ lb. celery, chopped.
- 1 lb. sweet onion, chopped.
- 1 oz. garlic, minced.
- 4 oz. vegetable oil
- 1-cup white vinegar
- 16 oz. canned tomatoes, chopped.
- 1-cup brown sugar
- 8 earl grey tea bags

Directions:

1. Put the water in a heat proof dish that fits your air fryer, add 1 lb. onion, 1 lb. carrot, ½ lb. celery, salt and pepper; stir and bring to a simmer over medium high heat
2. Add beef brisket and 8 tea bags; stir, transfer to your air fryer and cook at 300 °F, for 1 hour and 30 minutes.
3. Meanwhile, heat up a pan with the vegetable oil over medium high heat, add 1 lb. onion; stir and sauté for 10 minutes.
4. Add garlic, ½ lb. celery, tomatoes, sugar, vinegar, salt, pepper and 8 tea bags; stir, bring to a simmer, cook for 10 minutes and discard tea bags. Transfer beef brisket to a cutting board, slice, divide among plates, drizzle onion sauce all over and serve

Nutrition Values (Per Serving): Calories: 400; Fat: 12g; Fiber: 4g; Carbs: 38g; Protein: 34

258. Marinated Pork Chops and Onions Recipe

(Prep + Cooking Time: 24 hours 25 Minutes | **Serves:** 6)

Ingredients:

- 2 pork chops
- 1/4-cup olive oil
- 2 garlic cloves, minced.
- 2 yellow onions, sliced.
- ½-tsp. thyme; dried
- one-tsp. sweet paprika
- 2-tsp. mustard
- ½-tsp. oregano; dried
- A pinch of cayenne pepper
- Salt and black pepper to the taste.

Directions:

1. Take a bowl and mix oil with garlic, mustard, paprika, black pepper, oregano, thyme and cayenne and whisk well
2. Combine onions with meat and mustard mix, toss to coat, cover and keep in the fridge for 1 day.
3. Transfer meat and onions mix to a pan that fits your air fryer and cook at 360 °F, for 25 minutes.
4. Divide everything on plates and serve

Nutrition Values (Per Serving): Calories: 384; Fat: 4g; Fiber: 4g; Carbs: 17g; Protein: 25g

259. Beef and Green Onions Marinade Recipe.

(Prep + Cooking Time: 30 Minutes | **Serves:** 4)

Ingredients:

- 1 lb. lean beef
- 1-cup green onion, chopped.
- ½-cup water
- 1/4-cup brown sugar
- 1-cup soy sauce
- 1/4-cup sesame seeds
- 5 garlic cloves, minced.
- one-tsp. black pepper

Directions:

1. Take a bowl and mix onion with soy sauce, water, sugar, garlic, sesame seeds and pepper, whisk, add meat, toss and leave aside for 10 minutes.
2. Drain beef, transfer to your preheated air fryer and cook at 390 °F, for 20 minutes. Slice, divide among plates and serve with a side salad

Nutrition Values (Per Serving): Calories: 329; Fat: 8g; Fiber: 12g; Carbs: 26g; Protein: 22g

260. Beef Strips with Snow Peas and Mushrooms Recipe

(Prep + Cooking Time: 32 Minutes | **Serves:** 2)

Ingredients:

- 7 oz. snow peas
- 2 beef steaks; cut into strips
- 8 oz. white mushrooms, halved.
- 1 yellow onion; cut into rings
- 2-tbsp. soy sauce
- one-tsp. olive oil
- Salt and black pepper to the taste.

Directions:

1. Take a bowl and mix olive oil with soy sauce, whisk, add beef strips and toss
2. In another bowl, mix snow peas, onion and mushrooms with salt, pepper and the oil, toss well, put in a pan that fits your air fryer and cook at 350 °F, for 16 minutes.
3. Add beef strips to the pan as well and cook at 400 °F, for 6 minutes more.
4. Divide everything on plates and serve

Nutrition Values (Per Serving): Calories: 235; Fat: 8g; Fiber: 2g; Carbs: 22g; Protein: 24g

261. Oriental Fried Lamb Recipe.

(Prep + Cooking Time: 52 Minutes | **Serves:** 8)

Ingredients:

- 2 ½ lbs. lamb shoulder, chopped.
- 2 yellow onions, chopped.
- 2 garlic cloves, minced.
- 3 oz. almonds, peeled and chopped.
- 9 oz. plumps; pitted
- 8 oz. veggie stock
- 3-tbsp. olive oil
- 3-tbsp. honey
- one-tsp. ginger powder
- one-tsp. cinnamon powder.
- one-tsp. cumin powder
- one-tsp. turmeric powder
- Salt and black pepper to the tastes

Directions:

1. Take a bowl and mix cinnamon powder with ginger, cumin, turmeric, garlic, olive oil and lamb, toss to coat, place in your preheated air fryer and cook at 350 °F, for 8 minutes.
2. Transfer meat to a dish that fits your air fryer, add onions, stock, honey and plums; stir, introduce in your air fryer and cook at 350 °F, for 35 minutes. Divide everything on plates and serve with almond sprinkled on top.

Nutrition Values (Per Serving): Calories: 432; Fat: 23g; Fiber: 6g; Carbs: 30g; Protein: 20g

262. Crispy Lamb Recipe

(Prep + Cooking Time: 40 Minutes | **Serves:** 4)

Ingredients:

- 28 oz. rack of lamb
- 1 egg;
- 1 garlic clove, minced.
- 2-tbsp. macadamia nuts; toasted and crushed
- 1-tbsp. olive oil
- 1-tbsp. rosemary, chopped.
- 1-tbsp. bread crumbs
- Salt and black pepper to the taste.

Directions:

1. Take a bowl and mix oil with garlic and stir well.
2. Season lamb with salt, pepper and brush with the oil
3. In another bowl, mix nuts with breadcrumbs and rosemary.

4. Put the egg in a separate bowl and whisk well.
5. Dip lamb in egg, then in macadamia mix, place them in your air fryer's basket, cook at 360 °F and cook for 25 minutes; increase heat to 400 °F and cook for 5 minutes more. Divide among plates and serve right away

Nutrition Values (Per Serving): Calories: 230; Fat: 2g; Fiber: 2g; Carbs: 10g; Protein: 12g

263. Rib Eye Steak Recipe

(Prep + Cooking Time: 30 Minutes | **Serves:** 4)

Ingredients:

- 2 lbs. rib eye steak
- 1-tbsp. olive oil
- Salt and black pepper to the taste.

For the rub:

- 3-tbsp. sweet paprika
- 2-tbsp. garlic powder
- 1-tbsp. brown sugar
- 1-tbsp. cumin, ground.
- 2-tbsp. onion powder
- 2-tbsp. oregano; dried
- 1-tbsp. rosemary; dried

Directions:

1. Take a bowl and mix paprika with onion and garlic powder, sugar, oregano, rosemary, salt, pepper and cumin; stir and rub steak with this mix
2. Season steak with salt and pepper, rub again with the oil, put in your air fryer and cook at 400 °F, for 20 minutes; flipping them halfway. Transfer steak to a cutting board, slice and serve with a side salad.

Nutrition Values (Per Serving): Calories: 320; Fat: 8g; Fiber: 7g; Carbs: 22g; Protein: 21g

264. Asian Pork Recipe.

(Prep + Cooking Time: 45 Minutes | **Serves:** 4)

Ingredients:

- 14 oz. pork chops, cubed.
- 7 oz. coconut milk
- 3 oz. peanuts, ground.
- 2 garlic cloves, minced.
- 1 shallot, chopped.
- 3-tbsp. soy sauce
- 2-tbsp. olive oil
- 2-tsp. chili paste
- one-tsp. coriander, ground.
- one-tsp. ginger powder
- Salt and black pepper to the taste.

Directions:

1. Take a bowl and mix ginger with one-tsp. chili paste, half of the garlic, half of the soy sauce and half of the oil, whisk, add meat, toss and leave aside for 10 minutes.
2. Transfer meat to your air fryer's basket and cook at 400 °F, for 12 minutes; turning halfway.
3. Meanwhile, heat up a pan with the rest of the oil over medium high heat, add shallot, the rest of the garlic, coriander, coconut milk, the rest of the peanuts, the rest of the chili paste and the rest of the soy sauce; stir and cook for 5 minutes. Divide pork on plates, spread coconut mix on top and serve.

Nutrition Values (Per Serving): Calories: 423; Fat: 11g; Fiber: 4g; Carbs: 42g; Protein: 18g

265. Lamb Ribs Recipe

(Prep + Cooking Time: 55 Minutes | **Serves:** 8)

Ingredients:

- 8 lamb ribs
- 2 carrots, chopped.
- 2-cups veggie stock
- 4 garlic cloves, minced.

- 3-tbsp. white flour
- 1-tbsp. rosemary, chopped.
- 2-tbsp. extra virgin olive oil
- Salt and black pepper to the taste.

Directions:

1. Season lamb ribs with salt and pepper, rub with oil and garlic, put in preheated air fryer and cook at 360 °F, for 10 minutes
2. In a heat proof dish that fits your fryer, mix stock with flour and whisk well.
3. Add rosemary, carrots and lamb ribs, place in your air fryer and cook at 350 °F, for 30 minutes. Divide lamb mix on plates and serve hot

Nutrition Values (Per Serving): Calories: 302; Fat: 7g; Fiber: 2g; Carbs: 22g; Protein: 27

266. Greek Beef Meatballs Salad Recipe

(Prep + Cooking Time: 20 Minutes | **Serves:** 6)

Ingredients:

- 17 oz. beef, ground.
- 7 oz. Greek yogurt
- 7 oz. cherry tomatoes, halved.
- 1-cup baby spinach
- 1/4-cup milk
- 5 bread slices, cubed.
- 2 garlic cloves, minced.
- 1/4-cup mint, chopped.
- 1 egg, whisked.
- 1/4-cup parsley, chopped.
- 1 yellow onion, grated.
- 1 ½-tbsp. lemon juice
- 1-tbsp. olive oil
- 2 ½-tsp. oregano; dried
- Salt and black pepper to the taste.
- Cooking spray.

Directions:

1. Put torn bread Take a bowl and add milk, soak for a few minutes; squeeze and transfer to another bowl.
2. Add beef, egg, salt, pepper, oregano, mint, parsley, garlic and onion; stir and shape medium meatballs out of this mix
3. Spray them with cooking spray, place them in your air fryer and cook at 370 °F, for 10 minutes.
4. In a salad bowl, mix spinach with cucumber and tomato. Add meatballs, the oil, some salt, pepper, lemon juice and yogurt, toss and serve

Nutrition Values (Per Serving): Calories: 200; Fat: 4g; Fiber: 8g; Carbs: 13g; Protein: 27

267. Pork Chops and Green Beans Recipe

(Prep + Cooking Time: 25 Minutes | **Serves:** 4)

Ingredients:

- 4 pork chops; bone in
- 16 oz. green beans
- 3 garlic cloves, minced.
- 2-tbsp. parsley, chopped.
- 1-tbsp. sage, chopped.
- 2-tbsp. olive oil
- Salt and black pepper to the taste.

Directions:

1. In a pan that fits your air fryer, mix pork chops with olive oil, sage, salt, pepper, green beans, garlic and parsley, toss, introduce in your air fryer and cook at 360 °F, for 15 minutes.
2. Divide everything on plates and serve

Nutrition Values (Per Serving): Calories: 261; Fat: 7g; Fiber: 9g; Carbs: 14g; Protein: 20g

268. Simple Braised Pork Recipe

(Prep + Cooking Time: 1 hour 20 Minutes | **Serves:** 4)

Ingredients:

- 2 lbs. pork loin roast; boneless and cubed
- ½ lb. red grapes
- 1 thyme spring
- 1 bay leaf
- 2-cups chicken stock
- ½-cup dry white wine
- 2 garlic cloves, minced.
- ½ yellow onion, chopped.
- 2-tbsp. white flour
- 4-tbsp. butter, melted.
- one-tsp. thyme, chopped.
- Salt and black pepper to the taste.

Directions:

1. Season pork cubes with salt and pepper, rub with 2-tbsp. melted butter, put in your air fryer and cook at 370 °F, for 8 minutes
2. Meanwhile, heat up a pan that fits your air fryer with 2-tbsp. butter over medium high heat, add garlic and onion; stir and cook for 2 minutes.
3. Add wine, stock, salt, pepper, thyme, flour and bay leaf; stir well, bring to a simmer and take off heat.
4. Add pork cubes and grapes, toss, introduce in your air fryer and cook at 360 °F, for 30 minutes more.
5. Divide everything on plates and serve

Nutrition Values (Per Serving): Calories: 320; Fat: 4g; Fiber: 5g; Carbs: 29g; Protein: 38

269. Simple Fried Pork Shoulder Recipe

(Prep + Cooking Time: 1 hour and 50 minutes | **Serves:** 6)

Ingredients:

- 4 lbs. pork shoulder
- 3-tbsp. olive oil
- 3-tbsp. garlic, minced.
- Salt and black pepper to the taste.

Directions:

1. Take a bowl and mix olive oil with salt, pepper and oil, whisk well and brush pork shoulder with this mix
2. Place in preheated air fryer and cook at 390 °F, for 10 minutes.
3. Reduce heat to 300 °F and roast pork for 1 hour and 10 minutes. Slice pork shoulder, divide among plates and serve with a side salad.

Nutrition Values (Per Serving): Calories: 221; Fat: 4g; Fiber: 4g; Carbs: 7g; Protein: 10g

270. Marinated Lamb and Veggies Recipe

(Prep + Cooking Time: 40 Minutes | **Serves:** 4)

Ingredients:

- 3 oz. bean sprouts
- 1 onion, sliced.
- 8 oz. lamb loin, sliced.
- 1 carrot, chopped.
- ½-tbsp. olive oil

For the marinade:

- ½ apple, grated.
- 1 garlic clove, minced.
- 1 small yellow onion, grated.
- 5-tbsp. soy sauce
- 1-tbsp. sugar
- 2-tbsp. orange juice
- 1-tbsp. ginger, grated.
- Salt and black pepper to the taste.

Directions:

1. Take a bowl and mix 1 grated onion with the apple, garlic, 1-tbsp. ginger, soy sauce, orange juice, sugar and black pepper, whisk well, add lamb and leave aside for 10 minutes
2. Heat up a pan that fits your air fryer with the olive oil over medium high heat, add 1 sliced onion, carrot and bean sprouts; stir and cook for 3 minutes.
3. Add lamb and the marinade, transfer pan to your preheated air fryer and cook at 360 °F, for 25 minutes. Divide everything into bowls and serve

Nutrition Values (Per Serving): Calories: 265; Fat: 3g; Fiber: 7g; Carbs: 18g; Protein: 22g

271. Beef and Cabbage Mix Recipe

(Prep + Cooking Time: 50 Minutes | **Serves:** 6)

Ingredients:

- 2 ½ lbs. beef brisket
- 4 carrots, chopped.
- 2 bay leaves
- 1-cup beef stock
- 3 garlic cloves, chopped.
- 1 cabbage head; cut into medium wedges
- 3 turnips; cut into quarters
- Salt and black pepper to the taste.

Directions:

1. Put beef brisket and stock in a large pan that fits your air fryer, season beef with salt and pepper, add garlic and bay leaves, carrots, cabbage, potatoes and turnips, toss, introduce in your air fryer and cook at 360 °F and cook for 40 minutes. Divide among plates and serve.

Nutrition Values (Per Serving): Calories: 353; Fat: 16g; Fiber: 7g; Carbs: 20g; Protein: 24g

272. Beef Medallions Mix Recipe.

(Prep + Cooking Time: 2 hours 10 Minutes | **Serves:** 4)

Ingredients:

- 1-cup tomatoes; crushed
- 4 beef medallions
- 2-tbsp. lime juice
- 1-tbsp. hot pepper
- 2-tbsp. soy sauce
- 2-tsp. chili powder
- 2-tsp. onion powder
- Salt and black pepper to the taste.

Directions:

1. Take a bowl and mix tomatoes with hot pepper, soy sauce, chili powder, onion powder, a pinch of salt, black pepper and lime juice and whisk well
2. Arrange beef medallions in a dish, pour sauce over them, toss and leave them aside for 2 hours.
3. Discard tomato marinade, put beef in your preheated air fryer and cook at 360 °F, for 10 minutes. Divide steaks on plates and serve with a side salad

Nutrition Values (Per Serving): Calories: 230; Fat: 4g; Fiber: 1g; Carbs: 13g; Protein: 14g

273. Short Ribs and Beer Sauce Recipe

(Prep + Cooking Time: 60 Minutes | **Serves:** 6)

Ingredients:

- 4 lbs. short ribs; cut into small pieces
- 1/4-cup tomato paste
- 1-cup dark beer
- 1 Portobello mushroom; dried
- 1 bay leaf
- 6 thyme springs, chopped.
- 1 yellow onion, chopped.
- 1-cup chicken stock
- Salt and black pepper to the taste.

Directions:

1. Heat up a pan that fits your air fryer over medium heat, add tomato paste, onion, stock, beer, mushroom, bay leaves and thyme and bring to a simmer.
2. Add ribs, introduce in your air fryer and cook at 350 °F, for 40 minutes. Divide everything on plates and serve

Nutrition Values (Per Serving): Calories: 300; Fat: 7g; Fiber: 8g; Carbs: 18g; Protein: 23g

274. Creamy Pork Recipe

(Prep + Cooking Time: 32 Minutes | **Serves:** 6)

Ingredients:

- 2 lbs. pork meat; boneless and cubed
- 1 garlic clove, minced.
- 1 ½-cups sour cream
- 2 yellow onions, chopped.
- 3-cups chicken stock
- 1-tbsp. olive oil
- 2-tbsp. white flour
- 2-tbsp. dill, chopped.
- 2-tbsp. sweet paprika
- Salt and black pepper to the taste.

Directions:

1. In a pan that fits your air fryer, mix pork with salt, pepper and oil, toss, introduce in your air fryer and cook at 360 °F, for 7 minutes.
2. Add onion, garlic, stock, paprika, flour, sour cream and dill, toss and cook at 370 °F, for 15 minutes more. Divide everything on plates and serve right away

Nutrition Values (Per Serving): Calories: 300; Fat: 4g; Fiber: 10g; Carbs: 26g; Protein: 34

275. Beef Roast and Wine Sauce Recipe.

(Prep + Cooking Time: 55 Minutes | **Serves:** 6)

Ingredients:

- 3 lbs. beef roast
- 3 carrots, chopped.
- 5 potatoes, chopped.
- 1 yellow onion, chopped.
- 3 oz. red wine
- 17 oz. beef stock
- 4 garlic cloves, minced.
- ½-tsp. smoked paprika
- ½-tsp. chicken salt
- Salt and black pepper to the taste.

Directions:

1. Take a bowl and mix salt, pepper, chicken salt and paprika; stir, rub beef with this mix and put it in a big pan that fits your air fryer.
2. Add onion, garlic, stock, wine, potatoes and carrots, introduce in your air fryer and cook at 360 °F, for 45 minutes. Divide everything on plates and serve

Nutrition Values (Per Serving): Calories: 304; Fat: 20g; Fiber: 7g; Carbs: 20g; Protein: 32

276. Garlic and Bell Pepper Beef Recipe

(Prep + Cooking Time: 60 Minutes | **Serves:** 4)

Ingredients:

- 11 oz. steak fillets, sliced.
- 4 garlic cloves, minced.
- 1 red bell pepper; cut into strips
- ½-cup beef stock
- 4 green onions, sliced.
- 2-tbsp. fish sauce
- 2-tbsp. olive oil
- 1-tbsp. sugar
- 2-tsp. corn flour
- Black pepper to the taste

Directions:

1. In a pan that fits your air fryer mix beef with oil, garlic, black pepper and bell pepper; stir, cover and keep in the fridge for 30 minutes
2. Put the pan in your preheated air fryer and cook at 360 °F, for 14 minutes.
3. Take a bowl and mix sugar with fish sauce; stir well, pour over beef and cook at 360 °F, for 7 minutes more.
4. Add stock mixed with corn flour and green onions, toss and cook at 370 °F, for 7 minutes more. Divide everything on plates and serve

Nutrition Values (Per Serving): Calories: 343; Fat: 3g; Fiber: 12g; Carbs: 26g; Protein: 38

277. Beef Kabobs Recipe.

(Prep + Cooking Time: 20 Minutes | **Serves:** 4)

Ingredients:

- 2 lbs. sirloin steak; cut into medium pieces
- 2 red bell peppers, chopped.
- 1 red onion, chopped.
- 1 zucchini, sliced.
- 1/4-cup olive oil
- 1/4-cup salsa
- Juice form 1 lime
- ½-tbsp. cumin, ground.
- 2-tbsp. chili powder
- 2-tbsp. hot sauce
- Salt and black pepper to the taste.

Directions:

1. Take a bowl and mix salsa with lime juice, oil, hot sauce, chili powder, cumin, salt and black pepper and whisk well
2. Divide meat bell peppers, zucchini and onion on skewers, brush kabobs with the salsa mix you made earlier, put them in your preheated air fryer and cook them for 10 minutes at 370 °F, flipping kabobs halfway. Divide among plates and serve with a side salad.

Nutrition Values (Per Serving): Calories: 170; Fat: 5g; Fiber: 2g; Carbs: 13g; Protein: 16

278. Fryer Lamb Shanks Recipe

(Prep + Cooking Time: 55 Minutes | **Serves:** 4)

Ingredients:

- 4 lamb shanks
- 5 oz. dry sherry
- 1 yellow onion, chopped.
- 4 bay leaves
- 2 ½-cups chicken stock
- 2-tbsp. white flour
- 1-tbsp. olive oil
- 2-tsp. honey
- 4-tsp. coriander seeds; crushed
- Salt and pepper to the taste

Directions:

1. Season lamb shanks with salt and pepper, rub with half of the oil, put in your air fryer and cook at 360 °F, for 10 minutes.
2. Heat up a pan that fits your air fryer with the rest of the oil over medium high heat, add onion and coriander; stir and cook for 5 minutes
3. Add flour, sherry, stock, honey and bay leaves, salt and pepper; stir, bring to a simmer, add lamb, introduce everything in your air fryer and cook at 360 °F, for 30 minutes. Divide everything on plates and serve.

Nutrition Values (Per Serving): Calories: 283; Fat: 4g; Fiber: 2g; Carbs: 17g; Protein: 26

279. Lamb and Green Pesto Recipe

(Prep + Cooking Time: 1 hour 45 Minutes | **Serves:** 4)

Ingredients:

- 2 lbs. lamb riblets
- 1 small yellow onion; roughly chopped
- 1/3-cup pistachios, chopped.
- ½ onion, chopped.
- 1-cup mint
- 5 garlic cloves, minced.
- 1-cup parsley
- 5-tbsp. olive oil
- one-tsp. lemon zest, grated.
- Juice from 1 orange
- Salt and black pepper to the taste.

Directions:

1. In your food processor, mix parsley with mint, onion, pistachios, lemon zest, salt, pepper and oil and blend very well.
2. Rub lamb with this mix, place in a bowl; cover and leave in the fridge for 1 hour
3. Transfer lamb to a baking dish that fits your air fryer, also add garlic, drizzle orange juice and cook in your air fryer at 300 °F, for 45 minutes.

Nutrition Values (Per Serving): Calories: 200; Fat: 4g; Fiber: 6g; Carbs: 15g; Protein: 7g

280. Sirloin Steaks and Pico De Gallo Recipe

(Prep + Cooking Time: 20 Minutes | **Serves:** 4)

Ingredients:

- 4 medium sirloin steaks
- ½-tbsp. sweet paprika
- 2-tbsp. chili powder
- one-tsp. garlic powder
- one-tsp. cumin, ground.
- one-tsp. onion powder
- Salt and black pepper to the taste.

For the Pico de gallo:

- 1 jalapeno, chopped.
- 2 tomatoes, chopped.
- 1 small red onion, chopped.
- 1/4-cup cilantro, chopped.
- 1 small green bell pepper, chopped.
- 2 garlic cloves, minced.
- 2-tbsp. lime juice
- 1/4-tsp. cumin, ground.

Directions:

1. Take a bowl and mix chili powder with a pinch of salt, black pepper, onion powder, garlic powder, paprika and one-tsp. cumin; stir well, season steaks with this mix, put them in your air fryer and cook at 360 °F, for 10 minutes.
2. Take a bowl and mix red onion with tomatoes, garlic, lime juice, bell pepper, jalapeno, cilantro, black pepper to the taste and 1/4-tsp. cumin and toss. Top steaks with this mix and serve right away

Nutrition Values (Per Serving): Calories: 200; Fat: 12g; Fiber: 4g; Carbs: 15g; Protein: 18g

281. Garlic Lamb Chops Recipe.

(Prep + Cooking Time: 20 Minutes | **Serves:** 4)

Ingredients:

- 8 lamb chops
- 4 garlic cloves, minced.
- 1-tbsp. oregano, chopped.
- 1-tbsp. coriander, chopped.
- 3-tbsp. olive oil
- Salt and black pepper to the taste.

Directions:

1. Take a bowl and mix oregano with salt, pepper, oil, garlic and lamb chops and toss to coat
2. Transfer lamb chops to your air fryer and cook at 400 °F, for 10 minutes. Divide lamb chops on plates and serve with a side salad.

Nutrition Values (Per Serving): Calories: 231; Fat: 7g; Fiber: 5g; Carbs: 14g; Protein: 23g

282. Roasted Pork Belly and Apple Sauce Recipe

(Prep + Cooking Time: 50 Minutes | **Serves:** 6)

Ingredients:

- 17 oz. apples; cored and cut into wedges
- 2 lbs. pork belly; scored
- 1-quart water
- 2-tbsp. sugar
- 1-tbsp. lemon juice
- A drizzle of olive oil
- Salt and black pepper to the taste.

Directions:

1. In your blender, mix water with apples, lemon juice and sugar, pulse well, transfer to a bowl, add meat, toss well, drain, put in your air fryer and cook at 400 °F, for 40 minutes.
2. Pour the sauce in a pot, heat up over medium heat and simmer for 15 minutes. Slice pork belly, divide among plates, drizzle the sauce all over and serve

Nutrition Values (Per Serving): Calories: 456; Fat: 34g; Fiber: 4g; Carbs: 10g; Protein: 25g

283. Burgundy Beef Mix Recipe.

(Prep + Cooking Time: 1 hour 10 Minutes | **Serves:** 7)

Ingredients:

- ½ lbs. mushrooms, sliced.
- 2 lbs. beef chuck roast, cubed.
- 15 oz. canned tomatoes, chopped.
- 2 celery ribs, chopped.
- 2 yellow onions, chopped.
- 4 carrots, chopped.
- 1-cup water
- 1-cup beef stock
- 3-tbsp. almond flour
- 1-tbsp. thyme, chopped.
- ½-tsp. mustard powder
- Salt and black pepper to the taste.

Directions:

1. Heat up a heat proof pot that fits your air fryer over medium high heat, add beef; stir and brown them for a couple of minutes
2. Add tomatoes, mushrooms, onions, carrots, celery, salt, pepper mustard, stock and thyme and stir.
3. In a bowl mix water with flour; stir well, add this to the pot, toss, introduce in your air fryer and cook at 300 °F, for 1 hour. Divide into bowls and serve

Nutrition Values (Per Serving): Calories: 275; Fat: 13g; Fiber: 4g; Carbs: 17g; Protein: 28

284. Ham and Cauliflower Mix Recipe

(Prep + Cooking Time: 4 hours 10 Minutes | **Serves:** 6)

Ingredients:

- 8 oz. cheddar cheese, grated.
- 16 oz. cauliflower florets
- 14 oz. chicken stock
- 1/4-cup heavy cream
- 4-cups ham, cubed.
- 4 garlic cloves, minced.
- ½-tsp. garlic powder
- ½-tsp. onion powder
- Salt and black pepper to the taste.

Directions:

1. In a pot that fits your air fryer, mix ham with stock, cheese, cauliflower, garlic powder, onion powder, salt, pepper, garlic and heavy cream; stir, put in your air fryer and cook at 300 °F, for 1 hour. Divide into bowls and serve.

Nutrition Values (Per Serving): Calories: 320; Fat: 20g; Fiber: 3g; Carbs: 16g; Protein: 23g

285. Beef Stuffed Squash Recipe

(Prep + Cooking Time: 50 Minutes | **Serves:** 2)

Ingredients:

- 1 lb. beef, ground.
- 28 oz. canned tomatoes, chopped.
- 1 yellow onion, chopped.
- 1 green bell pepper, chopped.
- 1 Portobello mushroom, sliced.
- 1 spaghetti squash; pricked
- 3 garlic cloves, minced.
- ½-tsp. thyme; dried
- one-tsp. oregano; dried
- 1/4-tsp. cayenne pepper
- Salt and black pepper to the taste.

Directions:

1. Put spaghetti squash in your air fryer, cook at 350 °F, for 20 minutes; transfer to a cutting board, and cut into halves and discard seeds
2. Heat up a pan over medium high heat, add meat, garlic, onion and mushroom; stir and cook until meat browns.
3. Add salt, pepper, thyme, oregano, cayenne, tomatoes and green pepper; stir and cook for 10 minutes.
4. Stuff squash with this beef mix, introduce in the fryer and cook at 360 °F, for 10 minutes. Divide among plates and serve

Nutrition Values (Per Serving): Calories: 260; Fat: 7g; Fiber: 2g; Carbs: 14g; Protein: 10g

286. Short Ribs and Sauce Recipe

(Prep + Cooking Time: 46 Minutes | **Serves:** 4)

Ingredients:

- 4 lbs. short ribs
- 3 garlic cloves, minced.
- 3 ginger slices
- 2 green onions, chopped.
- 1/4-cup rice wine
- 1/4-cup pear juice
- ½-cup water
- ½-cup soy sauce
- one-tsp. vegetable oil
- 2-tsp. sesame oil

Directions:

1. Heat up a pan that fits your air fryer with the oil over medium heat, add green onions, ginger and garlic; stir and cook for 1 minute
2. Add ribs, water, wine, soy sauce, sesame oil and pear juice; stir, introduce in your air fryer and cook at 350 °F, for 35 minutes. Divide ribs and sauce on plates and serve.

Nutrition Values (Per Serving): Calories: 321; Fat: 12g; Fiber: 4g; Carbs: 20g; Protein: 14g

287. Chinese Steak and Broccoli Recipe

(Prep + Cooking Time: 57 Minutes | **Serves:** 4)

Ingredients:

- 3/4 lb. round steak; cut into strips
- 1 lb. broccoli florets
- 1/3-cup oyster sauce
- 1 garlic clove, minced.

- 1/3-cup sherry
- 1-tbsp. olive oil
- one-tsp. soy sauce
- 2-tsp. sesame oil
- one-tsp. sugar

Directions:

1. Take a bowl and mix sesame oil with oyster sauce, soy sauce, sherry and sugar; stir well, add beef, toss and leave aside for 30 minutes
2. Transfer beef to a pan that fits your air fryer, also add broccoli, garlic and oil, toss everything and cook at 380 °F, for 12 minutes. Divide among plates and serve.

Nutrition Values (Per Serving): Calories: 330; Fat: 12g; Fiber: 7g; Carbs: 23g; Protein: 23g

288. Mediterranean Steaks and Scallops Recipe.

(Prep + Cooking Time: 24 Minutes | **Serves:** 2)

Ingredients:

- 2 beef steaks
- 10 sea scallops
- 1/4-cup butter
- 1/4-cup veggie stock
- 4 garlic cloves, minced.
- 1 shallot, chopped.
- 2-tbsp. basil, chopped.
- 2-tbsp. lemon juice
- 2-tbsp. parsley, chopped.
- one-tsp. lemon zest
- Salt and black pepper to the taste.

Directions:

1. Season steaks with salt and pepper, put them in your air fryer, cook at 360 °F, for 10 minutes and transfer to a pan that fits the fryer
2. Add shallot, garlic, butter, stock, basil, lemon juice, parsley, lemon zest and scallops, toss everything gently and cook at 360 °F, for 4 minutes more. Divide steaks and scallops on plates and serve

Nutrition Values (Per Serving): Calories: 150; Fat: 2g; Fiber: 2g; Carbs: 14g; Protein: 17g

289. Creamy Lamb Recipe

(Prep + Cooking Time: 1 day 1 hour | **Serves:** 8)

Ingredients:

- 5 lbs. leg of lamb
- 2-cups low fat buttermilk
- 2 garlic cloves, minced.
- 1-cup white wine
- ½-cup sour cream
- ½-cup butter
- 2-tbsp. mustard
- 2-tbsp. basil, chopped.
- 2-tbsp. tomato paste
- 1-tbsp. cornstarch mixed with 1-tbsp. water
- Salt and black pepper to the taste.

Directions:

1. Put lamb roast in a big dish, add buttermilk, toss to coat, cover and keep in the fridge for 24 hours.
2. Pat dry lamb and put in a pan that fits your air fryer.
3. Take a bowl and mix butter with tomato paste, mustard, basil, rosemary, salt, pepper and garlic, whisk well, spread over lamb, introduce everything in your air fryer and cook at 300 °F, for 1 hour.
4. Slice lamb, divide among plates, leave aside for now and heat up cooking juices from the pan on your stove. Add wine, cornstarch mix, salt, pepper and sour cream; stir, take off heat, drizzle this sauce over lamb and serve

Nutrition Values (Per Serving): Calories: 287; Fat: 4g; Fiber: 7g; Carbs: 19g; Protein: 25g

290. Beef Curry Recipe.

(Prep + Cooking Time: 55 Minutes | **Serves:** 4)

Ingredients:

- 2 lbs. beef steak, cubed.
- 10 oz. canned coconut milk
- 3 potatoes, cubed.
- 2 yellow onions, chopped.
- 2 garlic cloves, minced.
- 2-tbsp. olive oil
- 1-tbsp. wine mustard
- 2 ½-tbsp. curry powder
- 2-tbsp. tomato sauce
- Salt and black pepper to the taste.

Directions:

1. Heat up a pan that fits your air fryer with the oil over medium high heat, add onions and garlic; stir and cook for 4 minutes.
2. Add potatoes and mustard; stir and cook for 1 minute
3. Add beef, curry powder, salt, pepper, coconut milk and tomato sauce; stir, transfer to your air fryer and cook at 360 °F, for 40 minutes. Divide into bowls and serve.

Nutrition Values (Per Serving): Calories: 432; Fat: 16g; Fiber: 4g; Carbs: 20g; Protein: 27

291. Stuffed Pork Steaks Recipe.

(Prep + Cooking Time: 30 Minutes | **Serves:** 4)

Ingredients:

- 4 pork loin steaks
- 2 pickles, chopped.
- 4 ham slices
- 3/4-cup olive oil
- 1-cup cilantro, chopped.
- 1-cup mint, chopped.
- 6 Swiss cheese slices
- Zest from 1 orange, grated.
- Zest from 2 limes, grated.
- Juice from 2 limes
- Juice from 1 orange
- 2-tbsp. mustard
- 4-tsp. garlic, minced.
- one-tsp. oregano; dried
- 2-tsp. cumin, ground.
- Salt and black pepper to the taste.

Directions:

1. In your food processor, mix lime zest and juice with orange zest and juice, garlic, oil, cilantro, mint, oregano, cumin, salt and pepper and blend well
2. Season steaks with salt and pepper, place them into a bowl, add marinade and toss to coat.
3. Place steaks on a working surface, divide pickles, cheese, mustard and ham on them, roll and secure with toothpicks.
4. Put stuffed pork steaks in your air fryer and cook at 340 °F, for 20 minutes. Divide among plates and serve with a side salad

Nutrition Values (Per Serving): Calories: 270; Fat: 7g; Fiber: 2g; Carbs: 13g; Protein: 20g

292. Fried Sausage and Mushrooms Recipe.

(Prep + Cooking Time: 50 Minutes | **Serves:** 6)

Ingredients:

- 2 lbs. pork sausage, sliced.
- 2 lbs. Portobello mushrooms, sliced.
- 2 sweet onions, chopped.
- 3 red bell peppers, chopped.
- 1-tbsp. brown sugar
- one-tsp. olive oil
- Salt and black pepper to the taste.

Directions:

1. In a baking dish that fits your air fryer, mix sausage slices with oil, salt, pepper, bell pepper, mushrooms, onion and sugar, toss, introduce in your air fryer and cook at 300 °F, for 40 minutes. Divide among plates and serve right away.

Nutrition Values (Per Serving): Calories: 130; Fat: 12g; Fiber: 1g; Carbs: 13g; Protein: 18g

293. Mustard Marinated Beef Recipe

(Prep + Cooking Time: 55 Minutes | **Serves:** 6)

Ingredients:

- 3 lbs. beef roast
- 3/4-cup red wine
- 3 garlic cloves, minced.
- 1 ¾-cup beef stock
- 6 bacon strips
- 1-tbsp. horseradish
- 1-tbsp. mustard
- 2-tbsp. butter
- Salt and black pepper to the taste.

Directions:

1. Take a bowl and mix butter with mustard, garlic, salt, pepper and horseradish, whisk and rub beef with this mix.
2. Arrange bacon strips on a cutting board, place beef on top, fold bacon around beef, transfer to your air fryer's basket, cook at 400 °F, for 15 minutes and transfer to a pan that fits your fryer
3. Add stock and wine to beef, introduce pan in your air fryer and cook at 360 °F, for 30 minutes more.
4. Carve beef, divide among plates and serve with a side salad

Nutrition Values (Per Serving): Calories: 500; Fat: 9g; Fiber: 4g; Carbs: 29g; Protein: 36

294. Beef Patties and Mushroom Sauce Recipe

(Prep + Cooking Time: 35 Minutes | **Serves:** 6)

Ingredients:

- 2 lbs. beef, ground.
- 1/4-cup beef stock
- 3/4-cup flour
- 1-tbsp. parsley, chopped.
- 1-tbsp. onion flakes
- 1-tbsp. soy sauce
- ½-tsp. garlic powder
- Salt and black pepper to the taste.

For the sauce:

- 1-cup yellow onion, chopped.
- 1/4-cup sour cream
- ½-cup beef stock
- 2-cups mushrooms, sliced.
- 2-tbsp. bacon fat
- 2-tbsp. butter
- ½-tsp. soy sauce
- Salt and black pepper to the taste.

Directions:

1. Take a bowl and mix beef with salt, pepper, garlic powder, 1-tbsp. soy sauce, 1/4-cup beef stock, flour, parsley and onion flakes; stir well, shape 6 patties, place them in your air fryer and cook at 350 °F, for 14 minutes.
2. Meanwhile, heat up a pan with the butter and the bacon fat over medium heat, add mushrooms; stir and cook for 4 minutes
3. Add onions; stir and cook for 4 minutes more.
4. Add ½-tsp. soy sauce, sour cream and ½-cup stock; stir well, bring to a simmer and take off heat. Divide beef patties on plates and serve with mushroom sauce on top

Nutrition Values (Per Serving): Calories: 435; Fat: 23g; Fiber: 4g; Carbs: 6g; Protein: 32

295. Lamb and Creamy Brussels Sprouts Recipe.

(Prep + Cooking Time: 1 hour and 20 minutes **| Serves:** 4)

Ingredients:

- 1 ½ lbs. Brussels sprouts; trimmed
- 2 lbs. leg of lamb; scored
- ½-cup sour cream
- 1 garlic clove, minced.
- 1-tbsp. lemon thyme, chopped.
- 1-tbsp. butter, melted.
- 2-tbsp. olive oil
- 1-tbsp. rosemary, chopped.
- Salt and black pepper to the taste.

Directions:

1. Season leg of lamb with salt, pepper, thyme and rosemary, brush with oil, place in your air fryer's basket, cook at 300 °F, for 1 hour, transfer to a plate and keep warm
2. In a pan that fits your air fryer, mix Brussels sprouts with salt, pepper, garlic, butter and sour cream, toss, put in your air fryer and cook at 400 °F, for 10 minutes. Divide lamb on plates, add Brussels sprouts on the side and serve.

Nutrition Values (Per Serving): Calories: 440; Fat: 23g; Fiber: 0g; Carbs: 2g; Protein: 49

296. Beef Casserole Recipe

(Prep + Cooking Time: 65 Minutes **| Serves:** 12)

Ingredients:

- 2 lbs. beef, ground.
- 16 oz. tomato sauce
- 28 oz. canned tomatoes, chopped.
- 2-cups eggplant, chopped.
- 2-cups mozzarella, grated.
- 1-tbsp. olive oil
- 2-tbsp. parsley, chopped.
- 2-tsp. mustard
- one-tsp. oregano; dried
- 2-tsp. gluten free Worcestershire sauce
- Salt and black pepper to the taste.

Directions:

1. Take a bowl and mix eggplant with salt, pepper and oil and toss to coat
2. In another bowl, mix beef with salt, pepper, mustard and Worcestershire sauce; stir well and spread on the bottom of a pan that fits your air fryer.
3. Add eggplant mix, tomatoes, tomato sauce, parsley, oregano and sprinkle mozzarella at the end.
4. Introduce in your air fryer and cook at 360 °F, for 35 minutes Divide among plates and serve hot

Nutrition Values (Per Serving): Calories: 200; Fat: 12g; Fiber: 2g; Carbs: 16g; Protein: 15g

297. Tasty Ham and Greens Recipe

(Prep + Cooking Time: 26 Minutes **| Serves:** 8)

Ingredients:

- 14 oz. canned black-eyed peas; drained
- 4-cups ham, chopped.
- 3-cups chicken stock
- 5 oz. onion, chopped.
- 16 oz. collard greens, chopped.
- 2-tbsp. flour
- 2-tbsp. olive oil
- ½-tsp. red pepper; crushed

Directions:

1. Drizzle the oil in a pan that fits your air fryer, add ham, stock and flour and whisk
2. Also add onion, black eyed peas, red pepper and collard greens, introduce in your air fryer and cook at 390 °F, for 16 minutes. Divide everything on plates and serve.

Nutrition Values (Per Serving): Calories: 322; Fat: 6g; Fiber: 8g; Carbs: 12g; Protein: 5g

298. Pork Chops and Mushrooms Mix Recipe

(Prep + Cooking Time: 50 Minutes | **Serves:** 3)

Ingredients:

- 3 pork chops; boneless
- 8 oz. mushrooms, sliced.
- ½-cup olive oil
- 1 yellow onion, chopped.
- 1-cup mayonnaise
- 1-tbsp. balsamic vinegar
- one-tsp. nutmeg
- one-tsp. garlic powder

Directions:

1. Heat up a pan that fits your air fryer with the oil over medium heat, add mushrooms and onions; stir and cook for 4 minutes
2. Add pork chops, nutmeg and garlic powder and brown on both sides.
3. Introduce pan your air fryer at 330 °F and cook for 30 minutes. Add vinegar and mayo; stir, divide everything on plates and serve

Nutrition Values (Per Serving): Calories: 600; Fat: 10g; Fiber: 1g; Carbs: 8g; Protein: 30

299. Filet Mignon and Mushrooms Sauce Recipe

(Prep + Cooking Time: 35 Minutes | **Serves:** 4)

Ingredients:

- 12 mushrooms, sliced.
- 1 shallot, chopped.
- 4 fillet mignons
- 2 garlic cloves, minced.
- 1/4-cup Dijon mustard
- 1/4-cup wine
- 1¼-cup coconut cream
- 2-tbsp. parsley, chopped.
- 2-tbsp. olive oil
- Salt and black pepper to the taste.

Directions:

1. Heat up a pan with the oil over medium high heat, add garlic and shallots; stir and cook for 3 minutes.
2. Add mushrooms; stir and cook for 4 minutes more
3. Add wine; stir and cook until it evaporates.
4. Add coconut cream, mustard, parsley, a pinch of salt and black pepper to the taste; stir, cook for 6 minutes more and take off heat.
5. Season fillets with salt and pepper, put them in your air fryer and cook at 360 °F, for 10 minutes. Divide fillets on plates and serve with the mushroom sauce on top

Nutrition Values (Per Serving): Calories: 340; Fat: 12g; Fiber: 1g; Carbs: 14g; Protein: 23g

300. Mexican Beef Mix Recipe.

(Prep + Cooking Time: 1 hour and 20 minutes | **Serves:** 8)

Ingredients:

- 2 lbs. beef roast, cubed.
- 14 oz. canned tomatoes, chopped.
- ½-cup black olives; pitted and chopped.
- ½-cup water
- 6 garlic cloves, minced.
- 2 green bell peppers, chopped.
- 1 habanero pepper, chopped.
- 4 jalapenos, chopped.
- 2 yellow onions, chopped.
- 2-tbsp. cilantro, chopped.
- 2-tbsp. olive oil
- one-tsp. oregano; dried
- 1 ½-tsp. cumin, ground.
- Salt and black pepper to the taste.

Directions:

1. In a pan that fits your air fryer, combine beef with oil, green bell peppers, onions, jalapenos, habanero pepper, tomatoes, garlic, water, cilantro, oregano, cumin, salt and pepper; stir, put in your air fryer and cook at 300 °F, for 1 hour and 10 minutes. Add olives; stir, divide into bowls and serve.

Nutrition Values (Per Serving): Calories: 305; Fat: 14g; Fiber: 4g; Carbs: 18g; Protein: 25g

301. Lamb Racks and Fennel Mix Recipe

(Prep + Cooking Time: 26 Minutes | **Serves:** 4)

Ingredients:

- 12 oz. lamb racks
- 4 figs; cut into halves
- 1/8-cup apple cider vinegar
- 2 fennel bulbs, sliced.
- 1-tbsp. brown sugar
- 2-tbsp. olive oil
- Salt and black pepper to the taste.

Directions:

1. Take a bowl and mix fennel with figs, vinegar, sugar and oil, toss to coat well, transfer to a baking dish that fits your air fryer, introduce in your air fryer and cook at 350 °F, for 6 minutes
2. Season lamb with salt and pepper, add to the baking dish with the fennel mix and air fry for 10 minutes more. Divide everything on plates and serve.

Nutrition Values (Per Serving): Calories: 240; Fat: 9g; Fiber: 3g; Carbs: 15g; Protein: 12g

302. Coffee Flavored Steaks Recipe

(Prep + Cooking Time: 25 Minutes | **Serves:** 4)

Ingredients:

- 1 ½-tbsp. coffee, ground.
- 4 rib eye steaks
- ½-tbsp. sweet paprika
- 2-tbsp. chili powder
- 2-tsp. onion powder
- 1/4-tsp. ginger, ground.
- 2-tsp. garlic powder
- 1/4 teaspoon; coriander, ground
- A pinch of cayenne pepper
- Black pepper to the taste

Directions:

1. Take a bowl and mix coffee with paprika, chili powder, garlic powder, onion powder, ginger, coriander, cayenne and black pepper; stir, rub steaks with this mix, put in preheated air fryer and cook at 360 °F, for 15 minutes. Divide steaks on plates and serve with a side salad.

Nutrition Values (Per Serving): Calories: 160; Fat: 10g; Fiber: 8g; Carbs: 14g; Protein: 12g

303. Balsamic Beef Recipe.

(Prep + Cooking Time: 1 hour 10 Minutes | **Serves:** 6)

Ingredients:

- ½-cup balsamic vinegar
- 1-cup beef stock
- 4 garlic cloves, minced.
- 1 medium beef roast
- 1-tbsp. soy sauce
- 1-tbsp. Worcestershire sauce
- 1-tbsp. honey

Directions:

1. In a heat proof dish that fits your air fryer, mix roast with roast with Worcestershire sauce, vinegar, stock, honey, soy sauce and garlic, toss well, introduce in your air fryer and cook at 370 °F, for 1 hour
2. Slice roast, divide among plates, drizzle the sauce all over and serve

Nutrition Values (Per Serving): Calories: 311; Fat: 7g; Fiber: 12g; Carbs: 20g; Protein: 16

304. Sausage and Kale Recipe

(Prep + Cooking Time: 30 Minutes | **Serves:** 4)

Ingredients:

- 1 ½ lb. Italian pork sausage, sliced.
- 5 lbs. kale, chopped.
- 1/4-cup red hot chili pepper, chopped.
- ½-cup red bell pepper, chopped.
- 1-cup water
- 1-cup yellow onion, chopped.
- one-tsp. garlic, minced.
- Salt and black pepper to the taste.

Directions:

1. In a pan that fits your air fryer, mix sausage with onion, bell pepper, salt, pepper, kale, garlic, water and chili pepper, toss, introduce in preheated air fryer and cook at 300 °F, for 20 minutes. Divide everything on plates and serve.

Nutrition Values (Per Serving): Calories: 150; Fat: 4g; Fiber: 1g; Carbs: 12g; Protein: 14g

305. Pork Chops and Roasted Peppers Recipe

(Prep + Cooking Time: 26 Minutes | **Serves:** 4)

Ingredients:

- 4 pork chops; bone in
- 3 garlic cloves, minced.
- 2 roasted bell peppers, chopped.
- 2-tbsp. thyme, chopped.
- 3-tbsp. olive oil
- 3-tbsp. lemon juice
- 1-tbsp. smoked paprika
- Salt and black pepper to the taste.

Directions:

1. In a pan that fits your air fryer, mix pork chops with oil, lemon juice, smoked paprika, thyme, garlic, bell peppers, salt and pepper, toss well, introduce in your air fryer and cook at 400 °F, for 16 minutes
2. Divide pork chops and peppers mix on plates and serve right away.

Nutrition Values (Per Serving): Calories: 321; Fat: 6g; Fiber: 8g; Carbs: 14g; Protein: 17g

306. Ham and Veggie Air Fried Mix Recipe.

(Prep + Cooking Time: 30 Minutes | **Serves:** 6)

Ingredients:

- 2-cups ham, chopped.
- 1-cup baby carrots
- 6 oz. sweet peas
- 4 oz. mushrooms, halved.
- 3-cups milk
- 1/4-cup butter
- 1/4-cup flour
- ½-tsp. thyme; dried

Directions:

1. Heat up a large pan that fits your air fryer with the butter over medium heat, melt it, add flour and whisk well
2. Add milk and, well again and take off heat.
3. Add thyme, ham, peas, mushrooms and baby carrots, toss, put in your air fryer and cook at 360 °F, for 20 minutes. Divide everything on plates and serve.

Nutrition Values (Per Serving): Calories: 311; Fat: 6g; Fiber: 8g; Carbs: 12g; Protein: 7g

307. Lamb and Spinach Mix Recipe.

(Prep + Cooking Time: 45 Minutes | **Serves:** 6)

Ingredients:

- 1 lb. lamb meat, cubed.
- 1 lb. spinach
- 14 oz. canned tomatoes, chopped.
- 2 garlic cloves, minced.
- 1 red onion, chopped.
- 2-tbsp. ginger, grated.
- 2-tsp. cumin powder
- one-tsp. garam masala
- 2-tsp. cardamom, ground.
- ½-tsp. chili powder
- one-tsp. turmeric
- 2-tsp. coriander, ground.

Directions:

1. In a heat proof dish that fits your air fryer, mix lamb with spinach, tomatoes, ginger, garlic, onion, cardamom, cloves, cumin, garam masala, chili, turmeric and coriander; stir, introduce in preheated air fryer and cook at 360 °F, for 35 minutes Divide into bowls and serve.

Nutrition Values (Per Serving): Calories: 160; Fat: 6g; Fiber: 3g; Carbs: 17g; Protein: 20g

308. Pork Chops and Sage Sauce Recipe

(Prep + Cooking Time: 25 Minutes | **Serves:** 2)

Ingredients:

- 2 pork chops
- 1 handful sage, chopped.
- 1 shallot, sliced.
- 2-tbsp. butter
- 1-tbsp. olive oil
- one-tsp. lemon juice
- Salt and black pepper to the taste.

Directions:

1. Season pork chops with salt and pepper, rub with the oil, put in your air fryer and cook at 370 °F, for 10 minutes; flipping them halfway
2. Meanwhile, heat up a pan with the butter over medium heat, add shallot; stir and cook for 2 minutes.
3. Add sage and lemon juice; stir well, cook for a few more minutes and take off heat
4. Divide pork chops on plates, drizzle sage sauce all over and serve.

Nutrition Values (Per Serving): Calories: 265; Fat: 6g; Fiber: 8g; Carbs: 19g; Protein: 12g

Side Dish Recipes

309. Green Beans Dish.

(Prep + Cooking Time: 35 Minutes | **Serves:** 4)

Ingredients:

- 1 ½ lbs. green beans; trimmed and steamed for 2 minutes
- ½ lb. shallots, chopped.
- 1/4-cup almonds; toasted
- 2-tbsp. olive oil
- Salt and black pepper to the taste.

Directions:

1. In your air fryer's basket, mix green beans with salt, pepper, shallots, almonds and oil; toss well and cook at 400 °F, for 25 minutes. Divide among plates and serve as a side dish

Nutrition Values (Per Serving): Calories: 152; Fat: 3g; Fiber: 6g; Carbs: 7g; Protein: 4g

310. Special Risotto

(Prep + Cooking Time: 40 Minutes | **Serves:** 4)

Ingredients:

- 2 yellow onions, chopped.
- 1 ½-cups rice
- ½-cup parmesan, grated.
- 2-cups chicken stock
- 1-cup mushrooms, sliced.
- 2-cups beer
- 2-tbsp. olive oil
- 1-tbsp. butter
- one-tsp. oregano; dried
- one-tsp. basil; dried

Directions:

1. In a dish that fits your air fryer, mix oil with onions, mushrooms, basil and oregano and stir
2. Add rice, beer, butter, stock and butter; stir again, place in your air fryer's basket and cook at 350 °F, for 30 minutes. Divide among plates and serve with grated parmesan on top as a side dish.

Nutrition Values (Per Serving): Calories: 142; Fat: 4g; Fiber: 4g; Carbs: 6g; Protein: 4g

311. Cauliflower Rice Dish.

(Prep + Cooking Time: 50 Minutes | **Serves:** 8)

Ingredients:

- 15 oz. mushrooms, chopped.
- 9 oz. water chestnuts; drained
- 3 garlic cloves, minced.
- 1 cauliflower head; riced
- 3/4-cup peas
- 1 egg, whisked.
- 1-tbsp. peanut oil
- 1-tbsp. sesame oil
- 4-tbsp. soy sauce
- 1-tbsp. ginger, grated.
- Juice from ½ lemon

Directions:

1. In your air fryer; mix cauliflower rice with peanut oil, sesame oil, soy sauce, garlic, ginger and lemon juice; stir, cover and cook at 350 °F, for 20 minutes.

2. Add chestnuts, peas, mushrooms and egg; toss and cook at 360 °F, for 20 minutes more. Divide among plates and serve for breakfast

Nutrition Values (Per Serving): Calories: 142; Fat: 3g; Fiber: 2g; Carbs: 6g; Protein: 4g

312. Yummy Biscuits

(Prep + Cooking Time: 30 Minutes | **Serves:** 8)

Ingredients:

- 2 ⅓-cup self-rising flour
- 1 ⅓-cup buttermilk
- 1-cup flour
- ½-cup butter+ 1 tablespoon, melted.
- ½-cup cheddar cheese, grated.
- 2-tbsp. sugar

Directions:

1. Take a bowl and mix self-rising flour with ½-cup butter, sugar, cheddar cheese and buttermilk and stir until you obtain a dough.
2. Spread 1-cup flour on a working surface, roll dough, flatten it, cut 8 circles with a cookie cutter and coat them with flour.
3. Line your air fryer's basket with tin foil, add biscuits, brush them with melted butter and cook them at 380 °F, for 20 minutes. Divide among plates and serve as a side

Nutrition Values (Per Serving): Calories: 221; Fat: 3g; Fiber: 8g; Carbs: 12g; Protein: 4g

313. Hassel-Back Potatoes

(Prep + Cooking Time: 30 Minutes | **Serves:** 2)

Ingredients:

- 2 potatoes, peeled and thinly sliced almost all the way horizontally
- 2-tbsp. olive oil
- one-tsp. garlic, minced.
- ½-tsp. oregano; dried
- ½-tsp. basil; dried
- ½-tsp. sweet paprika
- Salt and black pepper to the taste.

Directions:

1. Take a bowl and mix oil with garlic, salt, pepper, oregano, basil and paprika and whisk really well.
2. Rub potatoes with this mix; place them in your air fryer's basket and fry them at 360 °F, for 20 minutes. Divide them on plates and serve as a side dish.

Nutrition Values (Per Serving): Calories: 172; Fat: 6g; Fiber: 6g; Carbs: 9g; Protein: 6g

314. Special Sweet Potato Fries

(Prep + Cooking Time: 30 Minutes | **Serves:** 2)

Ingredients:

- 2 sweet potatoes, peeled and cut into medium fries
- 1/4-cup ketchup
- 2-tbsp. mayonnaise
- 2-tbsp. olive oil
- 1/4-tsp. coriander, ground.
- ½-tsp. cumin, ground.
- ½-tsp. curry powder
- A pinch of ginger powder
- A pinch of cinnamon powder.
- Salt and black pepper to the taste.

Directions:

1. In your air fryer's basket; mix sweet potato fries with salt, pepper, coriander, curry powder and oil; toss well and cook at 370 °F, for 20 minutes; flipping them once.
2. Meanwhile, in a bowl, mix ketchup with mayo, cumin, ginger and cinnamon and whisk well. Divide fries on plates; drizzle ketchup mix over them and serve as a side dish.

Nutrition Values (Per Serving): Calories: 200; Fat: 5g; Fiber: 8g; Carbs: 9g; Protein: 7g

315. Yummy Garlic Potatoes

(Prep + Cooking Time: 30 Minutes | **Serves:** 6)

Ingredients:

- 3 lbs. red potatoes, halved.
- 5 garlic cloves, minced.
- 1/3-cup parmesan, grated.
- 2-tbsp. olive oil
- 2-tbsp. butter
- 2-tbsp. parsley, chopped.
- ½-tsp. oregano; dried
- one-tsp. thyme; dried
- ½-tsp. basil; dried
- Salt and black pepper to the taste.

Directions:

1. Take a bowl and mix potato halves with parsley, garlic, basil, oregano, thyme, salt, pepper, oil and butter; toss really well and transfer to your air fryer's basket.
2. Cover and cook at 400 °F, for 20 minutes; flipping them once. Sprinkle parmesan on top, divide potatoes on plates and serve as a side dish

Nutrition Values (Per Serving): Calories: 162; Fat: 5g; Fiber: 5g; Carbs: 7g; Protein: 5g

316. Delicious Cauliflower Cakes

(Prep + Cooking Time: 20 Minutes | **Serves:** 6)

Ingredients:

- 3 ½-cups cauliflower rice
- 1/4-cup white flour
- ½-cup parmesan, grated.
- 2 eggs
- Salt and black pepper to the taste.
- Cooking spray.

Directions:

1. Take a bowl and mix cauliflower rice with salt and pepper, stir and squeeze excess water.
2. Transfer cauliflower to another bowl; add eggs, salt, pepper, flour and parmesan; stir really well and shape your cakes
3. Grease your air fryer with cooking spray, heat it up at 400 degrees; add cauliflower cakes and cook them for 10 minutes flipping them halfway. Divide cakes on plates and serve as a side dish.

Nutrition Values (Per Serving): Calories: 125; Fat: 2g; Fiber: 6g; Carbs: 8g; Protein: 3g

317. Zucchini Fries Dish

(Prep + Cooking Time: 22 Minutes | **Serves:** 4)

Ingredients:

- 1 zucchini; cut into medium sticks
- 1-cup bread crumbs
- 2 eggs, whisked.
- ½-cup flour
- A drizzle of olive oil
- Salt and black pepper to the taste.

Directions:

1. Put flour in a bowl and mix with salt and pepper and stir.
2. Put breadcrumbs in another bowl
3. In a third bowl mix eggs with a pinch of salt and pepper.
4. Dredge zucchini fries in flour; then in eggs and in bread crumbs at the end.
5. Grease your air fryer with some olive oil, heat up at 400 degrees F; add zucchini fries and cook them for 12 minutes. Serve them as a side dish

Nutrition Values (Per Serving): Calories: 172; Fat: 3g; Fiber: 3g; Carbs: 7g; Protein: 3g

318. Easy Creamy Endives.

(Prep + Cooking Time: 20 Minutes | **Serves:** 6)

Ingredients:

- 6 endives; trimmed and halved
- ½-cup Greek yogurt
- 3-tbsp. lemon juice
- ½-tsp. curry powder
- one-tsp. garlic powder
- Salt and black pepper to the taste.

Directions:

1. In a bowl mix endives with garlic powder, yogurt, curry powder, salt, pepper and lemon juice; toss, leave aside for 10 minutes and transfer to your preheated air fryer at 350 degrees F. Cook endives for 10 minutes; divide them on plates and serve as a side dish.

Nutrition Values (Per Serving): Calories: 100; Fat: 2g; Fiber: 2g; Carbs: 7g; Protein: 4g

319. Tasty Barley Risotto

(Prep + Cooking Time: 40 Minutes | **Serves:** 8)

Ingredients:

- 2 lbs. sweet potato, peeled and chopped.
- 3/4 lb. barley
- 5-cups veggie stock
- 3 oz. mushrooms, sliced.
- 2 oz. skim milk
- 2 yellow onions, chopped.
- 2 garlic cloves, minced.
- 3-tbsp. olive oil
- one-tsp. thyme; dried
- one-tsp. tarragon; dried
- Salt and black pepper to the taste.

Directions:

1. Put stock in a pot, add barley; stir, bring to a boil over medium heat and cook for 15 minutes.
2. Heat up your air fryer at 350 degrees F; add oil and heat it up.
3. Add barley, onions, garlic, mushrooms, milk, salt, pepper, tarragon and sweet potato; stir and cook for 15 minutes more. Divide among plates and serve as a side dish

Nutrition Values (Per Serving): Calories: 124; Fat: 4g; Fiber: 4g; Carbs: 6g; Protein: 4g

320. Roasted Pumpkin Side Dish

(Prep + Cooking Time: 22 Minutes | **Serves:** 4)

Ingredients:

- 1 ½ lb. pumpkin; deseeded, sliced and roughly chopped.
- 3 garlic cloves, minced.
- 1-tbsp. olive oil

- A pinch of brown sugar
- A pinch of cinnamon powder.
- A pinch of nutmeg, ground.
- A pinch of sea salt

Directions:

1. In your air fryer's basket, mix pumpkin with garlic, oil, salt, brown sugar, cinnamon and nutmeg; toss well, cover and cook at 370 °F, for 12 minutes. Divide among plates and serve as a side dish.

Nutrition Values (Per Serving): Calories: 200; Fat: 5g; Fiber: 4g; Carbs: 7g; Protein: 4g

321. Parmesan Button Mushrooms.

(Prep + Cooking Time: 25 Minutes | **Serves:** 3)

Ingredients:

- 9 button mushroom caps
- 1 egg white
- 3 cream cracker slices, crumbled.
- 1-tbsp. butter, melted.
- 2-tbsp. parmesan, grated.
- one-tsp. Italian seasoning
- A pinch of salt and black pepper

Directions:

1. Take a bowl and mix crackers with egg white, parmesan, Italian seasoning, butter, salt and pepper; stir well and stuff mushrooms with this mix.
2. Arrange mushrooms in your air fryer's basket and cook them at 360 °F, for 15 minutes. Divide among plates and serve as a side dish

Nutrition Values (Per Serving): Calories: 124; Fat: 4g; Fiber: 4g; Carbs: 7g; Protein: 3g

322. Amazing Potato Wedges

(Prep + Cooking Time: 35 Minutes | **Serves:** 4)

Ingredients:

- 2 potatoes; cut into wedges
- 2-tbsp. sweet chili sauce
- 3-tbsp. sour cream
- 1-tbsp. olive oil
- Salt and black pepper to the taste.

Directions:

1. Take a bowl and mix potato wedges with oil, salt and pepper, toss well, add to air fryer's basket and cook at 360 °F, for 25 minutes; flipping them once. Divide potato wedges on plates; drizzle sour cream and chili sauce all over and serve them as a side dish

Nutrition Values (Per Serving): Calories: 171; Fat: 8g; Fiber: 9g; Carbs: 18g; Protein: 7g

323. Eggplant Fries Dish.

(Prep + Cooking Time: 15 Minutes | **Serves:** 4)

Ingredients:

- 1 eggplant, peeled and cut into medium fries
- 2-cups panko bread crumbs
- ½-cup Italian cheese, shredded.
- 1 egg, whisked.
- 2-tbsp. milk
- A pinch of salt and black pepper to the taste
- Cooking spray.

Directions:

1. Take a bowl and mix egg with milk, salt and pepper and whisk well.
2. In another bowl; mix panko with cheese and stir
3. Dip eggplant fries in egg mix, then coat in panko mix, place them in your air fryer greased with cooking spray and cook at 400 °F, for 5 minutes. Divide among plates and serve as a side dish.

Nutrition Values (Per Serving): Calories: 162; Fat: 5g; Fiber: 5g; Carbs: 7g; Protein: 6g

324. Mushrooms and Cream

(Prep + Cooking Time: 20 Minutes | **Serves:** 6)

Ingredients:

- 2 bacon strips, chopped.
- 24 mushr ooms; stems removed
- ½-cup sour cream
- 1-cup cheddar cheese, grated.
- 1 green bell pepper, chopped.
- 1 yellow onion, chopped.
- 1 carrot, grated.
- Salt and black pepper to the taste.

Directions:

1. Heat up a pan over medium high heat; add bacon, onion, bell pepper and carrot; stir and cook for 1 minute.
2. Add salt, pepper and sour cream, stir cook for 1 minute more; take off heat and cool down
3. Stuff mushrooms with this mix, sprinkle cheese on top and cook at 360 °F, for 8 minutes. Divide among plates and serve as a side dish.

Nutrition Values (Per Serving): Calories: 211; Fat: 4g; Fiber: 7g; Carbs: 8g; Protein: 3g

325. Roasted Carrots

(Prep + Cooking Time: 30 Minutes | **Serves:** 4)

Ingredients:

- 1 lb. baby carrots
- 4-tbsp. orange juice
- 2-tsp. olive oil
- one-tsp. herbs de Provence

Directions:

1. In your air fryer's basket, mix carrots with herbs de Provence, oil and orange juice; toss and cook at 320 °F, for 20 minutes. Divide among plates and serve as a side dish.

Nutrition Values (Per Serving): Calories: 112; Fat: 2g; Fiber: 3g; Carbs: 4g; Protein: 3g

326. Herbed Tomatoes Dish.

(Prep + Cooking Time: 25 Minutes | **Serves:** 4)

Ingredients:

- 4 big tomatoes, halved.and insides scooped out
- 2 garlic cloves, minced.
- 1-tbsp. olive oil
- ½-tsp. thyme, chopped.
- Salt and black pepper to the taste.

Directions:

1. In your air fryer, mix tomatoes with salt, pepper, oil, garlic and thyme; toss and cook at 390 °F, for 15 minutes. Divide among plates and serve them as a side dish.

Nutrition Values (Per Serving): Calories: 112; Fat: 1g; Fiber: 3g; Carbs: 4g; Protein: 4g

327. Roasted Parsnips Dish

(Prep + Cooking Time: 50 Minutes | **Serves:** 6)

Ingredients:

- 2 lbs. parsnips, peeled and cut into medium chunks
- 2-tbsp. maple syrup
- 1-tbsp. parsley flakes; dried
- 1-tbsp. olive oil

Directions:

1. Preheat your air fryer at 360 degrees F; add oil and heat it up as well
2. Add parsnips, parsley flakes and maple syrup; toss and cook them for 40 minutes. Divide among plates and serve as a side dish.

Nutrition Values (Per Serving): Calories: 124; Fat: 3g; Fiber: 3g; Carbs: 7g; Protein: 4g

328. Button Mushroom Dish

(Prep + Cooking Time: 18 Minutes | **Serves:** 4)

Ingredients:

- 10 button mushrooms; stems removed
- 2-tbsp. mozzarella, grated.
- 1-tbsp. dill, chopped.
- 1-tbsp. Italian seasoning
- 2-tbsp. cheddar cheese, grated.
- 1-tbsp. olive oil
- Salt and black pepper to the taste.

Directions:

1. Take a bowl and mix mushrooms with Italian seasoning, salt, pepper, oil and dill and rub well.
2. Arrange mushrooms in your air fryer's basket; sprinkle mozzarella and cheddar in each and cook them at 360 °F, for 8 minutes. Divide them on plates and serve them as a side dish

Nutrition Values (Per Serving): Calories: 241; Fat: 7g; Fiber: 8g; Carbs: 14g; Protein: 6g

329. Roasted Eggplant Dish.

(Prep + Cooking Time: 30 Minutes | **Serves:** 6)

Ingredients:

- 1 ½ lbs. eggplant, cubed.
- 2 bay leaves
- 1-tbsp. olive oil
- one-tsp. onion powder
- one-tsp. sumac
- one-tsp. garlic powder
- 2-tsp. za'atar
- Juice from ½ lemon

Directions:

1. In your air fryer; mix eggplant cubes with oil, garlic powder, onion powder, sumac, za'atar, lemon juice and bay leaves; toss and cook at 370 °F, for 20 minutes. Divide among plates and serve as a side dish

Nutrition Values (Per Serving): Calories: 172; Fat: 4g; Fiber: 7g; Carbs: 12g; Protein: 3g

330. Corn with Cheese and Lime

(Prep + Cooking Time: 25 Minutes | **Serves:** 2)

Ingredients:

- 2 corns on the cob; husks removed
- ½-cup feta cheese, grated.
- 2-tsp. sweet paprika
- A drizzle of olive oil
- Juice from 2 limes

Directions:

1. Rub corn with oil and paprika, place in your air fryer and cook at 400 °F, for 15 minutes; flipping once. Divide corn on plates; sprinkle cheese on top, drizzle lime juice and serve as a side dish.

Nutrition Values (Per Serving): Calories: 200; Fat: 5g; Fiber: 2g; Carbs: 6g; Protein: 6g

331. Creamy Fried Potato Dish.

(Prep + Cooking Time: 1 hour and 30 minutes | **Serves:** 2)

Ingredients:

- 2 bacon strips, cooked and chopped.
- 1/3-cup cheddar cheese, shredded.
- 1 big potato
- 2-tbsp. heavy cream
- 1-tbsp. green onions, chopped.
- 1-tbsp. butter
- one-tsp. olive oil
- Salt and black pepper to the taste.

Directions:

1. Rub potato with oil, season with salt and pepper, place in preheated air fryer and cook at 400 °F, for 30 minutes.
2. Flip potato, cook for 30 minutes more; transfer to a cutting board, cool it down, slice in half lengthwise and scoop pulp in a bowl
3. Add bacon, cheese, butter, heavy cream, green onions, salt and pepper; stir well and stuff potato skins with this mix.
4. Return potatoes to your air fryer and cook them at 400 °F, for 20 minutes. Divide among plates and serve as a side dish

Nutrition Values (Per Serving): Calories: 172; Fat: 5g; Fiber: 7g; Carbs: 9g; Protein: 4g

332. Carrots and Rhubarb Dish

(Prep + Cooking Time: 50 Minutes | **Serves:** 4)

Ingredients:

- 1 lb. rhubarb; roughly chopped.
- 1 lb. baby carrots
- 1 orange, peeled, cut into medium segments and zest grated
- ½-tsp. stevia
- 2-tsp. walnut oil
- ½-cup walnuts, halved.

Directions:

1. Put the oil in your air fryer, add carrots; toss and fry them at 380 °F, for 20 minutes.
2. Add rhubarb, orange zest, stevia and walnuts; toss and cook for 20 minutes more. Add orange segments; toss and serve as a side dish

Nutrition Values (Per Serving): Calories: 172; Fat: 2g; Fiber: 3g; Carbs: 4g; Protein: 4g

333. Vermouth White Mushrooms.

(Prep + Cooking Time: 35 Minutes | **Serves:** 4)

Ingredients:

- 2 lbs. white mushrooms
- 2 garlic cloves, minced.
- 2-tbsp. white vermouth
- 1-tbsp. olive oil
- 2-tsp. herbs de Provence

Directions:

1. In your air fryer; mix oil with mushrooms, herbs de Provence and garlic; toss and cook at 350 °F, for 20 minutes.
2. Add vermouth, toss and cook for 5 minutes more. Divide among plates and serve as a side dish

Nutrition Values (Per Serving): Calories: 121; Fat: 2g; Fiber: 5g; Carbs: 7g; Protein: 4g

334. Fried Broccoli

(Prep + Cooking Time: 30 Minutes | **Serves:** 4)

Ingredients:

- 1 broccoli head; florets separated
- 3 garlic cloves, minced.
- 1-tbsp. duck fat
- 1-tbsp. sesame seeds
- Juice from ½ lemon

Directions:

1. Heat up your air fryer at 350 degrees F; add duck fat and heat as well
2. Add broccoli, garlic, lemon juice and sesame seeds; toss and cook for 20 minutes. Divide among plates and serve as a side dish.

Nutrition Values (Per Serving): Calories: 132; Fat: 3g; Fiber: 3g; Carbs: 6g; Protein: 4g

335. Onion Rings Dish

(Prep + Cooking Time: 20 Minutes | **Serves:** 3)

Ingredients:

- 1 onion cut into medium slices and rings separated
- 1 egg
- 1-cup milk
- 1¼-cups white flour
- 3/4-cup bread crumbs
- one-tsp. baking powder.
- A pinch of salt

Directions:

1. Take a bowl and mix flour with salt and baking powder; stir, dredge onion rings in this mix and place them on a separate plate.
2. Add milk and egg to flour mix and whisk well
3. Dip onion rings in this mix, dredge them in breadcrumbs; put them in your air fryer's basket and cook them at 360 °F, for 10 minutes. Divide among plates and serve as a side dish for a steak

Nutrition Values (Per Serving): Calories: 140; Fat: 8g; Fiber: 20g; Carbs: 12g; Protein: 3g

336. Veggie Fries Dish

(Prep + Cooking Time: 40 Minutes | **Serves:** 4)

Ingredients:

- 2 sweet potatoes cut into medium sticks
- 4 parsnips; cut into medium sticks
- 4 mixed carrots cut into medium sticks
- 2-tbsp. olive oil
- 1-tbsp. flour
- 2-tbsp. rosemary, chopped.
- ½-tsp. garlic powder
- Salt and black pepper to the taste.

Directions:

1. Put veggie fries in a bowl; add oil, garlic powder, salt, pepper, flour and rosemary and toss to coat.
2. Put sweet potatoes in your preheated air fryer; cook them for 10 minutes at 350 °F and transfer them to a platter
3. Put parsnip fries in your air fryer; cook for 5 minutes and transfer over potato fries.
4. Put carrot fries in your air fryer; cook for 15 minutes at 350 °F and transfer to the platter with the other fries. Divide veggie fries on plates and serve them as a side dish

Nutrition Values (Per Serving): Calories: 100; Fat: 0g; Fiber: 4g; Carbs: 7g; Protein: 4g

337. Potato Chips

(Prep + Cooking Time: 60 Minutes | **Serves:** 4)

Ingredients:

- 4 potatoes; scrubbed, peeled into thin chips, soaked in water for 30 minutes, drained and pat dried
- 1-tbsp. olive oil
- 2-tsp. rosemary, chopped.
- Salt to taste

Directions:

1. Take a bowl and mix potato chips with salt and oil toss to coat, place them in your air fryer's basket and cook at 330 °F, for 30 minutes. Divide among plates; sprinkle rosemary all over and serve as a side dish.

Nutrition Values (Per Serving): Calories: 200; Fat: 4g; Fiber: 4g; Carbs: 14g; Protein: 5g

338. Eggplant Dish

(Prep + Cooking Time: 20 Minutes | **Serves:** 4)

Ingredients:

- 8 baby eggplants; scooped in the center and pulp reserved
- 1 bunch coriander, chopped.
- 1 tomato chopped
- A pinch of oregano; dried
- 1 green bell pepper, chopped.
- 1 yellow onion, chopped.
- 1-tbsp. olive oil
- 1-tbsp. tomato paste
- ½-tsp. garlic powder
- Salt and black pepper to the taste.

Directions:

1. Heat up a pan with the oil over medium heat, add onion; stir and cook for 1 minute.
2. Add salt, pepper, eggplant pulp, oregano, green bell pepper, tomato paste, garlic power, coriander and tomato; stir, cook for 1-2 minutes more, take off heat and cool down

3. Stuff eggplants with this mix, place them in your air fryer's basket and cook at 360 °F, for 8 minutes. Divide eggplants on plates and serve them as a side dish

Nutrition Values (Per Serving): Calories: 200; Fat: 3g; Fiber: 7g; Carbs: 12g; Protein: 4g

339. Roasted Peppers Dish

(Prep + Cooking Time: 20 Minutes | **Serves:** 4)

Ingredients:

- 1 red bell pepper
- 1 oz. rocket leaves
- 1 green bell pepper
- 1 yellow bell pepper
- 1 lettuce head; cut into strips
- 2-tbsp. olive oil
- 1-tbsp. lemon juice
- 3-tbsp. Greek yogurt
- Salt and black pepper to the taste.

Directions:

1. Place bell peppers in your air fryer's basket, cook at 400 °F, for 10 minutes; transfer to a bowl, leave aside for 10 minutes; peel them, discard seeds, cut them in strips, transfer to a larger bowl; add rocket leaves and lettuce strips and toss
2. Take a bowl and mix oil with lemon juice, yogurt, salt and pepper and whisk well. Add this over bell peppers mix, toss to coat, divide among plates and serve as a side salad.

Nutrition Values (Per Serving): Calories: 170; Fat: 1g; Fiber: 1g; Carbs: 2g; Protein: 6g

340. Brussels Sprouts Dish

(Prep + Cooking Time: 25 Minutes | **Serves:** 4)

Ingredients:

- 1 lb. Brussels sprouts; trimmed and halved
- ½-cup mayonnaise
- 2-tbsp. roasted garlic; crushed
- 6-tsp. olive oil
- ½-tsp. thyme, chopped.
- Salt and black pepper to the taste.

Directions:

1. In your air fryer; mix Brussels sprouts with salt, pepper and oil; toss well and cook them at 390 °F, for 15 minutes.
2. Meanwhile, in a bowl, mix thyme with mayo and garlic and whisk well. Divide Brussels sprouts on plates; drizzle garlic sauce all over and serve as a side dish

Nutrition Values (Per Serving): Calories: 172; Fat: 6g; Fiber: 8g; Carbs: 12g; Protein: 6g

341. Coconut Potatoes

(Prep + Cooking Time: 30 Minutes | **Serves:** 4)

Ingredients:

- 2 potatoes, sliced.
- 4 oz. coconut cream
- 2 eggs, whisked.
- 1-tbsp. flour
- 1-tbsp. cheddar cheese, grated.
- Salt and black pepper to the taste.

Directions:

1. Place potato slices in your air fryer's basket and cook at 360 °F, for 10 minutes.
2. Meanwhile, in a bowl, mix eggs with coconut cream, salt, pepper and flour.

3. Arrange potatoes in your air fryer's pan, add coconut cream mix over them, sprinkle cheese, return to air fryer's basket and cook at 400 °F, for 10 minutes more. Divide among plates and serve as a side dish

Nutrition Values (Per Serving): Calories: 170; Fat: 4g; Fiber: 1g; Carbs: 15g; Protein: 17g

342. Cajun Onion Wedges Dish.

(Prep + Cooking Time: 25 Minutes | **Serves:** 4)

Ingredients:

- 2 big white onions; cut into wedges
- 1/4-cup milk
- 1/3-cup panko
- 2 eggs
- ½-tsp. Cajun seasoning
- 1 ½-tsp. paprika
- one-tsp. garlic powder
- A drizzle of olive oil
- Salt and black pepper to the taste.

Directions:

1. Take a bowl and mix panko with Cajun seasoning and oil and stir.
2. In another bowl; mix egg with milk, salt and pepper and stir
3. Sprinkle onion wedges with paprika and garlic powder, dip them in egg mix, then in bread crumbs mix; place in your air fryer's basket, cook at 360 °F, for 10 minutes; flip and cook for 5 minutes more. Divide among plates and serve as a side dish

Nutrition Values (Per Serving): Calories: 200; Fat: 2g; Fiber: 2g; Carbs: 14g; Protein: 7g

343. Greek Veggie Dish

(Prep + Cooking Time: 55 Minutes | **Serves:** 4)

Ingredients:

- 2 onions, chopped.
- 1 zucchini, sliced.
- 4 tomatoes; cut into quarters
- 2 red bell peppers, chopped.
- 2 garlic cloves, minced.
- 1 eggplant, sliced.
- 1 thyme spring, chopped.
- 3-tbsp. olive oil
- 1 bay leaf
- Salt and black pepper to the taste.

Directions:

1. In your air fryer's pan; mix eggplant slices with zucchini ones, bell peppers, garlic, oil, bay leaf, thyme, onions, tomatoes, salt and pepper; toss and cook them at 300 °F, for 35 minutes. Divide among plates and serve as a side dish.

Nutrition Values (Per Serving): Calories: 200; Fat: 1g; Fiber: 3g; Carbs: 7g; Protein: 6g

344. Air Fried Tomatoes.

(Prep + Cooking Time: 15 Minutes | **Serves:** 4)

Ingredients:

- ½-tbsp. Creole seasoning
- 1-cup buttermilk
- 1-cup panko bread crumbs
- 2 green tomatoes, sliced.
- Salt and black pepper to the taste.
- ½-cup flour
- Cooking spray.

Directions:

1. Season tomato slices with salt and pepper.
2. Put flour in a bowl; buttermilk in another and panko crumbs and Creole seasoning in a third one
3. Dredge tomato slices in flour; then in buttermilk and panko bread crumbs, place them in your air fryer's basket greased with cooking spray and cook them at 400 °F, for 5 minutes. Divide among plates and serve as a side dish

Nutrition Values (Per Serving): Calories: 124; Fat: 5g; Fiber: 7g; Carbs: 9g; Protein: 4g

345. Rice and Sausage Dish

(Prep + Cooking Time: 30 Minutes | **Serves:** 4)

Ingredients:

- 1 pork sausage, chopped.
- 2-cups white rice; already boiled
- 4 garlic cloves, minced.
- 1-tbsp. butter
- 2-tbsp. mozzarella cheese, shredded.
- 2-tbsp. carrot, chopped.
- 3-tbsp. cheddar cheese, grated.
- Salt and black pepper to the taste.

Directions:

1. Heat up your air fryer at 350 degrees F; add butter, melt it, add garlic, stir and brown for 2 minutes.
2. Add sausage, salt, pepper, carrots and rice; stir and cook at 350 °F, for 10 minutes. Add cheddar and mozzarella; toss, divide among plates and serve as a side dish.

Nutrition Values (Per Serving): Calories: 240; Fat: 12g; Fiber: 5g; Carbs: 20g; Protein: 13g

346. Brussels Sprouts and Pomegranate Seeds Dish.

(Prep + Cooking Time: 15 Minutes | **Serves:** 4)

Ingredients:

- 1 lb. Brussels sprouts; trimmed and halved
- 1/4-cup pine nuts; toasted
- 1-cup pomegranate seeds
- 1-tbsp. olive oil
- 2-tbsp. veggie stock
- Salt and black pepper to the taste.

Directions:

1. In a heat proof dish that fits your air fryer; mix Brussels sprouts with salt, pepper, pomegranate seeds, pine nuts, oil and stock; stir, place in your air fryer's basket and cook at 390 °F, for 10 minutes.
2. Divide among plates and serve as a side dish

Nutrition Values (Per Serving): Calories: 152; Fat: 4g; Fiber: 7g; Carbs: 12g; Protein: 3g

347. Quick Wild Rice Pilaf.

(Prep + Cooking Time: 35 Minutes | **Serves:** 12)

Ingredients:

- 1 shallot, chopped.
- 1-cup farro
- 3/4-cup cherries; dried
- 3/4-cup wild rice
- 4-cups chicken stock
- ½-cup hazelnuts; toasted and chopped
- A drizzle of olive oil
- 1-tbsp. parsley, chopped.
- one-tsp. garlic, minced.
- Salt and black pepper to the taste.
- Chopped chives for serving

Directions:

1. In a dish that fits your air fryer; mix shallot with garlic, oil, faro, wild rice, stock, salt, pepper, parsley, hazelnuts and cherries; stir, place in your air fryer's basket and cook at 350 °F, for 25 minutes. Divide among plates and serve as a side dish.

Nutrition Values (Per Serving): Calories: 142; Fat: 4g; Fiber: 4g; Carbs: 16g; Protein: 4g

348. Yummy Zucchini Croquettes.

(Prep + Cooking Time: 20 Minutes | **Serves:** 4)

Ingredients:

- 2 slices of bread, crumbled.
- 1 carrot, grated.
- 1 zucchini, grated.
- 1 egg
- 1-tbsp. corn flour
- 2-tbsp. parmesan cheese, grated.
- one-tsp. garlic, minced.
- ½-tsp. sweet paprika
- Salt and black pepper to the taste.

Directions:

1. Put zucchini in a bowl; add salt, leave aside for 10 minutes; squeeze excess water and transfer them to another bowl
2. Add carrots, salt, pepper, paprika, garlic, flour, parmesan, egg and bread crumbs; stir well, shape 8 croquettes, place them in your air fryer and cook at 360 °F, for 10 minutes. Divide among plates and serve as a side dish

Nutrition Values (Per Serving): Calories: 100; Fat: 3g; Fiber: 1g; Carbs: 7g; Protein: 4g

349. Colored Veggie Rice Recipe

(Prep + Cooking Time: 35 Minutes | **Serves:** 4)

Ingredients:

- 1-cup mixed carrots; peas, corn and green beans
- 2-cups basmati rice
- 2-cups water
- 5 black peppercorns
- 2 whole cardamoms
- 3 garlic cloves, minced.
- 2 bay leaves
- 3 whole cloves
- 2-tbsp. butter
- 1-tbsp. cumin seeds
- 1-tbsp. sugar
- one-tsp. cinnamon powder.
- ½-tsp. green chili, minced.
- ½-tsp. ginger, grated.
- Salt to the taste

Directions:

1. Pour the water in a heat proof dish that fits your air fryer
2. Add rice, mixed veggies, green chili, grated ginger, garlic cloves, cinnamon, cloves, butter, cumin seeds, bay leaves, cardamoms, black peppercorns, salt and sugar; stir, put in your air fryer's basket and cook at 370 °F, for 25 minutes
3. Divide among plates and serve as a side dish.

Nutrition Values (Per Serving): Calories: 283; Fat: 4g; Fiber: 8g; Carbs: 34g; Protein: 14g

350. Potato Casserole Dish

(Prep + Cooking Time: 55 Minutes | **Serves:** 4)

Ingredients:

- 3 lbs. sweet potatoes; scrubbed
- 1/4-cup milk
- 2-tbsp. white flour
- ½-tsp. nutmeg, ground.
- 1/4-tsp. allspice, ground.
- Salt to the taste

For the topping:

- 1/4-cup pecans; soaked, drained and ground
- 1/4-cup coconut, shredded.
- ½-cup almond flour
- ½-cup walnuts; soaked, drained and ground
- 1/4-cup sugar
- 5-tbsp. butter
- 1-tbsp. chia seeds
- one-tsp. cinnamon powder.

Directions:

1. Place potatoes in your air fryer's basket, prick them with a fork and cook at 360 °F, for 30 minutes.
2. Meanwhile, in a bowl, mix almond flour with pecans, walnuts, 1/4-cup coconut, 1/4-cup sugar, chia seeds, one-tsp. cinnamon and the butter and stir everything
3. Transfer potatoes to a cutting board, cool them, peel and place them in a baking dish that fits your air fryer.
4. Add milk, flour, salt, nutmeg and allspice and stir
5. Add crumble mix you've made earlier on top; place dish in your air fryer's basket and cook at 400 °F, for 8 minutes. Divide among plates and serve as a side dish

Nutrition Values (Per Serving): Calories: 162; Fat: 4g; Fiber: 8g; Carbs: 18g; Protein: 4g

351. Delightful Cauliflower and Broccoli.

(Prep + Cooking Time: 17 Minutes | **Serves:** 4)

Ingredients:

- 2 cauliflower heads; florets separated and steamed
- 4 anchovies
- 1 broccoli head; florets separated and steamed
- Zest from 1 orange, grated.
- Juice from 1 orange
- 4-tbsp. olive oil
- 1-tbsp. capers, chopped.
- A pinch of hot pepper flakes
- Salt and black pepper to the taste.

Directions:

1. Take a bowl and mix orange zest with orange juice, pepper flakes, anchovies, capers salt, pepper and olive oil and whisk well.
2. Add broccoli and cauliflower; toss well, transfer them to your air fryer's basket and cook at 400 °F, for 7 minutes. Divide among plates and serve as a side dish with some of the orange vinaigrette drizzled on top

Nutrition Values (Per Serving): Calories: 300; Fat: 4g; Fiber: 7g; Carbs: 28g; Protein: 4g

352. Flavored Cauliflower Dish

(Prep + Cooking Time: 20 Minutes | **Serves:** 4)

Ingredients:

- 12 cauliflower florets; steamed
- 2-tbsp. water
- 3-tbsp. white flour
- 1-tbsp. ginger, grated.
- 2-tsp. lemon juice
- 1/4-tsp. turmeric powder
- 1½-tsp. red chili powder
- ½-tsp. corn flour
- Salt and black pepper to the taste.
- Cooking spray.

Directions:

1. Take a bowl and mix chili powder with turmeric powder, ginger paste, salt, pepper, lemon juice, white flour, corn flour and water, stir, add cauliflower, toss well and transfer them to your air fryer's basket. Coat them with cooking spray, cook them at 400 °F, for 10 minutes, divide among plates and serve as a side dish.

Nutrition Values (Per Serving): Calories: 70; Fat: 1g; Fiber: 2g; Carbs: 12g; Protein: 3g

353. Delicious Tortilla Chips

(Prep + Cooking Time: 16 Minutes | **Serves:** 4)

Ingredients:

- 8 corn tortillas; cut into triangles
- 1-tbsp. olive oil
- A pinch of sweet paprika
- A pinch of garlic powder
- Salt and black pepper to the taste.

Directions:

1. Take a bowl and mix tortilla chips with oil, add salt, pepper, garlic powder and paprika; toss well, place them in your air fryer's basket and cook them at 400 °F, for 6 minutes. Serve them as a side for a fish dish.

Nutrition Values (Per Serving): Calories: 53; Fat: 1g; Fiber: 1g; Carbs: 6g; Protein: 4g

354. Maple Glazed Beets

(Prep + Cooking Time: 50 Minutes | **Serves:** 8)

Ingredients:

- 3 lbs. small beets; trimmed
- 4-tbsp. maple syrup
- 1-tbsp. duck fat

Directions:

1. Heat up your air fryer at 360 degrees F; add duck fat and heat it up
2. Add beets and maple syrup; toss and cook for 40 minutes. Divide among plates and serve as a side dish.

Nutrition Values (Per Serving): Calories: 121; Fat: 3g; Fiber: 2g; Carbs: 3g; Protein: 4g

355. Brussels Sprouts and Potatoes

(Prep + Cooking Time: 18 Minutes | **Serves:** 4)

Ingredients:

- 1 ½ lbs. Brussels sprouts; washed and trimmed
- 1-cup new potatoes, chopped.
- 1 ½-tbsp. bread crumbs
- 1 ½-tbsp. butter
- Salt and black pepper to the taste.

Directions:

1. Put Brussels sprouts and potatoes in your air fryer's pan, add bread crumbs, salt, pepper and butter
2. Toss well and cook at 400 °F, for 8 minutes.
3. Divide among plates and serve as a side dish

Nutrition Values (Per Serving): Calories: 152; Fat: 3g; Fiber: 7g; Carbs: 17g; Protein: 4g

356. Tasty Potatoes Patties.

(Prep + Cooking Time: 18 Minutes | **Serves:** 4)

Ingredients:

- 4 potatoes; cubed, boiled and mashed
- 1-cup parmesan, grated.
- 2 egg yolks
- 3-tbsp. chives, chopped.
- 2-tbsp. white flour
- A pinch of nutmeg
- Salt and black pepper to the taste.

For the breading:

- 1/4-cup bread crumbs
- 2 eggs, whisked.
- 1/4-cup white flour
- 3-tbsp. vegetable oil

Directions:

1. Take a bowl and mix mashed potatoes with egg yolks, salt, pepper, nutmeg, parmesan, chives and 2-tbsp. flour; stir well, shape medium cakes and place them on a plate.
2. In another bowl; mix vegetable oil with bread crumbs and stir.
3. Put whisked eggs in a third bowl and 1/4-cup flour in a forth one. Dip cakes in flour, then in eggs and in breadcrumbs at the end; place them in your air fryer's basket, cook them at 390 °F, for 8 minutes; divide among plates and serve as a side dish

Nutrition Values (Per Serving): Calories: 140; Fat: 3g; Fiber: 4g; Carbs: 17g; Protein: 4g

357. Creamy Potatoes Dish

(Prep + Cooking Time: 30 Minutes | **Serves:** 4)

Ingredients:

- 1 ½ lbs. potatoes, peeled and cubed
- 1-cup Greek yogurt
- 1-tbsp. hot paprika
- 2-tbsp. olive oil
- Salt and black pepper to the taste.

Directions:

1. Put potatoes in a bowl; add water to cover, leave aside for 10 minutes; drain, pat dry them, transfer to another bowl; add salt, pepper, paprika and half of the oil and toss them well
2. Put potatoes in your air fryer's basket and cook at 360 °F, for 20 minutes.

3. Take a bowl and mix yogurt with salt, pepper and the rest of the oil and whisk. Divide potatoes on plates, drizzle yogurt dressing all over; toss them and serve as a side dish

Nutrition Values (Per Serving): Calories: 170; Fat: 3g; Fiber: 5g; Carbs: 20g; Protein: 5g

358. Roasted Peppers Dish

(Prep + Cooking Time: 30 Minutes | **Serves:** 4)

Ingredients:

- 4 yellow bell peppers; cut into medium strips
- 4 red bell peppers; cut into medium strips
- 1 yellow onion, chopped.
- 4 green bell peppers; cut into medium strips
- 1-tbsp. olive oil
- 1-tbsp. sweet paprika
- Salt and black pepper to the taste.

Directions:

1. In your air fryer; mix red bell peppers with green and yellow ones.
2. Add paprika, oil, onion, salt and pepper; toss and cook at 350 °F, for 20 minutes. Divide among plates and serve as a side dish.

Nutrition Values (Per Serving): Calories: 142; Fat: 4g; Fiber: 4g; Carbs: 7g; Protein: 4g

359. Lemony Artichokes Side Dish

(Prep + Cooking Time: 25 Minutes | **Serves:** 4)

Ingredients:

- 2 medium artichokes; trimmed and halved
- 2-tbsp. lemon juice
- Salt and black pepper to the taste.
- Cooking spray.

Directions:

1. Grease your air fryer with cooking spray, add artichokes; drizzle lemon juice and sprinkle salt and black pepper and cook them at 380 °F, for 15 minutes. Divide them on plates and serve as a side dish.

Nutrition Values (Per Serving): Calories: 121; Fat: 3g; Fiber: 6g; Carbs: 9g; Protein: 4g

360. Pumpkin Rice Dish.

(Prep + Cooking Time: 35 Minutes | **Serves:** 4)

Ingredients:

- 12 oz. white rice
- 1 small yellow onion, chopped.
- 2 garlic cloves, minced.
- 4-cups chicken stock
- 6 oz. pumpkin puree
- 2-tbsp. olive oil
- ½-tsp. nutmeg
- ½-tsp. cinnamon powder.
- ½-tsp. allspice
- one-tsp. thyme, chopped.
- ½-tsp. ginger, grated.
- 4 oz. heavy cream

Directions:

1. In a dish that fits your air fryer; mix oil with onion, garlic, rice, stock, pumpkin puree, nutmeg, thyme, ginger, cinnamon, allspice and cream; stir well,

2. place in your air fryer's basket and cook at 360 °F, for 30 minutes. Divide among plates and serve as a side dish.

Nutrition Values (Per Serving): Calories: 261; Fat: 6g; Fiber: 7g; Carbs: 29g; Protein: 4g

361. Air Fried Red Cabbage

(Prep + Cooking Time: 25 Minutes | **Serves:** 4)

Ingredients:

- ½-cup yellow onion, chopped.
- 6-cups red cabbage, chopped.
- 1-cup applesauce
- 1-cup veggie stock
- 4 garlic cloves, minced.
- 1-tbsp. olive oil
- 1-tbsp. apple cider vinegar
- Salt and black pepper to the taste.

Directions:

1. In a heat proof dish that fits your air fryer; mix cabbage with onion, garlic, oil, stock, vinegar, applesauce, salt and pepper; toss really well, place dish in your air fryer's basket and cook at 380 °F, for 15 minutes. Divide among plates and serve as a side dish.

Nutrition Values (Per Serving): Calories: 172; Fat: 7g; Fiber: 7g; Carbs: 14g; Protein: 5g

362. Simple Cauliflower Bars

(Prep + Cooking Time: 35 Minutes | **Serves:** 12)

Ingredients:

- 1 big cauliflower head; florets separated
- 1/4-cup egg whites
- ½-cup mozzarella, shredded.
- one-tsp. Italian seasoning
- Salt and black pepper to the taste.

Directions:

1. Put cauliflower florets in your food processor; pulse well, spread on a lined baking sheet that fits your air fryer, introduce in the fryer and cook at 360 °F, for 10 minutes
2. Transfer cauliflower to a bowl; add salt, pepper, cheese, egg whites and Italian seasoning; stir really well, spread this into a rectangle pan that fits your air fryer; press well, introduce in the fryer and cook at 360 °F, for 15 minutes more. Cut into 12 bars, arrange them on a platter and serve as a snack

Nutrition Values (Per Serving): Calories: 50; Fat: 1g; Fiber: 2g; Carbs: 3g; Protein: 3g

363. Artichokes and Tarragon Sauce Dish.

(Prep + Cooking Time: 28 Minutes | **Serves:** 4)

Ingredients:

- 4 artichokes; trimmed
- 1 celery stalk, chopped.
- ½-cup olive oil
- 2-tbsp. lemon juice
- 2-tbsp. chicken stock
- 2-tbsp. tarragon, chopped.
- Lemon zest from 2 lemons, grated.
- Salt to the taste

Directions:

1. In your food processor; mix tarragon, chicken stock, lemon zest, lemon juice, celery, salt and olive oil and pulse very well

2. Take a bowl and mix artichokes with tarragon and lemon sauce; toss well, transfer them to your air fryer's basket and cook at 380 °F, for 18 minutes.
3. Divide artichokes on plates; drizzle the rest of the sauce all over and serve as a side dish

Nutrition Values (Per Serving): Calories: 215; Fat: 3g; Fiber: 8g; Carbs: 28g; Protein: 6g

364. Avocado Fries Dish

(Prep + Cooking Time: 20 Minutes | **Serves:** 4)

Ingredients:

- 1 avocado; pitted, peeled, sliced and cut into medium fries
- 1 egg, whisked.
- ½-cup panko bread crumbs
- 1-tbsp. olive oil
- 1-tbsp. lemon juice
- Salt and black pepper to the taste.

Directions:

1. Take a bowl and mix panko with salt and pepper and stir.
2. In another bowl; mix egg with a pinch of salt and whisk
3. In a third bowl; mix avocado fries with lemon juice and oil and toss.
4. Dip fries in egg, then in panko, place them in your air fryer's basket and cook at 390 °F, for 10 minutes; shaking halfway. Divide among plates and serve as a side dish

Nutrition Values (Per Serving): Calories: 130; Fat: 11g; Fiber: 3g; Carbs: 16g; Protein: 4g

365. Easy Mushroom Cakes

(Prep + Cooking Time: 18 Minutes | **Serves:** 8)

Ingredients:

- 4 oz. mushrooms, chopped.
- 14 oz. milk
- 1 yellow onion, chopped.
- 1 ½-tbsp. flour
- 1-tbsp. bread crumbs
- 2-tbsp. olive oil
- 1-tbsp. butter
- ½-tsp. nutmeg, ground.
- Salt and black pepper to the taste.

Directions:

1. Heat up a pan with the butter over medium high heat; add onion and mushrooms; stir, cook for 3 minutes, add flour, stir well again and take off heat
2. Add milk gradually, salt, pepper and nutmeg; stir and leave aside to cool down completely.
3. Take a bowl and mix oil with bread crumbs and whisk.
4. Take spoonful of the mushroom filling, add to breadcrumbs mix, coat well, shape patties out of this mix; place them in your air fryer's basket and cook at 400 °F, for 8 minutes. Divide among plates and serve as a side for a steak

Nutrition Values (Per Serving): Calories: 192; Fat: 2g; Fiber: 1g; Carbs: 16g; Protein: 6g

366. Beet Wedges Dish.

(Prep + Cooking Time: 25 Minutes | **Serves:** 4)

Ingredients:

- 4 beets; washed, peeled and cut into large wedges
- 2 garlic cloves, minced.
- 1-tbsp. olive oil
- one-tsp. lemon juice
- Salt and black to the taste

Directions:

1. Take a bowl and mix beets with oil, salt, pepper, garlic and lemon juice; toss well, transfer to your air fryer's basket and cook them at 400 °F, for 15 minutes. Divide beets wedges on plates and serve as a side dish.

Nutrition Values (Per Serving): Calories: 182; Fat: 6g; Fiber: 3g; Carbs: 8g; Protein: 2g

367. Creamy Brussels Sprouts Side Dish.

(Prep + Cooking Time: 35 Minutes | **Serves:** 8)

Ingredients:

- 3 lbs. Brussels sprouts, halved.
- 1 lb. bacon, chopped.
- 1-cup milk
- 2-cups heavy cream
- 3 shallots, chopped.
- 3-tbsp. prepared horseradish
- 4-tbsp. butter
- 1/4-tsp. nutmeg, ground.
- A drizzle of olive oil
- Salt and black pepper to the taste.

Directions:

1. Preheated you air fryer at 370 degrees F; add oil, bacon, salt and pepper and Brussels sprouts and toss.
2. Add butter, shallots, heavy cream, milk, nutmeg and horseradish; toss again and cook for 25 minutes. Divide among plates and serve as a side dish.

Nutrition Values (Per Serving): Calories: 214; Fat: 5g; Fiber: 8g; Carbs: 12g; Protein: 5g

368. Fried Creamy Cabbage

(Prep + Cooking Time: 30 Minutes | **Serves:** 4)

Ingredients:

- 4 bacon slices, chopped.
- 1 green cabbage head, chopped.
- 1-cup whipped cream
- 1 yellow onion, chopped.
- 2-tbsp. cornstarch
- Salt and black pepper to the taste.

Directions:

1. Put cabbage, bacon and onion in your air fryer.
2. Take a bowl and mix cornstarch with cream, salt and pepper, stir and add over cabbage. Toss, cook at 400 °F, for 20 minutes; divide among plates and serve as a side dish

Nutrition Values (Per Serving): Calories: 208; Fat: 10g; Fiber: 3g; Carbs: 16g; Protein: 5g

369. Yellow Squash and Zucchinis Dish

(Prep + Cooking Time: 45 Minutes | **Serves:** 4)

Ingredients:

- ½ lb. carrots, cubed.
- 1 lb. zucchinis, sliced.
- 1 yellow squash; halved, deseeded and cut into chunks
- 1-tbsp. tarragon, chopped.
- 6-tsp. olive oil
- Salt and white pepper to the taste

Directions:

1. In your air fryer's basket; mix zucchinis with carrots, squash, salt, pepper and oil; toss well and cook at 400 °F, for 25 minutes. Divide them on plates and serve as a side dish with tarragon sprinkled on top.

Nutrition Values (Per Serving): Calories: 160; Fat: 2g; Fiber: 1g; Carbs: 5g; Protein: 5g

Vegetable Recipes

370. Swiss Chard and Sausage Recipe.

(Prep + Cooking Time: 30 Minutes | **Serves:** 8)

Ingredients:

- 1 lb. sausage, chopped.
- 8-cups Swiss chard, chopped.
- ½-cup onion, chopped.
- 2-cups ricotta cheese
- 1-cup mozzarella, shredded.
- 1/4-cup parmesan, grated.
- 1 garlic clove, minced.
- 3 eggs
- 1-tbsp. olive oil
- A pinch of nutmeg
- Salt and black pepper to the taste.

Directions:

1. Heat up a pan that fits your air fryer with the oil over medium heat, add onions, garlic, Swiss chard, salt, pepper and nutmeg; stir, cook for 2 minutes and take off heat
2. Take a bowl and whisk eggs with mozzarella, parmesan and ricotta; stir, pour over Swiss chard mix, toss, introduce in your air fryer and cook at 320 °F, for 17 minutes. Divide among plates and serve.

Nutrition Values (Per Serving): Calories: 332; Fat: 13g; Fiber: 3g; Carbs: 14g; Protein: 23g

371. Fried Leeks Recipe

(Prep + Cooking Time: 17 Minutes | **Serves:** 4)

Ingredients:

- 4 leeks; washed, ends cut off and halved
- 1-tbsp. lemon juice
- 1-tbsp. butter, melted.
- Salt and black pepper to the taste.

Directions:

1. Rub leeks with melted butter, season with salt and pepper, put in your air fryer and cook at 350 °F, for 7 minutes.
2. Arrange on a platter, drizzle lemon juice all over and serve

Nutrition Values (Per Serving): Calories: 100; Fat: 4g; Fiber: 2g; Carbs: 6g; Protein: 2g

372. Okra and Corn Salad Recipe

(Prep + Cooking Time: 22 Minutes | **Serves:** 6)

Ingredients:

- 1 lb. okra; trimmed
- 28 oz. canned tomatoes, chopped.
- 3 green bell peppers, chopped.
- 6 scallions, chopped.
- 1-cup con
- 2-tbsp. olive oil
- one-tsp. sugar
- Salt and black pepper to the taste.

Directions:

1. Heat up a pan that fits your air fryer with the oil over medium high heat, add scallions and bell peppers; stir and cook for 5 minutes
2. Add okra, salt, pepper, sugar, tomatoes and corn; stir, introduce in your air fryer and cook at 360 °F, for 7 minutes. Divide okra mix on plates and serve warm.

Nutrition Values (Per Serving): Calories: 152; Fat: 4g; Fiber: 3g; Carbs: 18g; Protein: 4g

373. Flavored Fennel Recipe

(Prep + Cooking Time: 18 Minutes | **Serves:** 4)

Ingredients:

- 2 fennel bulbs; cut into quarters
- 3/4-cup veggie stock
- 1/4-cup white wine
- 1 garlic clove, minced.
- 1 red chili pepper, chopped.
- 1/4-cup parmesan, grated.
- 3-tbsp. olive oil
- Juice from ½ lemon
- Salt and black pepper to the taste.

Directions:

1. Heat up a pan that fits your air fryer with the oil over medium high heat, add garlic and chili pepper; stir and cook for 2 minutes
2. Add fennel, salt, pepper, stock, wine, lemon juice, and parmesan, toss to coat, introduce in your air fryer and cook at 350 °F, for 6 minutes. Divide among plates and serve right away.

Nutrition Values (Per Serving): Calories: 100; Fat: 4g; Fiber: 8g; Carbs: 4g; Protein: 4g

374. Beet Salad and Parsley Dressing Recipe

(Prep + Cooking Time: 24 Minutes | **Serves:** 4)

Ingredients:

- 4 beets
- 1 garlic clove, chopped.
- 2-tbsp. balsamic vinegar
- 2-tbsp. capers
- 1-tbsp. extra virgin olive oil
- Salt and black pepper to the taste.
- A bunch of parsley, chopped.

Directions:

1. Put beets in your air fryer and cook them at 360 °F, for 14 minutes.
2. Meanwhile, in a bowl, mix parsley with garlic, salt, pepper, olive oil and capers and stir very well
3. Transfer beets to a cutting board, leave them to cool down, peel them, slice put them in a salad bowl
4. Add vinegar, drizzle the parsley dressing all over and serve.

Nutrition Values (Per Serving): Calories: 70; Fat: 2g; Fiber: 1g; Carbs: 6g; Protein: 4g

375. Stuffed Baby Peppers Recipe

(Prep + Cooking Time: 16 Minutes | **Serves:** 4)

Ingredients:

- 1 lb. shrimp; cooked, peeled and deveined
- 12 baby bell peppers; cut into halves lengthwise
- 1-tbsp. lemon juice
- 1-tbsp. olive oil
- 6-tbsp. jarred basil pesto

- 1/4-tsp. red pepper flakes; crushed
- Salt and black pepper to the taste.
- A handful parsley, chopped.

Directions:

1. Take a bowl and mix shrimp with pepper flakes, pesto, salt, black pepper, lemon juice, oil and parsley, whisk very well and stuff bell pepper halves with this mix
2. Place them in your air fryer and cook at 320 °F, for 6 minutes; Arrange peppers on plates and serve.

Nutrition Values (Per Serving): Calories: 130; Fat: 2g; Fiber: 1g; Carbs: 3g; Protein: 15g

376. Radish Hash Recipe.

(Prep + Cooking Time: 17 Minutes | **Serves:** 4)

Ingredients:

- 1 lb. radishes, sliced.
- 1/3-cup parmesan, grated.
- 4 eggs
- ½-tsp. garlic powder
- ½-tsp. onion powder
- Salt and black pepper to the taste.

Directions:

1. Take a bowl and mix radishes with salt, pepper, onion and garlic powder, eggs and parmesan and stir well
2. Transfer radishes to a pan that fits your air fryer and cook at 350 °F, for 7 minutes
3. Divide hash on plates and serve.

Nutrition Values (Per Serving): Calories: 80; Fat: 5g; Fiber: 2g; Carbs: 5g; Protein: 7g

377. Peppers Stuffed with Beef Recipe.

(Prep + Cooking Time: 65 Minutes | **Serves:** 4)

Ingredients:

- 1-pound beef, ground.
- one-tsp. coriander, ground.
- 1 onion, chopped.
- 3 garlic cloves, minced.
- 1 egg
- 4 bell peppers; cut into halves and seeds removed
- 1/3-cup raisins
- 1/3-cup walnuts, chopped.
- 2-tbsp. olive oil
- 1-tbsp. ginger, grated.
- 1-tbsp. hot curry powder
- ½-tsp. cumin, ground.
- ½-tsp. turmeric powder
- Salt and black pepper to the taste.

Directions:

1. Heat up a pan with the oil over medium high heat, add onion; stir and cook for 4 minutes.
2. Add garlic and beef; stir and cook for 10 minutes
3. Add coriander, ginger, cumin, curry powder, salt, pepper, turmeric, walnuts and raisins; stir take off heat and mix with the egg.
4. Stuff pepper halves with this mix, introduce them in your air fryer and cook at 320 °F, for 20 minutes. Divide among plates and serve.

Nutrition Values (Per Serving): Calories: 170; Fat: 4g; Fiber: 3g; Carbs: 7g; Protein: 12g

378. Beet, Tomato and Goat Cheese Mix Recipe

(Prep + Cooking Time: 44 Minutes | **Serves:** 8)

Ingredients:

- 8 small beets; trimmed, peeled and halved
- 1 pint mixed cherry tomatoes, halved.
- 2 oz. pecans
- 4 oz. goat cheese, crumbled.
- 1 red onion, sliced.
- 1-tbsp. balsamic vinegar
- 2-tbsp. sugar
- 2-tbsp. olive oil
- Salt and black pepper to the taste.

Directions:

1. Put beets in your air fryer, season them with salt and pepper, cook at 350 °F, for 14 minutes and transfer to a salad bowl
2. Add onion, cherry tomatoes and pecans and toss
3. In another bowl, mix vinegar with sugar and oil, whisk well until sugar dissolves and add to salad. Also add goat cheese, toss and serve.

Nutrition Values (Per Serving): Calories: 124; Fat: 7g; Fiber: 5g; Carbs: 12g; Protein: 6g

379. Brussels Sprouts and Tomatoes Mix Recipe

(Prep + Cooking Time: 15 Minutes | **Serves:** 4)

Ingredients:

- 1 lb. Brussels sprouts; trimmed
- 1/4-cup green onions, chopped.
- 6 cherry tomatoes, halved.
- 1-tbsp. olive oil
- Salt and black pepper to the taste.

Directions:

1. Season Brussels sprouts with salt and pepper, put them in your air fryer and cook at 350 °F, for 10 minutes
2. Transfer them to a bowl, add salt, pepper, cherry tomatoes, green onions and olive oil, toss well and serve.

Nutrition Values (Per Serving): Calories: 121; Fat: 4g; Fiber: 4g; Carbs: 11g; Protein: 4g

380. Spinach Pie Recipe

(Prep + Cooking Time: 25 Minutes | **Serves:** 4)

Ingredients:

- 3 oz. cottage cheese
- 7oz. spinach
- 7 oz. flour
- 1 yellow onion, chopped.
- 2 eggs
- 1-tbsp. olive oil
- 2-tbsp. milk
- 2-tbsp. butter
- Salt and black pepper to the taste.

Directions:

1. In your food processor, mix flour with butter, 1 egg, milk, salt and pepper, blend well, transfer to a bowl, knead, cover and leave for 10 minutes
2. Heat up a pan with the oil over medium high heat, add onion and spinach; stir and cook for 2 minutes.
3. Add salt, pepper, the remaining egg and cottage cheese; stir well and take off heat

4. Divide dough in 4 pieces, roll each piece, place on the bottom of a ramekin, add spinach filling over dough, place ramekins in your air fryer's basket and cook at 360 °F, for 15 minutes.

Nutrition Values (Per Serving): Calories: 250; Fat: 12g; Fiber: 2g; Carbs: 23g; Protein: 12g

381. Cherry Tomatoes Skewers Recipe

(Prep + Cooking Time: 36 Minutes | **Serves:** 4)

Ingredients:

- 24 cherry tomatoes
- 3 garlic cloves, minced.
- 2-tbsp. olive oil
- 1-tbsp. thyme, chopped.
- 3-tbsp. balsamic vinegar
- Salt and black pepper to the taste.

For the dressing:

- 4-tbsp. olive oil
- 2-tbsp. balsamic vinegar
- Salt and black pepper to the taste.

Directions:

1. Take a bowl and mix 2-tbsp. oil with 3-tbsp. vinegar, 3 garlic cloves, thyme, salt and black pepper and whisk well.
2. Add tomatoes, toss to coat and leave aside for 30 minutes
3. Arrange 6 tomatoes on one skewer and repeat with the rest of the tomatoes.
4. Introduce them in your air fryer and cook at 360 °F, for 6 minutes
5. In another bowl, mix 2-tbsp. vinegar with salt, pepper and 4-tbsp. oil and whisk well. Arrange tomato skewers on plates and serve with the dressing drizzled on top.

Nutrition Values (Per Serving): Calories: 140; Fat: 1g; Fiber: 1g; Carbs: 2g; Protein: 7g

382. Broccoli Salad Recipe.

(Prep + Cooking Time: 18 Minutes | **Serves:** 4)

Ingredients:

- 6 garlic cloves, minced.
- 1 broccoli head; florets separated
- 1-tbsp. peanut oil
- 1-tbsp. Chinese rice wine vinegar
- Salt and black pepper to the taste.

Directions:

1. Take a bowl and mix broccoli with salt, pepper and half of the oil, toss, transfer to your air fryer and cook at 350 °F, for 8 minutes; shaking the fryer halfway
2. Transfer broccoli to a salad bowl, add the rest of the peanut oil, garlic and rice vinegar, toss really well and serve.

Nutrition Values (Per Serving): Calories: 121; Fat: 3g; Fiber: 4g; Carbs: 4g; Protein: 4g

383. Cheesy Brussels Sprouts Recipe

(Prep + Cooking Time: 18 Minutes | **Serves:** 4)

Ingredients:

- 1 lb. Brussels sprouts; washed
- 3-tbsp. parmesan, grated.
- 2-tbsp. butter
- Juice of 1 lemon
- Salt and black pepper to the taste.

Directions:

1. Put Brussels sprouts in your air fryer, cook them at 350 °F, for 8 minutes and transfer them to a bowl
2. Heat up a pan with the butter over medium heat, add lemon juice, salt and pepper, whisk well and add to Brussels sprouts. Add parmesan, toss until parmesan melts and serve.

Nutrition Values (Per Serving): Calories: 152; Fat: 6g; Fiber: 6g; Carbs: 8g; Protein: 12g

384. Eggplant and Garlic Sauce Recipe

(Prep + Cooking Time: 20 Minutes | **Serves:** 4)

Ingredients:

- 3 eggplants, halved.and sliced
- 1 red chili pepper, chopped.
- 2 garlic cloves, minced.
- 1 green onion stalk, chopped.
- 1-tbsp. ginger, grated.
- 2-tbsp. olive oil
- 1-tbsp. balsamic vinegar
- 1-tbsp. soy sauce

Directions:

1. Heat up a pan that fits your air fryer with the oil over medium high heat, add eggplant slices and cook for 2 minutes
2. Add chili pepper, garlic, green onions, ginger, soy sauce and vinegar, introduce in your air fryer and cook at 320 °F, for 7 minutes. Divide among plates and serve.

Nutrition Values (Per Serving): Calories: 130; Fat: 2g; Fiber: 4g; Carbs: 7g; Protein: 9g

385. Herbed Eggplant and Zucchini Mix Recipe.

(Prep + Cooking Time: 18 Minutes | **Serves:** 4)

Ingredients:

- 3 zucchinis; roughly cubed
- 1 eggplant; roughly cubed
- 3-tbsp. olive oil
- 2-tbsp. lemon juice
- one-tsp. oregano; dried
- one-tsp. thyme; dried
- Salt and black pepper to the taste.

Directions:

1. Put eggplant in a dish that fits your air fryer, add zucchinis, lemon juice, salt, pepper, thyme, oregano and olive oil, toss, introduce in your air fryer and cook at 360 °F, for 8 minutes
2. Divide among plates and serve right away.

Nutrition Values (Per Serving): Calories: 152; Fat: 5g; Fiber: 7g; Carbs: 19g; Protein: 5g

386. Sweet Baby Carrots Dish Recipe.

(Prep + Cooking Time: 20 Minutes | **Serves:** 4)

Ingredients:

- 2-cups baby carrots
- ½-tbsp. butter, melted.
- 1-tbsp. brown sugar
- A pinch of salt and black pepper

Directions:

1. In a dish that fits your air fryer, mix baby carrots with butter, salt, pepper and sugar, toss, introduce in your air fryer and cook at 350 °F, for 10 minutes. Divide among plates and serve

Nutrition Values (Per Serving): Calories: 100; Fat: 2g; Fiber: 3g; Carbs: 7g; Protein: 4g

387. Balsamic Artichokes Recipe

(Prep + Cooking Time: 17 Minutes | **Serves:** 4)

Ingredients:

- 4 big artichokes; trimmed
- 1/4-cup extra virgin olive oil
- 2 garlic cloves, minced.
- 2-tbsp. lemon juice
- one-tsp. oregano; dried
- 2-tsp. balsamic vinegar
- Salt and black pepper to the taste.

Directions:

1. Season artichokes with salt and pepper, rub them with half of the oil and half of the lemon juice, put them in your air fryer and cook at 360 °F, for 7 minutes
2. Meanwhile, in a bowl, mix the rest of the lemon juice with vinegar, the remaining oil, salt, pepper, garlic and oregano and stir very well
3. Arrange artichokes on a platter, drizzle the balsamic vinaigrette over them and serve.

Nutrition Values (Per Serving): Calories: 200; Fat: 3g; Fiber: 6g; Carbs: 12g; Protein: 4g

388. Flavored Fried Tomatoes Recipe

(Prep + Cooking Time: 25 Minutes | **Serves:** 8)

Ingredients:

- 2 lbs. cherry tomatoes, halved.
- 1/4-cup olive oil
- ½-cup parmesan, grated.
- 1/4-cup basil, chopped.
- 1 jalapeno pepper, chopped.
- 4 garlic cloves, minced.
- ½-tsp. oregano; dried
- Salt and black pepper to the taste.

Directions:

1. Take a bowl and mix tomatoes with garlic, jalapeno, season with salt, pepper and oregano and drizzle the oil, toss to coat, introduce in your air fryer and cook at 380 °F, for 15 minutes
2. Transfer tomatoes to a bowl, add basil and parmesan, toss and serve.

Nutrition Values (Per Serving): Calories: 140; Fat: 2g; Fiber: 2g; Carbs: 6g; Protein: 8g

389. Beets and Arugula Salad time Recipe

(Prep + Cooking Time: 20 Minutes | **Serves:** 4)

Ingredients:

- 1 ½ lbs. beets, peeled and quartered
- ½-cup orange juice
- 2-cups arugula
- 2 scallions, chopped.
- 2-tbsp. cider vinegar
- 2-tbsp. brown sugar
- 2-tsp. mustard
- 2-tsp. orange zest, grated.
- A drizzle of olive oil

Directions:

1. Rub beets with the oil and orange juice, place them in your air fryer and cook at 350 °F, for 10 minutes
2. Transfer beet quarters to a bowl, add scallions, arugula and orange zest and toss
3. Now, take a separate bowl, mix sugar with mustard and vinegar, whisk well, add to salad, toss and serve.

Nutrition Values (Per Serving): Calories: 121; Fat: 2g; Fiber: 3g; Carbs: 11g; Protein: 4g

390. Cheesy Artichokes Recipe

(Prep + Cooking Time: 16 Minutes | **Serves:** 6)

Ingredients:

- 14 oz. canned artichoke hearts
- 10 oz. spinach
- 8 oz. mozzarella, shredded.
- 3 garlic cloves, minced.
- 8 oz. cream cheese
- 16 oz. parmesan cheese, grated.
- ½-cup chicken stock
- ½-cup mayonnaise
- ½-cup sour cream
- one-tsp. onion powder

Directions:

1. In a pan that fits your air fryer, mix artichokes with stock, garlic, spinach, cream cheese, sour cream, onion powder and mayo, toss, introduce in your air fryer and cook at 350 °F, for 6 minutes
2. Add mozzarella and parmesan; stir well and serve.

Nutrition Values (Per Serving): Calories: 261; Fat: 12g; Fiber: 2g; Carbs: 12g; Protein: 15g

391. Stuffed Tomatoes Recipe.

(Prep + Cooking Time: 25 Minutes | **Serves:** 4)

Ingredients:

- 4 tomatoes; tops cut off and pulp scooped and chopped.
- 1 yellow onion, chopped.
- 1-cup cottage cheese
- ½-cup mushrooms, chopped.
- 1-tbsp. bread crumbs
- 2-tbsp. celery, chopped.
- 1-tbsp. parsley, chopped.
- 1-tbsp. butter
- 1/4-tsp. caraway seeds
- Salt and black pepper to the taste.

Directions:

1. Heat up a pan with the butter over medium heat, melt it, add onion and celery; stir and cook for 3 minutes
2. Add tomato pulp and mushrooms; stir and cook for 1 minute more
3. Add salt, pepper, crumbled bread, cheese, caraway seeds and parsley; stir, cook for 4 minutes more and take off heat.
4. Stuff tomatoes with this mix, place them in your air fryer and cook at 350 °F, for 8 minutes. Divide stuffed tomatoes on plates and serve

Nutrition Values (Per Serving): Calories: 143; Fat: 4g; Fiber: 6g; Carbs: 4g; Protein: 4g

392. Crispy Potatoes and Parsley Recipe.

(Prep + Cooking Time: 20 Minutes | **Serves:** 4)

Ingredients:

- 1 lb. gold potatoes; cut into wedges
- 2-tbsp. olive
- 1/4-cup parsley leaves, chopped.
- Juice from ½ lemon
- Salt and black pepper to the taste.

Directions:

1. Rub potatoes with salt, pepper, lemon juice and olive oil, put them in your air fryer and cook at 350 °F, for 10 minutes
2. Divide among plates, sprinkle parsley on top and serve.

Nutrition Values (Per Serving): Calories: 152; Fat: 3g; Fiber: 7g; Carbs: 17g; Protein: 4g

393. Collard Greens Mix Recipe

(Prep + Cooking Time: 20 Minutes | **Serves:** 4)

Ingredients:

- 1 bunch collard greens; trimmed
- 3 garlic cloves, minced.
- 1 yellow onion, chopped.
- 2-tbsp. tomato puree
- 1-tbsp. balsamic vinegar
- 2-tbsp. olive oil
- one-tsp. sugar
- Salt and black pepper to the taste.

Directions:

1. In a dish that fits your air fryer, mix oil, garlic, vinegar, onion and tomato puree and whisk,
2. Add collard greens, salt, pepper and sugar, toss, introduce in your air fryer and cook at 320 °F, for 10 minutes. Divide collard greens mix on plates and serve

Nutrition Values (Per Serving): Calories: 121; Fat: 3g; Fiber: 3g; Carbs: 7g; Protein: 3g

394. Creamy Green Beans Recipe

(Prep + Cooking Time: 25 Minutes | **Serves:** 4)

Ingredients:

- 2 lbs. green beans
- 1-cup mozzarella, shredded.
- ½-cup heavy cream
- 2/3-cup parmesan, grated.
- 2-tsp. lemon zest, grated.
- Salt and black pepper to the taste.
- A pinch of red pepper flakes

Directions:

1. Put the beans in a dish that fits your air fryer, add heavy cream, salt, pepper, lemon zest, pepper flakes, mozzarella and parmesan, toss, introduce in your air fryer and cook at 350 °F, for 15 minutes
2. Divide among plates and serve right away.

Nutrition Values (Per Serving): Calories: 231; Fat: 6g; Fiber: 7g; Carbs: 8g; Protein: 5g

395. Collard Greens and Turkey Wings Recipe

(Prep + Cooking Time: 30 Minutes | **Serves:** 6)

Ingredients:

- 2 ½ lbs. collard greens, chopped.
- 3 garlic cloves, minced.
- 2 smoked turkey wings
- 1 sweet onion, chopped.
- 2-tbsp. olive oil
- 2-tbsp. apple cider vinegar
- 1-tbsp. brown sugar
- ½-tsp. crushed red pepper
- Salt and black pepper to the taste.

Directions:

1. Heat up a pan that fits your air fryer with the oil over medium high heat, add onions; stir and cook for 2 minutes
2. Add garlic, greens, vinegar, salt, pepper, crushed red pepper, sugar and smoked turkey, introduce in preheated air fryer and cook at 350 °F, for 15 minutes
3. Divide greens and turkey on plates and serve.

Nutrition Values (Per Serving): Calories: 262; Fat: 4g; Fiber: 8g; Carbs: 12g; Protein: 4g

396. Beets and Blue Cheese Salad Recipe

(Prep + Cooking Time: 24 Minutes | **Serves:** 6)

Ingredients:

- 1/4-cup blue cheese, crumbled.
- 6 beets, peeled and quartered
- 1-tbsp. olive oil
- Salt and black pepper to the taste.

Directions:

1. Put beets in your air fryer, cook them at 350 °F, for 14 minutes and transfer them to a bowl.
2. Add blue cheese, salt, pepper and oil, toss and serve

Nutrition Values (Per Serving): Calories: 100; Fat: 4g; Fiber: 4g; Carbs: 10g; Protein: 5g

397. Green Beans and Parmesan Recipe.

(Prep + Cooking Time: 18 Minutes | **Serves:** 4)

Ingredients:

- 12 oz. green beans
- 1 egg, whisked.
- 1/3-cup parmesan, grated.
- 2-tbsp. olive oil
- 2-tsp. garlic, minced.
- Salt and black pepper to the taste.

Directions:

1. Take a bowl and mix oil with salt, pepper, garlic and egg and whisk well.
2. Add green beans to this mix, toss well and sprinkle parmesan all over
3. Transfer green beans to your air fryer and cook them at 390 °F, for 8 minutes. Divide green beans on plates and serve them right away

Nutrition Values (Per Serving): Calories: 120; Fat: 8g; Fiber: 2g; Carbs: 7g; Protein: 4g

398. Artichokes and Special Sauce Recipe.

(Prep + Cooking Time: 16 Minutes | **Serves:** 2)

Ingredients:

- 2 garlic cloves, minced.
- 2 artichokes; trimmed
- A drizzle of olive oil
- 1-tbsp. lemon juice

For the sauce:

- 3 anchovy fillets
- 1/4-cup extra virgin olive oil
- 3 garlic cloves
- 1/4-cup coconut oil

Directions:

1. Take a bowl and mix artichokes with oil, 2 garlic cloves and lemon juice, toss well, transfer to your air fryer, cook at 350 °F, for 6 minutes and divide among plates
2. In your food processor, mix coconut oil with anchovy, 3 garlic cloves and olive oil, blend very well, drizzle over artichokes and serve.

Nutrition Values (Per Serving): Calories: 261; Fat: 4g; Fiber: 7g; Carbs: 20g; Protein: 12g

399. Asian Potatoes Recipe

(Prep + Cooking Time: 22 Minutes | **Serves:** 4)

Ingredients:

- 5 potatoes; boiled, peeled and cubed
- 1-tbsp. coriander seeds
- 1-tbsp. pickled mango, chopped.
- 2-tbsp. olive oil
- 1-tbsp. cumin seeds
- 2-tsp. fenugreek; dried
- ½-tsp. turmeric powder
- ½-tsp. red chili powder
- one-tsp. pomegranate powder
- Salt and black pepper to the taste.

Directions:

1. Heat up a pan that fits your air fryer with the oil over medium heat, add coriander and cumin seeds; stir and cook for 2 minutes
2. Add salt, pepper, turmeric, chili powder, pomegranate powder, mango, fenugreek and potatoes, toss, introduce in your air fryer and cook at 360 °F, for 10 minutes.
3. Divide among plates and serve hot

Nutrition Values (Per Serving): Calories: 251; Fat: 7g; Fiber: 4g; Carbs: 12g; Protein: 7g

400. Spicy Cabbage Recipe

(Prep + Cooking Time: 18 Minutes | **Serves:** 4)

Ingredients:

- 1/4-cups apple juice
- 1 carrot, grated.
- 1/4-cup apple cider vinegar
- 1 cabbage; cut into 8 wedges
- 1-tbsp. sesame seed oil
- ½-tsp. cayenne pepper
- one-tsp. red pepper flakes; crushed

Directions:

1. In a pan that fits your air fryer, combine cabbage with oil, carrot, vinegar, apple juice, cayenne and pepper flakes, toss, introduce in preheated air fryer and cook at 350 °F, for 8 minutes
2. Divide cabbage mix on plates and serve.

Nutrition Values (Per Serving): Calories: 100; Fat: 4g; Fiber: 2g; Carbs: 11g; Protein: 7g

401. Eggplant Hash Recipe.

(Prep + Cooking Time: 30 Minutes | **Serves:** 4)

Ingredients:

- ½ lb. cherry tomatoes, halved.
- 1/4-cup mint, chopped.
- 1 eggplant; roughly chopped.
- 1/4-cup basil, chopped.
- ½-cup olive oil
- one-tsp. Tabasco sauce
- Salt and black pepper to the taste.

Directions:

1. Heat up a pan that fits your air fryer with half of the oil over medium high heat, add eggplant pieces, cook for 3 minutes; flip, cook them for 3 minutes more and transfer to a bowl.
2. Heat up the same pan with the rest of the oil over medium high heat, add tomatoes; stir and cook for 1-2 minutes.
3. Return eggplant pieces to the pan, add salt, black pepper, basil, mint and Tabasco sauce, introduce in your air fryer and cook at 320 °F, for 6 minutes. Divide among plates and serve

Nutrition Values (Per Serving): Calories: 120; Fat: 1g; Fiber: 4g; Carbs: 8g; Protein: 15g

402. Stuffed Eggplants Recipe

(Prep + Cooking Time: 40 Minutes | **Serves:** 4)

Ingredients:

- 2 ½ lbs. tomatoes; cut into halves and grated
- 4 small eggplants, halved.lengthwise
- 3 oz. feta cheese, crumbled.
- ½-cup cauliflower, chopped.
- ½-cup parsley, chopped.
- 1 green bell pepper, chopped.
- 1 yellow onion, chopped.
- 10-tbsp. olive oil
- 1-tbsp. garlic, minced.
- one-tsp. oregano, chopped.
- Salt and black pepper to the taste.

Directions:

1. Season eggplants with salt, pepper and 4-tbsp. oil, toss, put them in your air fryer and cook at 350 °F, for 16 minutes.
2. Meanwhile, heat up a pan with 3-tbsp. oil over medium high heat, add onion; stir and cook for 5 minutes.
3. Add bell pepper, garlic and cauliflower; stir, cook for 5 minutes; take off heat, add parsley, tomato, salt, pepper, oregano and cheese and whisk everything
4. Stuff eggplants with the veggie mix, drizzle the rest of the oil over them, put them in your air fryer and cook at 350 °F, for 6 minutes more. Divide among plates and serve right away

Nutrition Values (Per Serving): Calories: 240; Fat: 4, fiber, 2g; Carbs: 19g; Protein: 2g

403. Brussels Sprouts and Butter Sauce Recipe

(Prep + Cooking Time: 14 Minutes | **Serves:** 4)

Ingredients:

- 1 lb. Brussels sprouts; trimmed
- ½-cup bacon, cooked and chopped.
- 1-tbsp. butter
- 1-tbsp. mustard
- 2-tbsp. dill; finely chopped.
- Salt and black pepper to the taste.

Directions:

1. Put Brussels sprouts in your air fryer and cook them at 350 °F, for 10 minutes.
2. Heat up a pan with the butter over medium high heat, add bacon, mustard and dill and whisk well. Divide Brussels sprouts on plates, drizzle butter sauce all over and serve

Nutrition Values (Per Serving): Calories: 162; Fat: 8g; Fiber: 8g; Carbs: 14g; Protein: 5g

404. Broccoli and Tomatoes Fried Stew Recipe

(Prep + Cooking Time: 30 Minutes | **Serves:** 4)

Ingredients:

- 28 oz. canned tomatoes; pureed
- 1 broccoli head; florets separated
- 1 small ginger piece, chopped.
- 1 yellow onion, chopped.
- 1 garlic clove, minced.
- 1-tbsp. olive oil
- 2-tsp. coriander seeds
- A pinch of red pepper; crushed
- Salt and black pepper to the taste.

Directions:

1. Heat up a pan that fits your air fryer with the oil over medium heat, add onions, salt, pepper and red pepper; stir and cook for 7 minutes
2. Add ginger, garlic, coriander seeds, tomatoes and broccoli; stir, introduce in your air fryer and cook at 360 °F, for 12 minutes. Divide into bowls and serve.

Nutrition Values (Per Serving): Calories: 150; Fat: 4g; Fiber: 2g; Carbs: 7g; Protein: 12g

405. Mexican Peppers Recipe

(Prep + Cooking Time: 35 Minutes | **Serves:** 4)

Ingredients:

- 4 bell peppers; tops cut off and seeds removed
- 4 chicken breasts
- 1/4-cup yellow onion, chopped.
- 1/4-cup green peppers, chopped.
- 2-cups tomato sauce
- 1-cup tomatoes, chopped.
- ½-cup tomato juice
- 2-tbsp. jarred jalapenos, chopped.
- ½-tsp. garlic powder
- one-tsp. cumin, ground.
- 2-tsp. onion powder
- ½-tsp. red pepper; crushed
- one-tsp. chili powder
- Salt and black pepper to the taste.

Directions:

1. In a pan that fits your air fryer, mix chicken breasts with tomato juice, jalapenos, tomatoes, onion, green peppers, salt, pepper, onion powder, red pepper, chili powder, garlic powder, oregano and cumin; stir well, introduce in your air fryer and cook at 350 °F, for 15 minutes
2. Shred meat using 2 forks; stir, stuff bell peppers with this mix, place them in your air fryer and cook at 320 °F, for 10 minutes more. Divide stuffed peppers on plates and serve

Nutrition Values (Per Serving): Calories: 180; Fat: 4g; Fiber: 3g; Carbs: 7g; Protein: 14g

406. Tomato and Basil Tart Recipe

(Prep + Cooking Time: 24 Minutes | **Serves:** 2)

Ingredients:

- 1 bunch basil, chopped.
- ½-cup cherry tomatoes, halved.
- 1/4-cup cheddar cheese, grated.
- 1 garlic clove, minced.
- 4 eggs
- Salt and black pepper to the taste.

Directions:

1. Take a bowl and mix eggs with salt, black pepper, cheese and basil and whisk well.
2. Pour this into a baking dish that fits your air fryer, arrange tomatoes on top, introduce in the fryer and cook at 320 °F, for 14 minutes
3. Slice and serve right away.

Nutrition Values (Per Serving): Calories: 140; Fat: 1g; Fiber: 1g; Carbs: 2g; Protein: 10g

407. Stuffed Poblano Peppers Recipe

(Prep + Cooking Time: 25 Minutes | **Serves:** 4)

Ingredients:

- 10 poblano peppers; tops cut off and deseeded
- ½-cup cilantro, chopped.
- 8 oz. mushrooms, chopped.
- 1 white onion, chopped.
- 1-tbsp. olive oil
- 2-tsp. garlic, minced.
- Salt and black pepper to the taste.

Directions:

1. Heat up a pan with the oil over medium high heat, add onion and mushrooms; stir and cook for 5 minutes.
2. Add garlic, cilantro, salt and black pepper; stir and cook for 2 minutes
3. Divide this mix into poblanos, introduce them in your air fryer and cook at 350 °F, for 15 minutes. Divide among plates and serve.

Nutrition Values (Per Serving): Calories: 150; Fat: 3g; Fiber: 2g; Carbs: 7g; Protein: 10g

408. Zucchini Mix Recipe.

(Prep + Cooking Time: 24 Minutes | **Serves:** 6)

Ingredients:

- 6 zucchinis, halved.and then sliced
- 2 oz. parmesan, grated.
- 3 garlic cloves, minced.
- ½-cup yellow onion, chopped.
- 3/4-cup heavy cream
- 1-tbsp. butter
- one-tsp. oregano; dried
- Salt and black pepper to the taste.

Directions:

1. Heat up a pan that fits your air fryer with the butter over medium high heat, add onion; stir and cook for 4 minutes
2. Add garlic, zucchinis, oregano, salt, pepper and heavy cream, toss, introduce in your air fryer and cook at 350 °F, for 10 minutes. Add parmesan; stir, divide among plates and serve.

Nutrition Values (Per Serving): Calories: 160; Fat: 4g; Fiber: 2g; Carbs: 8g; Protein: 8g

409. Spanish Greens Recipe

(Prep + Cooking Time: 18 Minutes | **Serves:** 4)

Ingredients:

- 1 yellow onion, sliced.
- 1/4-cup pine nuts; toasted
- 1/4-cup balsamic vinegar
- 1 apple; cored and chopped.
- 1/4-cup raisins
- 6 garlic cloves, chopped.

- 5-cups mixed spinach and chard
- 3-tbsp. olive oil
- Salt and black pepper to the taste.
- A pinch of nutmeg

Directions:

1. Heat up a pan that fits your air fryer with the oil over medium high heat, add onion; stir and cook for 3 minutes
2. Add apple, garlic, raisins, vinegar, mixed spinach and chard, nutmeg, salt and pepper; stir, introduce in preheated air fryer and cook at 350 °F, for 5 minutes
3. Divide among plates, sprinkle pine nuts on top and serve.

Nutrition Values (Per Serving): Calories: 120; Fat: 1g; Fiber: 2g; Carbs: 3g; Protein: 6g

410. Swiss Chard Salad Recipe.

(Prep + Cooking Time: 23 Minutes | **Serves:** 4)

Ingredients:

- 1 bunch Swiss chard; torn
- 1/4-cup raisins
- 1/4-cup pine nuts; toasted
- 1-tbsp. balsamic vinegar
- 2-tbsp. olive oil
- 1 small yellow onion, chopped.
- A pinch of red pepper flakes
- Salt and black pepper to the taste.

Directions:

1. Heat up a pan that fits your air fryer with the oil over medium heat, add chard and onions; stir and cook for 5 minutes
2. Add salt, pepper, pepper flakes, raisins, pine nuts and vinegar; stir, introduce in your air fryer and cook at 350 °F, for 8 minutes. Divide among plates and serve.

Nutrition Values (Per Serving): Calories: 120; Fat: 2g; Fiber: 1g; Carbs: 8g; Protein: 8g

411. Asian Turnips Salad Recipe

(Prep + Cooking Time: 22 Minutes | **Serves:** 4)

Ingredients:

- 20 oz. turnips, peeled and chopped.
- 2 yellow onions, chopped.
- 2 green chilies, chopped.
- 2 tomatoes, chopped.
- 2-tbsp. butter
- one-tsp. cumin, ground.
- one-tsp. coriander, ground.
- one-tsp. garlic, minced.
- one-tsp. ginger, grated.
- ½-tsp. turmeric powder
- Salt and black pepper to the taste.
- A handful coriander leaves, chopped.

Directions:

1. Heat up a pan that fits your air fryer with the butter, melt it, add green chilies, garlic and ginger; stir and cook for 1 minute
2. Add onions, salt, pepper, tomatoes, turmeric, cumin, ground coriander and turnips; stir, introduce in your air fryer and cook at 350 °F, for 10 minutes
3. Divide among plates, sprinkle fresh coriander on top and serve.

Nutrition Values (Per Serving): Calories: 100; Fat: 3g; Fiber: 6g; Carbs: 12g; Protein: 4g

412. Greek Potato Mix Recipe.

(Prep + Cooking Time: 30 Minutes | **Serves:** 2)

Ingredients:

- 2 medium potatoes; cut into wedges
- ½-cup chicken stock
- 1 small carrot; roughly chopped.
- 1 bay leaf
- 1 yellow onion, chopped.
- 2-tbsp. Greek yogurt
- 1 ½-tbsp. flour
- 2-tbsp. butter
- Salt and black pepper to the taste.

Directions:

1. Heat up a pan that fits your air fryer with the butter over medium high heat, add onion and carrot; stir and cook for 3-4 minutes
2. Add potatoes, flour, chicken stock, salt, pepper and bay leaf; stir, introduce in your air fryer and cook at 320 °F, for 16 minutes. Add Greek yogurt, toss, divide among plates and serve

Nutrition Values (Per Serving): Calories: 198; Fat: 3g; Fiber: 2g; Carbs: 6g; Protein: 8g

413. Collard Greens and Bacon Recipe.

(Prep + Cooking Time: 22 Minutes | **Serves:** 4)

Ingredients:

- 1 lb. collard greens
- 3 bacon strips, chopped.
- 1/4-cup cherry tomatoes, halved.
- 2-tbsp. chicken stock
- 1-tbsp. apple cider vinegar
- Salt and black pepper to the taste.

Directions:

1. Heat up a pan that fits your air fryer over medium heat, add bacon; stir and cook 1-2 minutes
2. Add tomatoes, collard greens, vinegar, stock, salt and pepper; stir, introduce in your air fryer and cook at 320 °F, for 10 minutes. Divide among plates and serve.

Nutrition Values (Per Serving): Calories: 120; Fat: 3g; Fiber: 1g; Carbs: 3g; Protein: 7g

414. Portobello Mushrooms Recipe

(Prep + Cooking Time: 22 Minutes | **Serves:** 4)

Ingredients:

- 4 Portobello mushrooms; stems removed and chopped.
- 10 basil leaves
- 1/4-cup olive oil
- 3 garlic cloves, chopped.
- 1-cup almonds; roughly chopped.
- 8 cherry tomatoes, halved.
- 1-cup baby spinach
- 1-tbsp. parsley
- Salt and black pepper to the taste.

Directions:

1. In your food processor, mix basil with spinach, garlic, almonds, parsley, oil, salt, black pepper to the taste and mushroom stems and blend well
2. Stuff each mushroom with this mix, place them in your air fryer and cook at 350 °F, for 12 minutes. Divide mushrooms on plates and serve.

Nutrition Values (Per Serving): Calories: 145; Fat: 3g; Fiber: 2g; Carbs: 6g; Protein: 17g

415. Sesame Mustard Greens Recipe

(Prep + Cooking Time: 21 Minutes | **Serves:** 4)

Ingredients:

- 1 lb. mustard greens; torn
- 2 garlic cloves, minced.
- ½-cup yellow onion, sliced.
- 1-tbsp. olive oil
- 3-tbsp. veggie stock
- 1/4-tsp. dark sesame oil
- Salt and black pepper to the taste.

Directions:

1. Heat up a pan that fits your air fryer with the oil over medium heat, add onions; stir and brown them for 5 minutes
2. Add garlic, stock, greens, salt and pepper; stir, introduce in your air fryer and cook at 350 °F, for 6 minutes. Add sesame oil, toss to coat, divide among plates and serve.

Nutrition Values (Per Serving): Calories: 120; Fat: 3g; Fiber: 1g; Carbs: 3g; Protein: 7g

416. Green Beans and Potatoes Recipe.

(Prep + Cooking Time: 25 Minutes | **Serves:** 5)

Ingredients:

- 2 lbs. green beans
- 6 bacon slices, cooked and chopped.
- 6 new potatoes, halved.
- A drizzle of olive oil
- Salt and black pepper to the taste.

Directions:

1. Take a bowl and mix green beans with potatoes, salt, pepper and oil, toss, transfer to your air fryer and cook at 390 °F, for 15 minutes. Divide among plates and serve with bacon sprinkled on top

Nutrition Values (Per Serving): Calories: 374; Fat: 15g; Fiber: 12g; Carbs: 28g; Protein: 12g

417. Green Beans and Tomatoes Recipe.

(Prep + Cooking Time: 25 Minutes | **Serves:** 4)

Ingredients:

- 1 lb. green beans
- 1-pint cherry tomatoes
- 2-tbsp. olive oil
- Salt and black pepper to the taste.

Directions:

1. Take a bowl and mix cherry tomatoes with green beans, olive oil, salt and pepper, toss, transfer to your air fryer and cook at 400 °F, for 15 minutes. Divide among plates and serve right away

Nutrition Values (Per Serving): Calories: 162; Fat: 6g; Fiber: 5g; Carbs: 8g; Protein: 9g

418. Sweet Potatoes Mix Recipe.

(Prep + Cooking Time: 25 Minutes | **Serves:** 4)

Ingredients:

- ½ lb. bacon, chopped.
- 3 sweet potatoes, cubed.
- 4 garlic cloves, minced.
- A handful dill, chopped.
- 2 green onions, chopped.
- 4-tbsp. olive oil

- 2-tbsp. balsamic vinegar
- Juice from 1 lime
- A pinch of cinnamon powder.
- A pinch of red pepper flakes
- Salt and black pepper to the taste.

Directions:

1. Arrange bacon and sweet potatoes in your air fryer's basket, add garlic and half of the oil, toss well and cook at 350 °F and bake for 15 minutes
2. Meanwhile, in a bowl, mix vinegar with lime juice, olive oil, green onions, pepper flakes, dill, salt, pepper and cinnamon and whisk. Transfer bacon and sweet potatoes to a salad bowl, add salad dressing, toss well and serve right away.

Nutrition Values (Per Serving): Calories: 170; Fat: 3g; Fiber: 2g; Carbs: 5g; Protein: 12g

419. Rutabaga and Cherry Tomatoes Mix Recipe

(Prep + Cooking Time: 25 Minutes | **Serves:** 4)

Ingredients:

- ½-cup veggie stock
- 3/4-cup cashews; soaked for a couple of hours and drained
- 1 garlic clove, minced.
- 1-tbsp. shallot, chopped.
- 2-tbsp. nutritional yeast
- 2-tsp. lemon juice
- Salt and black pepper to the taste.

For the pasta:

- 2 rutabagas, peeled and cut into thick noodles
- 1-cup cherry tomatoes, halved.
- 1/4-tsp. garlic powder
- 5-tsp. olive oil

Directions:

1. Place tomatoes and rutabaga noodles into a pan that fits your air fryer, drizzle the oil over them, season with salt, black pepper and garlic powder, toss to coat and cook in your air fryer at 350 °F, for 15 minutes
2. Meanwhile, in a food processor, mix garlic with shallots, cashews, veggie stock, nutritional yeast, lemon juice, a pinch of sea salt and black pepper to the taste and blend well
3. Divide rutabaga pasta on plates, top with tomatoes, drizzle the sauce over them and serve.

Nutrition Values (Per Serving): Calories: 160; Fat: 2g; Fiber: 5g; Carbs: 10g; Protein: 8g

420. Simple Tomatoes and Bell Pepper Sauce Recipe

(Prep + Cooking Time: 25 Minutes | **Serves:** 4)

Ingredients:

- 1 lb. cherry tomatoes, halved.
- 2 red bell peppers, chopped.
- 3 bay leaves
- 2 garlic cloves, minced.
- 1-tbsp. balsamic vinegar
- 2-tbsp. olive oil
- one-tsp. rosemary; dried
- Salt and black pepper to the taste.

Directions:

1. In a bowl mix tomatoes with garlic, salt, black pepper, rosemary, bay leaves, half of the oil and half of the vinegar, toss to coat, introduce in your air fryer and roast them at 320 °F, for 15 minutes

2. Meanwhile, in your food processor, mix bell peppers with a pinch of sea salt, black pepper, the rest of the oil and the rest of the vinegar and blend very well.
3. Divide roasted tomatoes on plates, drizzle the bell peppers sauce over them and serve.

Nutrition Values (Per Serving): Calories: 123; Fat: 1g; Fiber: 1g; Carbs: 8g; Protein: 10g

421. Italian Eggplant Stew Recipe

(Prep + Cooking Time: 25 Minutes | **Serves:** 4)

Ingredients:

- 1 red onion, chopped.
- 1 handful green olives, pitted and sliced.
- 2 garlic cloves, chopped.
- 5 tomatoes, chopped.
- 2 eggplants; cut into medium chunks
- 1 bunch parsley, chopped.
- 2-tbsp. capers, chopped.
- 2-tbsp. olive oil
- 3-tbsp. herb vinegar
- one-tsp. oregano; dried
- Salt and black pepper to the taste.

Directions:

1. Heat up a pan that fits your air fryer with the oil over medium heat, add eggplant, oregano, salt and pepper; stir and cook for 5 minutes
2. Add garlic, onion, parsley, capers, olives, vinegar and tomatoes; stir, introduce in your air fryer and cook at 360 °F, for 15 minutes. Divide into bowls and serve.

Nutrition Values (Per Serving): Calories: 170; Fat: 13g; Fiber: 3g; Carbs: 5g; Protein: 7g

422. Garlic Tomatoes Recipe

(Prep + Cooking Time: 25 Minutes | **Serves:** 4)

Ingredients:

- 1 lb. mixed cherry tomatoes
- 1/4-cup olive oil
- 3 thyme springs, chopped.
- 4 garlic cloves; crushed
- Salt and black pepper to the taste.

Directions:

1. Take a bowl and mix tomatoes with salt, black pepper, garlic, olive oil and thyme, toss to coat, introduce in your air fryer and cook at 360 °F, for 15 minutes. Divide tomatoes mix on plates and serve

Nutrition Values (Per Serving): Calories: 100; Fat: 0g; Fiber: 1g; Carbs: 1g; Protein: 6g

423. Broccoli Hash Recipe

(Prep + Cooking Time: 38 Minutes | **Serves:** 2)

Ingredients:

- 10 oz. mushrooms, halved.
- 1 yellow onion, chopped.
- 1 avocado, peeled and pitted
- A pinch of red pepper flakes
- 1 broccoli head; florets separated
- 1 garlic clove, minced.
- 1-tbsp. olive oil
- 1-tbsp. balsamic vinegar
- one-tsp. basil; dried
- Salt and black pepper

Directions:

1. Take a bowl and mix mushrooms with broccoli, onion, garlic and avocado.

2. In another bowl, mix vinegar, oil, salt, pepper and basil and whisk well
3. Pour this over veggies, toss to coat, leave aside for 30 minutes; transfer to your air fryer's basket and cook at 350 °F, for 8 minutes; Divide among plates and serve with pepper flakes on top.

Nutrition Values (Per Serving): Calories: 182; Fat: 3g; Fiber: 3g; Carbs: 5g; Protein: 8g

424. Delicious Green Beans Recipe

(Prep + Cooking Time: 25 Minutes | **Serves:** 4)

Ingredients:

- 1 lb. red potatoes; cut into wedges
- 1 lb. green beans
- 2 garlic cloves, minced.
- 2-tbsp. olive oil
- ½-tsp. oregano; dried
- Salt and black pepper to the taste.

Directions:

1. In a pan that fits your air fryer, combine potatoes with green beans, garlic, oil, salt, pepper and oregano, toss, introduce in your air fryer and cook at 380 °F, for 15 minutes. Divide among plates and serve

Nutrition Values (Per Serving): Calories: 211; Fat: 6g; Fiber: 7g; Carbs: 8g; Protein: 5g

425. Potatoes and Tomatoes Mix Recipe

(Prep + Cooking Time: 26 Minutes | **Serves:** 4)

Ingredients:

- 1 ½ lbs. red potatoes, quartered.
- 1-pint cherry tomatoes
- 3 garlic cloves, minced.
- 1-tbsp. rosemary, chopped.
- 2-tbsp. olive oil
- one-tsp. sweet paprika
- Salt and black pepper to the taste.

Directions:

1. Take a bowl and mix potatoes with tomatoes, oil, paprika, rosemary, garlic, salt and pepper, toss, transfer to your air fryer and cook at 380 °F, for 16 minutes. Divide among plates and serve

Nutrition Values (Per Serving): Calories: 192; Fat: 4g; Fiber: 4g; Carbs: 30g; Protein: 3g

426. Balsamic Potatoes Recipe

(Prep + Cooking Time: 30 Minutes | **Serves:** 4)

Ingredients:

- 1 ½ lbs. baby potatoes, halved.
- 9 oz. cherry tomatoes
- 2 garlic cloves, chopped.
- 2 red onions, chopped.
- 2 thyme springs, chopped.
- 3-tbsp. olive oil
- 1 ½-tbsp. balsamic vinegar
- Salt and black pepper to the taste.

Directions:

1. In your food processor, mix garlic with onions, oil, vinegar, thyme, salt and pepper and pulse really well.
2. Take a bowl and mix potatoes with tomatoes and balsamic marinade, toss well, transfer to your air fryer and cook at 380 °F, for 20 minutes. Divide among plates and serve

Nutrition Values (Per Serving): Calories: 301; Fat: 6g; Fiber: 8g; Carbs: 18g; Protein: 6g

427. Zucchini Noodles Recipe

(Prep + Cooking Time: 30 Minutes | **Serves:** 6)

Ingredients:

- 3 zucchinis; cut with a spiralizer
- 16 oz. mushrooms, sliced.
- 2-cups tomatoes sauce
- 1/4-cup sun dried tomatoes, chopped.
- ½-cup cherry tomatoes, halved.
- 2-cups spinach; torn
- 2-tbsp. olive oil
- one-tsp. garlic, minced.
- A handful basil, chopped.
- Salt and black pepper to the taste.

Directions:

1. Put zucchini noodles in a bowl, season salt and black pepper and leave them aside for 10 minutes
2. Heat up a pan that fits your air fryer with the oil over medium high heat, add garlic; stir and cook for 1 minute
3. Add mushrooms, sun dried tomatoes, cherry tomatoes, spinach, cayenne, sauce and zucchini noodles; stir, introduce in your air fryer and cook at 320 °F, for 10 minutes
4. Divide among plates and serve with basil sprinkled on top.

Nutrition Values (Per Serving): Calories: 120; Fat: 1g; Fiber: 1g; Carbs: 2g; Protein: 9g

428. Potatoes and Special Tomato Sauce Recipe.

(Prep + Cooking Time: 26 Minutes | **Serves:** 4)

Ingredients:

- 2 lbs. potatoes, cubed.
- 1-cup tomato sauce
- 1 yellow onion, chopped.
- 4 garlic cloves, minced.
- 2-tbsp. basil, chopped.
- 2-tbsp. olive oil
- ½-tsp. oregano; dried
- ½-tsp. parsley; dried

Directions:

1. Heat up a pan that fits your air fryer with the oil over medium heat, add onion; stir and cook for 1-2 minutes.
2. Add garlic, potatoes, parsley, tomato sauce and oregano; stir, introduce in your air fryer and cook at 370 °F and cook for 16 minutes. Add basil, toss everything, divide among plates and serve

Nutrition Values (Per Serving): Calories: 211; Fat: 6g; Fiber: 8g; Carbs: 14g; Protein: 6g

429. Fried Asparagus Recipe

(Prep + Cooking Time: 25 Minutes | **Serves:** 4)

Ingredients:

- 2 lbs. fresh asparagus; trimmed
- 4 oz. feta cheese, crumbled.
- 4 garlic cloves, minced.
- 1/4-cup olive oil
- 2-tbsp. parsley; finely chopped.
- one-tsp. lemon zest
- ½-tsp. oregano; dried
- 1/4-tsp. red pepper flakes
- Salt and black pepper to the taste.
- Juice from 1 lemon

Directions:

1. Take a bowl and mix oil with lemon zest, garlic, pepper flakes and oregano and whisk
2. Add asparagus, cheese, salt and pepper, toss, transfer to your air fryer's basket and cook at 350 °F, for 8 minutes.
3. Divide asparagus on plates, drizzle lemon juice and sprinkle parsley on top and serve.

Nutrition Values (Per Serving): Calories: 162; Fat: 13g; Fiber: 5g; Carbs: 12g; Protein: 8g

Snack and Appetizer Recipes

430. Jerky Beef Snack

(Prep + Cooking Time: 3 hour and 30 minutes | **Serves:** 6)

Ingredients:

- 2 lbs. beef round, sliced.
- ½-cup Worcestershire sauce
- 2-cups soy sauce
- 2-tbsp. black pepper
- 2-tbsp. black peppercorns

Directions:

1. Take a bowl and mix soy sauce with black peppercorns, black pepper and Worcestershire sauce and whisk well.
2. Add beef slices; toss to coat and leave aside in the fridge for 6 hours
3. Introduce beef rounds in your air fryer and cook them at 370 °F, for 1 hour and 3
4. 0 minutes. Transfer to a bowl and serve cold.

Nutrition Values (Per Serving): Calories: 300; Fat: 12g; Fiber: 4g; Carbs: 3g; Protein: 8g

431. Herbed Tomatoes

(Prep + Cooking Time: 30 Minutes | **Serves:** 2)

Ingredients:

- 2 tomatoes, halved.
- one-tsp. oregano; dried
- one-tsp. rosemary; dried
- one-tsp. parsley; dried
- one-tsp. basil; dried
- Cooking spray.
- Salt and black pepper to the taste.

Directions:

1. Spray tomato halves with cooking oil, season with salt, pepper, parsley, basil, oregano and rosemary over them.
2. Place them in your air fryer's basket and cook at 320 °F, for 20 minutes. Arrange them on a platter and serve as an appetizer.

Nutrition Values (Per Serving): Calories: 100; Fat: 1g; Fiber: 1g; Carbs: 4g; Protein: 1g

432. Tasty Banana Chips

(Prep + Cooking Time: 25 Minutes | **Serves:** 4)

Ingredients:

- 4 bananas, peeled and sliced
- ½-tsp. chaat masala
- one-tsp. olive oil
- ½-tsp. turmeric powder
- A pinch of salt

Directions:

1. Take a bowl and mix banana slices with salt, turmeric, chaat masala and oil; toss and leave aside for 10 minutes.
2. Transfer banana slices to your preheated air fryer at 360 °F and cook them for 15 minutes flipping them once. Serve as a snack.

Nutrition Values (Per Serving): Calories: 121; Fat: 1g; Fiber: 2g; Carbs: 3g; Protein: 3g

433. Sweet Potato Spread

(Prep + Cooking Time: 20 Minutes | **Serves:** 10)

Ingredients:

- 19 oz. canned garbanzo beans; drained
- 5 garlic cloves, minced.
- 1-cup sweet potatoes, peeled and chopped.
- 1/4-cup tahini
- 1-tbsp. olive oil
- 2-tbsp. water
- 2-tbsp. lemon juice
- ½-tsp. cumin, ground.
- A pinch of salt and white pepper

Directions:

1. Put potatoes in your air fryer's basket, cook them at 360 °F, for 15 minutes; cool them down, peel, put them in your food processor and pulse well. basket,
2. Add sesame paste, garlic, beans, lemon juice, cumin, water and oil and pulse really well. Add salt and pepper, pulse again; divide into bowls and serve.

Nutrition Values (Per Serving): Calories: 200; Fat: 3g; Fiber: 10g; Carbs: 20g; Protein: 11g

434. Chestnut and Shrimp Rolls.

(Prep + Cooking Time: 25 Minutes | **Serves:** 4)

Ingredients:

- ½ lb. already cooked shrimp, chopped.
- ½ lb. shiitake mushrooms, chopped.
- 8 oz. water chestnuts, chopped.
- 3 scallions, chopped.
- 1 egg yolk
- 6 spring roll wrappers
- 2-cups cabbage, chopped.
- 1 garlic clove, minced.
- 1-tbsp. water
- 2-tbsp. olive oil
- one-tsp. ginger, grated.
- Salt and black pepper to the taste.

Directions:

1. Heat up a pan with the oil over medium high heat, add cabbage, shrimp, chestnuts, mushrooms, garlic, ginger, scallions, salt and pepper; stir and cook for 2 minutes.
2. Take a bowl and mix egg with water and stir well. Arrange roll wrappers on a working surface, divide shrimp and veggie mix on them, seal edges with egg wash, place them all in your air fryer's basket, cook at 360 °F, for 15 minutes; transfer to a platter and serve as an appetizer.

Nutrition Values (Per Serving): Calories: 140; Fat: 3g; Fiber: 1g; Carbs: 12g; Protein: 3g

435. Sweet Popcorn Snack

(Prep + Cooking Time: 15 Minutes | **Serves:** 4)

Ingredients:

- 2 oz. brown sugar
- 2 ½-tbsp. butter
- 2-tbsp. corn kernels

Directions:

1. Put corn kernels in your air fryer's pan, cook at 400 °F, for 6 minutes; transfer them to a tray, spread and leave aside for now
2. Heat up a pan over low heat, add butter, melt it, add sugar and stir until it dissolves.

3. Add popcorn, toss to coat, take off heat and spread on the tray again. Cool down, divide into bowls and serve as a snack.

Nutrition Values (Per Serving): Calories: 70; Fat: 0.2g; Fiber: 0g; Carbs: 1g; Protein: 1g

436. Salmon Patties

(Prep + Cooking Time: 30 Minutes | **Serves:** 4)

Ingredients:

- 1 big salmon fillet; skinless, boneless
- 3 big potatoes; boiled, drained and mashed
- 1 egg
- 2-tbsp. parsley, chopped.
- 2-tbsp. dill, chopped.
- 2-tbsp. bread crumbs
- Salt and black pepper to the taste.
- Cooking spray.

Directions:

1. Place salmon in your air fryer's basket and cook for 10 minutes at 360 degrees F.
2. Transfer salmon to a cutting board, cool it down; flake it and put it in a bowl
3. Add mashed potatoes, salt, pepper, dill, parsley, egg and bread crumbs; stir well and shape 8 patties out of this mix. Place salmon patties in your air fryer's basket, spry them with cooking oil, cook at 360 °F, for 12 minutes; flipping them halfway, transfer them to a platter and serve as an appetizer

Nutrition Values (Per Serving): Calories: 231; Fat: 3g; Fiber: 7g; Carbs: 14g; Protein: 4g

437. Cauliflower Snack.

(Prep + Cooking Time: 25 Minutes | **Serves:** 4)

Ingredients:

- 4-cups cauliflower florets
- 1/4-cup buffalo sauce
- 1/4-cup butter, melted.
- 1-cup panko bread crumbs
- Mayonnaise for serving

Directions:

1. Take a bowl and mix buffalo sauce with butter and whisk well
2. Dip cauliflower florets in this mix and coat them in panko bread crumbs.
3. Place them in your air fryer's basket and cook at 350 °F, for 15 minutes. Arrange them on a platter and serve with mayo on the side.

Nutrition Values (Per Serving): Calories: 241; Fat: 4g; Fiber: 7g; Carbs: 8g; Protein: 4g

438. Amazing Pesto Crackers

(Prep + Cooking Time: 27 Minutes | **Serves:** 6)

Ingredients:

- 1¼-cups flour
- 1 garlic clove, minced.
- 3-tbsp. butter
- 2-tbsp. basil pesto
- ½-tsp. baking powder.
- 1/4-tsp. basil; dried
- Salt and black pepper to the taste.

Directions:

1. Take a bowl and mix salt, pepper, baking powder, flour, garlic, cayenne, basil, pesto and butter and stir until you obtain a dough.

2. Spread this dough on a lined baking sheet that fits your air fryer; introduce in the fryer at 325 °F and bake for 17 minutes. Leave aside to cool down, cut crackers and serve them as a snack.

Nutrition Values (Per Serving): Calories: 200; Fat: 20g; Fiber: 1g; Carbs: 4g; Protein: 7g

439. Quick Zucchini Cakes

(Prep + Cooking Time: 22 Minutes | **Serves:** 12)

Ingredients:

- ½-cup whole wheat flour
- 1 egg
- 2 garlic cloves, minced.
- ½-cup dill, chopped.
- 3 zucchinis, grated.
- 1 yellow onion, chopped.
- Cooking spray.
- Salt and black pepper to the taste.

Directions:

1. Take a bowl and mix zucchinis with garlic, onion, flour, salt, pepper, egg and dill; stir well, shape small patties out of this mix, spray them with cooking spray; place them in your air fryer's basket and cook at 370 °F, for 6 minutes on each side. Serve them as a snack right away.

Nutrition Values (Per Serving): Calories: 60; Fat: 1g; Fiber: 2g; Carbs: 6g; Protein: 2g

440. Crispy Shrimp Snack.

(Prep + Cooking Time: 15 Minutes | **Serves:** 4)

Ingredients:

- 12 big shrimp; deveined and peeled
- 1-cup coconut, shredded.
- 1-cup white flour
- 1-cup panko bread crumbs
- 2 egg whites
- Salt and black pepper to the taste.

Directions:

1. Take a bowl and mix panko with coconut and stir
2. Put flour, salt and pepper in a second bowl and whisk egg whites in a third one.
3. Dip shrimp in flour, egg whites mix and coconut, place them all in your air fryer's basket; cook at 350 °F, for 10 minutes flipping halfway. Arrange on a platter and serve as an appetizer.

Nutrition Values (Per Serving): Calories: 140; Fat: 4g; Fiber: 0g; Carbs: 3g; Protein: 4g

441. Tasty Crab Sticks

(Prep + Cooking Time: 30 Minutes | **Serves:** 4)

Ingredients:

- 10 crabsticks, halved.
- 2-tsp. sesame oil
- 2-tsp. Cajun seasoning

Directions:

1. Put crab sticks in a bowl; add sesame oil and Cajun seasoning; toss, transfer them to your air fryer's basket and cook at 350 °F, for 12 minutes. Arrange on a platter and serve as an appetizer.

Nutrition Values (Per Serving): Calories: 110; Fat: 0g; Fiber: 1g; Carbs: 4g; Protein: 2g5

442. Bread Sticks Snack

(Prep + Cooking Time: 20 Minutes | **Serves:** 2)

Ingredients:

- 4 bread slices; each cut into 4 sticks
- 2 eggs
- 1/4-cup milk
- 1/4-cup brown sugar
- 1-tbsp. honey
- one-tsp. cinnamon powder.
- A pinch of nutmeg

Directions:

1. Take a bowl and mix eggs with milk, brown sugar, cinnamon, nutmeg and honey and whisk well.
2. Dip bread sticks in this mix; place them in your air fryer's basket and cook at 360 °F, for 10 minutes. Divide bread sticks into bowls and serve as a snack.

Nutrition Values (Per Serving): Calories: 140; Fat: 1g; Fiber: 4g; Carbs: 8g; Protein: 4g

443. Fried Dill Pickles.

(Prep + Cooking Time: 15 Minutes | **Serves:** 4)

Ingredients:

- 16 oz. jarred dill pickles; cut into wedges and pat dried
- 1/4-cup ranch sauce
- 1/4-cup milk
- ½-cup white flour
- 1 egg
- ½-tsp. sweet paprika
- ½-tsp. garlic powder
- Cooking spray.

Directions:

1. Take a bowl and combine milk with egg and whisk well
2. In a second bowl; mix flour with salt, garlic powder and paprika and stir as well
3. Dip pickles in flour, then in egg mix and again in flour and place them in your air fryer. Grease them with cooking spray, cook pickle wedges at 400 °F, for 5 minutes; transfer to a bowl and serve with ranch sauce on the side.

Nutrition Values (Per Serving): Calories: 109; Fat: 2g; Fiber: 2g; Carbs: 10g; Protein: 4g

444. Chicken Breast Sticks

(Prep + Cooking Time: 26 Minutes | **Serves:** 4)

Ingredients:

- 1 lb. chicken breast; skinless, boneless and cut into medium sticks
- 1 egg, whisked.
- 3/4-cup white flour
- 1-cup panko bread crumbs
- ½-tbsp. olive oil
- one-tsp. sweet paprika
- Zest from 1 lemon, grated.
- Salt and black pepper to the taste.

Directions:

1. Take a bowl and mix paprika with flour, salt, pepper and lemon zest and stir
2. Put whisked egg in another bowl and the panko breadcrumbs in a third one.

3. Dredge chicken pieces in flour, egg and panko and place them in your lined air fryer's basket; drizzle the oil over them, cook at 400 °F, for 8 minutes; flip and cook for 8 more minutes. Arrange them on a platter and serve as a snack.

Nutrition Values (Per Serving): Calories: 254; Fat: 4g; Fiber: 7g; Carbs: 20g; Protein: 22g

445. Salmon Meatballs Snack

(Prep + Cooking Time: 22 Minutes | **Serves:** 4)

Ingredients:

- 1 lb. salmon; skinless and chopped.
- 1 small yellow onion, chopped.
- 1/4-cup panko
- 2 garlic cloves, minced.
- 1 egg white
- 3-tbsp. cilantro, minced.
- ½-tsp. paprika
- ½-tsp. oregano, ground.
- Salt and black pepper to the taste.
- Cooking spray.

Directions:

1. In your food processor, mix salmon with onion, cilantro, egg white, garlic cloves, salt, pepper, paprika and oregano and stir well
2. Add panko, blend again and shape meatballs from this mix using your palms.
3. Place them in your air fryer's basket; spray them with cooking spray and cook at 320 °F, for 12 minutes shaking the fryer halfway. Arrange meatballs on a platter and serve them as an appetizer.

Nutrition Values (Per Serving): Calories: 289; Fat: 12g; Fiber: 3g; Carbs: 22g; Protein: 23g

446. Honey Chicken Wings.

(Prep + Cooking Time: 1 hour and 22 minutes | **Serves:** 8)

Ingredients:

- 16 chicken wings, halved.
- 2-tbsp. lime juice
- 2-tbsp. honey
- 2-tbsp. soy sauce
- Salt and black pepper to the taste.

Directions:

1. Take a bowl and mix chicken wings with soy sauce, honey, salt, pepper and lime juice; toss well and keep in the fridge for 1 hour.
2. Transfer chicken wings to your air fryer and cook them at 360 °F, for 12 minutes; flipping them halfway. Arrange them on a platter and serve as an appetizer

Nutrition Values (Per Serving): Calories: 211; Fat: 4g; Fiber: 7g; Carbs: 14g; Protein: 3g

447. Tasty Fish Sticks

(Prep + Cooking Time: 22 Minutes | **Serves:** 2)

Ingredients:

- 4 white fish filets; boneless, skinless and cut into medium sticks
- 4 oz. bread crumbs
- 1 egg, whisked.
- 4-tbsp. olive oil
- Salt and black pepper to the taste.

Directions:

1. Take a bowl and mix bread crumbs with oil and stir well.

2. Put egg in a second bowl; add salt and pepper and whisk well
3. Dip fish stick in egg and them in bread crumb mix, place them in your air fryer's basket and cook at 360 °F, for 12 minutes. Arrange fish sticks on a platter and serve as an appetizer.

Nutrition Values (Per Serving): Calories: 160; Fat: 3g; Fiber: 5g; Carbs: 12g; Protein: 3g

448. Easy Zucchini Chips

(Prep + Cooking Time: 1 hour 10 Minutes | **Serves:** 6)

Ingredients:

- 3 zucchinis; thinly sliced
- 2-tbsp. balsamic vinegar
- 2-tbsp. olive oil
- Salt and black pepper to the taste.

Directions:

1. Take a bowl and mix oil with vinegar, salt and pepper and whisk well.
2. Add zucchini slices, toss to coat well; introduce in your air fryer and cook at 200 °F, for 1 hour. Serve zucchini chips cold as a snack.

Nutrition Values (Per Serving): Calories: 40; Fat: 3g; Fiber: 7g; Carbs: 3g; Protein: 7g

449. Delicious Shrimp Muffins.

(Prep + Cooking Time: 36 Minutes | **Serves:** 6)

Ingredients:

- 1 spaghetti squash, peeled and halved
- 1-cup mozzarella, shredded.
- 1 ½-cups panko
- 8 oz. shrimp, peeled, cooked and chopped
- 1 garlic clove, minced.
- 2-tbsp. mayonnaise
- one-tsp. parsley flakes
- Salt and black pepper to the taste.
- Cooking spray.

Directions:

1. Put squash halves in your air fryer; cook at 350 °F, for 16 minutes; leave aside to cool down and scrape flesh into a bowl.
2. Add salt, pepper, parsley flakes, panko, shrimp, mayo and mozzarella and stir well.
3. Spray a muffin tray that fits your air fryer with cooking spray and divide squash and shrimp mix in each cup.
4. Introduce in the fryer and cook at 360 °F, for 10 minutes. Arrange muffins on a platter and serve as a snack.

Nutrition Values (Per Serving): Calories: 60; Fat: 2g; Fiber: 0.4g; Carbs: 4g; Protein: 4g

450. Succulent Chicken Dip

(Prep + Cooking Time: 35 Minutes | **Serves:** 10)

Ingredients:

- 2-cups chicken meat; cooked and shredded
- 12 oz. cream cheese
- 1/3-cup raisins
- 1/4-cup cilantro, chopped.
- ½-cup almonds, sliced.
- 4 scallions, chopped.
- ½-cup chutney
- 6 oz. Monterey jack cheese, grated.
- 1-cup yogurt

- 3-tbsp. butter, melted.
- 2-tsp. curry powder
- Salt and black pepper to the taste.

Directions:

1. In a bowl mix cream cheese with yogurt and whisk using your mixer.
2. Add curry powder, scallions, chicken meat, raisins, cheese, cilantro, salt and pepper and stir everything. Spread this into a baking dish that fist your air fryer; sprinkle almonds on top, place in your air fryer, bake at 300 degrees for 25 minutes; divide into bowls, top with chutney and serve as an appetizer.

Nutrition Values (Per Serving): Calories: 240; Fat: 10g; Fiber: 2g; Carbs: 24g; Protein: 12g

451. Spicy Fish Nuggets

(Prep + Cooking Time: 22 Minutes | **Serves:** 4)

Ingredients:

- 28 oz. fish fillets; skinless and cut into medium pieces
- 3 oz. panko bread crumbs
- 1 egg, whisked.
- 5-tbsp. water
- 1-tbsp. garlic powder
- 1-tbsp. smoked paprika
- 4-tbsp. homemade mayonnaise
- 5-tbsp. flour
- one-tsp. dill; dried
- Lemon juice from ½ lemon
- Salt and black pepper to the taste.
- Cooking spray.

Directions:

1. Take a bowl and mix flour with water and stir well.
2. Add egg, salt and pepper and whisk well
3. In a second bowl; mix panko with garlic powder and paprika and stir well.
4. Dip fish pieces in flour and egg mix and then in panko mix, place them in your air fryer's basket, spray them with cooking oil and cook at 400 °F, for 12 minutes.
5. Meanwhile, in a bowl mix mayo with dill and lemon juice and whisk well. Arrange fish nuggets on a platter and serve with dill mayo on the side

Nutrition Values (Per Serving): Calories: 332; Fat: 12g; Fiber: 6g; Carbs: 17g; Protein: 15g

452. Cheering Chicken Breast Rolls

(Prep + Cooking Time: 32 Minutes | **Serves:** 4)

Ingredients:

- 4 chicken breasts; boneless and skinless
- 4 mozzarella slices
- 2-cups baby spinach
- 1-cup sun dried tomatoes, chopped.
- 1 ½-tbsp. Italian seasoning
- A drizzle of olive oil
- Salt and black pepper to the taste.

Directions:

1. Flatten chicken breasts using a meat tenderizer, divide tomatoes, mozzarella and spinach, season with salt, pepper and Italian seasoning, roll and seal them
2. Place them in your air fryer's basket; drizzle some oil over them and cook at 375 °F, for 17 minutes; flipping once. Arrange chicken rolls on a platter and serve them as an appetizer.

Nutrition Values (Per Serving): Calories: 300; Fat: 1g; Fiber: 4g; Carbs: 7g; Protein: 10g

453. Delightful Chickpeas Snack

(Prep + Cooking Time: 20 Minutes | **Serves:** 4)

Ingredients:

- 15 oz. canned chickpeas; drained
- 1-tbsp. olive oil
- ½-tsp. cumin, ground.
- one-tsp. smoked paprika
- Salt and black pepper to the taste.

Directions:

1. Take a bowl and mix chickpeas with oil, cumin, paprika, salt and pepper; toss to coat, place them in your fryer's basket and cook at 390 °F, for 10 minutes. Divide into bowls and serve as a snack.

Nutrition Values (Per Serving): Calories: 140; Fat: 1g; Fiber: 6g; Carbs: 20g; Protein: 6g

454. Yummy Spring Rolls.

(Prep + Cooking Time: 35 Minutes | **Serves:** 8)

Ingredients:

- 2-cups green cabbage, shredded.
- 2 yellow onions, chopped.
- ½ chili pepper, minced.
- 3 garlic cloves, minced.
- 1 carrot, grated.
- 10 spring roll sheets
- 1-tbsp. ginger, grated.
- 2-tbsp. olive oil
- 2-tbsp. corn flour
- 2-tbsp. water
- one-tsp. soy sauce
- one-tsp. sugar
- Salt and black pepper to the taste.

Directions:

1. Heat up a pan with the oil over medium heat, add cabbage, onions, carrots, chili pepper, ginger, garlic, sugar, salt, pepper and soy sauce; stir well, cook for 2-3 minutes; take off heat and cool down
2. Cut spring roll sheets in squares, divide cabbage mix on each and roll them.
3. Take a bowl and mix corn flour with water; stir well and seal spring rolls with this mix.
4. Place spring rolls in your air fryer's basket and cook them at 360 °F, for 10 minutes.
5. Flip roll and cook them for 10 minutes more. Arrange on a platter and serve them as an appetizer

Nutrition Values (Per Serving): Calories: 214; Fat: 4g; Fiber: 4g; Carbs: 12g; Protein: 4g

455. Amazing Seafood Appetizer

(Prep + Cooking Time: 35 Minutes | **Serves:** 4)

Ingredients:

- ½-cup yellow onion, chopped.
- 1-cup celery, chopped.
- 1-cup baby shrimp, peeled and deveined
- 1-cup green bell pepper, chopped.
- 1-cup crabmeat; flaked
- 1-cup homemade mayonnaise
- 1-tbsp. butter
- 2-tbsp. bread crumbs
- one-tsp. Worcestershire sauce
- one-tsp. sweet paprika
- Salt and black pepper to the taste.

Directions:

1. Take a bowl and mix shrimp with crab meat, bell pepper, onion, mayo, celery, salt and pepper and stir.

2. Add Worcestershire sauce; stir again and pour everything into a baking dish that fits your air fryer
3. Sprinkle bread crumbs and add butter, introduce in your air fryer and cook at 320 °F, for 25 minutes; shaking halfway. Divide into bowl and serve with paprika sprinkled on top as an appetizer.

Nutrition Values (Per Serving): Calories: 200; Fat: 1g; Fiber: 2g; Carbs: 5g; Protein: 1g

456. Chicken Wings

(Prep + Cooking Time: 1 hours 10 Minutes | **Serves:** 2)

Ingredients:

- 16 pieces' chicken wings
- 3/4-cup potato starch
- 1/4-cup butter
- 1/4-cup honey
- 4-tbsp. garlic, minced.
- Salt and black pepper to the taste.

Directions:

1. Take a bowl and mix chicken wings with salt, pepper and potato starch; toss well, transfer to your air fryer's basket, cook them at 380 °F, for 25 minutes and at 400 °F, for 5 minutes more
2. Meanwhile, heat up a pan with the butter over medium high heat, melt it, add garlic; stir, cook for 5 minutes and then mix with salt, pepper and honey.
3. Whisk well, cook over medium heat for 20 minutes and take off heat. Arrange chicken wings on a platter; drizzle honey sauce all over and serve as an appetizer.

Nutrition Values (Per Serving): Calories: 244; Fat: 7g; Fiber: 3g; Carbs: 19g; Protein: 8g

457. Mexican Style Apple Snack

(Prep + Cooking Time: 15 Minutes | **Serves:** 4)

Ingredients:

- 3 big apples; cored, peeled and cubed
- ½-cup dark chocolate chips
- ½-cup clean caramel sauce
- 1/4-cup pecans, chopped.
- 2-tsp. lemon juice

Directions:

1. Take a bowl and mix apples with lemon juice; stir and transfer to a pan that fits your air fryer
2. Add chocolate chips, pecans, drizzle the caramel sauce, toss; introduce in your air fryer and cook at 320 °F, for 5 minutes. Toss gently, divide into small bowls and serve right away as a snack.

Nutrition Values (Per Serving): Calories: 200; Fat: 4g; Fiber: 3g; Carbs: 20g; Protein: 3g

458. Party Beef Rolls.

(Prep + Cooking Time: 25 Minutes | **Serves:** 4)

Ingredients:

- 14 oz. beef stock
- 7 oz. white wine
- 4 beef cutlets
- 4 ham slices
- 8 sage leaves
- 1-tbsp. butter, melted.
- Salt and black pepper to the taste.

Directions:

1. Heat up a pan with the stock over medium high heat, add wine, cook until it reduces, take off heat and divide into small bowls

2. Season cutlets with salt and pepper; cover with sage and roll each in ham slices
3. Brush rolls with butter, place them in your air fryer's basket and cook at 400 °F, for 15 minutes. Arrange rolls on a platter and serve them with the gravy on the side.

Nutrition Values (Per Serving): Calories: 260; Fat: 12g; Fiber: 1g; Carbs: 22g; Protein: 21g

459. Greek Style Lamb Meatballs

(Prep + Cooking Time: 18 Minutes | **Serves:** 10)

Ingredients:

- 1 slice of bread; toasted and crumbled
- 4 oz. lamb meat, minced.
- ½-tbsp. lemon peel, grated.
- 1-tbsp. oregano, chopped.
- 2-tbsp. feta cheese, crumbled.
- Salt and black pepper to the taste.

Directions:

1. Take a bowl and combine meat with bread crumbs, salt, pepper, feta, oregano and lemon peel; stir well, shape 10 meatballs and place them in you air fryer. Cook at 400 °F, for 8 minutes; arrange them on a platter and serve as an appetizer.

Nutrition Values (Per Serving): Calories: 234; Fat: 12g; Fiber: 2g; Carbs: 20g; Protein: 30

460. Radish Chips.

(Prep + Cooking Time: 20 Minutes | **Serves:** 4)

Ingredients:

- 15 radishes, sliced.
- 1-tbsp. chives, chopped.
- Salt and black pepper to the taste.
- Cooking spray.

Directions:

1. Arrange radish slices in your air fryer's basket, spray them with cooking oil, season with salt and black pepper to the taste, cook them at 350 °F, for 10 minutes
2. Flipping them halfway, transfer to bowls and serve with chives sprinkled on top.

Nutrition Values (Per Serving): Calories: 80; Fat: 1g; Fiber: 1g; Carbs: 1g; Protein: 1g

461. Sausage Balls Snack.

(Prep + Cooking Time: 25 Minutes | **Serves:** 9)

Ingredients:

- 4 oz. sausage meat, ground.
- 1 small onion, chopped.
- 3-tbsp. breadcrumbs
- one-tsp. sage
- ½-tsp. garlic, minced.
- Salt and black pepper to the taste.

Directions:

1. Take a bowl and mix sausage with salt, pepper, sage, garlic, onion and breadcrumbs; stir well and shape small balls out of this mix. Put them in your air fryer's basket, cook at 360 °F, for 15 minutes; divide into bowls and serve as a snack.

Nutrition Values (Per Serving): Calories: 130; Fat: 7g; Fiber: 1g; Carbs: 13g; Protein: 4g

462. Healthy Spinach Balls

(Prep + Cooking Time: 17 Minutes | **Serves:** 30)

Ingredients:

- 1/3-cup parmesan, grated.
- 16 oz. spinach
- 1/3-cup feta cheese, crumbled.
- 2 eggs
- 1-cup flour
- 4-tbsp. butter, melted.
- 1-tbsp. onion powder
- 3-tbsp. whipping cream
- 1/4-tsp. nutmeg, ground.
- one-tsp. garlic powder
- Salt and black pepper to the taste.

Directions:

1. In your blender, mix spinach with butter, eggs, flour, feta cheese, parmesan, nutmeg, whipping cream, salt, pepper, onion and garlic pepper, blend very well and keep in the freezer for 10 minutes
2. Shape 30 spinach balls; place them in your air fryer's basket and cook at 300 °F, for 7 minutes. Serve as a party appetizer.

Nutrition Values (Per Serving): Calories: 60; Fat: 5g; Fiber: 1g; Carbs: 1g; Protein: 2g

463. Roasted Pepper Rolls

(Prep + Cooking Time: 20 Minutes | **Serves:** 8)

Ingredients:

- 4 oz. feta cheese, crumbled.
- 1 orange bell pepper, halved.
- 1 green onion, chopped.
- 1 yellow bell pepper, halved.
- 2-tbsp. oregano, chopped.
- Salt and black pepper to the taste.

Directions:

1. Take a bowl and mix cheese with onion, oregano, salt and pepper and whisk well.
2. Place bell pepper halves in your air fryer's basket, cook at 400 °F, for 10 minutes; transfer to a cutting board, cool down and peel. Divide cheese mix on each bell pepper half, roll, secure with toothpicks, arrange on a platter and serve as an appetizer.

Nutrition Values (Per Serving): Calories: 170; Fat: 1g; Fiber: 2g; Carbs: 8g; Protein: 5g

464. Delicious Tuna Cakes

(Prep + Cooking Time: 20 Minutes | **Serves:** 12)

Ingredients:

- 15 oz. canned tuna; drain and flaked
- ½-cup red onion, chopped.
- 3 eggs
- ½-tsp. dill; dried
- one-tsp. parsley; dried
- one-tsp. garlic powder
- Salt and black pepper to the taste.
- Cooking spray.

Directions:

1. Take a bowl and mix tuna with salt, pepper, dill, parsley, onion, garlic powder and eggs; stir well and shape medium cakes out of this mix
2. Place tuna cakes in your air fryer's basket, spray them with cooking oil and cook at 350 °F, for 10 minutes; flipping them halfway. Arrange them on a platter and serve as an appetizer.

Nutrition Values (Per Serving): Calories: 140; Fat: 2g; Fiber: 1g; Carbs: 8g; Protein: 6g

465. Pure Pumpkin Muffins

(Prep + Cooking Time: 25 Minutes | **Serves:** 18)

Ingredients:

- 3/4-cup pumpkin puree
- 1/4-cup flour
- 1/4-cup butter
- ½-cup sugar
- 1 egg
- 2-tbsp. flaxseed meal
- one-tsp. cinnamon powder.
- ½-tsp. nutmeg, ground.
- ½-tsp. baking soda
- ½-tsp. baking powder.

Directions:

1. Take a bowl and mix butter with pumpkin puree and egg and blend well.
2. Add flaxseed meal, flour, sugar, baking soda, baking powder, nutmeg and cinnamon and stir well
3. Spoon this into a muffin pan that fits your fryer introduce in the fryer at 350 °F and bake for 15 minutes. Serve muffins cold as a snack.

Nutrition Values (Per Serving): Calories: 50; Fat: 3g; Fiber: 1g; Carbs: 2g; Protein: 2g

466. Cheesy Chicken Rolls

(Prep + Cooking Time: 30 Minutes | **Serves:** 12)

Ingredients:

- 4 oz. blue cheese, crumbled.
- 12 egg roll wrappers
- ½-cup tomato sauce
- 2-cups chicken, cooked and chopped.
- 2 green onions, chopped.
- 2 celery stalks; finely chopped.
- Salt and black pepper to the taste.
- Cooking spray.

Directions:

1. Take a bowl and mix chicken meat with blue cheese, salt, pepper, green onions, celery and tomato sauce; stir well and keep in the fridge for 2 hours.
2. Place egg wrappers on a working surface, divide chicken mix on them, roll and seal edges. Place rolls in your air fryer's basket, spray them with cooking oil and cook at 350 °F, for 10 minutes; flipping them halfway.

Nutrition Values (Per Serving): Calories: 220; Fat: 7g; Fiber: 2g; Carbs: 14g; Protein: 10g

467. Tasty Cheese Sticks

(Prep + Cooking Time: 1 hour and 18 minutes | **Serves:** 4)

Ingredients:

- 8 mozzarella cheese strings; cut into halves
- 1 garlic clove, minced.
- 1-cup parmesan, grated.
- 2 eggs, whisked.
- 1-tbsp. Italian seasoning
- Salt and black pepper to the taste.
- Cooking spray.

Directions:

1. Take a bowl and mix parmesan with salt, pepper, Italian seasoning and garlic and stir well.
2. Put whisked eggs in another bowl.
3. Dip mozzarella sticks in egg mixture; then in cheese mix
4. Dip them again in egg and in parmesan mix and keep them in the freezer for 1 hour.

5. Spray cheese sticks with cooking oil; place them in your air fryer's basket and cook at 390 °F, for 8 minutes flipping them halfway. Arrange them on a platter and serve as an appetizer

Nutrition Values (Per Serving): Calories: 140; Fat: 5g; Fiber: 1g; Carbs: 3g; Protein: 4g

468. Appetizing Cajun Shrimp

(Prep + Cooking Time: 15 Minutes | **Serves:** 2)

Ingredients:

- 20 tiger shrimp, peeled and deveined
- 1-tbsp. olive oil
- 1/4-tsp. smoked paprika
- ½-tsp. old bay seasoning
- Salt and black pepper to the taste.

Directions:

1. Take a bowl and mix shrimp with oil, salt, pepper, old bay seasoning and paprika and toss to coat.
2. Place shrimp in your air fryer's basket and cook at 390 °F, for 5 minutes. Arrange them on a platter and serve as an appetizer.

Nutrition Values (Per Serving): Calories: 162; Fat: 6g; Fiber: 4g; Carbs: 8g; Protein: 14g

469. Cheesy Tasty Zucchini Snack

(Prep + Cooking Time: 18 Minutes | **Serves:** 4)

Ingredients:

- 1-cup mozzarella, shredded.
- 1 zucchini, sliced.
- 1/4-cup tomato sauce
- A pinch of cumin
- Salt and black pepper to the taste.
- Cooking spray.

Directions:

1. Arrange zucchini slices in your air fryer's basket; spray them with cooking oil, spread tomato sauce all over, them, season with salt, pepper, cumin, sprinkle mozzarella at the end and cook them at 320 °F, for 8 minutes. Arrange them on a platter and serve as a snack.

Nutrition Values (Per Serving): Calories: 150; Fat: 4g; Fiber: 2g; Carbs: 12g; Protein: 4g

470. Tasty Apple Chips

(Prep + Cooking Time: 20 Minutes | **Serves:** 2)

Ingredients:

- 1 apple; cored and sliced
- 1-tbsp. white sugar
- ½-tsp. cinnamon powder.
- A pinch of salt

Directions:

1. Take a bowl and mix apple slices with salt, sugar and cinnamon; toss, transfer to your air fryer's basket, cook for 10 minutes at 390 °F, flipping once. Divide apple chips in bowls and serve as a snack.

Nutrition Values (Per Serving): Calories: 70; Fat: 0g; Fiber: 4g; Carbs: 3g; Protein: 1g

471. Easy Broccoli Patties.

(Prep + Cooking Time: 20 Minutes | **Serves:** 12)

Ingredients:

- 4-cups broccoli florets
- 2-cups cheddar cheese, grated.
- 1 ½-cup almond flour
- 1/4-cup olive oil
- 2 eggs
- ½-tsp. apple cider vinegar
- ½-tsp. baking soda
- one-tsp. paprika
- one-tsp. garlic powder
- Salt and black pepper to the taste.

Directions:

1. Put broccoli florets in your food processor; add salt and pepper, blend well and transfer to a bowl
2. Add almond flour, salt, pepper, paprika, garlic powder, baking soda, cheese, oil, eggs and vinegar; stir well and shape 12 patties out of this mix.
3. Place them in your preheated air fryer's basket and cook at 350 °F, for 10 minutes. Arrange patties on a platter and serve as an appetizer

Nutrition Values (Per Serving): Calories: 203; Fat: 12g; Fiber: 2g; Carbs: 14g; Protein: 2g

472. Special Empanadas

(Prep + Cooking Time: 35 Minutes | **Serves:** 4)

Ingredients:

- 1 package empanada shells
- 1 lb. beef meat, ground.
- 1 yellow onion, chopped.
- 1/4-cup tomato salsa
- 1 egg yolk whisked with 1-tbsp. water
- 1 green bell pepper, chopped.
- 2 garlic cloves, minced.
- 1-tbsp. olive oil
- ½-tsp. cumin, ground.
- Salt and black pepper to the taste.

Directions:

1. Heat up a pan with the oil over medium high heat; add beef and brown on all sides.
2. Add onion, garlic, salt, pepper, bell pepper and tomato salsa; stir and cook for 15 minutes
3. Divide cooked meat in empanada shells, brush them with egg wash and seal.
4. Place them in your air fryer's steamer basket and cook at 350 °F, for 10 minutes. Arrange on a platter and serve as an appetizer

Nutrition Values (Per Serving): Calories: 274; Fat: 17g; Fiber: 14g; Carbs: 20g; Protein: 7g

473. Mouthwatering Beef Rolls

(Prep + Cooking Time: 24 Minutes | **Serves:** 4)

Ingredients:

- 2 lbs. beef steak; opened and flattened with a meat tenderizer
- 3 oz. red bell pepper; roasted and chopped.
- 6 slices provolone cheese
- 1-cup baby spinach
- 3-tbsp. pesto
- Salt and black pepper to the taste.

Directions:

1. Arrange flattened beef steak on a cutting board, spread pesto all over, add cheese in a single layer, add bell peppers, spinach, salt and pepper to the taste.
2. Roll your steak, secure with toothpicks, season again with salt and pepper; place roll in your air fryer's basket and cook at 400 °F, for 14 minutes; rotating roll halfway. Leave aside to cool down, cut into 2 inch smaller rolls, arrange on a platter and serve them as an appetizer

Nutrition Values (Per Serving): Calories: 230; Fat: 1g; Fiber: 3g; Carbs: 12g; Protein: 10g

474. Kale and Celery Crackers

(Prep + Cooking Time: 30 Minutes | **Serves:** 6)

Ingredients:

- 2-cups flax seed, ground.
- 2-cups flax seed; soaked overnight and drained
- 4 bunches kale, chopped.
- 4 garlic cloves, minced.
- 1/3-cup olive oil
- 1 bunch basil, chopped.
- ½ bunch celery, chopped.

Directions:

1. In your food processor mix ground flaxseed with celery, kale, basil and garlic and blend well
2. Add oil and soaked flaxseed and blend again, spread in your air fryer's pan; cut into medium crackers and cook them at 380 °F, for 20 minutes. Divide into bowls and serve as an appetizer.

Nutrition Values (Per Serving): Calories: 143; Fat: 1g; Fiber: 2g; Carbs: 8g; Protein: 4g

475. Onion Rings

(Prep + Cook Time: 30 minutes | **Serves:** 4)

Ingredients:

- 1 large onion; cut into ¼ inch slices
- 3/4 cup dry breadcrumbs
- 1 cup milk
- 1 egg
- 1¼ cups all-purpose flour
- One-tablespoon. baking powder
- Salt, as your liking.

Directions:

1. Separate the onion slices into rings. In a shallow dish, mix together the flour, baking powder and salt.
2. In a second dish, mix well milk and egg. In a third dish, put the breadcrumbs
3. Coat each onion ring with flour mixture, then dip into egg mixture and finally, coat evenly with the breadcrumbs.
4. Set the temperature of Air Fryer to 360°F. Place the onion rings in an Air Fryer basket in a single layer.
5. Air Fry for about 7 to 10 minutes. Serve hot

476. Salmon Croquettes

(Prep + Cook Time: 29 minutes | **Serves:** 16)

Ingredients:

- 1 large can red salmon, drained.
- 2 eggs, lightly beaten
- 1 cup breadcrumbs
- 1/3 cup vegetable oil
- 2 tbsp. fresh parsley, chopped.

- Salt and freshly ground black pepper, as needed.

Directions:

1. Set the temperature of Air Fryer to 390°F. In a bowl, add the salmon and mash it completely using a fork.
2. Add the eggs, parsley, salt and black pepper. Mix until well combined
3. Make 16 equal-sized croquettes from the mixture. In a shallow dish, mix together the oil and breadcrumbs. Coat the croquettes evenly with the breadcrumb mixture.
4. Place the croquettes in an Air Fryer basket in a single layer in 2 batches. Air Fry for about 7 minutes. Serve.

477. Broccoli Bites

(Prep + Cook Time: 27 minutes | **Serves:** 10)

Ingredients:

- 1/4 cup Parmesan cheese, grated.
- 2 cups broccoli florets
- 2 eggs, beaten
- 1¼ cups panko breadcrumbs
- 1¼ cups cheddar cheese, grated.
- Salt and freshly ground black pepper, as needed.

Directions:

1. In a food processor, add the broccoli and pulse until finely crumbled
2. Take a large bowl, mix together the broccoli and remaining ingredients.
3. Make small equal-sized balls from the mixture. Arrange the balls in a baking sheet and refrigerate for at least 30 minutes.
4. Set the temperature of Air Fryer to 350°F. Put the balls in an Air fryer basket Air Fry for about 12 minutes. Serve

478. Spicy Stuffed Peppers.

(Prep + Cooking Time: 30 Minutes | **Serves:** 6)

Ingredients:

- 1 lb. mini bell peppers, halved.
- 1 lb. beef meat, ground.
- 1½-cups cheddar cheese, shredded.
- 1-tbsp. chili powder
- 1/4-tsp. red pepper flakes
- one-tsp. cumin, ground.
- one-tsp. garlic powder
- one-tsp. sweet paprika
- ½-tsp. oregano; dried
- Sour cream for serving
- Salt and black pepper to the taste.

Directions:

1. Take a bowl and mix chili powder with paprika, salt, pepper, cumin, oregano, pepper flakes and garlic powder and stir.
2. Heat up a pan over medium heat, add beef; stir and brown for 10 minutes.
3. Add chili powder mix; stir, take off heat and stuff pepper halves with this mix
4. Sprinkle cheese all over, place peppers in your air fryer's basket and cook them at 350 °F, for 6 minutes. Arrange peppers on a platter and serve them with sour cream on the side

Nutrition Values (Per Serving): Calories: 170; Fat: 22g; Fiber: 3g; Carbs: 6g; Protein: 27

479. Shrimp and Calamari Snack.

(Prep + Cooking Time: 30 Minutes | **Serves:** 1)

Ingredients:

- 8 oz. calamari; cut into medium rings
- 7 oz. shrimp, peeled and deveined
- 1 egg
- 3-tbsp. white flour
- 1-tbsp. olive oil
- 2-tbsp. avocado, chopped.
- 1-tbsp. mayonnaise
- one-tsp. tomato paste
- ½-tsp. turmeric powder
- one-tsp. lemon juice
- A splash of Worcestershire sauce
- Salt and black pepper to the taste.

Directions:

1. Take a bowl and whisk egg with oil, add calamari rings and shrimp and toss to coat.
2. In another bowl; mix flour with salt, pepper and turmeric and stir
3. Dredge calamari and shrimp in this mix, place them in your air fryer's basket and cook at 350 °F, for 9 minutes; flipping them once.
4. Meanwhile, in a bowl, mix avocado with mayo and tomato paste and mash using a fork.
5. Add Worcestershire sauce, lemon juice, salt and pepper and stir well. Arrange calamari and shrimp on a platter and serve with the sauce on the side

Nutrition Values (Per Serving): Calories: 288; Fat: 23g; Fiber: 3g; Carbs: 10g; Protein: 15g

480. Egg White Chips Snack

(Prep + Cooking Time: 13 Minutes | **Serves:** 2)

Ingredients:

- 4 eggs whites
- 2-tbsp. parmesan, shredded.
- ½-tbsp. water
- Salt and black pepper to the taste.

Directions:

1. Take a bowl and mix egg whites with salt, pepper and water and whisk well
2. Spoon this into a muffin pan that fits your air fryer, sprinkle cheese on top; introduce in your air fryer and cook at 350 °F, for 8 minutes. Arrange egg white chips on a platter and serve as a snack.

Nutrition Values (Per Serving): Calories: 180; Fat: 2g; Fiber: 1g; Carbs: 12g; Protein: 7g

481. Delicious Wrapped Shrimp

(Prep + Cooking Time: 18 Minutes | **Serves:** 16)

Ingredients:

- 10 oz. already cooked shrimp, peeled and deveined
- 1/3-cup red wine
- 1/3-cup blackberries, ground.
- 11 prosciutto sliced
- 2-tbsp. olive oil
- 1-tbsp. mint, chopped.

Directions:

1. Wrap each shrimp in a prosciutto slices, drizzle the oil over them, rub well, place in your preheated air fryer at 390 °F and fry them for 8 minutes.

2. Meanwhile, heat up a pan with ground blackberries over medium heat, add mint and wine; stir, cook for 3 minutes and take off heat. Arrange shrimp on a platter, drizzle blackberries sauce over them and serve as an appetizer

Nutrition Values (Per Serving): Calories: 224; Fat: 12g; Fiber: 2g; Carbs: 12g; Protein: 14g

482. Mozzarella Sticks

(Prep + Cook Time: 39 minutes | **Serves:** 4)

Ingredients:

- 1 lb. Mozzarella cheese block cut into 3x½-inch sticks
- 1 cup plain breadcrumbs
- 2 eggs
- 1/4 cup white flour
- 3 tbsp. nonfat milk

Directions:

1. Add the flour in a shallow dish. In a second dish, mix together the eggs and milk. In a third dish, put the breadcrumbs
2. Coat the Mozzarella sticks with flour, then dip into egg mixture and finally, coat evenly with the breadcrumbs.
3. Arrange the Mozzarella sticks onto a baking sheet and freeze for about 1 to 2 hours.
4. Set the temperature of Air Fryer to 440°F.
5. Arrange the Mozzarella sticks in an Air Fryer basket in a single layer in 2 batches. Air Fry for about 12 minutes

483. Chocolate Cookie Dough Balls

(Prep + Cook Time: 35 minutes | **Serves:** 6)

Ingredients:

- 16½ oz. store-bought chilled chocolate chip cookie dough
- 1/2 cup chocolate cookie crumbs
- 1/4 cup butter, melted
- 2 tbsp. sugar

Directions:

1. Cut the cookie dough into 12 equal-sized pieces and then, shape each into a ball.
2. Add the melted butter in a shallow dish. In another dish, mix together the cookie crumbs and sugar
3. Dip each cookie ball in the melted butter and then evenly coat with the cookie crumbs.
4. In the bottom of a baking sheet, place the coated cookie balls and freeze for at least 2 hours
5. Preheat the air fryer to 350°F. Line the air fryer basket with a piece of foil. Place the cookies balls in an Air Fryer basket in a single layer in 2 batches. Air Fry for about 10 minutes.

484. Cauliflower Poppers

(Prep + Cook Time: 26 minutes | **Serves:** 6)

Ingredients:

- 1 large head cauliflower; cut into bite-sized florets
- 2 tbsp. olive oil
- Salt and freshly ground black pepper, as needed.

Directions:

1. Drizzle the cauliflower florets with oil. Sprinkle with salt and black pepper
2. Set the temperature of Air Fryer to 390°F. Place the cauliflower florets in a greased Air Fryer basket in a single layer in 2 batches.
3. Air Fry for about 8 minutes, shaking once halfway through. Serve hot

485. Potato Chips

(Prep + Cook Time: 45 minutes | **Serves:** 6)

Ingredients:

- 4 small russet potatoes, thinly sliced
- 2 tbsp. fresh rosemary, finely chopped.
- One-tablespoon olive oil
- 1/4 tsp. salt

Directions:

1. In a large bowl, add the water and potato slices. Set aside for about 30 minutes, changing the water once halfway through
2. Drain the potato slices well and pat them dry with the paper towels. Set the temperature of Air Fryer to 350°F.
3. In a bowl, mix together the potato slices, olive oil, rosemary and salt. Add the potato chips in an Air Fryer basket in a single layer. Air Fry for about 30 minutes. Serve.

486. Squash Fries

(Prep + Cook Time: 45 minutes | **Serves:** 2)

Ingredients:

- 14 oz. butternut squash, peeled, seeded and cut into strips
- 1/2 tsp. red chili powder
- 1/2 tsp. ground cinnamon
- 2 tsp. olive oil
- 1/4 tsp. garlic salt
- Salt and freshly ground black pepper, as needed.

Directions:

1. Set the temperature of Air Fryer to 440°F. Line a baking sheet with parchment paper. Take a bowl, add all the listed Ingredients and toss to coat well
2. Place the butternut squash strips onto the prepared baking sheet in a single layer. Arrange the baking sheet in an Air Fryer basket. Air Fry for about 35 minutes. Serve.

487. Party Pork Rolls

(Prep + Cooking Time: 50 Minutes | **Serves:** 4)

Ingredients:

- 1 (15 oz.) pork fillet
- 1 garlic clove, minced.
- 1 red onion, chopped.
- 2-tbsp. olive oil
- 3-tbsp. parsley, chopped.
- one-tsp. cinnamon powder.
- ½-tsp. chili powder
- 1 ½-tsp. cumin, ground.
- Salt and black pepper to the taste.

Directions:

1. Take a bowl and mix cinnamon with garlic, salt, pepper, chili powder, oil, onion, parsley and cumin and stir well
2. Put pork fillet on a cutting board, flatten it using a meat tenderizer. And use a meat tenderizer to flatten it
3. Spread onion mix on pork, roll tight, cut into medium rolls, place them in your preheated air fryer at 360 °F and cook them for 35 minutes. Arrange them on a platter and serve as an appetizer

Nutrition Values (Per Serving): Calories: 304; Fat: 12g; Fiber: 1g; Carbs: 15g; Protein: 23g

488. Zucchini Fries

(Prep + Cook Time: 30 minutes | **Serves:** 4)

Ingredients:

- 1 lb. zucchini, sliced into 2½-inch sticks
- 3/4 cup panko breadcrumbs
- 2 tbsp. olive oil
- Salt, as your liking.

Directions:

1. In a colander, add the zucchini and sprinkle with salt. Set aside for about 10 minutes. Set the temperature of Air Fryer to 390°F
2. Gently pat dry the zucchini sticks with the paper towels and coat with oil. In a shallow dish, add the breadcrumbs. Coat the zucchini sticks evenly with breadcrumbs.
3. Place the zucchini sticks in an Air Fryer basket in a single layer in 2 batches. Set the temperature of Air Fryer to 425°F and Air Fry for about 10 minutes. Serve

489. Carrot Sticks

(Prep + Cook Time: 22 minutes | **Serves:** 2)

Ingredients:

- 1 large carrot, peeled and cut into sticks
- One-tablespoon fresh rosemary, finely chopped.
- One-tablespoon olive oil
- 2 tsp. sugar
- 1/4 tsp. cayenne pepper
- Salt and freshly ground black pepper, as needed.

Directions:

1. Set the temperature of Air Fryer to 390°F. In a bowl, add all the Ingredients and toss to coat well
2. Place the carrot sticks in an Air Fryer basket in a single layer.
3. Air Fry for about 12 minutes. Serve.

490. Bacon Jalapeno Balls

(Prep + Cooking Time: 14 Minutes | **Serves:** 3)

Ingredients:

- 3 bacon slices; cooked and crumbled
- 1 jalapeno pepper, chopped.
- 3 oz. cream cheese
- 1/4-tsp. garlic powder
- 1/4-tsp. onion powder
- ½-tsp. parsley; dried
- Salt and black pepper to the taste.

Directions:

1. Take a bowl and mix cream cheese with jalapeno pepper, onion and garlic powder, parsley, bacon salt and pepper and stir well. Shape small balls out of this mix, place them in your air fryer's basket, cook at 350 °F, for 4 minutes; arrange on a platter and serve as an appetizer.

Nutrition Values (Per Serving): Calories: 172; Fat: 4g; Fiber: 1g; Carbs: 12g; Protein: 5g

491. Simple Roasted Peanuts

(Prep + Cook Time: 19 minutes | **Serves:** 10)

Ingredients:

- 2½ cups raw peanuts
- One-tablespoon olive oil
- Salt, as your liking.

Directions:

1. Set the temperature of Air Fryer to 320°F. Add the peanuts in an Air Fryer basket in a single layer
2. Air Fry for about 9 minutes, tossing twice. Remove the peanuts from Air Fryer basket and transfer into a bowl.
3. Add the oil and salt and toss to coat well.
4. Return the nuts mixture into Air Fryer basket.
5. Air Fry for about 5 minutes. Once done, transfer the hot nuts in a glass or steel bowl and serve.

492. Pepper Rolls

(Prep + Cook Time: 20 minutes | **Serves:** 8)

Ingredients:

- 4 oz. feta cheese; crumbled
- 1 orange bell pepper, deseeded and halved.
- 1 yellow bell pepper, deseeded and halved.
- 1 green onion, chopped.
- 2 tbsp. oregano, chopped.
- Salt and black pepper to taste.

Directions:

1. Place the bell pepper halves in your air fryer's basket and cook at 400°F for 10 minutes
2. Transfer the bell peppers to a cutting board, cool down, peel and arrange them on a working surface.
3. In a bowl, mix the cheese, salt, pepper, cilantro and green onions, stir well
4. Spread the cheese mixture on each pepper half, roll the peppers and secure them with toothpicks. Serve as an appetizer, or even as a great side

493. Tasty Banana Snack.

(Prep + Cooking Time: 15 Minutes | **Serves:** 8)

Ingredients:

- 1 banana, peeled and sliced into 16 pieces
- 3/4-cup chocolate chips
- 16 baking-cups crust
- 1/4-cup peanut butter
- 1-tbsp. vegetable oil

Directions:

1. Put chocolate chips in a small pot, heat up over low heat; stir until it melts and take off heat.

2. Take a bowl and mix peanut butter with coconut oil and whisk well.
3. Spoon one-tsp. chocolate mix in a cup, add 1 banana slice and top with one-tsp. butter mix. Repeat with the rest of the cups, place them all into a dish that fits your air fryer, cook at 320 °F, for 5 minutes; transfer to a freezer and keep there until you serve them as a snack.

Nutrition Values (Per Serving): Calories: 70; Fat: 4g; Fiber: 1g; Carbs: 10g; Protein: 1g

494. Broccoli Poppers

(Prep + Cook Time: 25 minutes | **Serves:** 4)

Ingredients:

- 1 lb. broccoli; cut into small florets
- 2 tbsp. plain yogurt
- 2 tbsp. chickpea flour
- 1/4 tsp. ground turmeric
- 1/2 tsp. red chili powder
- 1/4 tsp. ground cumin
- Salt, to taste.

Directions:

1. In a bowl, mix together the yogurt and spices. Add the broccoli and generously coat with marinade
2. Refrigerate for about 20 minutes. Set the temperature of Air Fryer to 400°F.
3. Sprinkle the broccoli florets with chickpea flour. Add the broccoli florets in an Air Fryer basket in a single layer. Air Fry for about 10 minutes, tossing once halfway through. Serve hot

495. Simple Roasted Cashews

(Prep + Cook Time: 24 minutes | **Serves:** 8)

Ingredients:

- 2 cups raw cashew nuts
- One-tablespoon. butter, melted
- Salt and freshly ground black pepper, as needed.

Directions:

1. Set the temperature of Air Fryer to 355°F. In a bowl, mix together all the ingredients
2. Place the cashews nuts in an Air Fryer basket in a single layer. (you can lay a piece of grease-proof baking paper)
3. Air Fry for about 4 minutes, shaking once halfway through. Once done, transfer the hot nuts in a glass bowl and serve.

496. Tasty Stuffed Peppers

(Prep + Cooking Time: 18 Minutes | **Serves:** 8)

Ingredients:

- 3.5 oz. goat cheese; cut into 8 pieces
- 8 small bell peppers; tops cut off and seeds removed
- 1-tbsp. olive oil
- Salt and black pepper to the taste.

Directions:

1. Take a bowl and mix cheese with oil with salt and pepper and toss to coat. Stuff each pepper with goat cheese, place them in your air fryer's basket, cook at 400 °F, for 8 minutes; arrange on a platter and serve as an appetizer.

Nutrition Values (Per Serving): Calories: 120; Fat: 1g; Fiber: 1g; Carbs: 12g; Protein: 8g

497. Yummy Olives Balls.

(Prep + Cooking Time: 14 Minutes | **Serves:** 6)

Ingredients:

- 8 black olives; pitted and minced
- 4 oz. cream cheese
- 14 pepperoni slices, chopped.
- 1-tbsp. basil, chopped.
- 2-tbsp. sun dried tomato pesto
- Salt and black pepper to the taste.

Directions:

1. Take a bowl and mix cream cheese with salt, pepper, basil, pepperoni, pesto and black olives; stir well and shape small balls out of this mix. Place them in your air fryer's basket, cook at 350 °F, for 4 minutes; arrange on a platter and serve as a snack.

Nutrition Values (Per Serving): Calories: 100; Fat: 1g; Fiber: 0g; Carbs: 8g; Protein: 3g

498. Traditional Sweet Bacon Snack.

(Prep + Cooking Time: 40 Minutes | **Serves:** 16)

Ingredients:

- 3 oz. dark chocolate
- 16 bacon slices
- 1-tbsp. avocado oil
- ½-tsp. cinnamon powder.
- one-tsp. maple extract

Directions:

1. Arrange bacon slices in your air fryer's basket; sprinkle cinnamon mix over them and cook them at 300 °F, for 30 minutes
2. Heat up a pot with the oil over medium heat, add chocolate and stir until it melts.
3. Add maple extract; stir, take off heat and leave aside to cool down a bit.
4. Take bacon strips out of the oven; leave them to cool down, dip each in chocolate mix; place them on a parchment paper and leave them to cool down completely. Serve cold as a snack

Nutrition Values (Per Serving): Calories: 200; Fat: 4g; Fiber: 5g; Carbs: 12g; Protein: 3g

499. Dill Pickle Fries

(Prep + Cook Time: 43 minutes | **Serves:** 12)

Ingredients:

- 1½ (16-oz.) jars spicy dill pickle spears, drained. and pat dried
- 1 egg, beaten
- 1 cup panko breadcrumbs
- 1 cup all-purpose flour
- 1/4 cup milk
- 1/2 tsp. paprika
- Nonstick cooking spray

Directions:

1. In a shallow dish, mix together the flour and paprika. In a second dish, mix well milk and egg
2. In a third dish, put the breadcrumbs. Coat the pickle spears with flour mixture, then dip into egg mixture and finally, coat evenly with the breadcrumbs.
3. Spray the pickle spears evenly with cooking spray. Set the temperature of Air Fryer to 440°F. Arrange the pickle spears in an Air Fryer basket in a single layer in 2 batches. Air Fry for about 14 minutes, flipping once halfway through. Serve.

500. Easy Spicy Chickpeas

(Prep + Cook Time: 25 minutes | **Serves:** 4)

Ingredients:

- 1 (15-oz.) can chickpeas, rinsed and drained
- One-tablespoon olive oil
- 1/2 tsp. ground cumin
- 1/2 tsp. smoked paprika
- 1/2 tsp. cayenne pepper
- Salt, to taste

Directions:

1. Set the temperature of Air Fryer to 390°F. In a bowl, add all the Ingredients and toss to coat well
2. Add the chickpeas in an Air Fryer basket in 2 batches. (you can lay a piece of grease-proof baking paper)
3. Air Fry for about 8 to 10 minutes. Once done, transfer the hot nuts in a glass or steel bowl and serve.

501. Rice Bites

(Prep + Cook Time: 35 minutes | **Serves:** 4)

Ingredients:

- 3 oz. mozzarella cheese, cubed
- 1/3 cup Parmesan cheese, grated.
- 3/4 cup breadcrumbs
- 3 cups cooked risotto
- 1 egg, beaten

Directions:

1. In a bowl, mix together the risotto, Parmesan cheese and egg. Make 20 equal-sized balls from the mixture
2. Insert a mozzarella cube in the center of each ball and using your fingers, smooth the risotto mixture to cover the mozzarella.
3. In a shallow dish, add the breadcrumbs. Coat the balls evenly with breadcrumbs.
4. Set the temperature of Air Fryer to 390°F
5. Arrange the balls in an Air Fryer basket in a single layer in 2 batches. Air Fry for about 10 minutes or until they turn golden brown. Serve.

502. Crispy Prawns

(Prep + Cook Time: 23 minutes | **Serves:** 4)

Ingredients:

- 1/2 lb. nacho chips, crushed.
- 18 prawns, peeled and deveined
- 1 egg

Directions:

1. In a shallow dish, crack the egg and beat well. Put the crushed nacho chips in another dish.
2. dip the prawn into beaten egg and then, coat with the nacho chips
3. Set the temperature of Air Fryer to 355°F. Place the prawns in an Air Fryer basket in a single layer.
4. Air Fry for about 8 minutes. Serve hot.

503. Balsamic Zucchini Slices

(Prep + Cook Time: 55 minutes | **Serves:** 6)

Ingredients:

- 3 zucchinis; thinly sliced
- 2 tbsp. balsamic vinegar
- 2 tbsp. avocado oil
- Salt and black pepper to taste.

Directions:

1. Add all of the ingredients to a bowl and mix. Put the zucchini mixture in your air fryer's basket and cook at 220°F for 50 minutes. Serve as a snack and enjoy!

504. Spring Rolls

(Prep + Cook Time: 35 minutes | **Serves:** 6)

Ingredients:

- 3½ oz. cooked shrimps
- 1¾ oz. fresh mushrooms, sliced
- 1 oz. canned water chestnuts, sliced
- 1 oz. bean sprouts
- 1 small carrot, peeled and cut into matchsticks
- 2 scallions (green part), chopped.
- 12 spring roll wrappers
- 1 egg, beaten
- 2 tbsp. vegetable oil; divided
- One-tablespoon. fresh ginger; finely grated
- One-tablespoon. Chinese five-spice powder
- One-tablespoon soy sauce

Directions:

1. Take a skillet, heat one tbsp. of oil over medium heat and sauté the mushrooms, water chestnuts and ginger for about 2 to 3 minutes
2. Add in the beans sprouts, carrot, scallion, soy sauce and five-spice powder. Sauté for about 1 minute.
3. Stir in the shrimps and remove from heat. Set aside to cool.
4. Divide the veggie mixture evenly between spring rolls. Roll the wrappers around the filling and seal with beaten egg. Coat each roll with the remaining oil.
5. Set the temperature of Air Fryer to 390°F. Grease an Air Fryer basket
6. Place rolls into the prepared Air Fryer basket in a single layer in 2 batches. Air Fry for about 5 minutes. Serve.

505. White Mushrooms Appetizer.

(Prep + Cooking Time: 20 Minutes | **Serves:** 4)

Ingredients:

- 4 oz. cream cheese, soft.
- 24 oz. white mushroom caps
- 1-cup shrimp; cooked, peeled, deveined and chopped.
- 1/4-cup mayonnaise
- 1 small yellow onion, chopped.
- ½-cup Mexican cheese, shredded.
- 1/4-cup sour cream
- one-tsp. curry powder
- one-tsp. garlic powder
- Salt and black pepper to the taste.

Directions:

1. Take a bowl and mix mayo with garlic powder, onion, curry powder, cream cheese, sour cream, Mexican cheese, shrimp, salt and pepper to the taste and whisk well
2. Stuff mushrooms with this mix; place them in your air fryer's basket and cook at 300 °F, for 10 minutes. Arrange on a platter and serve as an appetizer.

Nutrition Values (Per Serving): Calories: 200; Fat: 20g; Fiber: 3g; Carbs: 16g; Protein: 14g

506. Veggie Bread Rolls

(Prep + Cook Time: 53 minutes | **Serves:** 8)

Ingredients:

- 5 large potatoes, peeled
- 2 green chilies, seeded and chopped
- 2 curry leaves
- 8 bread slices, trimmed
- 2 small onions, finely chopped.
- 2 tbsp. vegetable oil; divided
- 1/2 tsp. ground turmeric
- Salt, as your liking.

Directions:

1. In the pan of a boiling water, add the potatoes and cook for about 15 to 20 minutes.
2. Drain the potatoes well and with a potato masher, mash the potatoes
3. In a skillet, heat One-tablespoon. of oil over a medium heat and sauté the onion for about 4 to 5 minutes.
4. Add the green chilies, curry leaves and turmeric. Sauté for about 1 minute.
5. Add in the mashed potatoes and salt and mix them well. Once done, remove from the heat and set aside to cool completely.
6. Make 8 equal-sized oval-shaped patties from the mixture. Wet the bread slices completely with water.
7. Using your hands, press each bread slice between your hands to remove the excess water.
8. Place 1 bread slice in your palm and place 1 patty in the center.
9. Roll the bread slice in a spindle shape and seal the edges to secure the filling
10. Coat the roll with some oil. Repeat with the remaining slices, filling and oil.
11. Set the temperature of Air Fryer to 390°F. Grease the Air Fryer basket with cooking spray
12. Add rolls into the prepared basket in a single layer. Air Fry for about 12 to 13 minutes. Serve.

507. Simple Roasted Mixed Nuts

(Prep + Cook Time: 25 minutes | **Serves:** 6)

Ingredients:

- 1 packet stevia
- 1/2 cup walnuts
- 1/2 cup pecans
- 1/2 cup almonds
- 2 tbsp. egg white
- 1/2 tbsp. ground cinnamon
- A pinch of cayenne pepper

Directions:

1. Set the temperature of Air Fryer to 320°F. Take a bowl and mix together all the listed ingredients
2. Place the nuts in an Air Fryer basket in a single layer. (you can lay a piece of grease-proof baking paper)
3. Air Fry for about 20 minutes, stirring once halfway through.
4. Once done, transfer the hot nuts in a glass or steel bowl and serve

508. Lentils Snack

(Prep + Cook Time: 17 minutes | **Serves:** 4)

Ingredients:

- 15 oz. canned lentils; drained
- One-tablespoon. sweet paprika
- One-tablespoon olive oil
- 1/2 tsp. cumin; ground
- Salt and black pepper to taste.

Directions:

1. Place all ingredients in a bowl and mix well. Transfer the mixture to your air fryer and cook at 400°F for 12 minutes
2. Divide into bowls and serve as a snack (or a side, or appetizer!)

509. Spinach Rolls

(Prep + Cook Time: 24 minutes | **Serves:** 6)

Ingredients:

- 1 (16-oz.) package frozen spinach, thawed
- 1/2 cup Romano cheese, grated.
- 1 red onion, chopped.
- 1 cup fresh parsley, chopped.
- 1 cup fresh mint leaves, chopped.
- 1 egg
- 1 package frozen filo dough, thawed
- 1 cup feta cheese, crumbled
- 2 tbsp. olive oil
- 1/4 tsp. ground cardamom
- Salt and freshly ground black pepper, as needed.

Directions:

1. Put all the listed Ingredients except filo dough and oil in a food processor and pulse until smooth
2. Place one filo sheet on the cutting board and cut into three rectangular strips. Brush each strip with the oil.
3. Add about one tsp. of spinach mixture along with the short side of a strip.
4. Roll the dough to secure the filling. Repeat with the remaining filo sheets and spinach mixture.
5. Set the temperature of Air Fryer to 355°F. Grease an Air Fryer basket. Place rolls into the prepared basket in a single layer. Air Fry for about 4 minutes

510. Bacon Wrapped Shrimp

(Prep + Cook Time: 22 minutes | **Serves:** 6)

Ingredients:

- 1 lb. shrimp, peeled and deveined
- 1 lb. bacon, thinly sliced

Directions:

1. Wrap each shrimp with one bacon slice. Add the shrimp in a baking dish and refrigerate for about 20 minutes
2. Set the temperature of Air Fryer to 390°F.
3. Add the shrimp in an Air Fryer basket in a single layer. Air Fry for about 5 to 7 minutes.

511. Beet Chips

(Prep + Cook Time: 25 minutes | **Serves:** 6)

Ingredients:

- 4 medium beetroots, peeled and thinly sliced.
- 2 tbsp. olive oil
- 1/2 tsp. salt
- 1/4 tsp. smoked paprika

Directions:

1. Set the temperature of Air Fryer to 325°F. In a bowl, add all the Ingredients and toss to coat well
2. Arrange the beet slices in an Air Fryer basket in a single layer. Air Fry for about 12 to 15 minutes. Serve.

512. Banana Chips

(Prep + Cook Time: 20 minutes | **Serves:** 8)

Ingredients:

- 2 raw bananas, peeled and sliced
- 2 tbsp. olive oil
- Salt and freshly ground black pepper, as needed.

Directions:

1. Set the temperature of Air Fryer to 355°F. Drizzle the banana slices evenly with oil
2. Arrange the banana slices in an Air Fryer basket in a single layer. Air Fry for about 10 minutes. Sprinkle with salt and black pepper. Serve.

513. Tomatoes and Dates Salsa

(Prep + Cook Time: 20 minutes | **Serves:** 12)

Ingredients:

- 1½ lbs. tomatoes; peeled and cubed
- 1 apple; cored and cubed
- 3 oz. dates, roughly chopped.
- 1 yellow onion, chopped.
- 6 oz. sultanas, chopped.
- One-tablespoon balsamic vinegar
- One-tablespoon. whole spice
- 1/2 tbsp. brown sugar
- Salt and black pepper to taste.

Directions:

1. In a pan that fits your air fryer, add and toss all the ingredients. Place the pan in the fryer and cook at 370°F for 15 minutes
2. Remove the salsa, place in a bowl and chill. Serve the salsa cold as a snack or appetizer

514. Coco Chicken Bites

(Prep + Cooking Time: 23 Minutes | **Serves:** 4)

Ingredients:

- 8 chicken tenders
- 3/4-cup panko bread crumbs
- 3/4-cup coconut, shredded.
- 2 eggs
- 2-tsp. garlic powder
- Salt and black pepper to the taste.
- Cooking spray.

Directions:

1. Take a bowl and mix eggs with salt, pepper and garlic powder and whisk well
2. In another bowl; mix coconut with panko and stir well.
3. Dip chicken tenders in eggs mix and then coat in coconut one well.
4. Spray chicken bites with cooking spray, place them in your air fryer's basket and cook them at 350 °F, for 10 minutes. Arrange them on a platter and serve as an appetizer

Nutrition Values (Per Serving): Calories: 252; Fat: 4g; Fiber: 2g; Carbs: 14g; Protein: 24g

515. Eggplant Slices

(Prep + Cook Time: 31 minutes | **Serves:** 4)

Ingredients:

- 1 medium eggplant, peeled and cut into 1/2-inch round slices
- 2 eggs, beaten
- 1/4 cup olive oil
- 1 cup Italian-style breadcrumbs
- 1/2 cup all-purpose flour
- Salt, as your liking.

Directions:

1. In a colander, add the eggplant slices and sprinkle with salt. Set aside for about 45 minutes and pat dry the eggplant slices
2. Add the flour in a shallow dish. Crack the eggs in a second dish and beat well. In a third dish, mix together the oil and breadcrumbs.
3. Coat each eggplant slice with flour, then dip into beaten eggs and finally, evenly coat with the breadcrumbs mixture. Set the temperature of Air Fryer to 390°F. Arrange the eggplant slices in an Air Fryer basket in a single layer in 2 batches. Air Fry for about 8 minutes. Serve

516. Buttered Corn

(Prep + Cook Time: 25 minutes | **Serves:** 2)

Ingredients:

- 2 corn on the cob
- 2 tbsp. butter, softened. and divided
- Salt and freshly ground black pepper, as needed.

Directions:

1. Set the temperature of Air Fryer to 320°F. Sprinkle the cobs evenly with salt and black pepper.
2. After that, rub with One-tablespoon of butter
3. With 1 piece of foil, wrap each cob and place in an Air Fryer basket. Air Fry for about 20 minutes.
4. Top with the remaining butter and serve.

517. Cheesy Chicken Wings

(Prep + Cooking Time: 22 Minutes | **Serves:** 6)

Ingredients:

- 6 lb. chicken wings, halved.
- ½-cup parmesan cheese, grated.
- 1 egg
- 2-tbsp. butter
- one-tsp. garlic powder
- ½-tsp. Italian seasoning
- A pinch of red pepper flakes; crushed
- Salt and black pepper to the taste.

Directions:

1. Arrange chicken wings in your air fryer's basket and cook at 390 °F and cook for 9 minutes.
2. Meanwhile, in your blender, mix butter with cheese, egg, salt, pepper, pepper flakes, garlic powder and Italian seasoning and blend very well.
3. Take chicken wings out; pour cheese sauce over them, toss to coat well and cook in your air fryer's basket at 390 °F, for 3 minutes. Serve them as an appetizer

Nutrition Values (Per Serving): Calories: 204; Fat: 8g; Fiber: 1g; Carbs: 18g; Protein: 14g

518. Fried Corn

(Prep + Cook Time: 15 minutes | **Serves:** 4)

Ingredients:

- 2 tbsp. corn kernels
- 2½ tbsp. butter

Directions:

1. In a pan that fits your air fryer, mix the corn with the butter
2. Place the pan in the fryer and cook at 400°F for 10 minutes. Serve as a snack and enjoy!

519. Holyday Beef Patties.

(Prep + Cooking Time: 18 Minutes | **Serves:** 4)

Ingredients:

- 1 leek, chopped.
- 14 oz. beef, minced.
- 2-tbsp. ham; cut into strips
- 3-tbsp. bread crumbs
- ½-tsp. nutmeg, ground.
- Salt and black pepper to the taste.

Directions:

1. Take a bowl and mix beef with leek, salt, pepper, ham, breadcrumbs and nutmeg; stir well and shape small patties out of this mix. Place them in your air fryer's basket, cook at 400 °F, for 8 minutes; arrange on a platter and serve as an appetizer.

Nutrition Values (Per Serving): Calories: 260; Fat: 12g; Fiber: 3g; Carbs: 12g; Protein: 21g

520. Potato Croquettes

(Prep + Cook Time: 38 minutes | **Serves:** 4)

Ingredients:

- 2 medium Russet potatoes, peeled and cubed
- 1/2 cup breadcrumbs
- 1/2 cup Parmesan cheese, grated.
- 1 egg yolk
- 2 eggs
- 2 tbsp. chives; minced
- 2 tbsp. vegetable oil
- 2 tbsp. all-purpose flour
- Salt and freshly ground black pepper, as needed.
- A pinch of ground nutmeg

Directions:

1. Add potatoes in the pan of a boiling water and cook for about 15 minutes. Drain the potatoes well and transfer into a large bowl
2. With a potato masher, mash the potatoes and set aside to cool completely.

3. In the same bowl of mashed potatoes, add in the flour, Parmesan cheese, egg yolk, chives, nutmeg, salt and black pepper. Whisk until well combined. Make small equal-sized balls from the mixture. Now, roll each ball into a cylinder shape.
4. In a shallow dish, crack the eggs and beat well. In another dish, mix together the breadcrumbs and oil.
5. Dip the croquettes in egg mixture and then evenly coat with the breadcrumbs mixture
6. Set the temperature of Air Fryer to 390°F. Place the croquettes in an Air Fryer basket in a single layer. Air Fry for about 7 to 8 minutes.

521. Pork Bites

(Prep + Cook Time: 25 minutes | **Serves:** 4)

Ingredients:

- 1 lb. ground pork
- 2 eggs
- 3/4 cup coconut, shredded.
- 3/4 cup panko breadcrumbs
- 2 tsp. garlic powder
- A drizzle of olive oil
- Salt and black pepper to taste.

Directions:

1. In a bowl, mix coconut with panko and stir well. In another bowl, mix the pork, salt, pepper, eggs and garlic powder and then shape medium meatballs out of this mix
2. Dredge the meatballs in the coconut mix, place them in your air fryer's basket, introduce in the air fryer and cook at 350°F for 15 minutes. Serve and enjoy!

522. Basil and Cilantro Crackers

(Prep + Cook Time: 26 minutes | **Serves:** 6)

Ingredients:

- 1 garlic clove; minced
- 1¼ cups flour
- 2 tbsp. basil; minced
- 2 tbsp. cilantro; minced
- 4 tbsp. butter, melted.
- 1/2 tsp. baking powder
- Salt and black pepper to taste.

Directions:

1. Add all of the ingredients to a bowl and stir until you obtain a dough.
2. Spread this on a lined baking sheet that fits your air fryer. Place the baking sheet in the fryer at 325°F and cook for 16 minutes. Cool down, cut and serve

523. French Fries

(Prep + Cook Time: 45 minutes | **Serves:** 8)

Ingredients:

- 1¾ lbs. potatoes, peeled and cut into strips
- 1/4 cup olive oil
- One-tablespoon. onion powder
- One-tablespoon. garlic powder
- 2 tsp. paprika

Directions:

1. In a large bowl, add the water and potato strips. Set aside for about 1 hour
2. Drain the potato strips well and pat them dry with the paper towels.
3. Take a large bowl, add the potato strips and the remaining ingredients. Toss to coat well.

4. Set the temperature of Air Fryer to 375°F
5. Add the potato strips in an Air Fryer basket in a single layer. Air Fry for about 30 minutes. Serve.

524. Avocado Fries

(Prep + Cook Time: 27 minutes | **Serves:** 2)

Ingredients:

- 1 avocado, peeled, pitted and sliced into 8 pieces
- 1/2 cup panko breadcrumbs
- 1 egg
- 1/4 cup all-purpose flour
- One-tablespoon. water
- Non stick cooking spray
- Salt and freshly ground black pepper, as needed.

Directions:

1. In a shallow bowl, mix together the flour, salt and black pepper. In a second bowl, mix well egg and water. In a third bowl, put the breadcrumbs
2. Coat the avocado slices with flour mixture, then dip into egg mixture and finally, coat evenly with the breadcrumbs
3. spray the avocado slices evenly with cooking spray. Set the temperature of Air Fryer to 400°F.
4. Place the avocado slices in an Air Fryer basket in a single layer. Air Fry for about 7 minutes, flipping once halfway through. Enjoy!

525. Minty Shrimp Mix

(Prep + Cook Time: 13 minutes | **Serves:** 12)

Ingredients:

- 10 oz. shrimp; peeled and deveined
- 1/3 cup red wine
- 2 tbsp. olive oil
- One-tablespoon mint, chopped.

Directions:

1. In your air fryer, mix / toss all the ingredients.
2. Cook at 390°F for 8 minutes. Divide into bowls and serve as an appetizer

526. Cauliflower Poppers

(Prep + Cook Time: 30 minutes | **Serves:** 4)

Ingredients:

- 4 cups cauliflower florets
- 1 large egg white
- 3/4 cup panko breadcrumbs
- 3 tbsp. ketchup
- 2 tbsp. hot sauce

Directions:

1. In a bowl, mix together the egg white, ketchup and hot sauce. Add the breadcrumbs in another bowl. Dip the cauliflower florets in ketchup mixture and then evenly coat with the breadcrumbs
2. Set the temperature of Air Fryer to 320°F. Arrange the cauliflower florets in an Air Fryer basket in a single layer. Air Fry for about 20 minutes. Serve.

527. Cheesy Sandwich

(Prep + Cook Time: 15 minutes | **Serves:** 2)

Ingredients:

- 4 white bread slices
- 1/2 cup sharp cheddar cheese, grated.
- 1/2 cup butter, softened.

Directions:

1. Set the temperature of Air Fryer to 355°F. Spread the butter evenly over one side of each bread slice.
2. Sprinkle the cheese over buttered side of 2 slices
3. Top with the remaining slices of bread. Place the sandwiches in an Air Fryer basket in a single layer. Air Fry for about 4 to 5 minutes. Serve

528. Squash Dip

(Prep + Cook Time: 35 minutes | **Serves:** 6)

Ingredients:

- 1 yellow onion, chopped.
- 8 garlic cloves; minced
- 1 bunch basil, chopped.
- 8 carrots, chopped.
- 2 butternut squash, chopped.
- 1 cup veggie stock
- 1/4 cup lemon juice
- 2 tbsp. olive oil
- Salt and black pepper to taste.

Directions:

1. In a pan that fits your air fryer, mix all the ingredients except the lemon juice
2. Place the pan in the fryer and cook at 380°F for 25 minutes
3. Transfer the entire mixture to a blender, add the lemon juice and pulse well. Divide into bowls and serve as a party dip or an appetizer

529. Apple Chips

(Prep + Cook Time: 26 minutes | **Serves:** 2)

Ingredients:

- 1 apple, peeled, cored and thinly sliced
- One-tablespoon sugar
- 1/2 tsp. ground cinnamon
- A pinch of ground cardamom
- A pinch of ground ginger
- A pinch of salt

Directions:

1. Set the temperature of Air Fryer to 390°F. In a bowl, add all the Ingredients and toss to coat well
2. Arrange the apple slices in an Air Fryer basket in a single layer in 2 batches. Air Fry for about 7 to 8 minutes, flipping once halfway through. Serve

530. Polenta Sticks

(Prep + Cook Time: 16 minutes | **Serves:** 4)

Ingredients:

- 2½ cups cooked polenta
- 1/4 cup Parmesan cheese, shredded.
- Salt, as your liking.

Directions:

1. Add the polenta evenly into a greased baking dish and with the back of a spoon, smooth the top surface.
2. Cover the baking dish and refrigerate for about 1 hour or until set
3. Remove from the refrigerator and cut down the polenta into the desired size slices. Set the temperature of Air Fryer to 350°F. Grease a baking dish.
4. Arrange the polenta sticks into the prepared baking dish in a single layer and sprinkle with salt
5. Place the baking dish into an Air Fryer basket. Air Fry for about 5 to 6 minutes. Top with the cheese and serve.

531. Kale Chips

(Prep + Cook Time: 23 minutes | **Serves:** 4)

Ingredients:

- 1 head fresh kale; stems and ribs removed and cut into 1½ inch pieces
- One-tablespoon. soy sauce
- One-tablespoon olive oil
- 1/8 tsp. cayenne pepper
- A pinch of freshly ground black pepper

Directions:

1. Set the temperature of Air Fryer to 390°F. Take a large bowl and mix together all the ingredients
2. Place the kale leaves in an Air Fryer basket in a single layer
3. Air Fry for about 2 to 3 minutes, tossing once halfway through. Serve.

532. Coconut Shrimp Snack

(Prep + Cook Time: 22 minutes | **Serves:** 4)

Ingredients:

- 12 large shrimp; deveined and peeled
- 2 cups coconut, shredded.
- 2 eggs, whisked.
- 1 cup white flour
- Salt and black pepper to taste.

Directions:

1. Put the coconut in one bowl, the flour in a second one and the eggs in a third
2. Season the shrimp with the salt and pepper, then dredge them in the flour, then the eggs and then the coconut.
3. Place the shrimp in your air fryer's basket and cook at 360°F for 12 minutes, flipping them halfway
4. Divide the shrimp into bowls and serve as a snack (or an appetizer, or even an entrée!)

533. Lemon Biscuits

(Prep + Cook Time: 20 minutes | **Serves:** 10)

Ingredients:

- 3½ oz. caster sugar
- 3½ oz. cold butter
- 1 small egg
- 8½ oz. Self rising flour
- One-tablespoon. fresh lemon zest; finely grated
- One-tablespoon. vanilla extract
- 2 tbsp. fresh lemon juice

Directions:

1. In a bowl, mix together the flour and sugar. Using two forks; cut in the butter until coarse crumb forms.

2. Add in the egg, vanilla extract, lemon juice and zest. Mix until a soft dough forms
3. After that, take out the dough from bowl and put onto a floured surface. Now, roll it into an even thickness. (1/2 inch)
4. Cut the dough into medium-sized biscuits using a cookie cutter. Set the temperature of Air Fryer to 355°F. Place the biscuits in a baking sheet in a single layer
5. Put the baking sheet in an Air Fryer basket. Air Fry for about 5 minutes or until golden brown.

534. Turmeric Carrot Chips

(Prep + Cook Time: 30 minutes | **Serves:** 4)

Ingredients:

- 4 carrots; thinly sliced
- One-tablespoon. olive oil
- 1/2 tsp. turmeric powder
- 1/2 tsp. chaat masala
- Salt and black pepper to taste.

Directions:

1. Place all ingredients in a bowl and toss well. Put the mixture in your air fryer's basket and cook at 370°F for 25 minutes, shaking the fryer from time to time. Serve as a snack

535. Coconut Cookies

(Prep + Cook Time: 27 minutes | **Serves:** 8)

Ingredients:

- 2¼ oz. caster sugar
- 5 oz. Self-rising flour
- 3½ oz. butter
- 1 small egg
- 1¼ oz. white chocolate, chopped.
- 3 tbsp. desiccated coconut
- One-tablespoon. vanilla extract

Directions:

1. In a large bowl, add the sugar and butter and beat until fluffy and light
2. Add the egg and vanilla extract and whisk until well combined. Now, add the flour and chocolate and mix well.
3. In a shallow bowl, place the coconut. With your hands, make small balls from the mixture and roll evenly into the coconut.
4. Place the balls onto an ungreased baking sheet about 1- inch apart and gently, press each ball.
5. Set the temperature of air fryer to 355°F. Place baking sheet into the air fryer basket. Air fry for about 8 minutes and then, another 4 minutes at 320°F
6. Remove from air fryer and place the baking sheet onto a wire rack to cool for about 5 minutes.
7. Invert the cookies onto wire rack to cool completely before serving. Serve.

536. Cheesy Pastries

(Prep + Cook Time: 20 minutes | **Serves:** 6)

Ingredients:

- 4 oz. feta cheese, crumbled
- 1 scallion, finely chopped.
- 1 egg yolk
- 2 frozen filo pastry sheets, thawed
- 2 tbsp. fresh parsley, finely chopped.
- 2 tbsp. olive oil
- Salt and ground black pepper, as needed

Directions:

1. In a large bowl, add the egg yolk and beat well. Add in the feta cheese, scallion, parsley, salt and black pepper. Mix well
2. Cut each filo pastry sheet in three strips. Add about One-tablespoon. of feta mixture on the underside of a strip.
3. Fold the tip of sheet over the filling in a zigzag manner to form a triangle.
4. Repeat with the remaining strips and fillings. Set the temperature of Air Fryer to 390°F. Coat each pastry evenly with oil.
5. Place the pastries in an Air Fryer basket in a single layer
6. Air Fry for about 3 minutes, then air fryer for about 2 minutes on 360°F. Serve.

537. Bacon Croquettes

(Prep + Cook Time: 23 minutes | **Serves:** 6)

Ingredients:

- 1 lb. sharp cheddar cheese block; cut into 1-inch rectangular pieces
- 1 lb. thin bacon slices
- 1 cup breadcrumbs
- 1 cup all-purpose flour
- 3 eggs
- 1/4 cup olive oil
- Salt, as your liking.

Directions:

1. Wrap 2 bacon slices around 1 piece of cheddar cheese, covering completely. Repeat with the remaining bacon and cheese pieces
2. Arrange the croquettes in a baking dish and freeze for about 5 minutes. Add the flour in a shallow dish.
3. In a second dish, crack the eggs and beat well. In a third dish, mix together the breadcrumbs, salt and oil.
4. Coat the croquettes with flour, then dip into beaten eggs and finally, evenly coat with the breadcrumbs mixture.
5. Set the temperature of Air Fryer to 390°F. Arrange the croquettes in an Air Fryer basket in a single layer. Air Fry for about 7 to 8 minutes. Serve hot

538. Buttermilk Biscuits

(Prep + Cook Time: 23 minutes | **Serves:** 4)

Ingredients:

- 3/4 cup buttermilk
- 1/4 cup cold unsalted butter; cut into cubes
- 1¼ cups all-purpose flour
- 1/2 cup cake flour
- One-tablespoon. granulated sugar
- 2 tbsp. butter, melted
- 1/2 tsp. baking powder
- 1/4 tsp. baking soda
- Salt, as your liking.

Directions:

1. In a large bowl, sift together the flours, baking soda, baking powder, sugar and salt. Using two forks; cut in the butter until coarse crumb forms. Slowly, add in the buttermilk and mix until a smooth dough forms

2. After that, take out the dough from bowl and put onto a floured surface. Using your hands, press it into 1/2 inch thickness.
3. With a 1 ¾-inch round cookie cutter; cut the biscuits.
4. Cut out the remaining biscuits from dough. Set the temperature of Air Fryer to 400°F. Place the biscuits in a pie pan in a single layer and coat with butter
5. Put the pie pan in an Air Fryer basket. Air Fry for about 8 minutes. Serve.

539. Tortilla Chips

(Prep + Cook Time: 16 minutes | **Serves:** 6)

Ingredients:

- 8 corn tortillas; cut into triangles
- One-tablespoon olive oil
- Salt, to taste.

Directions:

1. Set the temperature of Air Fryer to 390°F. Coat the tortilla chips with oil
2. Sprinkle each side of the tortillas with salt Place them in an Air Fryer basket in a single layer in 2 batches. Air Fry for about 3 minutes. Enjoy with your favorite salsa.

540. Cod Nuggets

(Prep + Cook Time: 25 minutes | **Serves:** 4)

Ingredients:

- 1 lb. cod; cut into 1x2½-inch strips
- 1 cup all-purpose flour
- 2 eggs
- 3/4 cup breadcrumbs
- 2 tbsp. olive oil
- A pinch of salt

Directions:

1. Add the flour in a shallow dish. Crack the eggs in a second dish and beat well. In a third dish, mix together the breadcrumbs, salt and oil
2. Coat the nuggets with flour, then dip into beaten eggs and finally, evenly coat with the breadcrumbs.
3. Set the temperature of Air Fryer to 390°F. Add the croquettes in an Air Fryer basket in a single layer.
4. Air Fry for about 8 to 10 minutes.

541. Cream Cheese Balls

(Prep + Cook Time: 10 minutes | **Serves:** 6)

Ingredients:

- 4 oz. cream cheese
- 8 black olives; pitted and minced
- 14 pepperoni slices, chopped.
- 2 tbsp. basil pesto
- One-tablespoon basil, chopped.
- Salt and black pepper to taste.

Directions:

1. In a bowl, place all of the ingredients and stir
2. Shape the mixture into medium balls and then place them in your lined air fryer's basket. Cook at 360°F for 5 minutes. Serve as a snack

542. Beef Dip

(Prep + Cook Time: 40 minutes | **Serves:** 6)

Ingredients:

- 2 lbs. ground beef; browned
- 4 garlic cloves; minced
- 2 celery ribs, chopped.
- 1 yellow onion, chopped.
- 28 oz. canned tomatoes, crushed.
- 1/4 cup beef stock
- 2 carrots, chopped.
- One-tablespoon olive oil
- A pinch of basil, dried.
- A pinch of oregano, dried.
- A splash of red wine
- Salt and black pepper to taste.

Directions:

1. Place all the ingredients in a pan that fits your air fryer and whisk
2. Put the pan in the fryer and cook at 380°F for 30 minutes. Divide into bowls and serve as a snack or appetizer

543. Lemony Apple Bites

(Prep + Cook Time: 10 minutes | **Serves:** 4)

Ingredients:

- 1/2 cup caramel sauce
- 3 big apples; cored, peeled and cubed
- 2 tsp. lemon juice

Directions:

1. In your air fryer, mix all the ingredients, toss well
2. Cook at 340°F for 5 minutes. Divide into cups and serve as a snack

544. Mushroom Salad

(Prep + Cook Time: 35 minutes | **Serves:** 6)

Ingredients:

- 10 oz. shiitake mushrooms, chopped.
- 10 oz. cremini mushrooms, chopped.
- 10 oz. Portobello mushrooms, chopped.
- 1 oz. parmesan cheese, grated.
- 1/4 cup olive oil
- 1/4 cup coconut cream
- 1 cup chicken stock
- 3 garlic cloves; minced
- 1 yellow onion, chopped.
- One-tablespoon thyme, chopped.
- One-tablespoon parsley; minced
- Salt and black pepper to taste.

Directions:

1. In a pan that fits your air fryer, heat up the oil over medium heat. Add the onions, garlic, thyme, salt and pepper, stir and cook for 3-4 minutes.
2. Add the stock and the mushrooms, stir and cook for 1-2 minutes more
3. Place the pan in the air fryer and cook at 350°F for 20 minutes
4. Add the cream, parmesan and parsley and stir well. Divide into bowls and serve as an appetizer

545. Veggie Pastries

(Prep + Cook Time: 57 minutes | **Serves:** 8)

Ingredients:

- 2 large potatoes, peeled
- 3 puff pastry sheets
- 1/2 cup onion, chopped.
- 2 garlic cloves; minced
- 1/2 cup carrot, peeled and chopped
- 1/2 cup green peas, shelled
- One-tablespoon olive oil
- 2 tbsp. fresh ginger; minced
- Salt and ground black pepper, as needed

Directions:

1. In the pan of a boiling water, put the potatoes and cook for about 15 to 20 minutes. Drain the potatoes well and with a potato masher, mash the potatoes
2. In a skillet, heat the oil over medium heat and sauté the carrot, onion, ginger and garlic for about 4 to 5 minutes. Drain all the fat from the skillet.
3. Stir in the mashed potatoes, peas, salt and black pepper. Cook for about 1 to 2 minutes.
4. Once done, remove the potato mixture from heat and set aside to cool completely
5. Put the puff pastry onto a smooth surface. Cut each puff pastry sheet into four pieces and then cut each piece in a round shape. Add about two tablespoons of veggie filling over each pastry round.
6. Moisten the edges using your wet fingers. Fold each pastry round in half to seal the filling
7. Using a fork, firmly press the edges. Set the temperature of Air Fryer to 390°F. Add the pastries in an Air Fryer basket in a single layer in 2 batches. Air Fry for about 5 minutes. Serve.

546. Carrot Dip

(Prep + Cook Time: 25 minutes | **Serves:** 6)

Ingredients:

- 2 cups carrots, grated.
- 4 tbsp. butter, melted.
- One-tablespoon chives
- A pinch of cayenne pepper
- Salt and black pepper to taste.

Directions:

1. Add all ingredients to a pan that fits your air fryer and mix. Place the pan in the fryer and cook at 380°F for 15 minutes.
2. Blend a bit using an immersion blender and then divide into bowls. Serve as a dip.

547. Minty Cauliflower Spread

(Prep + Cook Time: 20 minutes | **Serves:** 6)

Ingredients:

- 3 cups veggie stock
- 6 cups cauliflower florets
- 8 garlic cloves; minced
- 2 tbsp. butter, melted.
- A handful of mint, chopped.
- Salt and black pepper to taste.

Directions:

1. Place all the ingredients into a pan that fits your air fryer; mix well.
2. Put the pan into the air fryer and cook at 370°F for 15 minutes. Blend using an immersion blender, divide into bowls and serve.

548. Broccoli Bites

(Prep + Cook Time: 20 minutes | **Serves:** 6)

Ingredients:

- 1 broccoli head; florets separated
- One-tablespoon. olive oil
- One-tablespoon. butter, melted.
- 2 tsp. garlic powder
- Salt and black pepper to taste.

Directions:

1. Spread the broccoli florets on a lined baking sheet that fits your air fryer; then add all other ingredients and toss.
2. Cook at 450°F for 15 minutes. Divide into bowls and serve as a snack (or as a side)

549. Banana Chips

(Prep + Cook Time: 10 minutes | **Serves:** 8)

Ingredients:

- 1 banana; peeled and sliced into 16 pieces
- 1/4 cup peanut butter; soft
- One-tablespoon vegetable oil

Directions:

1. Put the banana slices in your air fryer's basket and drizzle the oil over them
2. Cook at 360°F for 5 minutes. Transfer to bowls and serve them dipped in peanut butter.

550. Kale Crackers

(Prep + Cook Time: 30 minutes | **Serves:** 6)

Ingredients:

- 4 cups flax seed; soaked overnight, drained. and ground
- 4 garlic cloves; minced
- 1 bunch basil, chopped.
- 4 bunches kale, chopped.
- 1/3 cup avocado oil

Directions:

1. Place all ingredients in your food processor and pulse well. Spread the mixture in your air fryer's pan and cut into medium crackers
2. Cook in the air fryer cook at 380°F for 20 minutes. Cool and serve as a snack

551. Chicken Sticks

(Prep + Cook Time: 26 minutes | **Serves:** 4)

Ingredients:

- 1 lb. chicken breast; skinless, boneless and cut in medium sticks
- 1 cup breadcrumbs
- 1 egg, whisked.
- 3/4 cup white flour
- 1/2 tbsp. olive oil
- Salt and black pepper to taste.

Directions:

1. Combine the flour, salt and pepper in a bowl. Put the egg in another bowl and the breadcrumbs in a third one.

2. Dredge the chicken pieces in the flour, then the egg and then the breadcrumbs.
3. Place the chicken pieces in your air fryer's basket, drizzle the oil over them and cook at 400°F for 16 minutes, flipping them halfway. Serve right away and enjoy

552. Leek Spread

(Prep + Cook Time: 20 minutes | **Serves:** 6)

Ingredients:

- 3 leeks, roughly chopped.
- 1/2 cup whipping cream
- 3 tbsp. lemon juice
- 2 tbsp. butter, melted.
- Salt and pepper to taste

Directions:

1. In a pan that fits your air fryer, mix the leeks, butter, lemon juice, salt and pepper, stir well.
2. Put the pan into the fryer and cook at 380°F for 15 minutes
3. Transfer the mixture to a blender, add the cream and pulse. Divide into bowls and serve cold.

553. Chili Dip

(Prep + Cook Time: 22 minutes | **Serves:** 4)

Ingredients:

- 6 ancho chilies, dried., seedless and chopped.
- 1 cup water
- 2 garlic cloves; minced
- 2 tbsp. apple cider vinegar
- 1½ tsp. sugar
- 1/2 tsp. oregano, dried.
- Salt and black pepper to taste.

Directions:

1. Mix all the ingredients together in a pan that fits your air fryer, stir well
2. Place the pan in the air fryer and cook at 380°F for 12 minutes. Transfer the mixture to a blender and pulse. Divide into bowls and serve as a dip

554. Coriander Bites

(Prep + Cook Time: 30 minutes | **Serves:** 4)

Ingredients:

- 12 oz. tofu; cubed
- 2 tbsp. soy sauce
- One-tablespoon. sweet paprika
- 2 tbsp. fish sauce
- 2 tsp. olive oil
- One-tablespoon coriander paste

Directions:

1. In a bowl, mix the tofu, paprika, One-tablespoon. of the oil, coriander paste, soy sauce and fish sauce, toss and set aside for 10 minutes.
2. Transfer the coriander tofu bites to your air fryer's basket, drizzle the remaining tsp. of the oil over them and cook at 350°F for 20 minutes, shaking halfway. Serve as a snack

555. Tomato Dip

(Prep + Cook Time: 15 minutes | **Serves:** 4)

Ingredients:

- 1 cup tomato puree
- 1 yellow onion, chopped.
- 2 garlic cloves; minced
- 4 tbsp. honey
- 4 tbsp. white vinegar
- One-tablespoon. liquid smoke
- One-tablespoon. Tabasco sauce
- One-tablespoon olive oil
- 1/8 tsp. cumin powder
- Salt and black pepper to taste.

Directions:

1. Place all the ingredients in a pan that fits your air fryer and mix well.
2. Put the pan into the fryer and cook at 370°F for 10 minutes. Whisk well, divide into bowls and serve as a dip.

556. Cheesy Beef Meatballs

(Prep + Cook Time: 18 minutes | **Serves:** 8)

Ingredients:

- 4 oz. beef meat; minced
- One-tablespoon oregano, chopped.
- One-tablespoon breadcrumbs
- 2 tbsp. feta cheese; crumbled
- 1/2 tbsp. lemon peel, grated.
- Salt and black pepper to taste.

Directions:

1. Place all of the ingredients in a bowl and stir well. Shape medium meatballs out of this mix.
2. Place the meatballs in your air fryer's basket and cook at 400°F for 8 minutes. Serve as an appetizer, or even as an entrée

557. Lentils Spread

(Prep + Cook Time: 25 minutes | **Serves:** 4)

Ingredients:

- 30 oz. canned tomatoes, crushed.
- 3 garlic cloves; minced
- 2 cups canned red lentils; drained
- 1 cup chicken stock
- Salt and black pepper to taste.

Directions:

1. Add all of the ingredients to a pan that fits your air fryer and stir.
2. Place the pan into the fryer and cook at 370°F for 20 minutes. Blend the mix with an immersion blender. Divide into bowls and serve as a snack or an appetizer

558. Lemony Endives Appetizer

(Prep + Cook Time: 20 minutes | **Serves:** 4)

Ingredients:

- 6 endives, halved. lengthwise
- 1/2 cup yogurt
- 3 tbsp. lemon juice
- One-tablespoon. garlic powder

- Salt and black pepper to taste.

Directions:

1. In a bowl, mix all ingredients except the endives; whisk. Now add the endives, toss and set them aside for 10 minutes.
2. Place the endives in your air fryer's basket and cook at 360°F for 10 minutes. Serve as an appetizer

559. Crab Bites

(Prep + Cook Time: 17 minutes | **Serves:** 6)

Ingredients:

- 10 crabsticks; cut into medium bites
- 2 tsp. olive oil
- Salt and black pepper to taste.

Directions:

1. Mix all the ingredients in your air fryer.
2. Cook at 350°F for 12 minutes. Divide into bowls and serve

560. Corn Dip

(Prep + Cook Time: 23 minutes | **Serves:** 4)

Ingredients:

- 2 cups corn kernels
- 1 cup chicken stock
- 1 yellow onion, chopped.
- One-tablespoon. thyme, chopped.
- One-tablespoon olive oil
- 2 tbsp. white wine
- 2 tsp. butter, melted.
- Salt and black pepper to taste.

Directions:

1. Put a pan that fits your air fryer over medium heat and add the oil and the butter; heat up.
2. Add the onion, stir and sauté for 3 minutes. Add the corn, stock, wine, salt, pepper and thyme, stir
3. Place the pan in the fryer and cook at 390°F for 15 minutes
4. Blend a bit using an immersion blender, divide into bowls and serve as a party dip or appetizer.

561. Sausage Bites

(Prep + Cook Time: 25 minutes | **Serves:** 9)

Ingredients:

- 5 oz. ground sausage meat
- 1 yellow onion, chopped.
- 3 tbsp. breadcrumbs
- 1/2 tsp. garlic; minced
- Salt and black pepper to taste.

Directions:

1. Mix all of the ingredients in a bowl, stir well. Shape medium balls out of this mix, place them in your air fryer and cook at 360°F for 15 minutes
2. Serve as an appetizer, or, would be a great breakfast food!

562. Zucchini and Mint Spread

(Prep + Cook Time: 22 minutes | **Serves:** 4)

Ingredients:

- 1½ lbs. zucchini, chopped.
- 1 bunch mint, chopped.
- 2 garlic cloves; minced
- 1/2 cup veggie stock
- 1 yellow onion, chopped.
- One-tablespoon olive oil
- Salt and white pepper to taste

Directions:

1. Over medium heat, heat up the oil in a pan that fits your air fryer.
2. Add the onions and garlic, stir and cook for 1-2 minutes. Add the remaining ingredients, stir well.
3. Place the pan in the air fryer and cook at 380°F for 10 minutes.
4. Blend using an immersion blender and serve as an appetizer or party spread

563. Italian Mozzarella Sticks

(Prep + Cook Time: 18 minutes | **Serves:** 12)

Ingredients:

- 1 cup parmesan cheese, grated.
- 2 eggs, whisked.
- A drizzle of olive oil
- 8 mozzarella cheese strings, halved.
- One-tablespoon Italian seasoning
- Salt and black pepper to taste.

Directions:

1. In a bowl, mix the parmesan, salt, pepper and Italian seasoning, stir. Put the whisked eggs in another bowl
2. Dip the mozzarella sticks in the egg mixture, then in the parmesan mix
3. Dip the sticks one more time in egg and parmesan and place them in your air fryer's basket. Drizzle the oil over them and cook at 390°F for 8 minutes, flipping them halfway. Serve as an appetizer

564. Chives Radish Snack

(Prep + Cook Time: 15 minutes | **Serves:** 4)

Ingredients:

- 16 radishes; sliced
- A drizzle of olive oil
- One-tablespoon chives, chopped.
- Salt and black pepper to taste.

Directions:

1. In a bowl, mix the radishes, salt, pepper and oil, toss well.
2. Place the radishes in your air fryer's basket and cook at 350°F for 10 minutes. Divide into bowls and serve with chives sprinkled on top

565. Zucchini Balls

(Prep + Cook Time: 22 minutes | **Serves:** 8)

Ingredients:

- 3 zucchinis, grated.
- 1 egg
- 1/2 cup white flour
- 2 garlic cloves; minced

- 1/2 cup dill, chopped.
- Cooking spray
- Salt and black pepper to taste.

Directions:

1. In a bowl, mix all the ingredients and stir. Shape the mix into medium balls and place them into your air fryer's basket.
2. Cook at 375°F for 12 minutes, flipping them halfway. Serve them as a snack right away.

566. Potato Chips

(Prep + Cook Time: 17 minutes | **Serves:** 4)

Ingredients:

- 4 potatoes; thinly sliced
- One-tablespoon olive oil
- Salt and black pepper to taste.
- Sour cream for serving

Directions:

1. Brush the potato slices with the oil and place them in your air fryer's basket. Cook at 400°F for 12 minutes, flipping them halfway. Serve as a snack along with the sour cream

567. Buttery Onion Dip

(Prep + Cook Time: 40 minutes | **Serves:** 8)

Ingredients:

- 2½ lbs. red onions, chopped.
- 6 tbsp. butter, softened.
- 1/2 tsp. baking soda
- Salt and black pepper to taste.

Directions:

1. Place the butter into a pan that fits your air fryer and heat over medium heat.
2. Add the onions and the baking soda, stir and sauté for 5 minutes. Transfer the pan to your air fryer and cook at 370°F for 25 minutes. Serve warm as a party dip

568. Cheesy Tomatoes and Sausage Dip

(Prep + Cook Time: 15 minutes | **Serves:** 4)

Ingredients:

- 5 oz. canned tomatoes, chopped.
- 1 cup Italian sausage; cooked and chopped.
- 2 cups processed cheese; cut into chunks
- 4 tbsp. chicken stock

Directions:

1. Place all the ingredients into a pan that fits your air fryer and mix well.
2. Put the pan into the fryer and cook at 378°F for 10 minutes. Stir well and serve as a party dip or appetizer; enjoy!

Dessert Recipes

569. Bread Dough and Amaretto Dessert Recipe

(Prep + Cooking Time: 22 Minutes | **Serves:** 12)

Ingredients:

- 1 lb. bread dough
- 12 oz. chocolate chips
- 1-cup sugar
- ½-cup butter, melted.
- 1-cup heavy cream
- 2-tbsp. amaretto liqueur

Directions:

1. Roll dough, cut into 20 slices and then cut each slice in halves.
2. Brush dough pieces with butter, sprinkle sugar, place them in your air fryer's basket after you've brushed it some butter, cook them at 350 °F, for 5 minutes; flip them, cook for 3 minutes more and transfer to a platter
3. Heat up a pan with the heavy cream over medium heat, add chocolate chips and stir until they melt. Add liqueur; stir again, transfer to a bowl and serve bread dippers with this sauce.

Nutrition Values (Per Serving): Calories: 200; Fat: 1g; Fiber: 0g; Carbs: 6g; Protein: 6g

570. Easy Cheesecake Recipe.

(Prep + Cooking Time: 25 Minutes | **Serves:** 15)

Ingredients:

- 1 lb. cream cheese
- 1-cup graham crackers, crumbled.
- 2 eggs
- 4-tbsp. sugar
- 2-tbsp. butter
- ½-tsp. vanilla extract

Directions:

1. Take a bowl and mix crackers with butter.
2. Press crackers mix on the bottom of a lined cake pan, introduce in your air fryer and cook at 350 °F, for 4 minutes
3. Meanwhile, in a bowl, mix sugar with cream cheese, eggs and vanilla and whisk well.
4. Spread filling over crackers crust and cook your cheesecake in your air fryer at 310 °F, for 15 minutes. Leave cake in the fridge for 3 hours, slice and serve.

Nutrition Values (Per Serving): Calories: 245; Fat: 12g; Fiber: 1g; Carbs: 20g; Protein: 3g

571. Banana Bread Recipe

(Prep + Cooking Time: 50 Minutes | **Serves:** 6)

Ingredients:

- 3/4-cup sugar
- 2 bananas; mashed
- 1 ½-cups flour
- 1/3-cup butter
- 1/3-cup milk
- 1 egg
- 1 ½-tsp. cream of tartar
- one-tsp. vanilla extract
- one-tsp. baking powder.
- ½-tsp. baking soda
- Cooking spray.

Directions:

1. Take a bowl and mix milk with cream of tartar, sugar, butter, egg, vanilla and bananas and stir everything.
2. In another bowl, mix flour with baking powder and baking soda
3. Combine the 2 mixtures; stir well, pour this into a cake pan greased with some cooking spray, introduce in your air fryer and cook at 320 °F, for 40 minutes. Take bread out, leave aside to cool down, slice and serve it.

Nutrition Values (Per Serving): Calories: 292; Fat: 7g; Fiber: 8g; Carbs: 28g; Protein: 4g

572. Pears and Espresso Cream Recipe

(Prep + Cooking Time: 40 Minutes | **Serves:** 4)

Ingredients:

- 4 pears, halved.and cored
- 1-tbsp. sugar
- 2-tbsp. butter
- 2-tbsp. water
- 2-tbsp. lemon juice

For the cream:

- 1-cup whipping cream
- 1/3-cup sugar
- 1-cup mascarpone
- 2-tbsp. espresso; cold

Directions:

1. Take a bowl and mix pears halves with lemon juice, 1-tbsp. sugar, butter and water, toss well, transfer them to your air fryer and cook at 360 °F, for 30 minutes
2. Meanwhile, in a bowl, mix whipping cream with mascarpone, ⅓-cup sugar and espresso, whisk really well and keep in the fridge until pears are done.
3. Divide pears on plates, top with espresso cream and serve them.

Nutrition Values (Per Serving): Calories: 211; Fat: 5g; Fiber: 7g; Carbs: 8g; Protein: 7g

573. Carrot Cake Recipe

(Prep + Cooking Time: 55 Minutes | **Serves:** 6)

Ingredients:

- 5 oz. flour
- 1/3-cup pecans; toasted and chopped.
- 1/3-cup coconut flakes, shredded.
- 1/4-cup pineapple juice
- ½-cup sugar
- 1/3-cup carrots, grated.
- 1 egg
- 3-tbsp. yogurt
- 4-tbsp. sunflower oil
- ½-tsp. baking soda
- ½-tsp. cinnamon powder.
- ½-tsp. allspice
- 3/4-tsp. baking powder.
- 1/4-tsp. nutmeg, ground.
- Cooking spray.

Directions:

1. Take a bowl and mix flour with baking soda and powder, salt, allspice, cinnamon and nutmeg and stir.
2. In another bowl, mix egg with yogurt, sugar, pineapple juice, oil, carrots, pecans and coconut flakes and stir well
3. Combine the two mixtures and stir well, pour this into a spring form pan that fits your air fryer which you've greased with some cooking spray, transfer to your air fryer and cook on 320 °F, for 45 minutes.

4. Leave cake to cool down, then cut and serve it

Nutrition Values (Per Serving): Calories: 200; Fat: 6g; Fiber: 20g; Carbs: 22g; Protein: 4g

574. Pumpkin Cookies Recipe

(Prep + Cooking Time: 25 Minutes | **Serves:** 24)

Ingredients:

- ½-cup pumpkin flesh; mashed
- ½-cup dark chocolate chips
- 2 ½-cups flour
- 1/4-cup honey
- 1-tbsp. flax seed, ground.
- 3-tbsp. water
- 2-tbsp. butter
- ½-tsp. baking soda
- one-tsp. vanilla extract

Directions:

1. Take a bowl and mix flax seed with water; stir and leave aside for a few minutes.
2. In another bowl, mix flour with salt and baking soda
3. In a third bowl, mix honey with pumpkin puree, butter, vanilla extract and flaxseed.
4. Combine flour with honey mix and chocolate chips and stir
5. Scoop 1-tbsp. of cookie dough on a lined baking sheet that fits your air fryer, repeat with the rest of the dough, introduce them in your air fryer and cook at 350 °F, for 15 minutes.
6. Leave cookies to cool down and serve

Nutrition Values (Per Serving): Calories: 140; Fat: 2g; Fiber: 2g; Carbs: 7g; Protein: 10g

575. Easy Granola Recipe.

(Prep + Cooking Time: 45 Minutes | **Serves:** 4)

Ingredients:

- ½-cup pumpkin seeds
- ½-cup sunflower seeds
- ½-cup pecans, chopped.
- 1-cup coconut, shredded.
- ½-cup almonds
- 2-tbsp. sugar
- 2-tbsp. sunflower oil
- one-tsp. apple pie spice mix
- one-tsp. nutmeg, ground.

Directions:

1. Take a bowl and mix almonds and pecans with pumpkin seeds, sunflower seeds, coconut, nutmeg and apple pie spice mix and stir well
2. Heat up a pan with the oil over medium heat, add sugar and stir well.
3. Pour this over nuts and coconut mix and stir well
4. Spread this on a lined baking sheet that fits your air fryer, introduce in your air fryer and cook at 300 °F and bake for 25 minutes. Leave your granola to cool down, cut and serve

Nutrition Values (Per Serving): Calories: 322; Fat: 7g; Fiber: 8g; Carbs: 12g; Protein: 7g

576. Tomato Cake Recipe

(Prep + Cooking Time: 40 Minutes | **Serves:** 4)

Ingredients:

- 1-cup tomatoes chopped
- ½-cup olive oil
- 3/4-cup maple syrup
- 1 ½-cups flour

- 2-tbsp. apple cider vinegar
- one-tsp. cinnamon powder.
- one-tsp. baking powder.
- one-tsp. baking soda

Directions:

1. Take a bowl and mix flour with baking powder, baking soda, cinnamon and maple syrup and stir well.
2. In another bowl, mix tomatoes with olive oil and vinegar and stir well
3. Combine the 2 mixtures; stir well, pour into a greased round pan that fits your air fryer, introduce in the fryer and cook at 360 °F, for 30 minutes. Leave cake to cool down, slice and serve.

Nutrition Values (Per Serving): Calories: 153; Fat: 2g; Fiber: 1g; Carbs: 25g; Protein: 4g

577. Strawberry Pie Recipe.

(Prep + Cooking Time: 30 Minutes **| Serves:** 12)

Ingredients:

For the crust: y

- 1-cup sunflower seeds
- 1-cup coconut, shredded.
- 1/4-cup butter

For the filling:

- 8 oz. strawberries, chopped for serving
- 4 oz. strawberries
- 8 oz. cream cheese
- ½-cup heavy cream
- 2-tbsp. water
- ½-tbsp. lemon juice
- one-tsp. gelatin
- 1/4-tsp. stevia

Directions:

1. In your food processor, mix sunflower seeds with coconut, a pinch of salt and butter, pulse and press this on the bottom of a cake pan that fits your air fryer.
2. Heat up a pan with the water over medium heat, add gelatin; stir until it dissolves, leave aside to cool down, add this to your food processor, mix with 4 oz. strawberries, cream cheese, lemon juice and stevia and blend well
3. Add heavy cream; stir well and spread this over crust.
4. Top with 8 oz. strawberries, introduce in your air fryer and cook at 330 °F, for 15 minutes. Keep in the fridge until you serve it

Nutrition Values (Per Serving): Calories: 234; Fat: 23g; Fiber: 2g; Carbs: 6g; Protein: 7g

578. Macaroons Recipe

(Prep + Cooking Time: 18 Minutes **| Serves:** 20)

Ingredients:

- 2-cup coconut, shredded.
- 4 egg whites
- 2-tbsp. sugar
- one-tsp. vanilla extract

Directions:

1. Take a bowl and mix egg whites with stevia and beat using your mixer
2. Add coconut and vanilla extract, whisk again, shape small balls out of this mix, introduce them in your air fryer and cook at 340 °F, for 8 minutes. Serve macaroons cold.

Nutrition Values (Per Serving): Calories: 55; Fat: 6g; Fiber: 1g; Carbs: 2g; Protein: 1g

579. Orange Cake Recipe.

(Prep + Cooking Time: 42 Minutes | **Serves:** 12)

Ingredients:

- 1 orange, peeled and cut into quarters
- 6 eggs
- 2 oz. sugar+ 2-tbsp.
- 4 oz. yogurt
- 4 oz. cream cheese
- 9 oz. flour
- 2-tbsp. orange zest
- one-tsp. baking powder.
- one-tsp. vanilla extract

Directions:

1. In your food processor, pulse orange very well
2. Add flour, 2-tbsp. sugar, eggs, baking powder, vanilla extract and pulse well again
3. Transfer this into 2 spring form pans, introduce each in your fryer and cook at 330 °F, for 16 minutes
4. Meanwhile, in a bowl, mix cream cheese with orange zest, yogurt and the rest of the sugar and stir well.
5. Place one cake layer on a plate, add half of the cream cheese mix, add the other cake layer and top with the rest of the cream cheese mix. Spread it well, slice and serve

Nutrition Values (Per Serving): Calories: 200; Fat: 13g; Fiber: 2g; Carbs: 9g; Protein: 8g

580. Cinnamon Rolls and Cream Cheese Dip Recipe

(Prep + Cooking Time: 2 hours 15 Minutes | **Serves:** 8)

Ingredients:

- 1 lb. bread dough
- 1/4-cup butter, melted.
- 3/4-cup brown sugar
- 1 ½-tbsp. cinnamon, ground.

For the cream cheese dip:

- 4 oz. cream cheese
- 1 ¼-cups sugar
- 2-tbsp. butter
- ½-tsp. vanilla

Directions:

1. Roll dough on a floured working surface; shape a rectangle and brush with 1/4-cup butter.
2. Take a bowl and mix cinnamon with sugar; stir, sprinkle this over dough, roll dough into a log, seal well and cut into 8 pieces
3. Leave rolls to rise for 2 hours, place them in your air fryer's basket, cook at 350 °F, for 5 minutes; flip them, cook for 4 minutes more and transfer to a platter
4. Take a bowl and mix cream cheese with butter, sugar and vanilla and whisk really well. Serve your cinnamon rolls with this cream cheese dip

Nutrition Values (Per Serving): Calories: 200; Fat: 1g; Fiber: 0g; Carbs: 5g; Protein: 6g

581. Crispy Apples Recipe.

(Prep + Cooking Time: 20 Minutes | **Serves:** 4)

Ingredients:

- 5 apples; cored and cut into chunks
- 3/4-cup old fashioned rolled oats
- 1/4-cup flour
- 1/4-cup brown sugar
- ½-cup water
- 4-tbsp. butter

- 1-tbsp. maple syrup
- 2-tsp. cinnamon powder.
- ½-tsp. nutmeg powder

Directions:

1. Put the apples in a pan that fits your air fryer, add cinnamon, nutmeg, maple syrup and water
2. Take a bowl and mix butter with oats, sugar, salt and flour; stir, drop spoonfuls of this mix on top of apples, introduce in your air fryer and cook at 350 °F, for 10 minutes. Serve warm.

Nutrition Values (Per Serving): Calories: 200; Fat: 6g; Fiber: 8g; Carbs: 29g; Protein: 12g

582. Fried Bananas Recipe.

(Prep + Cooking Time: 25 Minutes | **Serves:** 4)

Ingredients:

- 8 bananas, peeled and halved
- 2 eggs
- 1-cup panko
- ½-cup corn flour
- 3-tbsp. cinnamon sugar
- 3-tbsp. butter

Directions:

1. Heat up a pan with the butter over medium high heat, add panko; stir and cook for 4 minutes and then transfer to a bowl
2. Roll each in flour, eggs and panko mix, arrange them in your air fryer's basket, dust with cinnamon sugar and cook at 280 °F, for 10 minutes. Serve right away.

Nutrition Values (Per Serving): Calories: 164; Fat: 1g; Fiber: 4g; Carbs: 32g; Protein: 4g

583. Lentils and Dates Brownies Recipe

(Prep + Cooking Time: 25 Minutes | **Serves:** 8)

Ingredients:

- 28 oz. canned lentils; rinsed and drained
- 12 dates
- 1 banana, peeled and chopped.
- 4-tbsp. almond butter
- 1-tbsp. honey
- 2-tbsp. cocoa powder
- ½-tsp. baking soda

Directions:

1. In your food processor, mix lentils with butter, banana, cocoa, baking soda and honey and blend really well
2. Add dates, pulse a few more times, pour this into a greased pan that fits your air fryer, spread evenly, introduce in the fryer at 360 °F and bake for 15 minutes.
3. Take brownies mix out of the oven, cut, arrange on a platter and serve

Nutrition Values (Per Serving): Calories: 162; Fat: 4g; Fiber: 2g; Carbs: 3g; Protein: 4g

584. Strawberry Shortcakes Recipe.

(Prep + Cooking Time: 65 Minutes | **Serves:** 6)

Ingredients:

- 2-cups strawberries, sliced.
- ½-cup whipping cream
- 1 ½-cup flour
- 1/4-cup sugar+ 4-tbsp.
- 1/3-cup butter
- 1-cup buttermilk
- 1 egg, whisked.
- 1-tbsp. rum

- 1-tbsp. mint, chopped.
- one-tsp. lime zest, grated.
- 1/4-tsp. baking soda
- one-tsp. baking powder.
- Cooking spray.

Directions:

1. Take a bowl and mix flour with 1/4-cup sugar, baking powder and baking soda and stir
2. In another bowl, mix buttermilk with egg; stir, add to flour mix and whisk
3. Spoon this dough into 6 jars greased with cooking spray, cover with tin foil, arrange them in your air fryer cook at 360 °F, for 45 minutes
4. Meanwhile, in a bowl, mix strawberries with 3-tbsp. sugar, rum, mint and lime zest; stir and leave aside in a cold place
5. In another bowl, mix whipping cream with 1-tbsp. sugar and stir. Take jars out, divide strawberry mix and whipped cream on top and serve

Nutrition Values (Per Serving): Calories: 164; Fat: 2g; Fiber: 3g; Carbs: 5g; Protein: 2g

585. Chocolate Cake Recipe.

(Prep + Cooking Time: 40 Minutes | **Serves:** 12)

Ingredients:

- 8 oz. canned pumpkin puree
- 3/4-cup white flour
- 3/4-cup whole wheat flour
- 2/3-cup chocolate chips
- 1 banana; mashed
- ½-cup Greek yogurt
- 1 egg
- 3/4-cup sugar
- 2-tbsp. canola oil
- ½-tsp. vanilla extract
- one-tsp. baking soda
- 3/4-tsp. pumpkin pie spice
- ½-tsp. baking powder.
- Cooking spray.

Directions:

1. Take a bowl and mix white flour with whole wheat flour, salt, baking soda and powder and pumpkin spice and stir.
2. In another bowl, mix sugar with oil, banana, yogurt, pumpkin puree, vanilla and egg and stir using a mixer
3. Combine the 2 mixtures, add chocolate chips; stir, pour this into a greased Bundt pan that fits your air fryer.
4. Introduce in your air fryer and cook at 330 °F, for 30 minutes
5. Leave the cake to cool down, before cutting and serving it

Nutrition Values (Per Serving): Calories: 232; Fat: 7g; Fiber: 7g; Carbs: 29g; Protein: 4g

586. Cocoa Cookies Recipe

(Prep + Cooking Time: 24 Minutes | **Serves:** 12)

Ingredients:

- 4 oz. cream cheese
- 3 oz. cocoa powder
- 6 oz. coconut oil, melted.
- 6 eggs
- ½-tsp. baking powder.
- 5-tbsp. sugar
- 2-tsp. vanilla

Directions:

1. In a blender, mix eggs with coconut oil, cocoa powder, baking powder, vanilla, cream cheese and swerve and stir using a mixer
2. Pour this into a lined baking dish that fits your air fryer, introduce in the fryer at 320 °F and bake for 14 minutes. Slice cookie sheet into rectangles and serve.

Nutrition Values (Per Serving): Calories: 178; Fat: 14g; Fiber: 2g; Carbs: 3g; Protein: 5g

587. Chocolate Cookies Recipe

(Prep + Cooking Time: 35 Minutes | **Serves:** 12)

Ingredients:

- ½-cup unsweetened chocolate chips
- 2-cups flour
- ½-cup butter
- 1 egg
- 4-tbsp. sugar
- one-tsp. vanilla extract

Directions:

1. Heat up a pan with the butter over medium heat; stir and cook for 1 minute
2. Take a bowl and mix egg with vanilla extract and sugar and stir well
3. Add melted butter, flour and half of the chocolate chips and stir everything.
4. Transfer this to a pan that fits your air fryer, spread the rest of the chocolate chips on top, introduce in the fryer at 330 °F and bake for 25 minutes. Slice when it's cold and serve.

Nutrition Values (Per Serving): Calories: 230; Fat: 12g; Fiber: 2g; Carbs: 4g; Protein: 5g

588. Bread Pudding Recipe

(Prep + Cooking Time: 1 hour 10 Minutes | **Serves:** 4)

Ingredients:

- 6 glazed doughnuts, crumbled.
- 1/4-cup sugar
- ½-cup raisins
- 1-cup cherries
- ½-cup chocolate chips.
- 1 ½-cups whipping cream
- 4 egg yolks

Directions:

1. Take a bowl and mix cherries with egg yolks and whipping cream and stir well.
2. In another bowl, mix raisins with sugar, chocolate chips and doughnuts and stir
3. Combine the 2 mixtures, transfer everything to a greased pan that fits your air fryer and cook at 310 °F, for 1 hour. Chill pudding before cutting and serving it.

Nutrition Values (Per Serving): Calories: 302; Fat: 8g; Fiber: 2g; Carbs: 23g; Protein: 10g

589. Ginger Cheesecake Recipe

(Prep + Cooking Time: 2 hours and 30 Minutes | **Serves:** 6)

Ingredients:

- ½-cup ginger cookies, crumbled.
- 16 oz. cream cheese, soft.
- ½-cup sugar
- 2 eggs
- ½-tsp. nutmeg, ground.
- one-tsp. rum
- 2-tsp. butter, melted.
- ½-tsp. vanilla extract

Directions:

1. Grease a pan with the butter and spread cookie crumbs on the bottom
2. Take a bowl and beat cream cheese with nutmeg, vanilla, rum and eggs, whisk well and spread over the cookie crumbs.
3. Introduce in your air fryer and cook at 340 °F, for 20 minutes. Leave cheesecake to cool down and keep in the fridge for 2 hours before slicing and serving it.

Nutrition Values (Per Serving): Calories: 412; Fat: 12g; Fiber: 6g; Carbs: 20g; Protein: 6g

590. Apple Bread Recipe

(Prep + Cooking Time: 50 Minutes | **Serves:** 6)

Ingredients:

- 3-cups apples; cored and cubed
- 2-cups white flour
- 2 eggs
- 1 stick butter
- 1-cup water
- 1-cup sugar
- 1-tbsp. apple pie spice
- 1-tbsp. baking powder.
- 1-tbsp. vanilla

Directions:

1. In a bowl mix egg with 1 butter stick, apple pie spice and sugar and stir using your mixer.
2. Add apples and stir again well
3. In another bowl, mix baking powder with flour and stir.
4. Combine the 2 mixtures; stir and pour into a spring form pan
5. Put spring form pan in your air fryer and cook at 320 °F, for 40 minutes Slice and serve

Nutrition Values (Per Serving): Calories: 192; Fat: 6g; Fiber: 7g; Carbs: 14g; Protein: 7g

591. Wrapped Pears Recipe.

(Prep + Cooking Time: 25 Minutes | **Serves:** 4)

Ingredients:

- 14 oz. vanilla custard
- 2 pears, halved.
- 4 puff pastry sheets
- 1 egg, whisked.
- 2-tbsp. sugar
- ½-tsp. cinnamon powder.

Directions:

1. Place puff pastry slices on a working surface, add spoonfuls of vanilla custard in the center of each, top with pear halves and wrap
2. Brush pears with egg, sprinkle sugar and cinnamon, place them in your air fryer's basket and cook at 320 °F, for 15 minutes. Divide parcels on plates and serve.

Nutrition Values (Per Serving): Calories: 200; Fat: 2g; Fiber: 1g; Carbs: 14g; Protein: 3g

592. Pumpkin Pie Recipe.

(Prep + Cooking Time: 25 Minutes | **Serves:** 9)

Ingredients:

- 2-tbsp. water
- 2-tbsp. flour
- 1-tbsp. sugar
- 1-tbsp. butter

For the pumpkin pie filling:

- 3.5 oz. pumpkin flesh, chopped.
- 3 oz. water
- 1 egg, whisked.
- 1-tbsp. sugar
- one-tsp. mixed spice
- one-tsp. nutmeg

Directions:

1. Put 3 oz. water in a pot, bring to a boil over medium high heat, add pumpkin, egg, 1-tbsp. sugar, spice and nutmeg; stir, boil for 20 minutes; take off heat and blend using an immersion blender
2. Take a bowl and mix flour with butter, 1-tbsp. sugar and 2-tbsp. water and knead your dough well.
3. Grease a pie pan that fits your air fryer with butter, press dough into the pan, fill with pumpkin pie filling, place in your air fryer's basket and cook at 360 °F, for 15 minutes. Slice and serve warm.

Nutrition Values (Per Serving): Calories: 200; Fat: 5g; Fiber: 2g; Carbs: 5g; Protein: 6g

593. Coffee Cheesecakes Recipe

(Prep + Cooking Time: 30 Minutes | **Serves:** 6)

Ingredients:

For the cheesecakes:

- 8 oz. cream cheese
- 1/3-cup sugar
- 3 eggs
- 3-tbsp. coffee
- 1-tbsp. caramel syrup
- 2-tbsp. butter

For the frosting:

- 8 oz. mascarpone cheese, soft.
- 2-tbsp. sugar
- 3-tbsp. butter
- 3-tbsp. caramel syrup

Directions:

1. In your blender, mix cream cheese with eggs, 2-tbsp. butter, coffee, 1-tbsp. caramel syrup and ⅓-cup sugar and pulse very well, spoon into a cupcakes pan that fits your air fryer, introduce in the fryer and cook at 320 °F and bake for 20 minutes
2. Leave aside to cool down and then keep in the freezer for 3 hours. Meanwhile, in a bowl, mix 3-tbsp. butter with 3-tbsp. caramel syrup, 2-tbsp. sugar and mascarpone, blend well, spoon this over cheesecakes and serve them.

Nutrition Values (Per Serving): Calories: 254; Fat: 23g; Fiber: 0g; Carbs: 21g; Protein: 5g

594. Mini Lava Cakes Recipe

(Prep + Cooking Time: 30 Minutes | **Serves:** 3)

Ingredients:

- 1 egg
- 4-tbsp. milk
- 4-tbsp. flour
- 4-tbsp. sugar
- 2-tbsp. olive oil
- 1-tbsp. cocoa powder
- ½-tsp. orange zest
- ½-tsp. baking powder.

Directions:

1. Take a bowl and mix egg with sugar, oil, milk, flour, salt, cocoa powder, baking powder and orange zest; stir very well and pour this into greased ramekins
2. Add ramekins to your air fryer and cook at 320 °F, for 20 minutes. Serve lava cakes warm.

Nutrition Values (Per Serving): Calories: 201; Fat: 7g; Fiber: 8g; Carbs: 23g; Protein: 4g

595. Mandarin Pudding Recipe

(Prep + Cooking Time: 60 Minutes | **Serves:** 8)

Ingredients:

- 1 mandarin, peeled and sliced
- Juice from 2 mandarins
- 2-tbsp. brown sugar
- 3/4-cup white flour
- 3/4-cup almonds, ground.
- 4 oz. butter, soft.
- 2 eggs, whisked.
- 3/4-cup sugar
- Honey for serving

Directions:

1. Grease a loaf pan with some butter, sprinkle brown sugar on the bottom and arrange mandarin slices.
2. Take a bowl and mix butter with sugar, eggs, almonds, flour and mandarin juice; stir, spoon this over mandarin slices, place pan in your air fryer and cook at 360 °F, for 40 minutes
3. Transfer pudding to a plate and serve with honey on top.

Nutrition Values (Per Serving): Calories: 162; Fat: 3g; Fiber: 2g; Carbs: 3g; Protein: 6g

596. Plum Cake Recipe.

(Prep + Cooking Time: 1 hour and 20 Minutes | **Serves:** 8)

Ingredients:

- 1 ¾ lbs. plums; pitted and cut into quarters
- 7 oz. flour
- 3 oz. warm milk
- 1 oz. almond flakes
- 1 oz. butter, soft.
- 1 egg, whisked.
- 1 package dried yeast
- 5-tbsp. sugar
- Zest from 1 lemon, grated.

Directions:

1. Take a bowl and mix yeast with butter, flour and 3-tbsp. sugar and stir well
2. Add milk and egg and whisk for 4 minutes until you obtain a dough.
3. Arrange the dough in a spring form pan that fits your air fryer and which you've greased with some butter, cover and leave aside for 1 hour. Arrange plumps on top of the butter, sprinkle the rest of the sugar, introduce in your air fryer at 350 degrees F, bake for 36 minutes; cool down, sprinkle almond flakes and lemon zest on top, slice and serve.

Nutrition Values (Per Serving): Calories: 192; Fat: 4g; Fiber: 2g; Carbs: 6g; Protein: 7g

597. Sponge Cake Recipe.

(Prep + Cooking Time: 30 Minutes | **Serves:** 12)

Ingredients:

- 3-cups flour
- 1 ½-cup milk
- ½-cup cornstarch
- 1 ⅔-cup sugar
- 1/4-cup lemon juice
- 2-cups water
- 1-cup olive oil
- 3-tsp. baking powder.
- one-tsp. baking soda
- 2-tsp. vanilla extract

Directions:

1. Take a bowl and mix flour with cornstarch, baking powder, baking soda and sugar and whisk well.
2. In another bowl, mix oil with milk, water, vanilla and lemon juice and whisk
3. Combine the two mixtures; stir, pour in a greased baking dish that fits your air fryer, introduce in the fryer and cook at 350 °F, for 20 minutes. Leave cake to cool down, cut and serve.

Nutrition Values (Per Serving): Calories: 246; Fat: 3g; Fiber: 1g; Carbs: 6g; Protein: 2g

598. Cocoa and Almond Bars Recipe

(Prep + Cooking Time: 34 Minutes | **Serves:** 6)

Ingredients:

- 8 dates; pitted and soaked
- 1/4-cup coconut, shredded.
- 1/4-cup cocoa nibs
- 1/4-cup hemp seeds
- 1/4-cup goji berries
- 1-cup almonds; soaked and drained
- 2-tbsp. cocoa powder

Directions:

1. Put almonds in your food processor, blend, add hemp seeds, cocoa nibs, cocoa powder, goji, coconut and blend very well
2. Add dates, blend well again, spread on a lined baking sheet that fits your air fryer and cook at 320 °F, for 4 minutes. Cut into equal parts and keep in the fridge for 30 minutes before serving.

Nutrition Values (Per Serving): Calories: 140; Fat: 6g; Fiber: 3g; Carbs: 7g; Protein: 19g

599. Peach Pie Recipe.

(Prep + Cooking Time: 45 Minutes | **Serves:** 4)

Ingredients:

- 2 ¼ lbs. peaches; pitted and chopped.
- ½-cup sugar
- 1 pie dough
- 2-tbsp. cornstarch
- 1-tbsp. dark rum
- 1-tbsp. lemon juice
- 2-tbsp. flour
- 2-tbsp. butter, melted.
- A pinch of nutmeg, ground.

Directions:

1. Roll pie dough into a pie pan that fits your air fryer and press well.
2. Take a bowl and mix peaches with cornstarch, sugar, flour, nutmeg, rum, lemon juice and butter and stir well
3. Pour and spread this into pie pan, introduce in your air fryer and cook at 350 °F, for 35 minutes. Serve warm or cold

Nutrition Values (Per Serving): Calories: 231; Fat: 6g; Fiber: 7g; Carbs: 9g; Protein: 5g

600. Blueberry Scones Recipe

(Prep + Cooking Time: 20 Minutes | **Serves:** 10)

Ingredients:

- 1-cup blueberries
- ½-cup heavy cream
- ½-cup butter
- 1-cup white flour
- 2 eggs
- 5-tbsp. sugar
- 2-tsp. vanilla extract
- 2-tsp. baking powder.

Directions:

1. Take a bowl and mix flour, salt, baking powder and blueberries and stir
2. In another bowl, mix heavy cream with butter, vanilla extract, sugar and eggs and stir well.
3. Combine the 2 mixtures, knead until you obtain your dough, shape 10 triangles from this mix, place them on a lined baking sheet that fits your air fryer and cook them at 320 °F, for 10 minutes. Serve them cold.

Nutrition Values (Per Serving): Calories: 130; Fat: 2g; Fiber: 2g; Carbs: 4g; Protein: 3g

601. Cocoa Cake Recipe

(Prep + Cooking Time: 27 Minutes | **Serves:** 6)

Ingredients:

- 3.5 oz. butter, melted.
- 3 oz. sugar
- 3 oz. flour
- 3 eggs
- ½-tsp. lemon juice
- one-tsp. cocoa powder

Directions:

1. Take a bowl and mix 1-tbsp. butter with cocoa powder and whisk
2. In another bowl, mix the rest of the butter with sugar, eggs, flour and lemon juice, whisk well and pour half into a cake pan that fits your air fryer
3. Add half of the cocoa mix, spread, add the rest of the butter layer and top with the rest of cocoa.
4. Introduce in your air fryer and cook at 360 °F, for 17 minutes. Cool cake down before slicing and serving.

Nutrition Values (Per Serving): Calories: 340; Fat: 11g; Fiber: 3g; Carbs: 25g; Protein: 5g

602. Ricotta and Lemon Cake Recipe.

(Prep + Cooking Time: 1 hour and 10 Minutes | **Serves:** 4)

Ingredients:

- 3 lbs. ricotta cheese
- ½ lb. sugar
- 8 eggs, whisked.
- Zest from 1 orange, grated.
- Zest from 1 lemon, grated.
- Butter for the pan

Directions:

1. Take a bowl and mix eggs with sugar, cheese, lemon and orange zest and stir very well
2. Grease a baking pan that fits your air fryer with some batter, spread ricotta mixture, introduce in the fryer at 390 °F and bake for 30 minutes
3. Reduce heat at 380 °F and bake for 40 more minutes. Take out of the oven, leave cake to cool down and serve!

Nutrition Values (Per Serving): Calories: 110; Fat: 3g; Fiber: 2g; Carbs: 3g; Protein: 4g

603. Banana Cake Recipe

(Prep + Cooking Time: 40 Minutes | **Serves:** 4)

Ingredients:

- 1/3-cup brown sugar
- 1 egg
- 1 banana, peeled and mashed.
- 1-cup white flour
- 2-tbsp. honey
- 1-tbsp. butter, soft.

- one-tsp. baking powder.
- ½-tsp. cinnamon powder.
- Cooking spray.

Directions:

1. Spray a cake pan with some cooking spray and leave aside.
2. Take a bowl and mix butter with sugar, banana, honey, egg, cinnamon, baking powder and flour and whisk
3. Pour this into a cake pan greased with cooking spray, introduce in your air fryer and cook at 350 °F, for 30 minutes. Leave cake to cool down, slice and serve.

Nutrition Values (Per Serving): Calories: 232; Fat: 4g; Fiber: 1g; Carbs: 34g; Protein: 4g

604. Sweet Potato Pie

(Prep + Cook Time: 85 minutes | **Serves:** 6)

Ingredients:

- 1 (9-inches) prepared frozen pie dough, thawed
- 2 large eggs
- 6-oz sweet potato
- 1/4 cup heavy cream
- One-tablespoon. olive oil
- One-tablespoon light brown sugar
- 2 tbsp. maple syrup
- One-tablespoon butter, melted.
- 1/2 tsp. ground cinnamon
- 1/8 tsp. ground nutmeg
- 3/4 tsp. vanilla extract
- Salt, to taste.

Directions:

1. Set the temperature of air fryer to 400°F. Coat the sweet potato evenly with oil. Arrange the sweet potato into an air fryer basket. Air fry for about 30 minutes. Remove from air fryer and set aside to cool completely.
2. Peel the sweet potato and mash it completely. Place the pie dough onto a floured surface and cut into 8-inch pie shell.
3. Arrange the dough shell into a greased pie pan. In a large bowl; add the mashed sweet potato and remaining Ingredients and mix until well combined
4. Place sweet potato mixture evenly over the pie shell. Set the temperature of air fryer to 320°F.
5. Arrange the pie pan into an air fryer basket. Air fry for about 30 minutes. Remove from air fryer and place the pie pan onto a wire rack to cool for about 10 to 15 minutes before serving. Serve warm

605. Brown Butter Cookies Recipe

(Prep + Cooking Time: 20 Minutes | **Serves:** 6)

Ingredients:

- 1 ½-cups butter
- 2 eggs, whisked.
- ⅔-cup pecans, chopped.
- 3-cups flour
- 2-cups brown sugar
- 2-tsp. vanilla extract
- one-tsp. baking soda
- ½-tsp. baking powder.

Directions:

1. Heat up a pan with the butter over medium heat; stir until it melts, add brown sugar and stir until this dissolves

2. Take a bowl and mix flour with pecans, vanilla extract, baking soda, baking powder and eggs and stir well.
3. Add brown butter; stir well and arrange spoonfuls of this mix on a lined baking sheet that fits your air fryer.
4. Introduce in the fryer and cook at 340 °F, for 10 minutes. Leave cookies to cool down and serve.

Nutrition Values (Per Serving): Calories: 144; Fat: 5g; Fiber: 6g; Carbs: 19g; Protein: 2g

606. Strawberry Cobbler Recipe

(Prep + Cooking Time: 35 Minutes | **Serves:** 6)

Ingredients:

- 6-cups strawberries, halved.
- 3/4-cup sugar
- ½-cup flour
- ½-cup water
- 3 ½-tbsp. olive oil
- 1-tbsp. lemon juice
- 1/8-tsp. baking powder.
- A pinch of baking soda
- Cooking spray.

Directions:

1. Take a bowl and mix strawberries with half of sugar, sprinkle some flour, add lemon juice, whisk and pour into the baking dish that fits your air fryer and greased with cooking spray
2. In another bowl, mix flour with the rest of the sugar, baking powder and soda and stir well.
3. Add the olive oil and mix until the whole thing with your hands
4. Add ½-cup water and spread over strawberries.
5. Introduce in the fryer at 355 °F and bake for 25 minutes. Leave cobbler aside to cool down, slice and serve.

Nutrition Values (Per Serving): Calories: 221; Fat: 3g; Fiber: 3g; Carbs: 6g; Protein: 9g

607. Brownies Muffins

(Prep + Cook Time: 20 minutes | **Serves:** 12)

Ingredients:

- 1 package Betty Crocker fudge brownie mix
- 1 egg
- 1/3 cup vegetable oil
- 1/4 cup walnuts, chopped.
- 2 tsp. water

Directions:

1. In a bowl; mix well all the ingredients. Set the temperature of air fryer to 300°F.
2. Grease 12 muffin molds. Place mixture evenly into the prepared muffin molds
3. Arrange the molds into an Air Fryer basket. Air fry for 10 minutes or until a toothpick inserted in the center comes out clean
4. Remove the muffin molds from air fryer and place onto a wire rack to cool for about 10 minutes
5. Finally, invert the muffins onto wire rack to completely cool before serving

608. Yogurt Cake

(Prep + Cook Time: 35 minutes | **Serves:** 8)

Ingredients:

- 8 oz. canned pumpkin puree
- 1 banana, mashed.
- 1 egg
- 1½ cups white flour
- 1 cup Greek yogurt
- 1/2 tsp. vanilla extract
- 1/2 tsp. baking powder
- 3/4 cup sugar
- One-tablespoon. baking soda
- 2 tbsp. vegetable oil
- Cooking spray

Directions:

1. In a bowl, combine all ingredients (except the cooking spray) and stir well
2. Pour the mixture into a cake pan greased with cooking spray and put it in your air fryer's basket
3. Cook at 330°F for 30 minutes. Cool down, slice and serve.

609. Blueberry Pudding Recipe

(Prep + Cooking Time: 35 Minutes | **Serves:** 6)

Ingredients:

- 2-cups flour
- 2-cups rolled oats
- 1-cup walnuts, chopped.
- 8-cups blueberries
- 1 stick butter, melted.
- 2-tbsp. rosemary, chopped.
- 3-tbsp. maple syrup

Directions:

1. Spread blueberries in a greased baking pan and leave aside
2. In your food processor, mix rolled oats with flour, walnuts, butter, maple syrup and rosemary, blend well, layer this over blueberries, introduce everything in your air fryer and cook at 350 degrees for 25 minutes. Leave dessert to cool down, cut and serve.

Nutrition Values (Per Serving): Calories: 150; Fat: 3g; Fiber: 2g; Carbs: 7g; Protein: 4g

610. Plum and Currant Tart Recipe

(Prep + Cooking Time: 65 Minutes | **Serves:** 6)

Ingredients:

For the crumble:

- 1/4-cup almond flour
- 1-cup brown rice flour
- ½-cup cane sugar
- 1/4-cup millet flour
- 10-tbsp. butter, soft.
- 3-tbsp. milk

For the filling:

- 1 lb. small plums; pitted and halved
- 1-cup white currants
- 3-tbsp. sugar
- 2-tbsp. cornstarch
- 1/4-tsp. ginger powder
- one-tsp. lime juice
- ½-tsp. vanilla extract
- ½-tsp. cinnamon powder.

Directions:

1. Take a bowl and mix brown rice flour with ½-cup sugar, millet flour, almond flour, butter and milk and stir until you obtain a sand like dough.
2. Reserve 1/4 of the dough, press the rest of the dough into a tart pan that fits your air fryer and keep in the fridge for 30 minutes.
3. Meanwhile, in a bowl, mix plums with currants, 3-tbsp. sugar, cornstarch, vanilla extract, cinnamon, ginger and lime juice and stir well
4. Pour this over tart crust, crumble reserved dough on top, introduce in your air fryer and cook at 350 °F, for 35 minutes. Leave tart to cool down, slice and serve.

Nutrition Values (Per Serving): Calories: 200; Fat: 5g; Fiber: 4g; Carbs: 8g; Protein: 6g

611. Sweet Potato Cheese cake Recipe.

(Prep + Cooking Time: 15 Minutes **| Serves:** 4)

Ingredients:

- 6 oz. mascarpone, soft.
- 8 oz. cream cheese, soft.
- ⅔-cup graham crackers, crumbled.
- ⅔-cup sweet potato puree
- 3/4-cup milk
- 4-tbsp. butter, melted.
- one-tsp. vanilla extract
- 1/4-tsp. cinnamon powder.

Directions:

1. Take a bowl and mix butter with crumbled crackers; stir well, press on the bottom of a cake pan that fits your air fryer and keep in the fridge for now
2. In another bowl, mix cream cheese with mascarpone, sweet potato puree, milk, cinnamon and vanilla and whisk really well. Spread this over crust, introduce in your air fryer, cook at 300 °F, for 4 minutes and keep in the fridge for a few hours before serving.

Nutrition Values (Per Serving): Calories: 172; Fat: 4g; Fiber: 6g; Carbs: 8g; Protein: 3g

612. Strawberry Donuts Recipe

(Prep + Cooking Time: 25 Minutes **| Serves:** 4)

Ingredients:

- 8 oz. flour
- 4 oz. whole milk
- 1 egg
- 1-tbsp. white sugar
- 2 ½-tbsp. butter
- 1-tbsp. brown sugar
- one-tsp. baking powder.

For the strawberry icing:

- 3.5 oz. icing sugar
- 1/4-cup strawberries, chopped.
- 1-tbsp. whipped cream
- 2-tbsp. butter
- ½-tsp. pink coloring

Directions:

1. Take a bowl and mix butter, 1-tbsp. brown sugar, 1-tbsp. white sugar and flour and stir
2. In a second bowl, mix egg with 1 ½-tbsp. butter and milk and stir well.
3. Combine the 2 mixtures; stir, shape donuts from this mix, place them in your air fryer's basket and cook at 360 °F, for 15 minutes

4. Put 1-tbsp. butter, icing sugar, food coloring, whipped cream and strawberry puree and whisk well. Arrange donuts on a platter and serve with strawberry icing on top.

Nutrition Values (Per Serving): Calories: 250; Fat: 12g; Fiber: 1g; Carbs: 32g; Protein: 4g

613. Cashew Bars Recipe

(Prep + Cooking Time: 25 Minutes | **Serves:** 6)

Ingredients:

- 1/4-cup almond meal
- 4 dates, chopped.
- 1 ½-cups cashews, chopped.
- 3/4-cup coconut, shredded.
- 1/3-cup honey
- 1-tbsp. chia seeds
- 1-tbsp. almond butter

Directions:

1. Take a bowl and mix honey with almond meal and almond butter and stir well.
2. Add cashews, coconut, dates and chia seeds and stir well again
3. Spread this on a lined baking sheet that fits your air fryer and press well.
4. Introduce in the fryer and cook at 300 °F, for 15 minutes. Leave mix to cool down, cut into medium bars and serve

Nutrition Values (Per Serving): Calories: 121; Fat: 4g; Fiber: 7g; Carbs: 5g; Protein: 6g

614. Fruity Crumble

(Prep + Cook Time: 35 minutes | **Serves:** 4)

Ingredients:

- 1/2 lb. fresh apricots, pitted and cubed
- 1/3 cup sugar, divided
- 1 cup fresh blackberries
- 7/8 cup flour
- 1/4 cup chilled butter, cubed
- One-tablespoon fresh lemon juice
- One-tablespoon cold water
- Pinch of salt

Directions:

1. Set the temperature of air fryer to 390°F. Grease a baking pan. In a large bowl; mix well apricots, blackberries, 2 tbsp. of sugar and lemon juice.
2. Spread apricot mixture into the prepared baking pan. In another bowl; add the flour, remaining sugar, salt, water and butter. Mix until a crumbly mixture forms.
3. Spread the flour mixture evenly over apricot mixture. Place the pan in an air fryer basket.
4. Air fry for about 20 minutes. Remove the baking pan from air fryer and place onto a wire rack to cool for about 10 minutes. Serve warm

615. Orange Cookies Recipe

(Prep + Cooking Time: 22 Minutes | **Serves:** 8)

Ingredients:

- ½-cup butter, soft.
- 3/4-cup sugar
- 2-cups flour
- 1 egg, whisked.
- one-tsp. vanilla extract
- 1-tbsp. orange zest, grated.
- one-tsp. baking powder.

For the filling:

- 4 oz. cream cheese, soft.
- 2-cups powdered sugar
- ½-cup butter

Directions:

1. Take a bowl and mix cream cheese with ½-cup butter and 2-cups powdered sugar; stir well using your mixer and leave aside for now.
2. In another bowl, mix flour with baking powder.
3. In a third bowl, mix ½-cup butter with 3/4-cup sugar, egg, vanilla extract and orange zest and whisk well.
4. Combine flour with orange mix; stir well and scoop 1-tbsp. of the mix on a lined baking sheet that fits your air fryer
5. Repeat with the rest of the orange batter, introduce in the fryer and cook at 340 °F, for 12 minutes. Leave cookies to cool down, spread cream filling on half of them top with the other cookies and serve.

Nutrition Values (Per Serving): Calories: 124; Fat: 5g; Fiber: 6g; Carbs: 8g; Protein: 4g

616. Sweet Squares Recipe.

(Prep + Cooking Time: 40 Minutes | **Serves:** 6)

Ingredients:

- 1-cup flour
- 2 eggs, whisked.
- 1-cup sugar
- 1/4-cup powdered sugar
- ½-cup butter, soft.
- 2-tbsp. lemon juice
- ½-tsp. baking powder
- 2-tsp. lemon peel, grated.

Directions:

1. Take a bowl and mix flour with powdered sugar and butter; stir well, press on the bottom of a pan that fits your air fryer, introduce in the fryer and bake at 350 °F, for 14 minutes
2. In another bowl, mix sugar with lemon juice, lemon peel, eggs and baking powder; stir using your mixer and spread over baked crust. Bake for 15 minutes more, leave aside to cool down, cut into medium squares and serve cold.

Nutrition Values (Per Serving): Calories: 100; Fat: 4g; Fiber: 1g; Carbs: 12g; Protein: 1g

617. Apple Cake

(Prep + Cook Time: 60 minutes | **Serves:** 6)

Ingredients:

- 2 cups apples, peeled, cored and chopped
- 1 egg
- 1/3 cup brown sugar
- 1 cup all-purpose flour
- 5 tbsp. plus One-tablespoon. vegetable oil
- One-tablespoon. ground nutmeg
- One-tablespoon. ground cinnamon
- 1/2 tsp. baking soda
- 3/4 tsp. vanilla extract
- Salt, to taste.

Directions:

1. In a bowl, mix well flour, sugar, spices, baking soda and salt. In another bowl; add the egg and oil and whisk until smooth. Add the vanilla extract and whisk well. Slowly, add the flour mixture, whisking continuously until well combined.

2. Fold in the chopped apples. Set the temperature of air fryer to 355°F. Lightly, grease a cake pan. Place mixture evenly into the prepared cake pan
3. With a piece of foil, cover the pan and poke some holes using a fork. Arrange the cake pan into an air fryer basket. Now, set the temperature of air fryer to 320°F. Air fry for about 40 minutes.
4. Remove the foil and air fry for another 5 minutes or until a toothpick inserted in the center comes out clean. Remove the cake pan from air fryer and place onto a wire rack to cool for about 10 minutes.
5. invert the cake onto wire rack to completely cool before slicing. Cut the cake into desired size slices and serve.

618. Berries Mix Recipe

(Prep + Cooking Time: 11 Minutes | **Serves:** 4)

Ingredients:

- 1 lb. strawberries, halved.
- 1/4-cup basil leaves; torn
- 1 ½-cups blueberries
- 2-tbsp. lemon juice
- 1 ½-tbsp. maple syrup
- 1 ½-tbsp. champagne vinegar
- 1-tbsp. olive oil

Directions:

1. In a pan that fits your air fryer, mix lemon juice with maple syrup and vinegar, bring to a boil over medium high heat, add oil, blueberries and strawberries; stir.
2. Introduce in your air fryer and cook at 310 °F, for 6 minutes
3. Sprinkle basil on top and serve!

Nutrition Values (Per Serving): Calories: 163; Fat: 4g; Fiber: 4g; Carbs: 10g; Protein: 2.1

619. Apple Crumble

(Prep + Cook Time: 35 minutes | **Serves:** 4)

Ingredients:

- 1/4 cup butter, softened.
- 1 (14-oz) can apple pie filling
- 9 tbsp. self-rising flour
- 7 tbsp. caster sugar
- Pinch of salt

Directions:

1. Set the temperature of air fryer to 320°F. Lightly, grease a baking dish. Place apple pie filling evenly into the prepared baking dish. In a medium bowl; add the remaining Ingredients and mix until a crumbly mixture forms. Spread the mixture evenly over apple pie filling.
2. Arrange the baking dish in an air fryer basket. Air fry for about 25 minutes
3. Remove the baking dish from air fryer and place onto a wire rack to cool for about 10 minutes. Serve warm.

620. Rhubarb Pie Recipe

(Prep + Cooking Time: 1 hour 15 Minutes | **Serves:** 6)

Ingredients:

- 1 ¼-cups almond flour
- 8-tbsp. butter
- 5-tbsp. cold water
- one-tsp. sugar

For the filling:

- 3-cups rhubarb, chopped.
- 1 ½-cups sugar
- 2 eggs
- 3-tbsp. flour
- 1-tbsp. butter
- ½-tsp. nutmeg, ground.
- 2-tbsp. low fat milk

Directions:

1. Take a bowl and mix 1 ¼-cups flour with one-tsp. sugar, 8-tbsp. butter and cold water; stir and knead until you obtain a dough
2. Transfer dough to a floured working surface, shape a disk, flatten, wrap in plastic, keep in the fridge for about 30 minutes; roll and press on the bottom of a pie pan that fits your air fryer
3. Take a bowl and mix rhubarb with 1 ½-cups sugar, nutmeg, 3-tbsp. flour and whisk.
4. In another bowl, whisk eggs with milk, add to rhubarb mix, pour the whole mix into the pie crust, introduce in your air fryer and cook at 390 °F, for 45 minutes. Cut and serve it cold.

Nutrition Values (Per Serving): Calories: 200; Fat: 2g; Fiber: 1g; Carbs: 6g; Protein: 3g

621. Chocolate and Pomegranate Bars Recipe

(Prep + Cooking Time: 2 hours 10 Minutes | **Serves:** 6)

Ingredients:

- 1 ½-cups dark chocolate, chopped.
- ½-cup almonds, chopped.
- ½-cup pomegranate seeds
- ½-cup milk
- one-tsp. vanilla extract

Directions:

1. Heat up a pan with the milk over medium low heat, add chocolate; stir for 5 minutes; take off heat add vanilla extract, half of the pomegranate seeds and half of the nuts and stir
2. Pour this into a lined baking pan, spread, sprinkle a pinch of salt, the rest of the pomegranate arils and nuts, introduce in your air fryer and cook at 300 °F, for 4 minutes. Keep in the fridge for 2 hours before serving.

Nutrition Values (Per Serving): Calories: 68; Fat: 1g; Fiber: 4g; Carbs: 6g; Protein: 1g

622. Plum Bars Recipe

(Prep + Cooking Time: 26 Minutes | **Serves:** 8)

Ingredients:

- 2-cups dried plums
- 2-cup rolled oats
- 1-cup brown sugar
- 1 egg, whisked.
- 6-tbsp. water
- 2-tbsp. butter, melted.
- one-tsp. cinnamon powder.
- ½-tsp. baking soda
- Cooking spray.

Directions:

1. In your food processor, mix plums with water and blend until you obtain a sticky spread.
2. Take a bowl and mix oats with cinnamon, baking soda, sugar, egg and butter and whisk really well
3. Press half of the oats mix in a baking pan that fits your air fryer sprayed with cooking oil, spread plums mix and top with the other half of the oats mix
4. Introduce in your air fryer and cook at 350 °F, for 16 minutes. Leave mix aside to cool down, cut into medium bars and serve.

Nutrition Values (Per Serving): Calories: 111; Fat: 5g; Fiber: 6g; Carbs: 12g; Protein: 6g

623. Lemon Tart Recipe

(Prep + Cooking Time: 1 hour 35 Minutes | **Serves:** 6)

Ingredients:

For the crust:

- 2-cups white flour
- 2-tbsp. sugar
- 12-tbsp. cold butter
- 3-tbsp. ice water
- A pinch of salt

For the filling:

- 1 ¼-cup sugar
- 2 eggs, whisked.
- Zest from 2 lemons, grated.
- 10-tbsp. melted and chilled butter
- Juice from 2 lemons

Directions:

1. Take a bowl and mix 2-cups flour with a pinch of salt and 2-tbsp. sugar and whisk.
2. Add 12-tbsp. butter and the water, knead until you obtain a dough, shape a ball, wrap in foil and keep in the fridge for 1 hour
3. Transfer dough to a floured surface, flatten it, arrange on the bottom of a tart pan, prick with a fork, keep in the fridge for 20 minutes; introduce in your air fryer at 360 °F and bake for 15 minutes.
4. Take a bowl and mix 1 ¼-cup sugar with eggs, 10-tbsp. butter, lemon juice and lemon zest and whisk very well.
5. Pour this into pie crust, spread evenly, introduce in the fryer and cook at 360 °F, for 20 minutes. Cut and serve it.

Nutrition Values (Per Serving): Calories: 182; Fat: 4g; Fiber: 1g; Carbs: 2g; Protein: 3g

624. Fruity Oreo Muffins

(Prep + Cook Time: 25 minutes | **Serves:** 6)

Ingredients:

- 1 pack Oreo biscuits, crushed.
- 1 apple, peeled, cored and chopped
- 1 banana; peeled and chopped
- 1 cup milk
- One-tablespoon. cocoa powder
- One-tablespoon. honey
- One-tablespoon. fresh lemon juice
- 1/2 tsp. baking powder
- 1/4 tsp. baking soda
- A pinch of ground cinnamon

Directions:

1. In a bowl, add the milk, biscuits, cocoa powder, baking soda and baking powder. Mix until a smooth mixture forms.
2. Set the temperature of air fryer to 320°F. Grease 6 muffin cups. Place mixture evenly into the prepared muffin cups. Arrange the muffin cups into an air fryer basket. Air fry for 10 minutes or until a toothpick inserted in the center comes out clean
3. Remove from air fryer and place the muffin cups onto a wire rack to cool slightly.
4. Meanwhile; in another bowl; mix together the banana, apple, honey, lemon juice and cinnamon.
5. Carefully; scoop some portion of muffins from the center to make a cup. Fill each cup with fruit mixture. Refrigerate to chill before serving.

625. Walnut Brownies

(Prep + Cook Time: 37 minutes | **Serves:** 4)

Ingredients:

- 1/2 cup chocolate; roughly chopped
- 1/4 cup walnuts, chopped.
- 1/3 cup butter
- 1 egg, beaten
- 5 tbsp. sugar
- One-tablespoon. vanilla extract
- 5 tbsp. self-rising flour
- A pinch of salt

Directions:

1. In a microwave-safe bowl; add the chocolate and butter. Microwave on high heat for about 2 minutes, stirring after every 30 seconds. Remove from microwave and set aside to cool. Now, in a bowl; add the sugar, egg, vanilla extract and salt and whisk until creamy and light.
2. Add the chocolate mixture and whisk until well combined. Add the flour and walnuts and mix until well combined. Set the temperature of air fryer to 355°F. Line a baking pan with a greased parchment paper.
3. Place mixture evenly into the prepared pan and with the back of spatula, smooth the top surface
4. Arrange the baking pan into an air fryer basket. Air fry for about 20 minutes.
5. Remove the baking pan from air fryer and set aside to cool completely. Cut into 4 equal-sized squares and serve.

626. Lava Cake

(Prep + Cook Time: 27½ minutes | **Serves:** 4)

Ingredients:

- 1 cup confectioners' sugar
- 1/3 cup fresh raspberries
- 2 large eggs
- 2 large egg yolks
- 2/3 cup chocolate chips
- 1/2 cup unsalted butter, softened.
- 1/3 cup all-purpose flour plus more for dusting
- 2 tbsp. powdered sugar
- One-tablespoon. peppermint extract

Directions:

1. In a microwave-safe bowl; put the chocolate chips and butter. Microwave on high heat for about 30 seconds. Remove the bowl from microwave and stir the mixture well. Add the eggs, egg yolks and confectioners' sugar and whisk until well combined. Add the flour and gently, stir to combine
2. Set the temperature of air fryer to 375°F. Grease 4 ramekins and dust each with a little flour. Place mixture evenly into the prepared ramekins.
3. Arrange the ramekins into an air fryer basket. Air fry for about 10 to 12 minutes. Remove from air fryer and place the ramekins onto a wire rack for about 5 minutes.
4. Carefully run a knife around sides of each ramekin several times to loosen the cake. Finally, invert each cake onto a dessert plate and dust with powdered sugar. Garnish with raspberries and serve immediately.

627. Orange Cake

(Prep + Cook Time: 30 minutes | **Serves:** 3)

Ingredients:

- 1 egg
- One-tablespoon cocoa powder
- 4 tbsp. flour
- 2 tbsp. vegetable oil
- 4 tbsp. milk
- 2 tbsp. orange juice
- 4 tbsp. sugar
- 1/2 tsp. orange zest
- 1/2 tsp. baking powder

Directions:

1. Place all of the ingredients in a bowl and mix well.
2. Divide the mixture between 3 ramekins and place them in your air fryer
3. Cook at 320°F for 20 minutes. Serve the cakes warm and enjoy!

628. Special Brownies Recipe

(Prep + Cooking Time: 27 Minutes | **Serves:** 4)

Ingredients:

- 1/4-cup walnuts, chopped.
- 1/4-cup white flour
- 1/3-cup cocoa powder
- 1/3-cup sugar
- 1 egg
- 7-tbsp. butter
- 1-tbsp. peanut butter
- ½-tsp. baking powder.
- ½-tsp. vanilla extract

Directions:

1. Heat up a pan with 6-tbsp. butter and the sugar over medium heat; stir, cook for 5 minutes; transfer this to a bowl, add salt, vanilla extract, cocoa powder, egg, baking powder, walnuts and flour; stir the whole thing really well and pour into a pan that fits your air fryer
2. Take a bowl and mix 1-tbsp. butter with peanut butter, heat up in your microwave for a few seconds; stir well and drizzle this over brownies mix
3. Introduce in your air fryer and bake at 320 °F and bake for 17 minutes. Leave brownies to cool down, cut and serve.

Nutrition Values (Per Serving): Calories: 223; Fat: 32g; Fiber: 1g; Carbs: 3g; Protein: 6g

629. Lentils Cookies Recipe.

(Prep + Cooking Time: 35 Minutes | **Serves:** 36)

Ingredients:

- ½-cup brown sugar
- 1-cup canned lentils; drained and mashed
- 1-cup butter, soft.
- 1-cup white flour
- 1-cup whole wheat flour
- 1 egg
- 1-cup water
- 1-cup raisins
- 1-cup rolled oats
- 1-cup coconut; unsweetened and shredded
- ½-cup white sugar
- ½-tsp. nutmeg, ground.
- one-tsp. cinnamon powder.
- one-tsp. baking powder.
- 2-tsp. almond extract

Directions:

1. Take a bowl and mix white and whole wheat flour with salt, cinnamon, baking powder and nutmeg and stir.
2. Take a bowl and mix butter with white and brown sugar and stir using your kitchen mixer for 2 minutes
3. Add egg, almond extract, lentils mix, flour mix, oats, raisins and coconut and stir everything well.
4. Scoop-tbsp. of dough on a lined baking sheet that fits your air fryer, introduce them in the fryer and cook at 350 °F, for 15 minutes. Arrange cookies on a serving platter and serve.

Nutrition Values (Per Serving): Calories: 154; Fat: 2g; Fiber: 2g; Carbs: 4g; Protein: 7g

630. Black Tea Cake Recipe.

(Prep + Cooking Time: 45 Minutes | **Serves:** 12)

Ingredients:

- 3 ½-cups flour
- ½-cup olive oil
- 4 eggs
- 2-cups sugar
- 2-cups milk
- ½-cup butter
- 6-tbsp. black tea powder
- one-tsp. baking soda
- 2-tsp. vanilla extract
- 3-tsp. baking powder.

For the cream:

- 4-cups sugar
- 1-cup butter, soft.
- 6-tbsp. honey

Directions:

1. Put the milk in a pot, heat up over medium heat, add tea; stir well, take off heat and leave aside to cool down.
2. Take a bowl and mix ½-cup butter with 2-cups sugar, eggs, vegetable oil, vanilla extract, baking powder, baking soda and 3 ½-cups flour and stir everything really well
3. Pour this into 2 greased round pans, introduce each in the fryer at 330 °F and bake for 25 minutes.
4. Take a bowl and mix 1-cup butter with honey and 4-cups sugar and stir really well
5. Arrange one cake on a platter, spread the cream all over, top with the other cake and keep in the fridge until you serve it.

Nutrition Values (Per Serving): Calories: 200; Fat: 4g; Fiber: 4g; Carbs: 6g; Protein: 2g

631. Passion Fruit Pudding Recipe

(Prep + Cook Time: 50 Minutes | **Serves:** 6)

Ingredients:

- 1/2 cup almond flour
- 4 passion fruits; pulp and seeds
- 1 cup Paleo passion fruit curd
- 3 eggs
- 2-ounce ghee, melted.
- 3 ½-ounce almond milk
- 3 ½-ounce maple syrup
- 1/2 tsp. baking powder

Directions:

1. In a bowl, mix the half of the fruit curd with passion fruit seeds and pulp, stir and divide into 6 heat proof ramekins.

2. In a bowl, whisked eggs with maple syrup, ghee, the rest of the curd, baking powder, milk and flour and stir well
3. Divide this into the ramekins as well, introduce in the fryer and cook at 200°F, for 40 minutes. Leave puddings to cool down and serve!

632. Pear Pastry Pouch

(Prep + Cook Time: 30 minutes | **Serves:** 4)

Ingredients:

- 2 small pears, peeled, cored and halved
- 1 egg, lightly beaten
- 2 cups vanilla custard
- 4 puff pastry sheets
- 2 tbsp. sugar
- 2 tbsp. whipped cream
- Pinch of ground cinnamon

Directions:

1. Carefully; make small cuts in each pear half. In the center of each pastry sheet, place a spoonful of vanilla custard and top with a pear half. In a bowl; mix together the sugar and cinnamon. Sprinkle the sugar mixture evenly over pear halves. Pinch the corners to shape into a pouch.
2. coat each pear with egg. Set the temperature of air fryer to 330°F. Lightly, grease an air fryer basket. Arrange pear pouches into the prepared air fryer basket in a single layer. Air fry for about 15 minutes.
3. Remove from air fryer and transfer the pear pouches onto a platter. Top with whipped cream and serve with the remaining custard.

633. Lemon Bars Recipe

(Prep + Cooking Time: 35 Minutes | **Serves:** 6)

Ingredients:

- 1-cup butter, soft.
- 2-cups sugar
- 2 ¼-cups flour
- 4 eggs
- Juice from 2 lemons

Directions:

1. Take a bowl and mix butter with ½-cup sugar and 2-cups flour; stir well, press on the bottom of a pan that fits your air fryer, introduce in the fryer and cook at 350 °F, for 10 minutes
2. In another bowl, mix the rest of the sugar with the rest of the flour, eggs and lemon juice, whisk well and spread over crust. Introduce in the fryer at 350 °F, for 15 minutes more, leave aside to cool down, cut bars and serve them.

Nutrition Values (Per Serving): Calories: 125; Fat: 4g; Fiber: 4g; Carbs: 16g; Protein: 2g

634. Chocolate Yogurt Muffins

(Prep + Cook Time: 25 minutes | **Serves:** 9)

Ingredients:

- 1/4 cup mini chocolate chips
- 1/4 cup pecans, chopped.
- 1 ½ cups all-purpose flour
- 1/4 cup sugar
- 1 cup yogurt
- 1 egg
- 1/3 cup vegetable oil
- 2 tsp. vanilla extract
- 2 tsp. baking powder
- 1/2 tsp. salt

Directions:

1. Take a bowl, mix well flour, sugar, baking powder and salt. In another bowl; add the yogurt, oil, egg and vanilla extract and whisk until well combined. Add the flour mixture and mix until just combined. Fold in the chocolate chips and pecans. Set the temperature of air fryer to 355°F. Grease 9 muffin molds.
2. Place mixture evenly into the prepared muffin molds. Arrange the muffin molds into an air fryer basket. Air fry for 10 minutes or until a toothpick inserted in the center comes out clean
3. Remove the muffin molds from air fryer and place onto a wire rack to cool for about 10 minutes. Finally, invert the muffins onto wire rack to completely cool before serving.

635. Crispy Banana Split

(Prep + Cook Time: 19 minutes | **Serves:** 8)

Ingredients:

- 4 bananas; peeled and halved lengthwise
- 2 eggs
- 1/2 cup corn flour
- 1 cup panko breadcrumbs
- 3 tbsp. coconut oil
- 2 tbsp. walnuts, chopped.
- 3 tbsp. sugar
- 1/4 tsp. ground cinnamon

Directions:

1. In a medium skillet, heat the oil over medium heat and cook breadcrumbs for about 3 to 4 minutes or until golden browned and crumbled, stirring continuously. Transfer the breadcrumbs into a shallow bowl and set aside to cool. In a second bowl; place the corn flour. In a third bowl; whisk the eggs
2. Coat the banana slices with flour and then, dip into eggs and finally, coat evenly with the breadcrumbs. In a small bowl; mix together the sugar and cinnamon.
3. Set the temperature of air fryer to 280°F. Grease an air fryer basket. Arrange banana slices into the prepared air fryer basket in a single layer and sprinkle with cinnamon sugar
4. Air fry for about 10 minutes. Remove from air fryer and transfer the banana slices onto plates to cool slightly Sprinkle with chopped walnuts and serve.

636. Fried Apples Recipe

(Prep + Cooking Time: 27 Minutes | **Serves:** 4)

Ingredients:

- 4 big apples; cored
- A handful raisins
- 1-tbsp. cinnamon, ground.
- Raw honey to the taste

Directions:

1. Fill each apple with raisins, sprinkle cinnamon, drizzle honey, put them in your air fryer and cook at 367 °F, for 17 minutes. Leave them to cool down and serve.

Nutrition Values (Per Serving): Calories: 220; Fat: 3g; Fiber: 4g; Carbs: 6g; Protein: 10g

637. Figs and Coconut Butter Mix Recipe

(Prep + Cooking Time: 10 Minutes | **Serves:** 3)

Ingredients:

- 1-cup almonds; toasted and chopped
- 12 figs, halved.
- 1/4-cup sugar
- 2-tbsp. coconut butter

Directions:

1. Put butter in a pan that fits your air fryer and melt over medium high heat
2. Add figs, sugar and almonds, toss, introduce in your air fryer and cook at 300 °F, for 4 minutes.
3. Divide into bowls and serve cold.

Nutrition Values (Per Serving): Calories: 170; Fat: 4g; Fiber: 5g; Carbs: 7g; Protein: 9g

638. Cinnamon Apples

(Prep + Cook Time: 20 minutes | **Serves:** 4)

Ingredients:

- 4 apples; peeled, cored and cut into wedges
- 3 tbsp. butter, melted.
- 3 tbsp. cinnamon sugar

Directions:

1. In a pan that fits your air fryer, mix the apples with the sugar and the butter, toss
2. Place the pan in the fryer and cook at 370°F for 15 minutes. Serve warm.

639. Layered Cake

(Prep + Cook Time: 45 minutes | **Serves:** 8)

Ingredients:

For Cake:

- 3 ½-oz butter, softened.
- 2 medium eggs
- 3 ½-oz plain flour
- One-tablespoon. ground cinnamon
- 7 tbsp. sugar
- Pinch of salt

For Filling:

- 1¾-oz butter, softened.
- 2/3 cup icing sugar
- One-tablespoon whipped cream
- 2 tbsp. strawberry jam

Directions:

1. In a large bowl; mix well flour, cinnamon and salt. In another bowl; add the sugar and butter and whisk until creamy. Add in the eggs and whisk until well combined. Slowly, add the flour mixture whisking continuously until well combined Set the temperature of air fryer to 355°F. Grease a cake pan.
2. Place mixture evenly into the prepared cake pan. Air fry for about 15 minutes and then, another 10 minutes at 335°F
3. Remove the cake pan from air fryer and place onto a wire rack to cool for about 10 minutes. Now, invert the cake onto wire rack to completely cool before filling. After cooling, cut the cake into 2 equal-sized portions.
4. **For filling:** in a bowl; add the butter and whisk until creamy. Add the cream and icing sugar and whisk until a thick creamy mixture forms. Place one cake portion onto a serving platter, cut side up.
5. Spread the jam evenly over cake and top with butter mixture. Arrange another cake over filling, cut side down. Cut the cake into desired size slices and serve.

640. Shortbread Fingers

(Prep + Cook Time: 27 minutes | **Serves:** 10)

Ingredients:

- 1 2/3 cups plain flour
- 1/3 cup caster sugar
- 3/4 cup butter

Directions:

1. In a large bowl; mix together the sugar and flour. Add the butter and mix until a smooth dough forms. Cut the dough into 10 equal-sized fingers. With a fork, lightly prick the fingers. Set the temperature of air fryer to 355°F. Lightly, grease a baking sheet.
2. Arrange fingers into the prepared baking sheet in a single layer. Arrange the baking sheet into an air fryer basket.
3. Air fry for about 12 minutes. Remove the baking sheet from air fryer and place onto a wire rack to cool for about 5 to 10 minutes. invert the short bread fingers onto wire rack to completely cool before serving. Serve

641. Maple Cupcakes Recipe

(Prep + Cooking Time: 30 Minutes | **Serves:** 4)

Ingredients:

- ½ apple; cored and chopped.
- ½-cup pure applesauce
- 4 eggs
- 3/4-cup white flour
- 4-tbsp. butter
- 4-tsp. maple syrup
- ½-tsp. baking powder.
- 2-tsp. cinnamon powder.
- one-tsp. vanilla extract

Directions:

1. Heat up a pan with the butter over medium heat, add applesauce, vanilla, eggs and maple syrup; stir, take off heat and leave aside to cool down
2. Add flour, cinnamon, baking powder and apples, whisk, pour in a cupcake pan, introduce in your air fryer at 350 °F and bake for 20 minutes
3. Leave cupcakes them to cool down, transfer to a platter and serve them.

Nutrition Values (Per Serving): Calories: 150; Fat: 3g; Fiber: 1g; Carbs: 5g; Protein: 4g

642. Pecan Pie

(Prep + Cook Time: 50 minutes | **Serves:** 5)

Ingredients:

- 2 large eggs
- 1 frozen pie crust, thawed
- 1/4 cup caster sugar
- 3/4 cup brown sugar
- 1 cup pecan halves
- 1/3 cup butter, melted.
- One-tablespoon milk
- One-tablespoon. vanilla extract
- 1¾ tbsp. flour

Directions:

1. In a large bowl; mix well sugars and butter. Add the eggs and whisk until foamy. Add the flour, milk and vanilla extract and whisk until well combined. Fold in the pecan halves. Set the temperature of air fryer to 300°F. Grease a pie pan. Arrange the crust in the bottom of prepared pie pan.
2. Transfer pecan mixture evenly over the crust. Arrange the pan in an air fryer basket. Air fry for about 22 minutes and then, another 13 minutes at 285°F
3. Remove from air fryer and place the pie pan onto a wire rack to cool for about 10 to 15 minutes before serving. Serve warm.

643. Milky Doughnuts

(Prep + Cook Time: 39 minutes | **Serves:** 12)

Ingredients:

For Doughnuts:

- 1 cup whole wheat flour
- 3/4 cup sugar
- 1 cup all-purpose flour
- 1/2 cup milk
- 1 egg
- One-tablespoon butter, softened.
- 2 tsp. baking powder
- 2 tsp. vanilla extract
- Salt, to taste.

For Glaze:

- 2 tbsp. condensed milk
- One-tablespoon cocoa powder
- 2 tbsp. icing sugar

Directions:

1. In a large bowl; mix well flours, baking powder and salt. In another bowl; add the sugar and egg. Whisk until fluffy and light. Add the flour mixture and stir until well combined. Add the butter, milk and vanilla extract and mix until a soft dough forms.
2. Refrigerate the dough for at least 1 hour. Now, put the dough onto a lightly floured surface and roll into ½-inch thickness.
3. With a small doughnut cutter, cut 24 small doughnuts from the rolled dough. Set the temperature of air fryer to 390°F. Grease an air fryer basket
4. Place doughnuts into the prepared air fryer basket in 3 batches. Air fry for about 6 to 8 minutes. Remove from air fryer and transfer the doughnuts onto a platter to cool completely. In a small bowl; mix together the condensed milk and cocoa powder. Spread the glaze over doughnuts and sprinkle with icing sugar. Serve.

644. Tangerine Cake Recipe.

(Prep + Cooking Time: 30 Minutes | **Serves:** 8)

Ingredients:

- 2-cups flour
- 1/4-cup olive oil
- ½-cup milk
- 3/4-cup sugar
- ½-tsp. vanilla extract
- one-tsp. cider vinegar
- Juice and zest from 2 lemons
- Juice and zest from 1 tangerine
- Tangerine segments; for serving

Directions:

1. Take a bowl and mix flour with sugar and stir
2. In another bowl, mix oil with milk, vinegar, vanilla extract, lemon juice and zest and tangerine zest and whisk very well.
3. Add flour; stir well, pour this into a cake pan that fits your air fryer, introduce in the fryer and cook at 360 °F, for 20 minutes. Serve right away with tangerine segments on top.

Nutrition Values (Per Serving): Calories: 190; Fat: 1g; Fiber: 1g; Carbs: 4g; Protein: 4g

645. Butter Cake

(Prep + Cook Time: 30 minutes | **Serves:** 6)

Ingredients:

- 3-oz butter, softened.
- 1/2 cup milk
- 1/2 cup caster sugar
- 1 egg
- 1 ⅓ cups plain flour, sifted
- One-tablespoon icing sugar
- A pinch of salt

Directions:

1. In a bowl, add the butter and sugar and whisk until light and creamy. Add in the egg and whisk until smooth and fluffy. add the flour and salt and mix well alternately with the milk. Set the temperature of air fryer to 350°F. Grease a small Bundt cake pan.
2. Place mixture evenly into the prepared cake pan. Arrange the cake pan in an air fryer basket. Air fry for about 15 minutes or until a toothpick inserted into the center comes out clean
3. Remove the cake pan from air fryer and place onto a wire rack to cool for about 10 minutes. Now, invert the cake onto wire rack to completely cool before slicing. Dust the cake with icing sugar and cut into desired size slices. Serve.

646. Poppyseed Cake Recipe

(Prep + Cooking Time: 40 Minutes | **Serves:** 6)

Ingredients:

- 1 ¼-cups flour
- 3/4-cup sugar
- 1-cup milk
- ½-cup butter, soft.
- 2 eggs, whisked.
- 2-tbsp. poppy seeds
- 1-tbsp. orange zest, grated.
- ½-tsp. vanilla extract
- one-tsp. baking powder.
- 2-tsp. lime zest, grated.

For the cream:

- ½-cup passion fruit puree
- 4 egg yolks
- 1-cup sugar
- 3-tbsp. butter, melted

Directions:

1. Take a bowl and mix flour with baking powder, 3/4-cup sugar, orange zest and lime zest and stir.
2. Add ½-cup butter, eggs, poppy seeds, vanilla and milk; stir using your mixer, pour into a cake pan that fits your air fryer and cook at 350 °F, for about 30 minutes
3. Meanwhile, heat up a pan with 3-tbsp. butter over medium heat, add sugar and stir until it dissolves.
4. Take off heat, add passion fruit puree and egg yolks gradually and whisk really well.
5. Take cake out of the fryer, cool it down a bit and cut into halves horizontally.

6. Spread 1/4 of passion fruit cream over one half, top with the other cake half and spread 1/4 of the cream on top. Serve cold.

Nutrition Values (Per Serving): Calories: 211; Fat: 6g; Fiber: 7g; Carbs: 12g; Protein: 6g

647. Vanilla Soufflé

(Prep + Cook Time: 54 minutes | **Serves:** 6)

Ingredients:

- 4 egg yolks
- 1/2 cup plus 2 tbsp. sugar, divided
- 1/4 cup butter, softened.
- 5 egg whites
- 1/4 cup all-purpose flour
- 1 cup milk
- 2 tbsp. powdered sugar plus extra for dusting
- 3 tsp. vanilla extract, divided
- One-tablespoon. cream of tartar

Directions:

1. In a bowl; add the butter and flour and mix until a smooth paste forms. In a medium pan, mix together 1/2 cup of sugar and milk over medium-low heat and cook for about 3 minutes or until the sugar is dissolved, stirring continuously.
2. Add the flour mixture, whisking continuously and simmer for about 3 to 4 minutes or until mixture becomes thick. Remove from the heat and stir in One-tablespoon. of vanilla extract.
3. Set aside for about 10 minutes to cool. In a bowl, mix together the egg yolks and One-tablespoon. of vanilla extract. Add the egg yolk mixture into milk mixture and mix until well combined
4. In another bowl; add the egg whites, cream of tartar, remaining sugar and vanilla extract and whisk until stiff peaks form.
5. Fold the egg whites mixture into milk mixture. Set the temperature of air fryer to 330°F. Grease 6 ramekins and sprinkle each with a pinch of sugar
6. Place mixture evenly into the prepared ramekins and with the back of a spoon, smooth the top surface. Arrange the ramekins into an air fryer basket in 2 batches. Air fry for about 14-16 minutes. Remove from air fryer and set aside to cool slightly. Sprinkle with the powdered sugar and serve warm.

648. Lime Cheesecake Recipe

(Prep + Cooking Time: 4 hours and 14 minutes **| Serves:** 10)

Ingredients:

- 1/4-cup coconut, shredded.
- 4 oz. flour
- 2-tbsp. butter, melted.
- 2-tsp. sugar

For the filling:

- 1 lb. cream cheese
- 2 sachets lime jelly
- 2-cups hot water
- Juice form 1 lime
- Zest from 1 lime, grated.

Directions:

1. Take a bowl and mix coconut with flour, butter and sugar; stir well and press this on the bottom of a pan that fits your air fryer
2. Meanwhile, put the hot water in a bowl, add jelly sachets and stir until it dissolves.
3. Put cream cheese in a bowl, add jelly, lime juice and zest and whisk really well

4. Add this over the crust, spread, introduce in the air fryer and cook at 300 °F, for 4 minutes. Keep in the fridge for 4 hours before serving.

Nutrition Values (Per Serving): Calories: 260; Fat: 23g; Fiber: 2g; Carbs: 5g; Protein: 7g

649. Passion Fruit Pudding Recipe

(Prep + Cooking Time: 50 Minutes | **Serves:** 6)

Ingredients:

- 3 ½ oz. maple syrup
- 3 ½ oz. almond milk
- ½-cup almond flour
- 1-cup Paleo passion fruit curd
- 4 passion fruits; pulp and seeds
- 3 eggs
- 2 oz. ghee, melted.
- ½-tsp. baking powder.

Directions:

4. Take a bowl and mix the half of the fruit curd with passion fruit seeds and pulp; stir and divide into 6 heat proof ramekins.
5. In a bowl, whisk eggs with maple syrup, ghee, the rest of the curd, baking powder, milk and flour and stir well.
6. Divide this into the ramekins as well, introduce in the fryer and cook at 200 °F, for 40 minutes. Leave puddings to cool down and serve!

Nutrition Values (Per Serving): Calories: 430; Fat: 22g; Fiber: 3g; Carbs: 7g; Protein: 8g

650. Red Velvet Cupcakes

(Prep + Cook Time: 32 minutes | **Serves:** 12)

Ingredients:

For Cupcakes:

- 3/4 cup icing sugar
- 3/4 cup peanut butter
- 2 cups refined flour
- 3 eggs
- One-tablespoon. cocoa powder
- 2 tsp. beet powder

For Frosting:

- 1 (8-oz) package cream cheese, softened.
- 1 cup butter
- 4 ½ cups powdered sugar
- 2 tsp. vanilla extract
- 1/4 tsp. salt

For Garnishing:

- 1/2 cup fresh raspberries

Directions:

1. **For cupcakes:** in a bowl; put all the Ingredients and with an electric whisker, whisk until well combined. Place the mixture into silicon cups. Set the temperature of air fryer to 340°F. Arrange the silicon cups into an air fryer basket.
2. Air fry for about 10 to 12 minutes or until a toothpick inserted in the center comes out clean. Remove the silicon cups from air fryer and place onto a wire rack to cool for about 10 minutes
3. invert the cupcakes onto wire rack to completely cool before frosting.

4. **<u>For frosting:</u>** in a large bowl; mix well butter, cream cheese, vanilla extract and salt. Add the powdered sugar, one cup at a time, whisking well after each addition. Spread frosting evenly over each cupcake. Garnish with raspberries and serve.

651. Amaretto Cream

(Prep + Cook Time: 18 minutes | **Serves:** 8)

Ingredients:

- 12 oz. chocolate chips
- 1 cup heavy cream
- 1 cup sugar
- 1/2 cup butter, melted.
- 2 tbsp. amaretto liqueur

Directions:

1. Place all of the ingredients in a bowl and stir
2. Pour the mixture into small ramekins and place in the air fryer

Printed in Great Britain
by Amazon

45971606R00147